④

LOVE and LIES by MUSAWO

CONTENTS

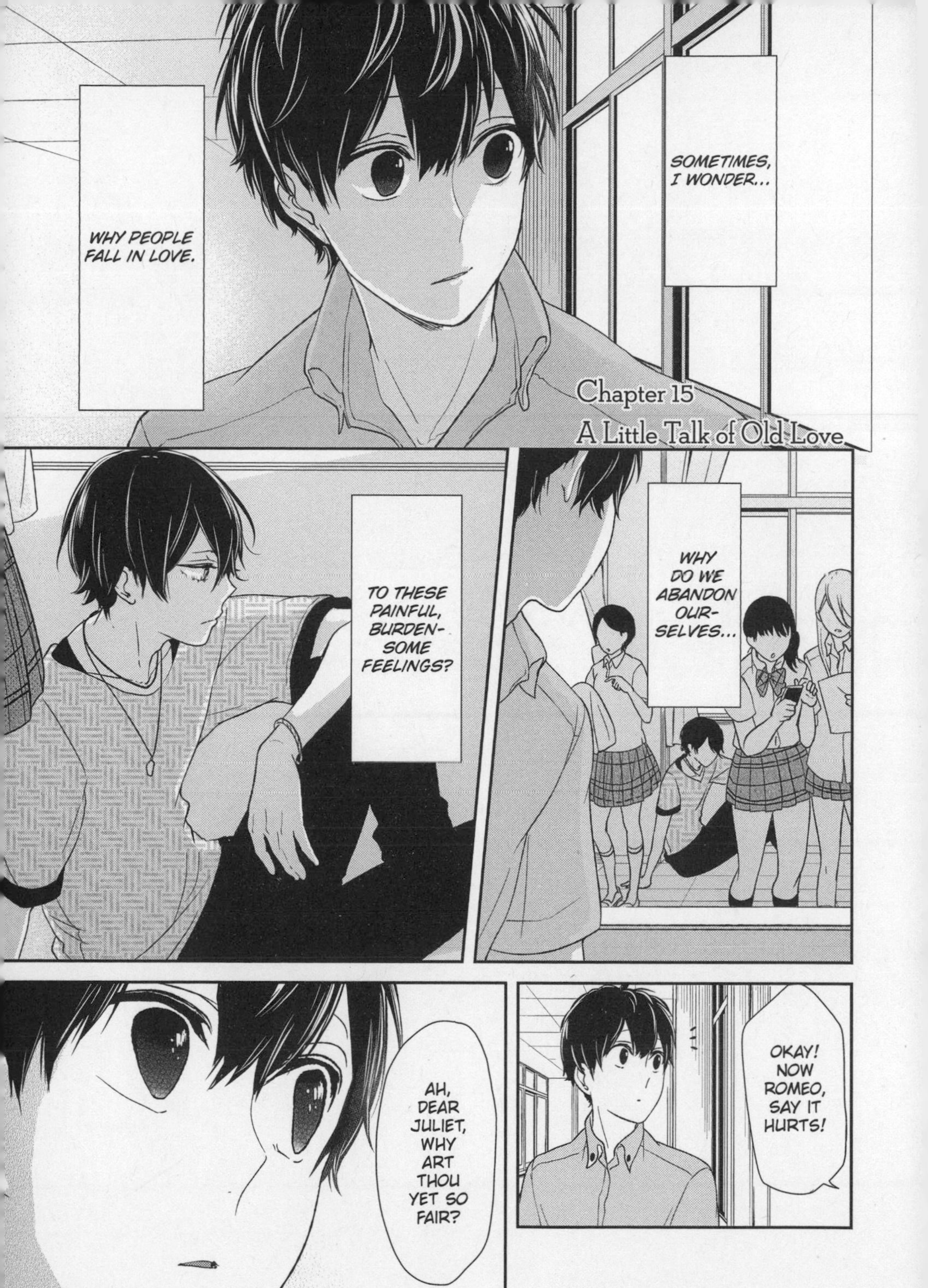
SOMETIMES, I WONDER...
WHY PEOPLE FALL IN LOVE.
Chapter 15
A Little Talk of Old Love
WHY DO WE ABANDON OURSELVES...
TO THESE PAINFUL, BURDENSOME FEELINGS?
OKAY! NOW ROMEO, SAY IT HURTS!
AH, DEAR JULIET, WHY ART THOU YET SO FAIR?

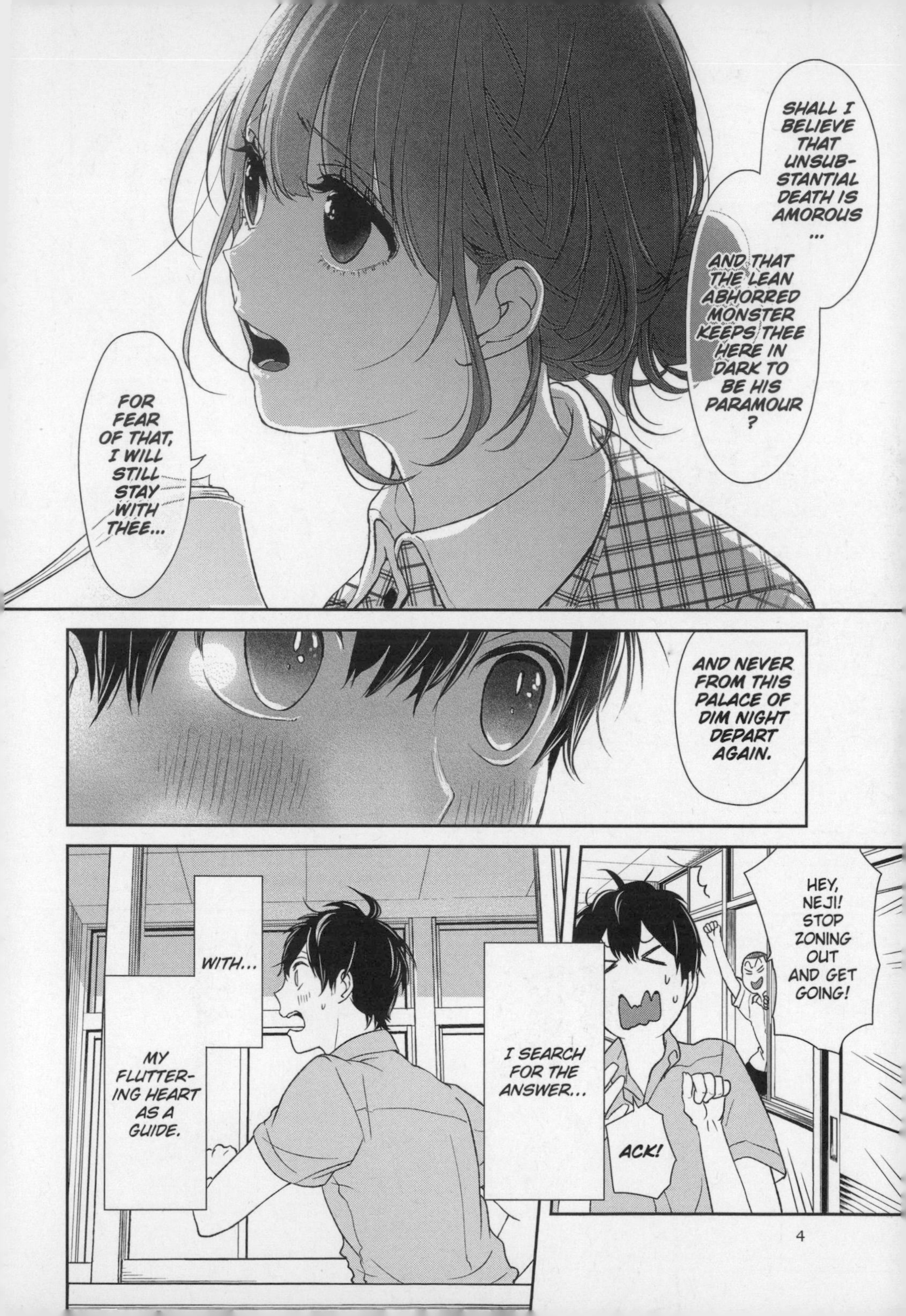
SHALL I BELIEVE THAT UNSUB-STANTIAL DEATH IS AMOROUS ...
AND THAT THE LEAN ABHORRED MONSTER KEEPS THEE HERE IN DARK TO BE HIS PARAMOUR ?
FOR FEAR OF THAT, I WILL STILL STAY WITH THEE...
AND NEVER FROM THIS PALACE OF DIM NIGHT DEPART AGAIN.
HEY, NEJI! STOP ZONING OUT AND GET GOING!
I SEARCH FOR THE ANSWER...
ACK!
WITH...
MY FLUTTER-ING HEART AS A GUIDE.

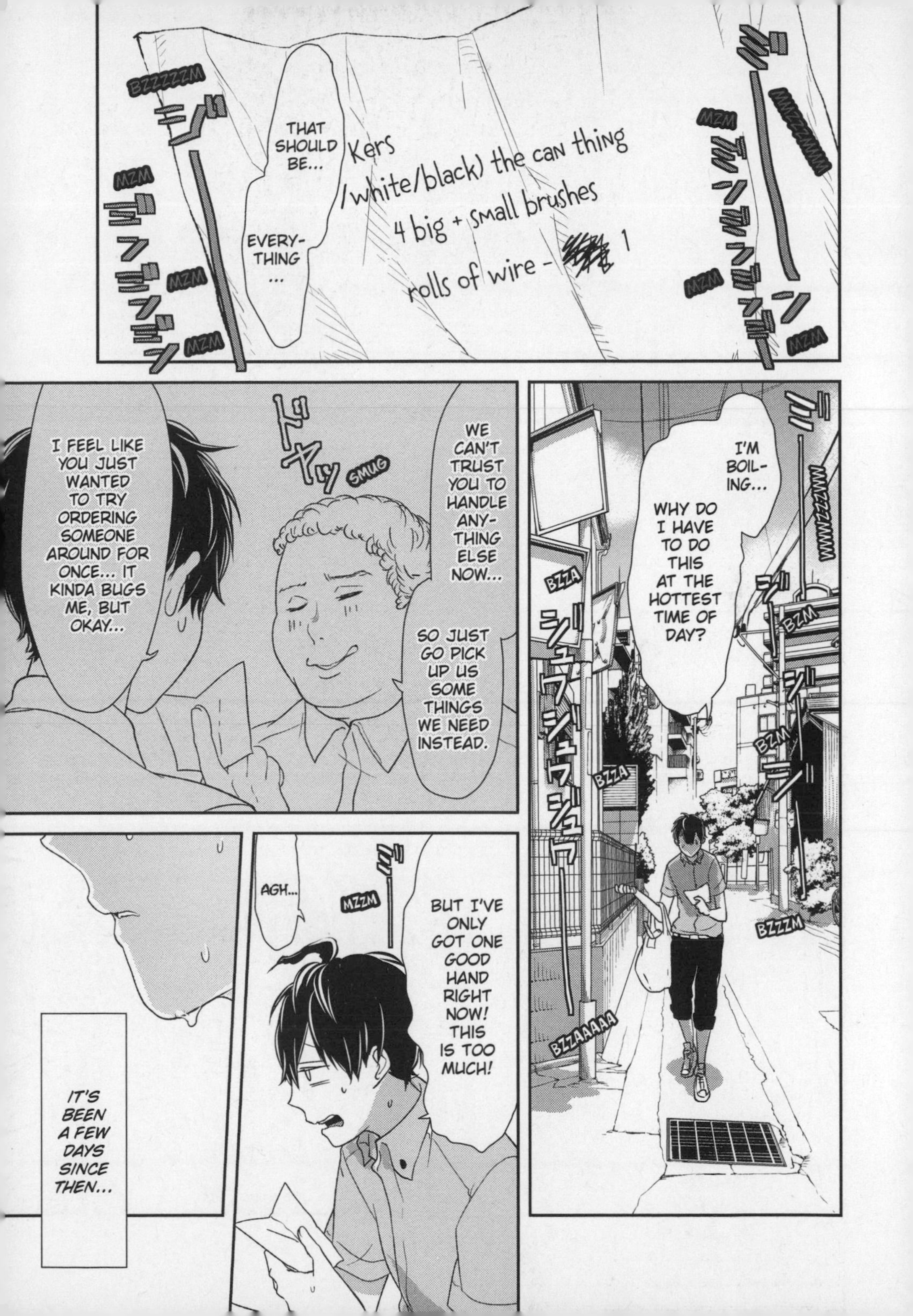
MZM
MZM
BZZZZZM
MZM
MZM
MZM
THAT SHOULD BE...
EVERYTHING...
Kers
/white/black) the can thing
4 big + small brushes
rolls of wire - 1
I'M BOILING...
WHY DO I HAVE TO DO THIS AT THE HOTTEST TIME OF DAY?
BZZA
BZM
BZM
BZZA
BZZZM
BZZAAAAA
WE CAN'T TRUST YOU TO HANDLE ANYTHING ELSE NOW...
SO JUST GO PICK UP US SOME THINGS WE NEED INSTEAD.
SMUG
I FEEL LIKE YOU JUST WANTED TO TRY ORDERING SOMEONE AROUND FOR ONCE... IT KINDA BUGS ME, BUT OKAY...
AGH...
MZZM
BUT I'VE ONLY GOT ONE GOOD HAND RIGHT NOW! THIS IS TOO MUCH!
IT'S BEEN A FEW DAYS SINCE THEN...

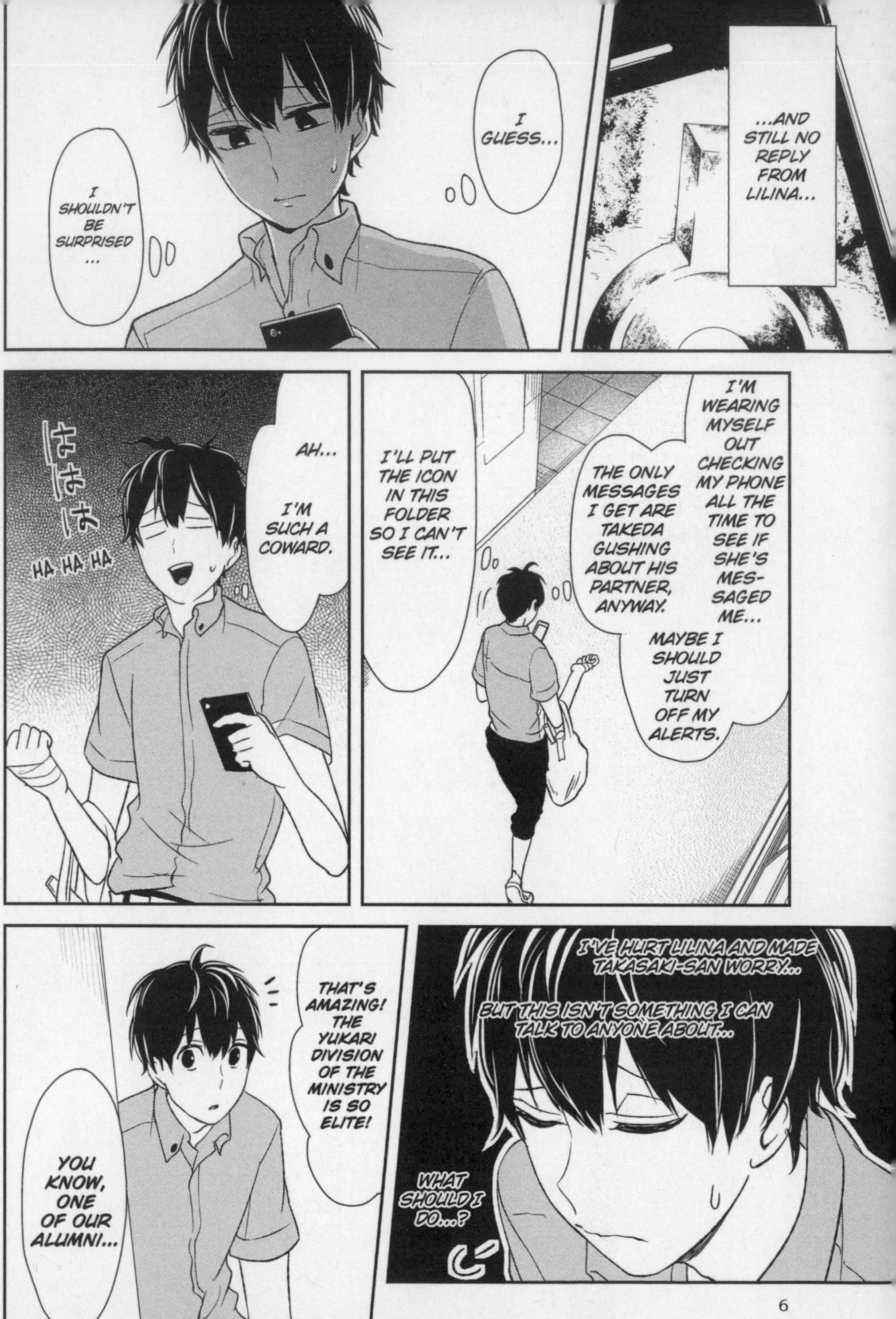
...AND STILL NO REPLY FROM LILINA...
I GUESS...
I SHOULDN'T BE SURPRISED...
I'M WEARING MYSELF OUT CHECKING MY PHONE ALL THE TIME TO SEE IF SHE'S MES-SAGED ME...
THE ONLY MESSAGES I GET ARE TAKEDA GUSHING ABOUT HIS PARTNER, ANYWAY.
MAYBE I SHOULD JUST TURN OFF MY ALERTS.
I'LL PUT THE ICON IN THIS FOLDER SO I CAN'T SEE IT...
AH...
I'M SUCH A COWARD.
ははは
HA HA HA
I'VE HURT LILINA AND MADE TAKASAKI-SAN WORRY...
BUT THIS ISN'T SOMETHING I CAN TALK TO ANYONE ABOUT...
WHAT SHOULD I DO...?
THAT'S AMAZING! THE YUKARI DIVISION OF THE MINISTRY IS SO ELITE!
YOU KNOW, ONE OF OUR ALUMNI...

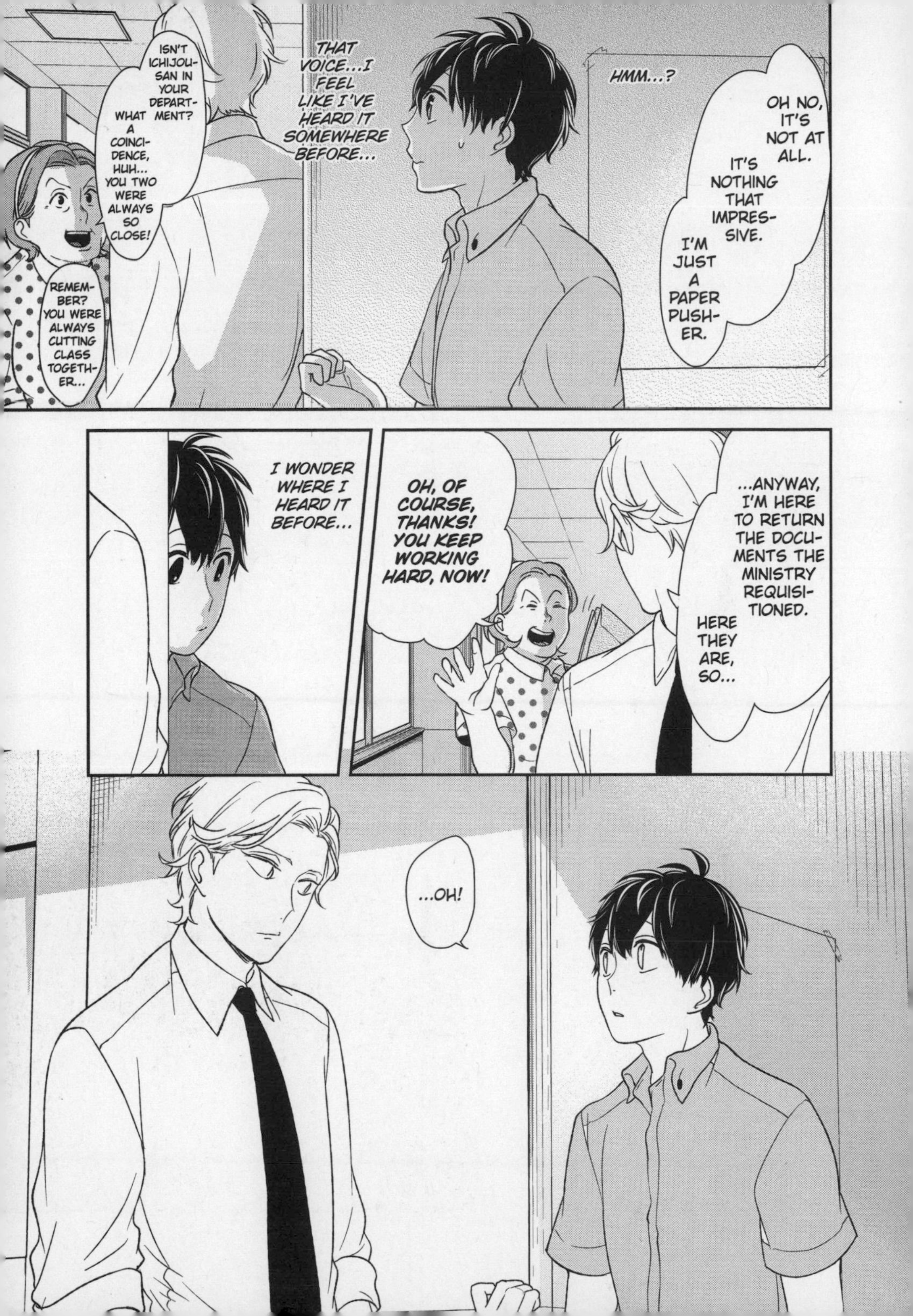
HMM...?
OH NO, IT'S NOT AT ALL.
IT'S NOTHING THAT IMPRESSIVE.
I'M JUST A PAPER PUSHER.
THAT VOICE...I FEEL LIKE I'VE HEARD IT SOMEWHERE BEFORE...
ISN'T ICHIJOU-SAN IN YOUR DEPARTMENT?
WHAT A COINCIDENCE, HUH... YOU TWO WERE ALWAYS SO CLOSE!
REMEMBER? YOU WERE ALWAYS CUTTING CLASS TOGETHER...
...ANYWAY, I'M HERE TO RETURN THE DOCUMENTS THE MINISTRY REQUISITIONED.
HERE THEY ARE, SO...
OH, OF COURSE, THANKS! YOU KEEP WORKING HARD, NOW!
I WONDER WHERE I HEARD IT BEFORE...
...OH!

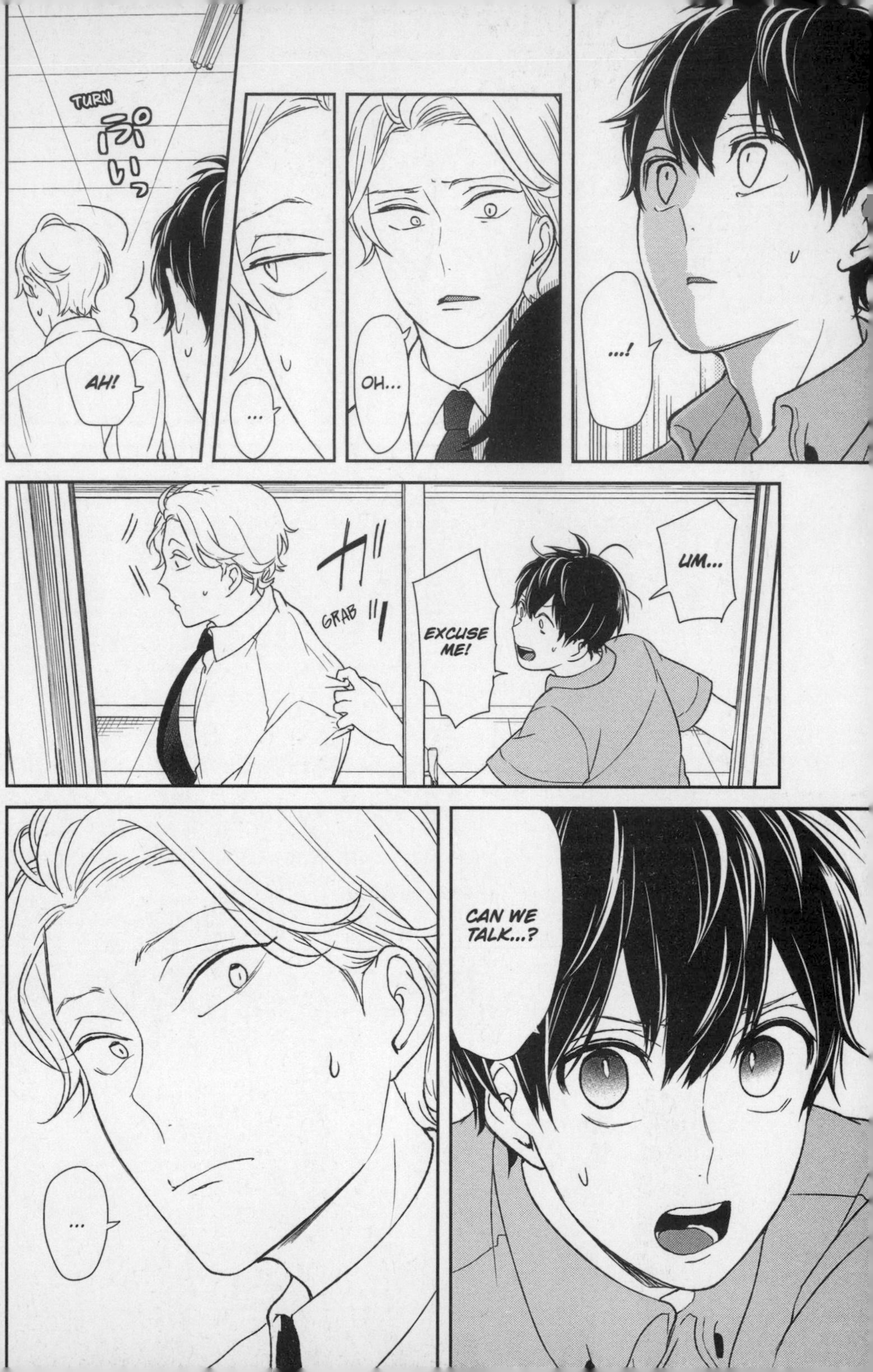
...!
OH...
...
TURN
ぷいっ
AH!
UM...
EXCUSE ME!
ガ
GRAB
CAN WE TALK...?
...

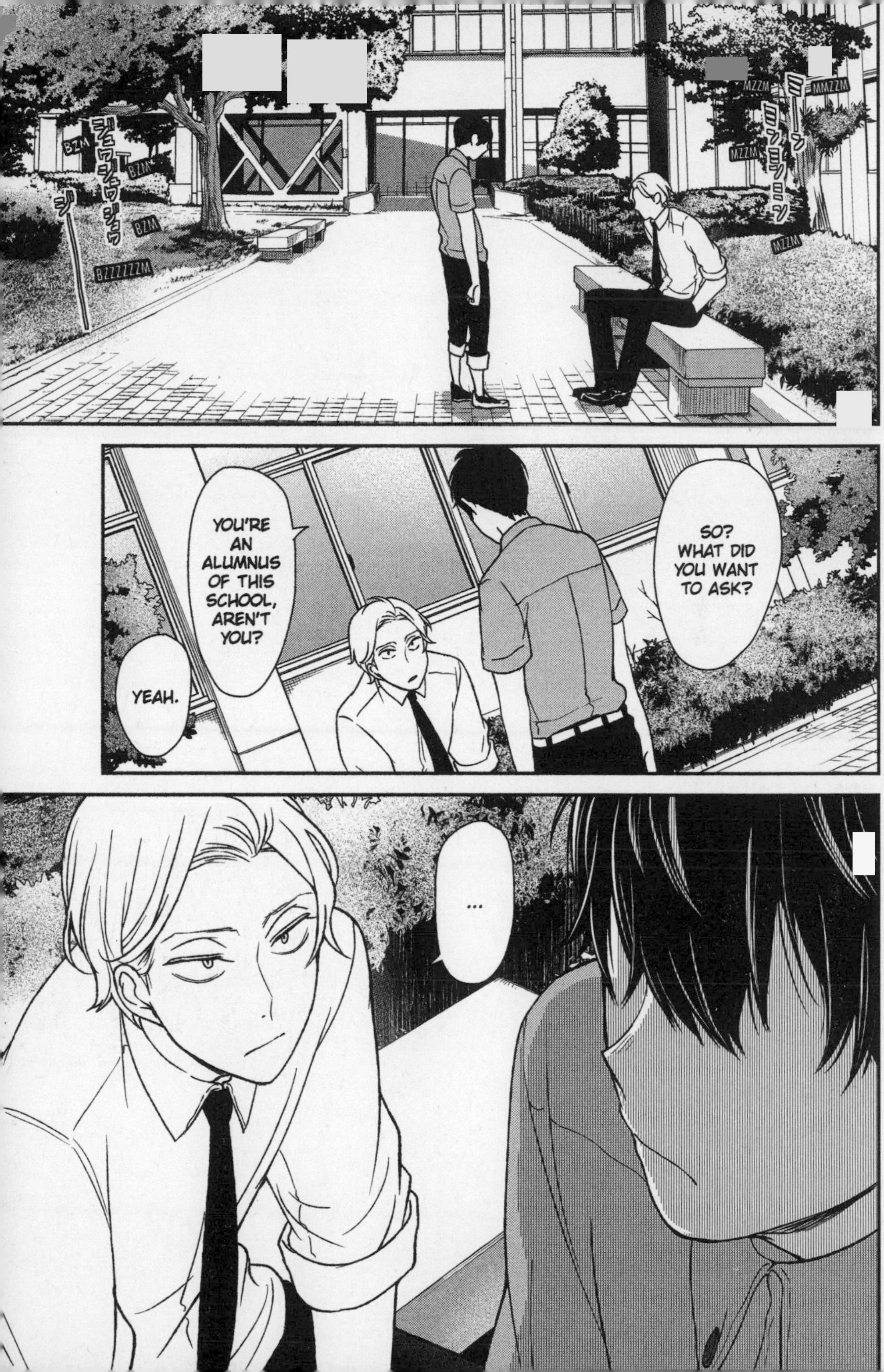
MZZM
MMZZM
MZZM
MZZM
BZM
BZM
BZM
BZZZZZM
SO? WHAT DID YOU WANT TO ASK?
YOU'RE AN ALUMNUS OF THIS SCHOOL, AREN'T YOU?
YEAH.
...

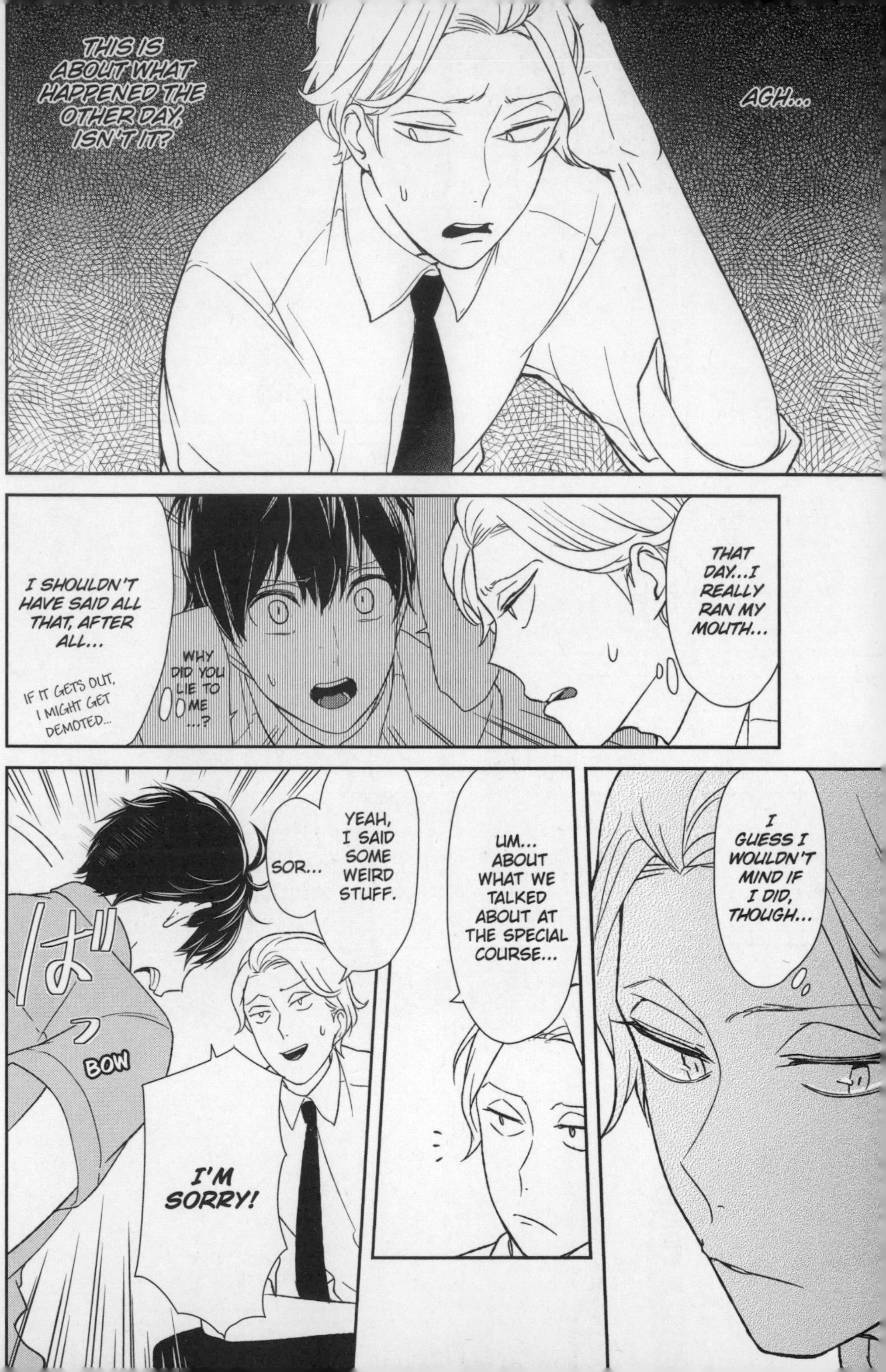
AGH...
THIS IS ABOUT WHAT HAPPENED THE OTHER DAY, ISN'T IT?
THAT DAY...I REALLY RAN MY MOUTH...
WHY DID YOU LIE TO ME ...?
I SHOULDN'T HAVE SAID ALL THAT, AFTER ALL...
IF IT GETS OUT, I MIGHT GET DEMOTED...
I GUESS I WOULDN'T MIND IF I DID, THOUGH...
UM... ABOUT WHAT WE TALKED ABOUT AT THE SPECIAL COURSE...
YEAH, I SAID SOME WEIRD STUFF.
SOR...
ばっ
BOW
I'M SORRY!

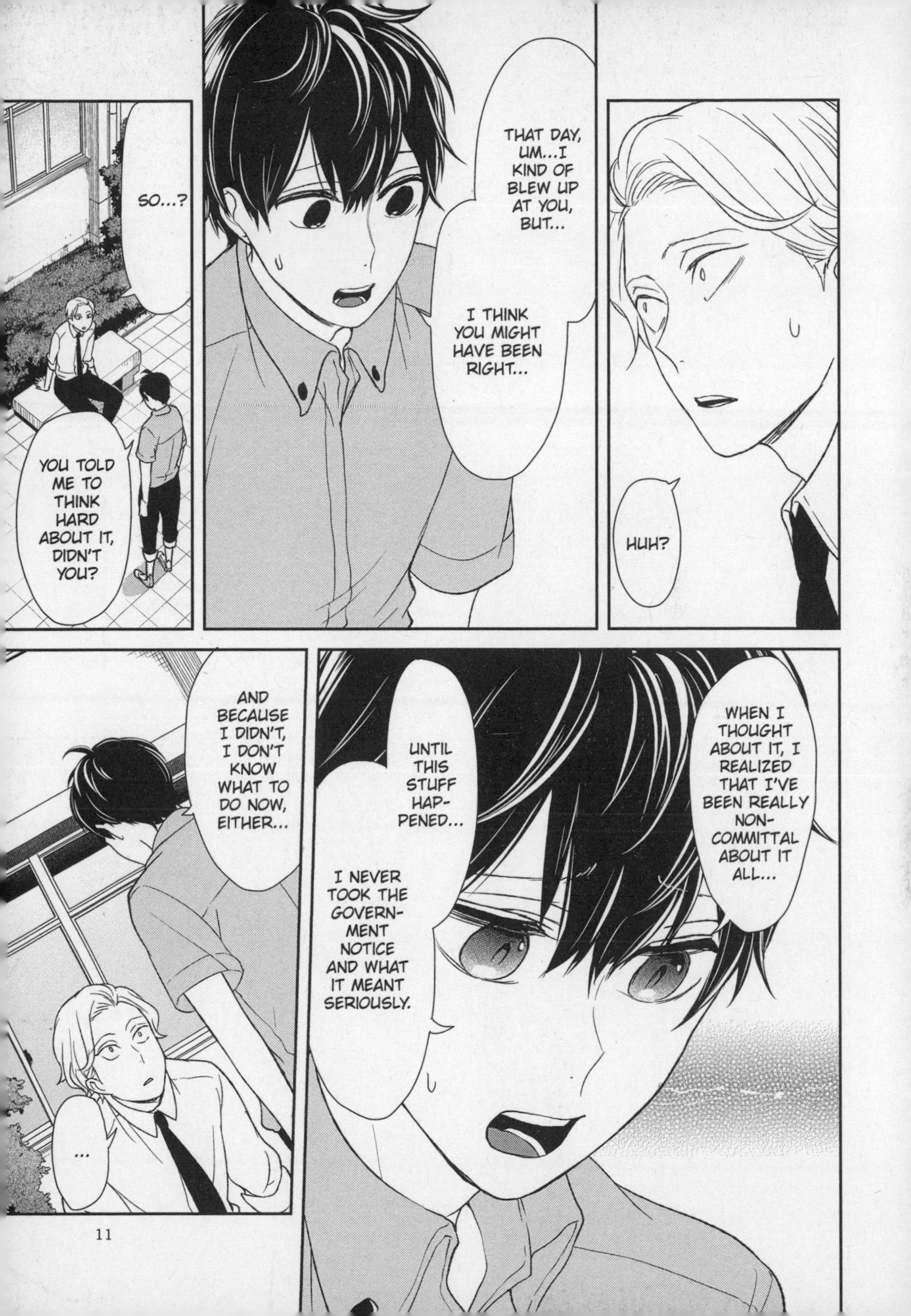
HUH?
THAT DAY, UM...I KIND OF BLEW UP AT YOU, BUT...
I THINK YOU MIGHT HAVE BEEN RIGHT...
SO...?
YOU TOLD ME TO THINK HARD ABOUT IT, DIDN'T YOU?
WHEN I THOUGHT ABOUT IT, I REALIZED THAT I'VE BEEN REALLY NON-COMMITTAL ABOUT IT ALL...
UNTIL THIS STUFF HAP-PENED...
I NEVER TOOK THE GOVERN-MENT NOTICE AND WHAT IT MEANT SERIOUSLY.
AND BECAUSE I DIDN'T, I DON'T KNOW WHAT TO DO NOW, EITHER...
...

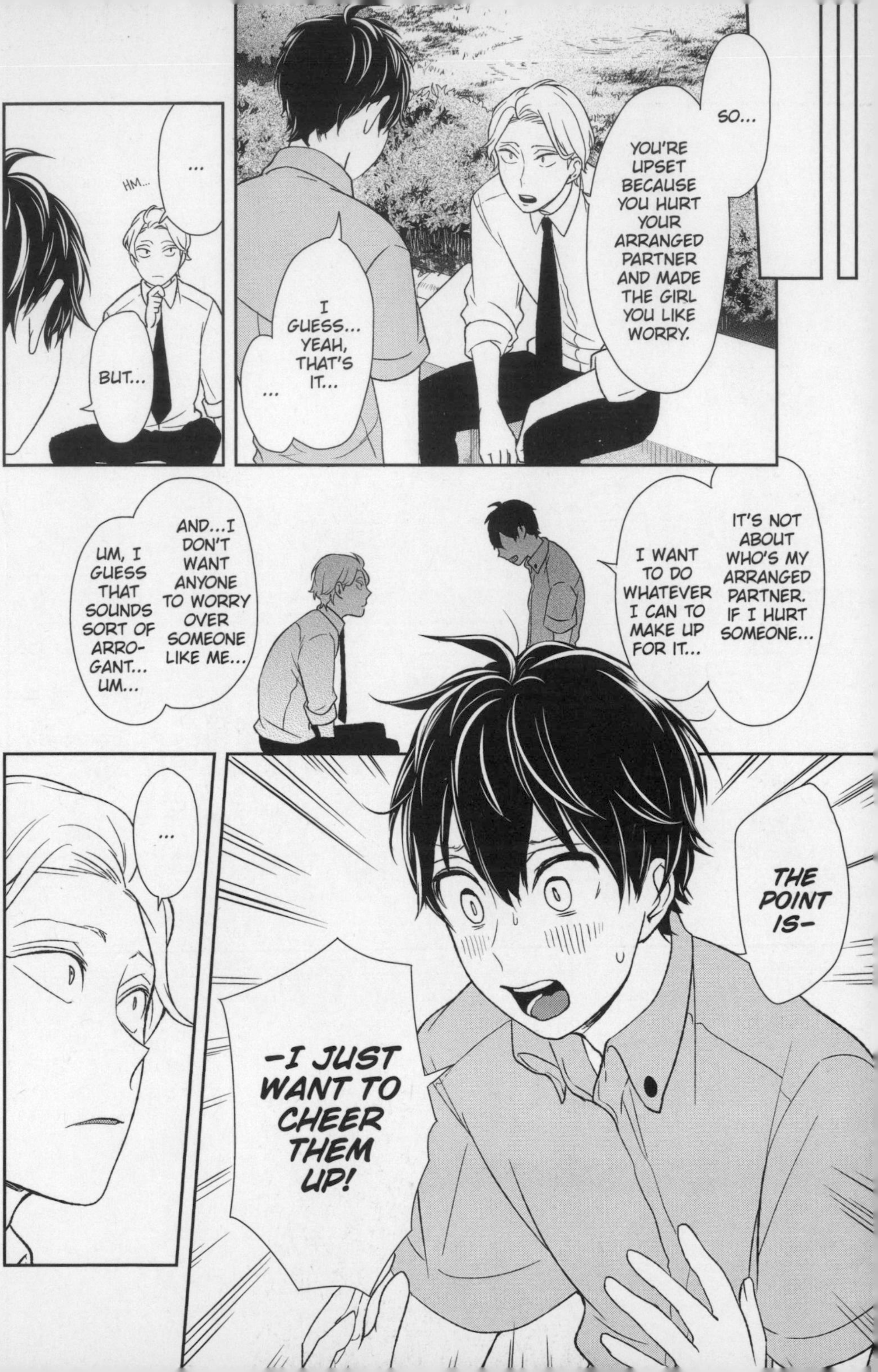
SO...
YOU'RE UPSET BECAUSE YOU HURT YOUR ARRANGED PARTNER AND MADE THE GIRL YOU LIKE WORRY.
I GUESS... YEAH, THAT'S IT...
...
...
HM...
BUT...
IT'S NOT ABOUT WHO'S MY ARRANGED PARTNER. IF I HURT SOMEONE...
I WANT TO DO WHATEVER I CAN TO MAKE UP FOR IT...
AND...I DON'T WANT ANYONE TO WORRY OVER SOMEONE LIKE ME...
UM, I GUESS THAT SOUNDS SORT OF ARRO-GANT... UM...
THE POINT IS-
-I JUST WANT TO CHEER THEM UP!
...

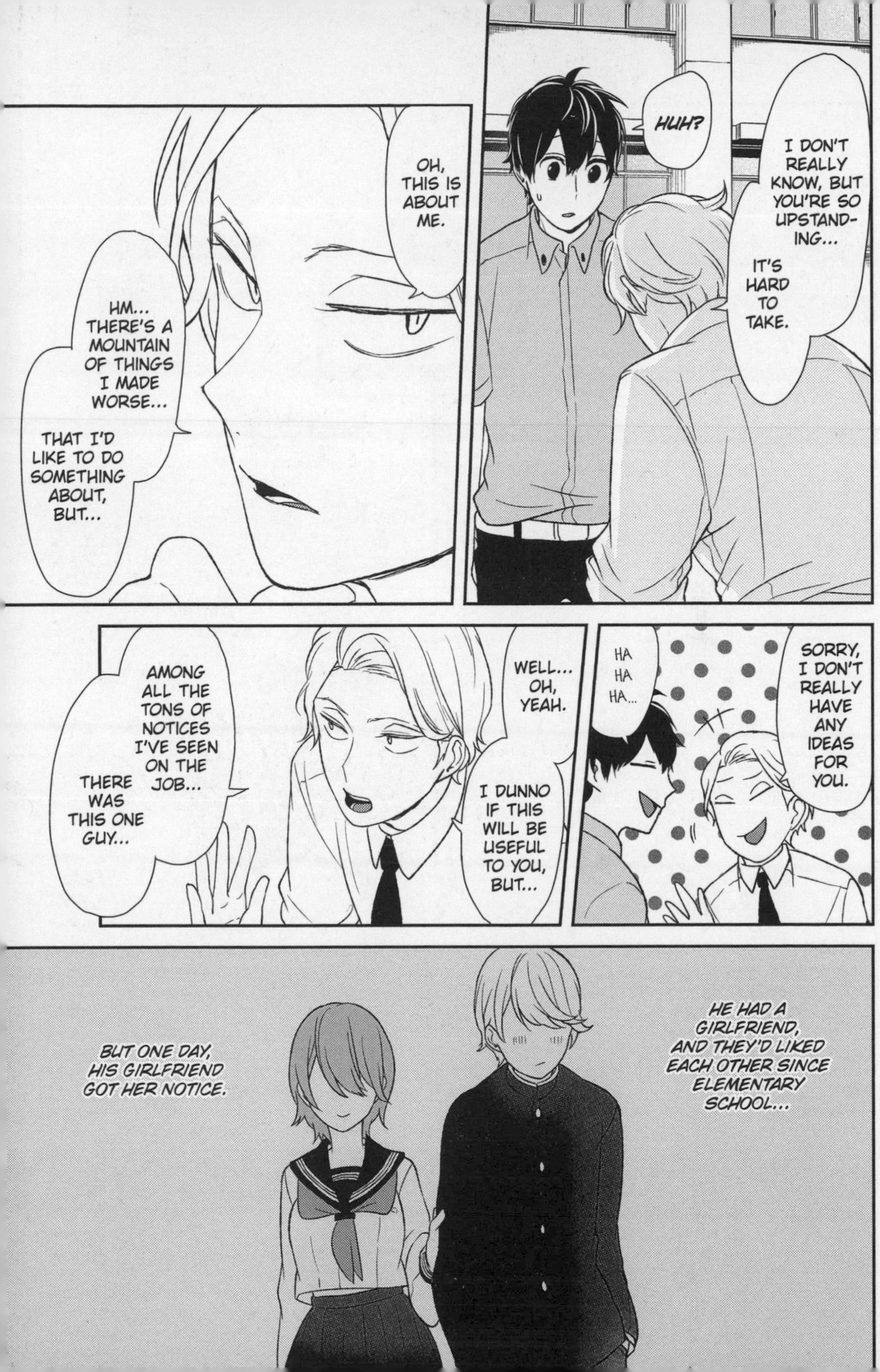
I DON'T REALLY KNOW, BUT YOU'RE SO UPSTANDING...
IT'S HARD TO TAKE.
HUH?
OH, THIS IS ABOUT ME.
HM... THERE'S A MOUNTAIN OF THINGS I MADE WORSE...
THAT I'D LIKE TO DO SOMETHING ABOUT, BUT...
SORRY, I DON'T REALLY HAVE ANY IDEAS FOR YOU.
HA HA HA...
WELL... OH, YEAH.
I DUNNO IF THIS WILL BE USEFUL TO YOU, BUT...
AMONG ALL THE TONS OF NOTICES I'VE SEEN ON THE JOB...
THERE WAS THIS ONE GUY...
HE HAD A GIRLFRIEND, AND THEY'D LIKED EACH OTHER SINCE ELEMENTARY SCHOOL...
BUT ONE DAY, HIS GIRLFRIEND GOT HER NOTICE.

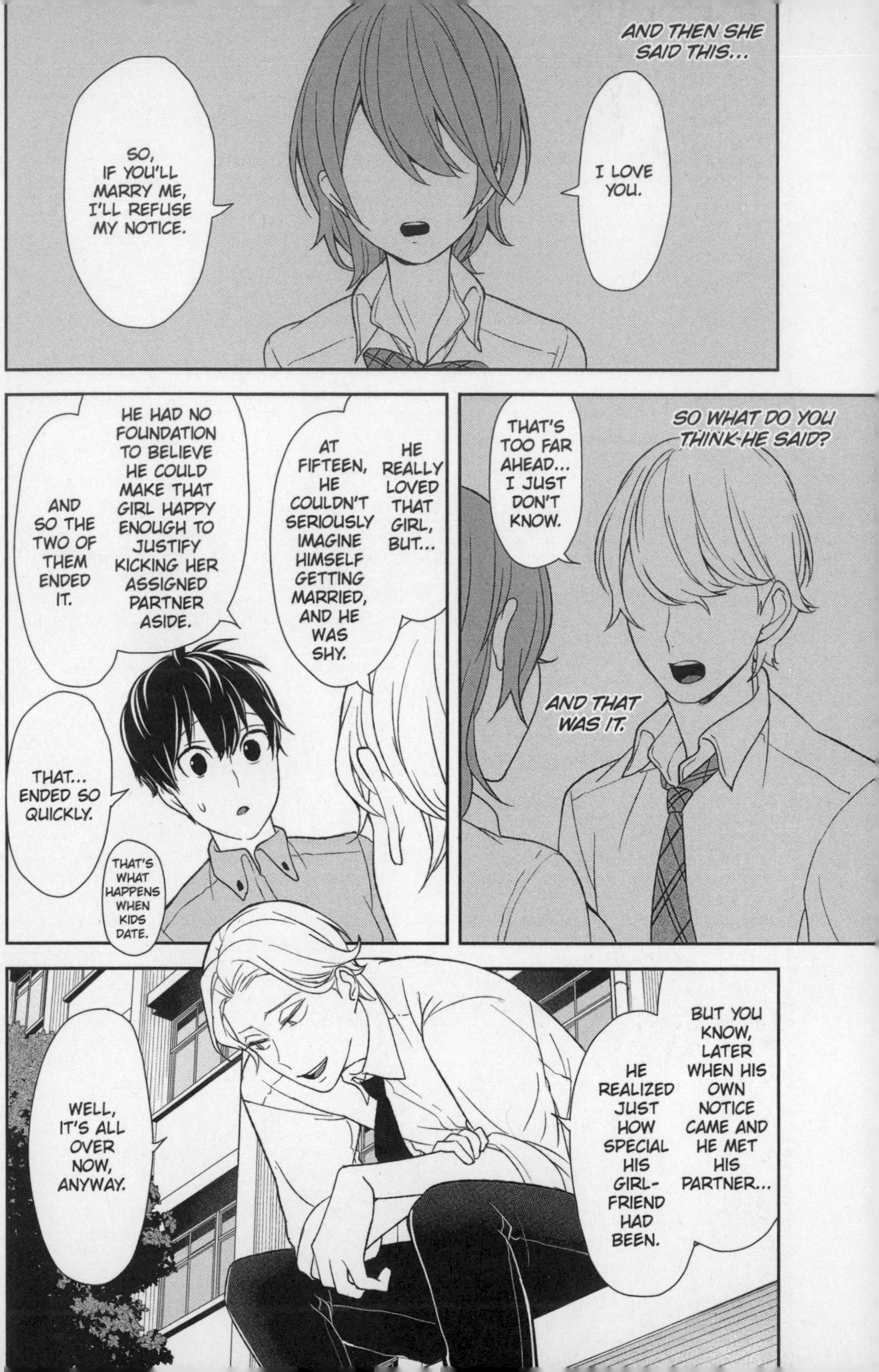
AND THEN SHE SAID THIS...
I LOVE YOU.
SO, IF YOU'LL MARRY ME, I'LL REFUSE MY NOTICE.
SO WHAT DO YOU THINK HE SAID?
THAT'S TOO FAR AHEAD... I JUST DON'T KNOW.
AND THAT WAS IT.
HE REALLY LOVED THAT GIRL, BUT...
AT FIFTEEN, HE COULDN'T SERIOUSLY IMAGINE HIMSELF GETTING MARRIED, AND HE WAS SHY.
HE HAD NO FOUNDATION TO BELIEVE HE COULD MAKE THAT GIRL HAPPY ENOUGH TO JUSTIFY KICKING HER ASSIGNED PARTNER ASIDE.
AND SO THE TWO OF THEM ENDED IT.
THAT... ENDED SO QUICKLY.
THAT'S WHAT HAPPENS WHEN KIDS DATE.
BUT YOU KNOW, LATER WHEN HIS OWN NOTICE CAME AND HE MET HIS PARTNER...
HE REALIZED JUST HOW SPECIAL HIS GIRL-FRIEND HAD BEEN.
WELL, IT'S ALL OVER NOW, ANYWAY.

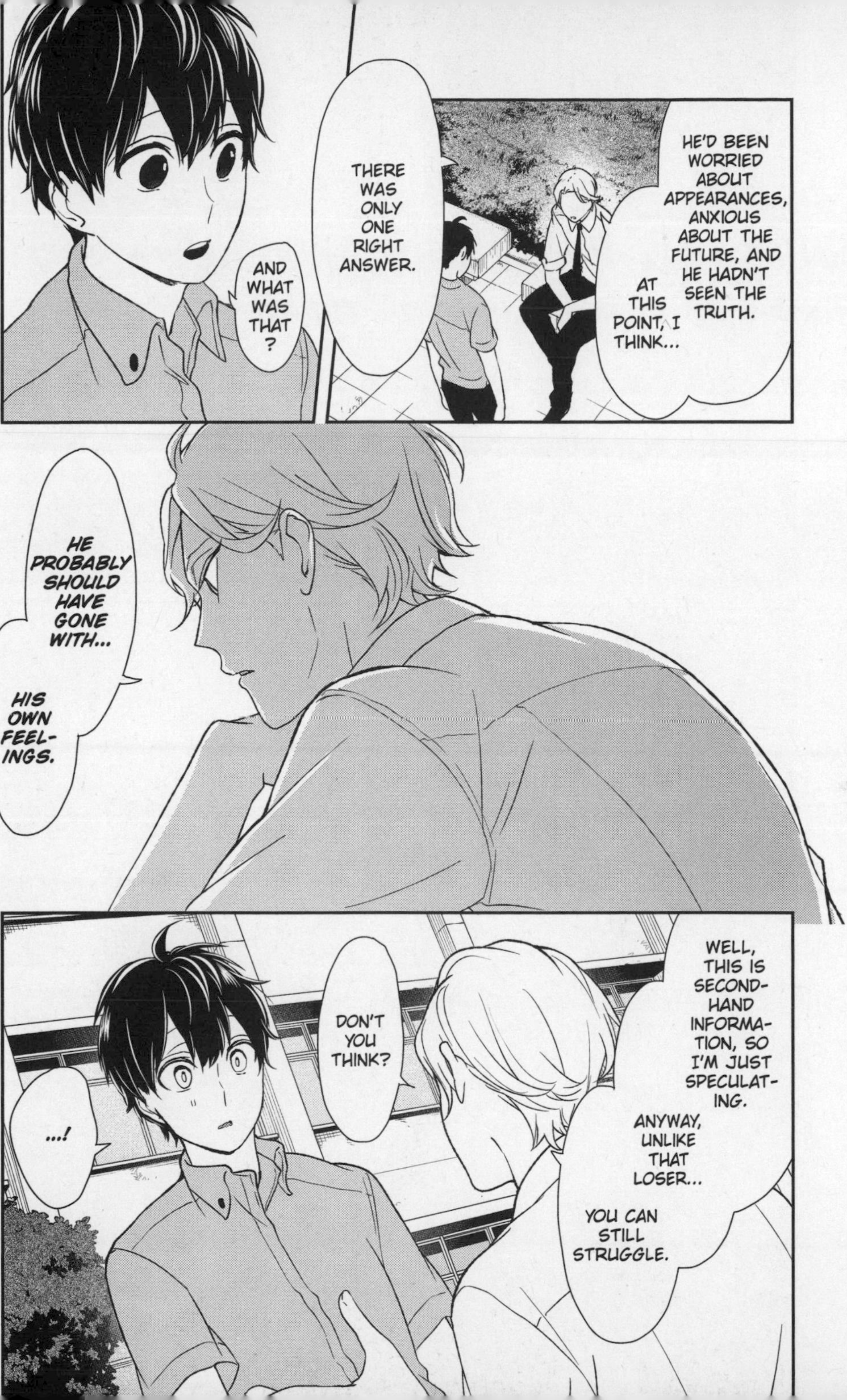
HE'D BEEN WORRIED ABOUT APPEARANCES, ANXIOUS ABOUT THE FUTURE, AND HE HADN'T SEEN THE TRUTH.
AT THIS POINT, I THINK...
THERE WAS ONLY ONE RIGHT ANSWER.
AND WHAT WAS THAT?
HE PROBABLY SHOULD HAVE GONE WITH...
HIS OWN FEEL-INGS.
WELL, THIS IS SECOND-HAND INFORMA-TION, SO I'M JUST SPECULAT-ING.
ANYWAY, UNLIKE THAT LOSER...
YOU CAN STILL STRUGGLE.
DON'T YOU THINK?
...!

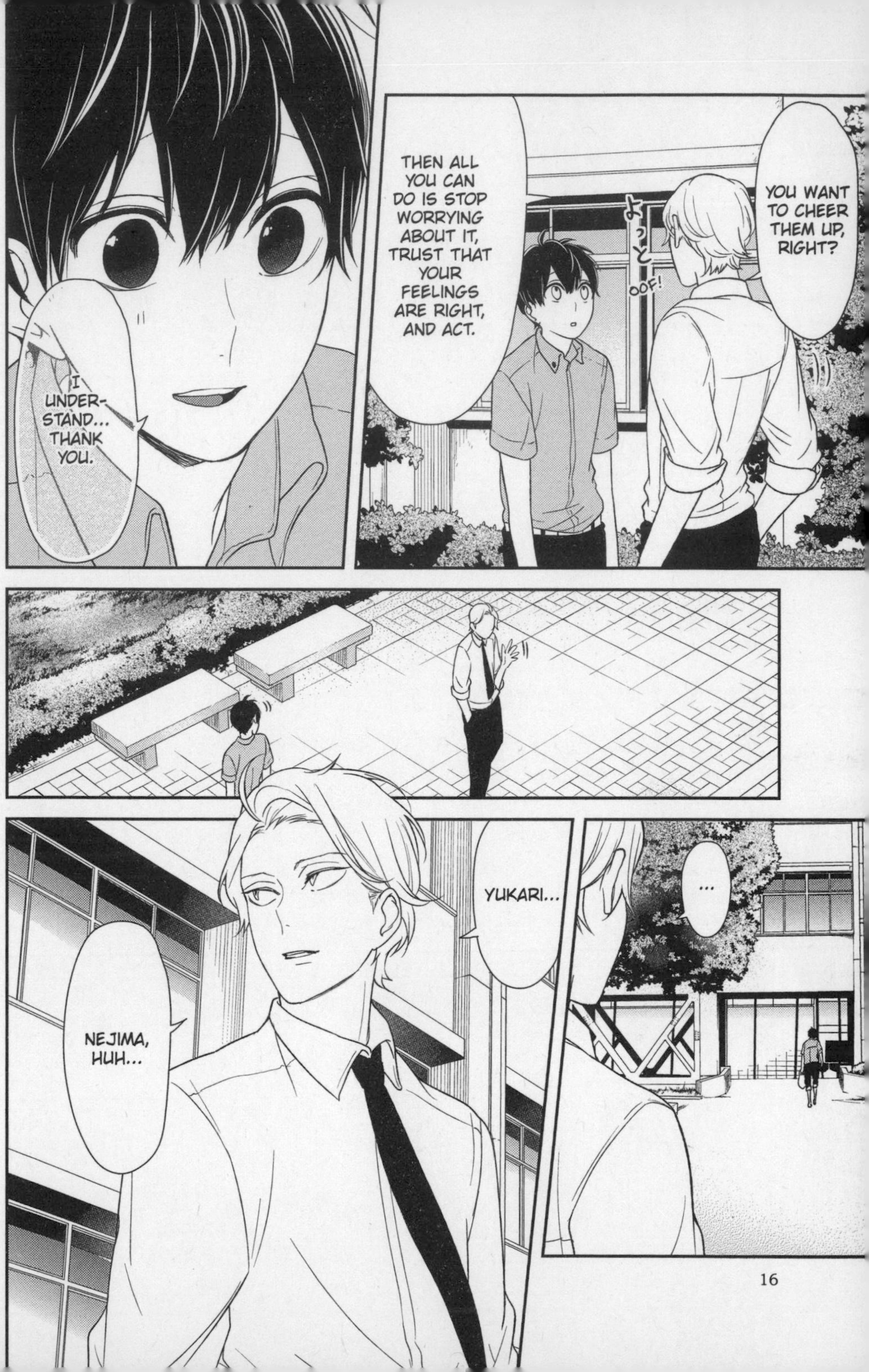
YOU WANT TO CHEER THEM UP, RIGHT?
よっと
OOF!
THEN ALL YOU CAN DO IS STOP WORRYING ABOUT IT, TRUST THAT YOUR FEELINGS ARE RIGHT, AND ACT.
I UNDER-STAND... THANK YOU.
...
YUKARI...
NEJIMA, HUH...

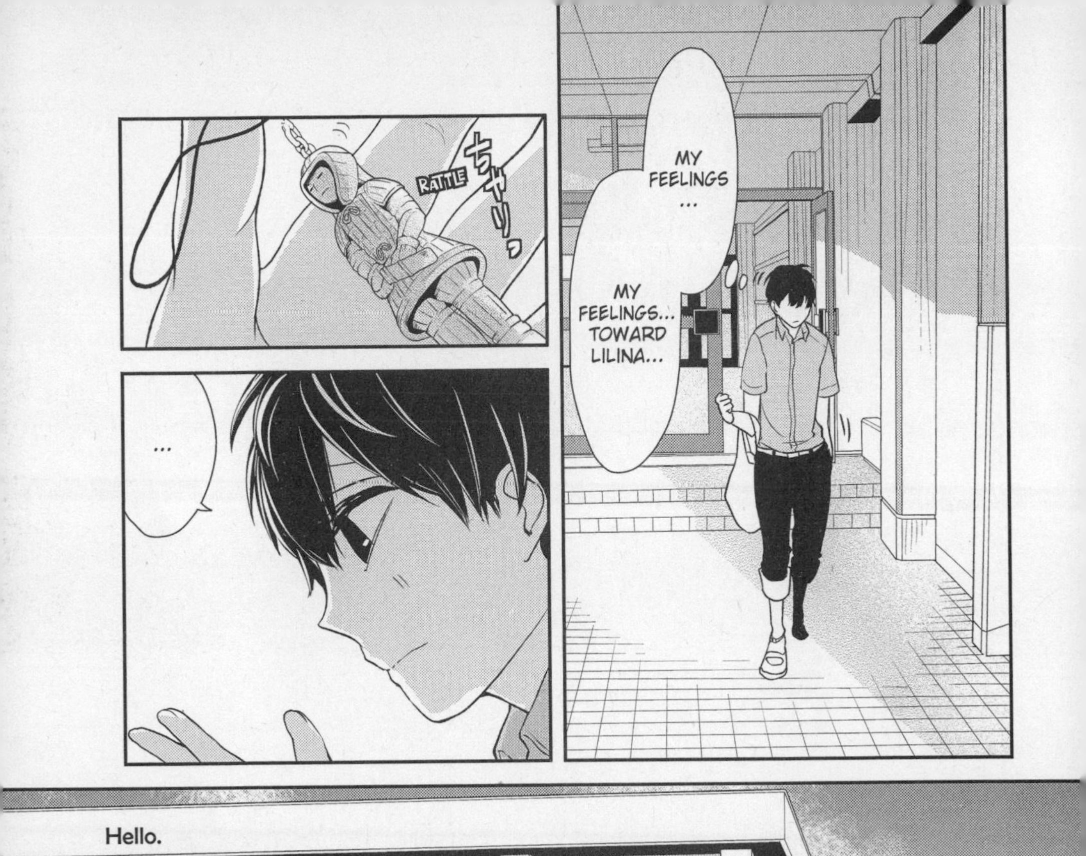
MY FEELINGS ...
MY FEELINGS... TOWARD LILINA...
RATTLE
ちゃりっ
...
Hello.
It's almost August, huh? What've you been up to during summer vacation? I'm basically going to school every day in preparation for the cultural festival, haha.
Um, remember how we talked about going to see a kofun together? Do you want to go, for real? I don't mean right now, but... I was really happy when you brought up the idea...
You're the first person who's ever taken me seriously when I talk about my dreams and kofun and stuff.
If you don't mind, I'd like to talk to you again.

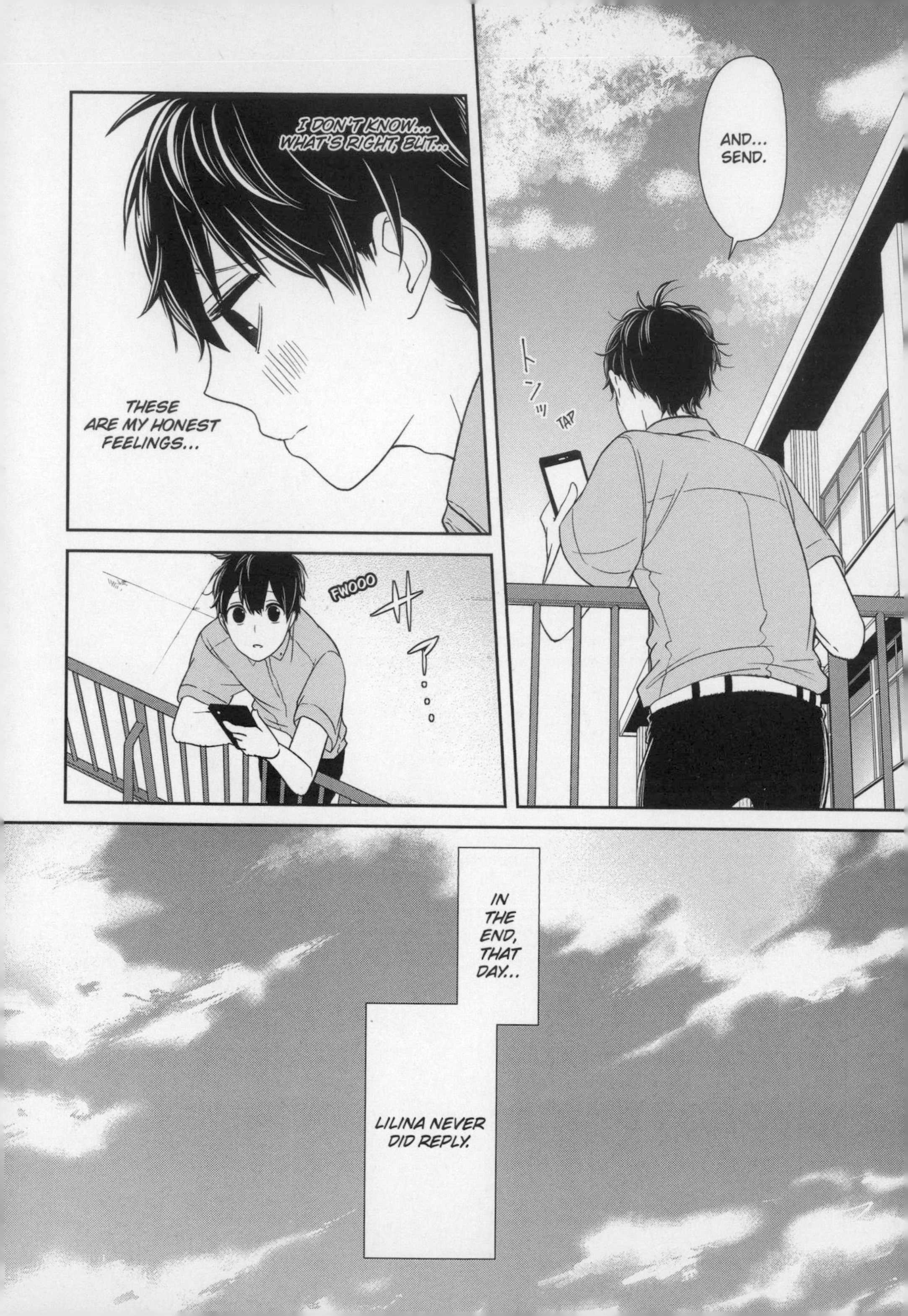
AND... SEND.
TAP
I DON'T KNOW... WHAT'S RIGHT, BUT...
THESE ARE MY HONEST FEELINGS...
FWOOO
IN THE END, THAT DAY...
LILINA NEVER DID REPLY.

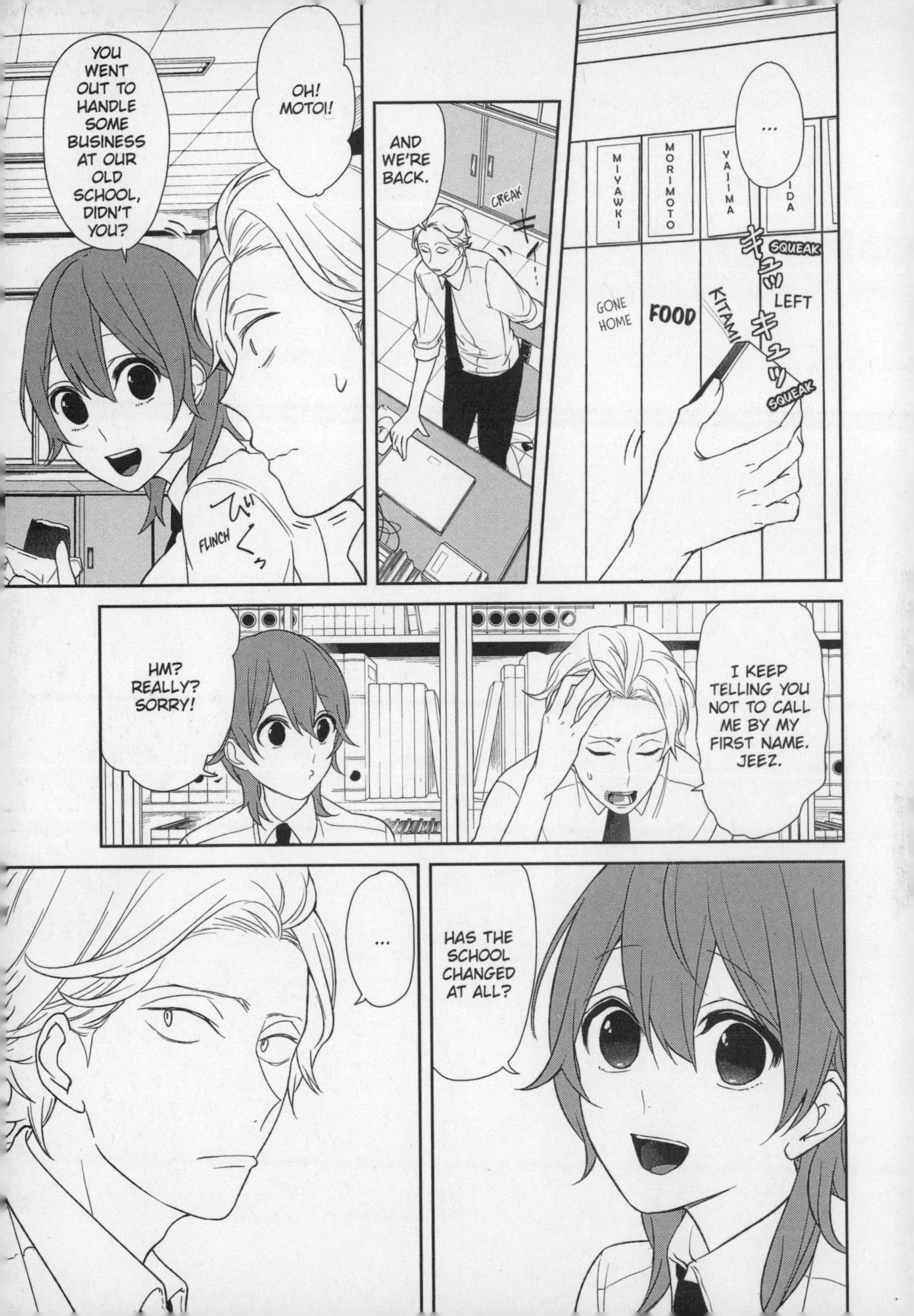
...
IDA
YAJIMA
MORIMOTO
MIYAWKI
SQUEAK
LEFT
KITAMI
FOOD
GONE HOME
SQUEAK
AND WE'RE BACK.
CREAK
OH! MOTOI!
YOU WENT OUT TO HANDLE SOME BUSINESS AT OUR OLD SCHOOL, DIDN'T YOU?
FLINCH
I KEEP TELLING YOU NOT TO CALL ME BY MY FIRST NAME. JEEZ.
HM? REALLY? SORRY!
HAS THE SCHOOL CHANGED AT ALL?
...

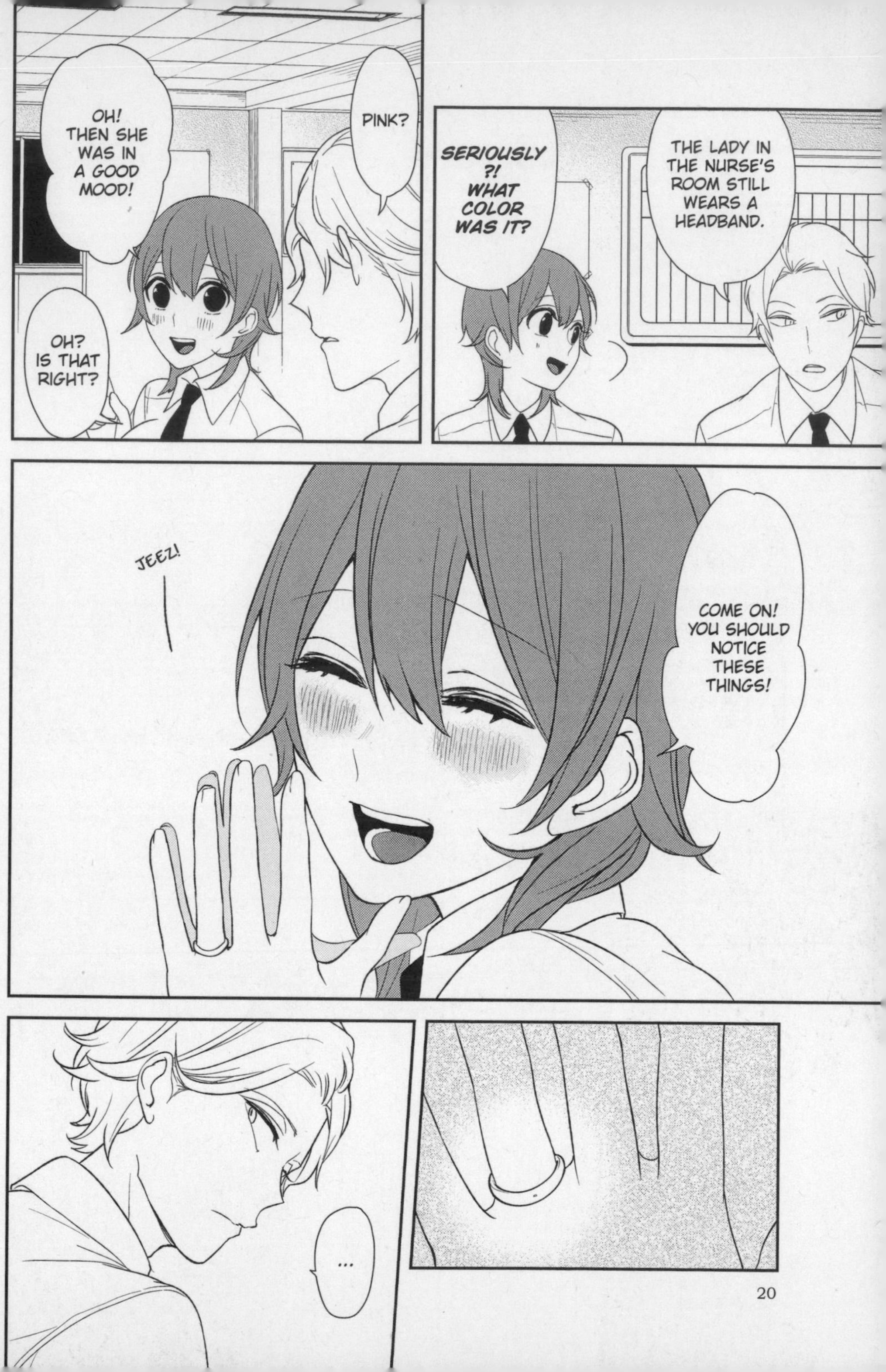
THE LADY IN THE NURSE'S ROOM STILL WEARS A HEADBAND.
SERIOUSLY?! WHAT COLOR WAS IT?
PINK?
OH! THEN SHE WAS IN A GOOD MOOD!
OH? IS THAT RIGHT?
COME ON! YOU SHOULD NOTICE THESE THINGS!
JEEZ!
...

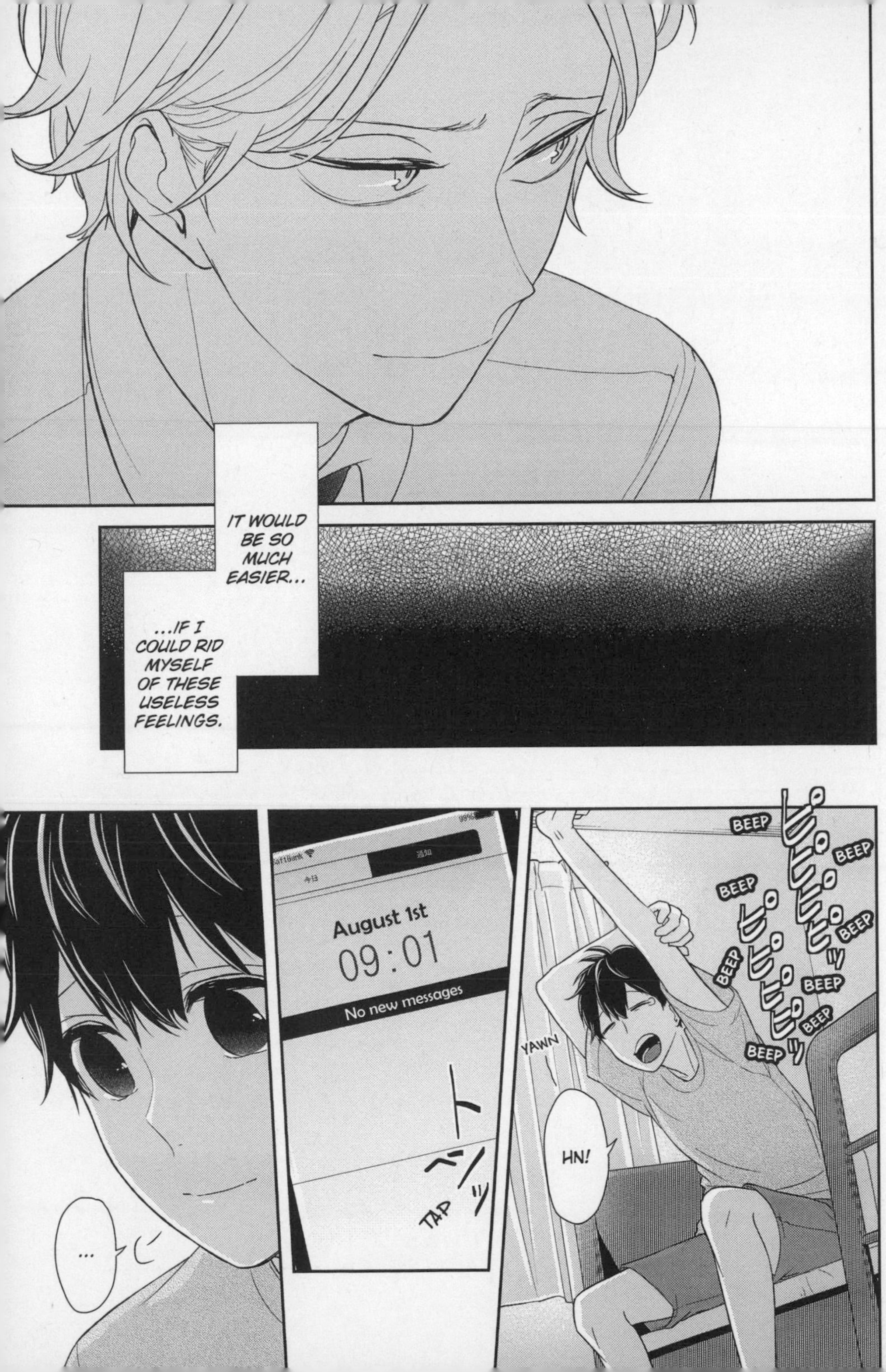
IT WOULD BE SO MUCH EASIER...
...IF I COULD RID MYSELF OF THESE USELESS FEELINGS.
BEEP
BEEP
BEEP
BEEP
BEEP
BEEP
BEEP
BEEP
YAWN
HN!
August 1st
09:01
No new messages
TAP
...

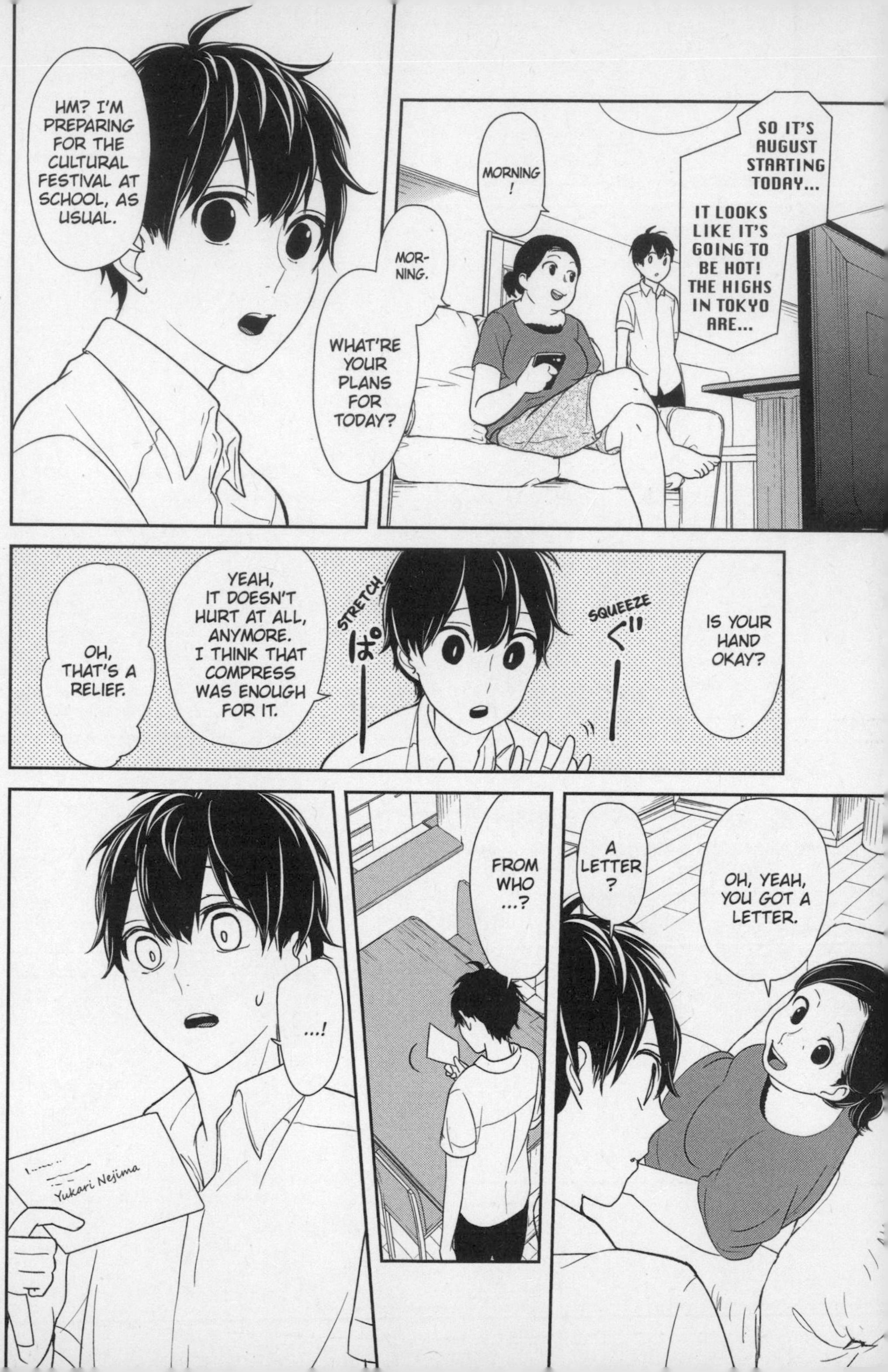
SO IT'S AUGUST STARTING TODAY...
IT LOOKS LIKE IT'S GOING TO BE HOT! THE HIGHS IN TOKYO ARE...
MORNING!
MORNING.
WHAT'RE YOUR PLANS FOR TODAY?
HM? I'M PREPARING FOR THE CULTURAL FESTIVAL AT SCHOOL, AS USUAL.
IS YOUR HAND OKAY?
SQUEEZE
STRETCH
YEAH, IT DOESN'T HURT AT ALL, ANYMORE. I THINK THAT COMPRESS WAS ENOUGH FOR IT.
OH, THAT'S A RELIEF.
OH, YEAH, YOU GOT A LETTER.
A LETTER?
FROM WHO...?
...!
Yukari Nejima

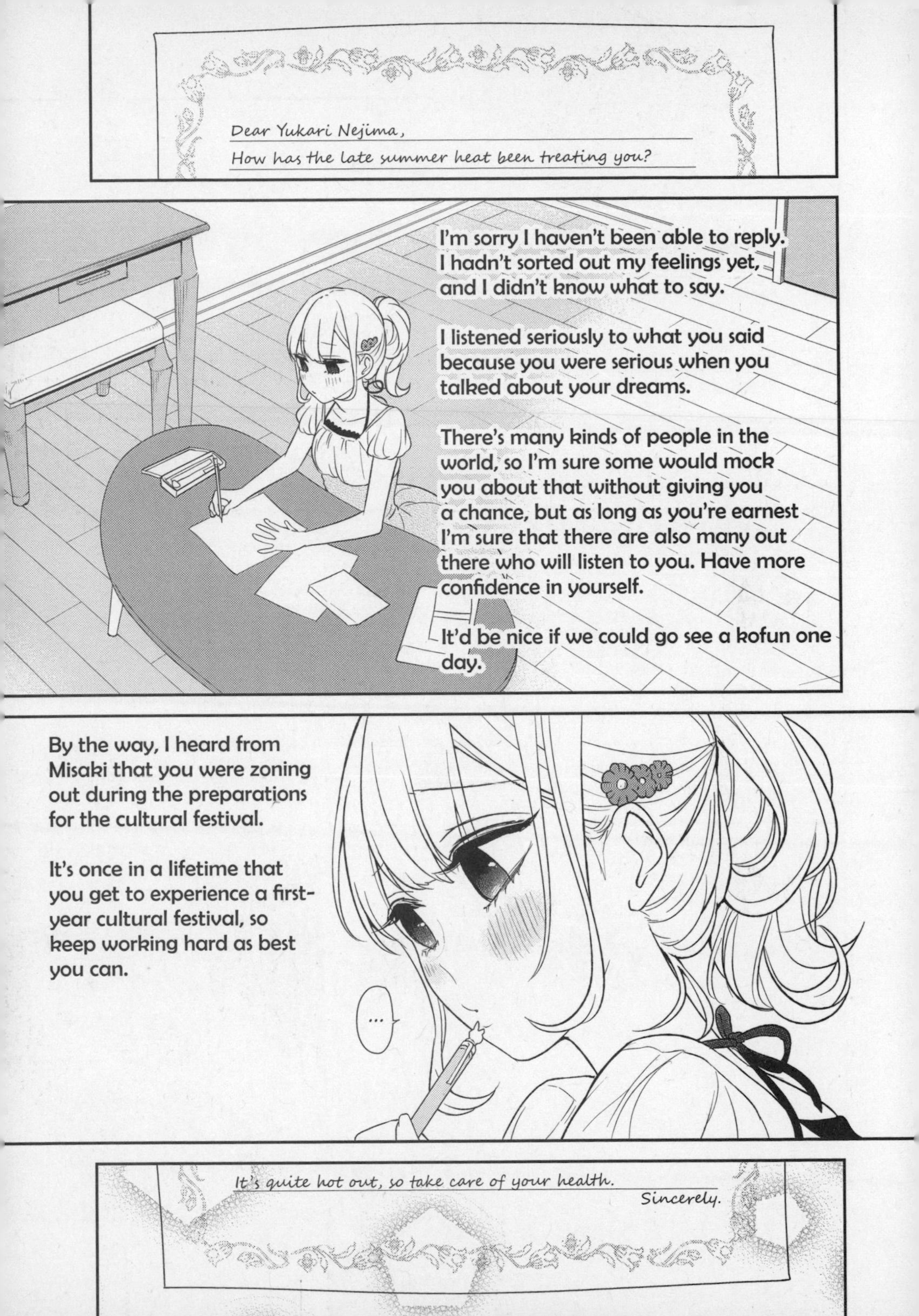
Dear Yukari Nejima,
How has the late summer heat been treating you?
I'm sorry I haven't been able to reply. I hadn't sorted out my feelings yet, and I didn't know what to say.
I listened seriously to what you said because you were serious when you talked about your dreams.
There's many kinds of people in the world, so I'm sure some would mock you about that without giving you a chance, but as long as you're earnest I'm sure that there are also many out there who will listen to you. Have more confidence in yourself.
It'd be nice if we could go see a kofun one day.
By the way, I heard from Misaki that you were zoning out during the preparations for the cultural festival.
It's once in a lifetime that you get to experience a first-year cultural festival, so keep working hard as best you can.
...
It's quite hot out, so take care of your health.
Sincerely.

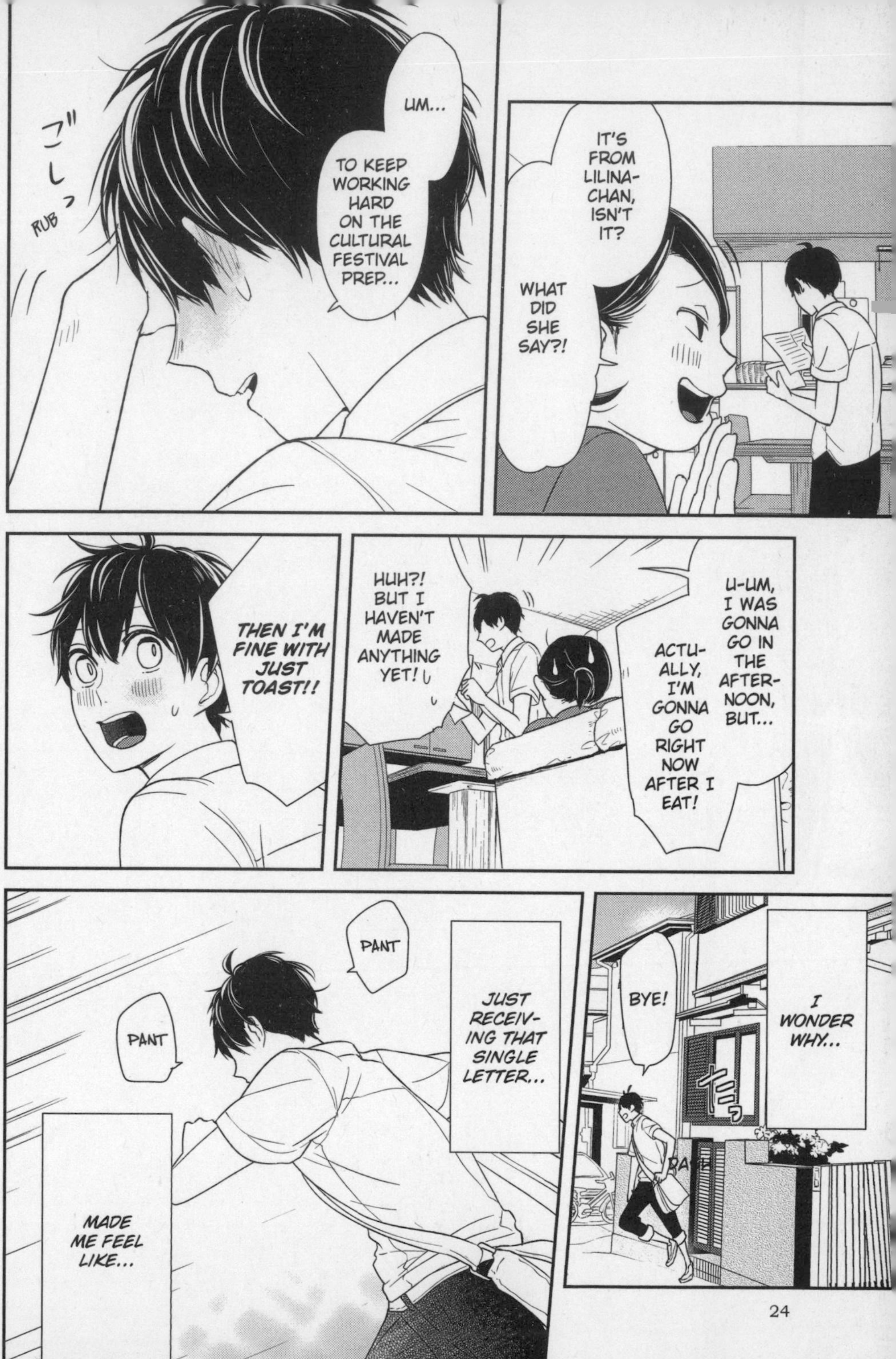
IT'S FROM LILINA-CHAN, ISN'T IT?
WHAT DID SHE SAY?!
ごしっ
RUB
UM...
TO KEEP WORKING HARD ON THE CULTURAL FESTIVAL PREP...
U-UM, I WAS GONNA GO IN THE AFTER-NOON, BUT...
ACTU-ALLY, I'M GONNA GO RIGHT NOW AFTER I EAT!
HUH?! BUT I HAVEN'T MADE ANYTHING YET!
THEN I'M FINE WITH JUST TOAST!!
I WONDER WHY...
BYE!
PANT
JUST RECEIV-ING THAT SINGLE LETTER...
PANT
MADE ME FEEL LIKE...

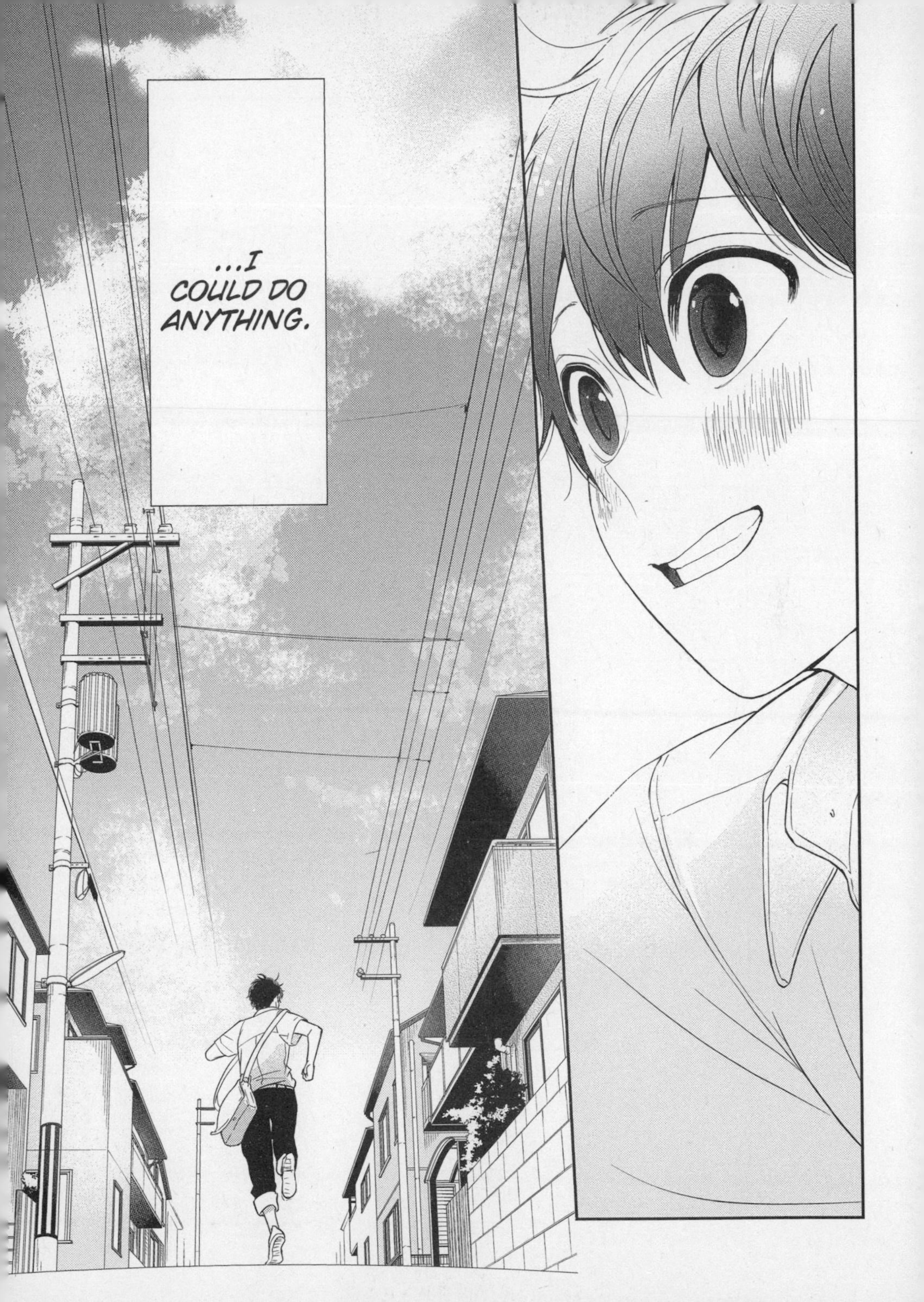
...I COULD DO ANYTHING.

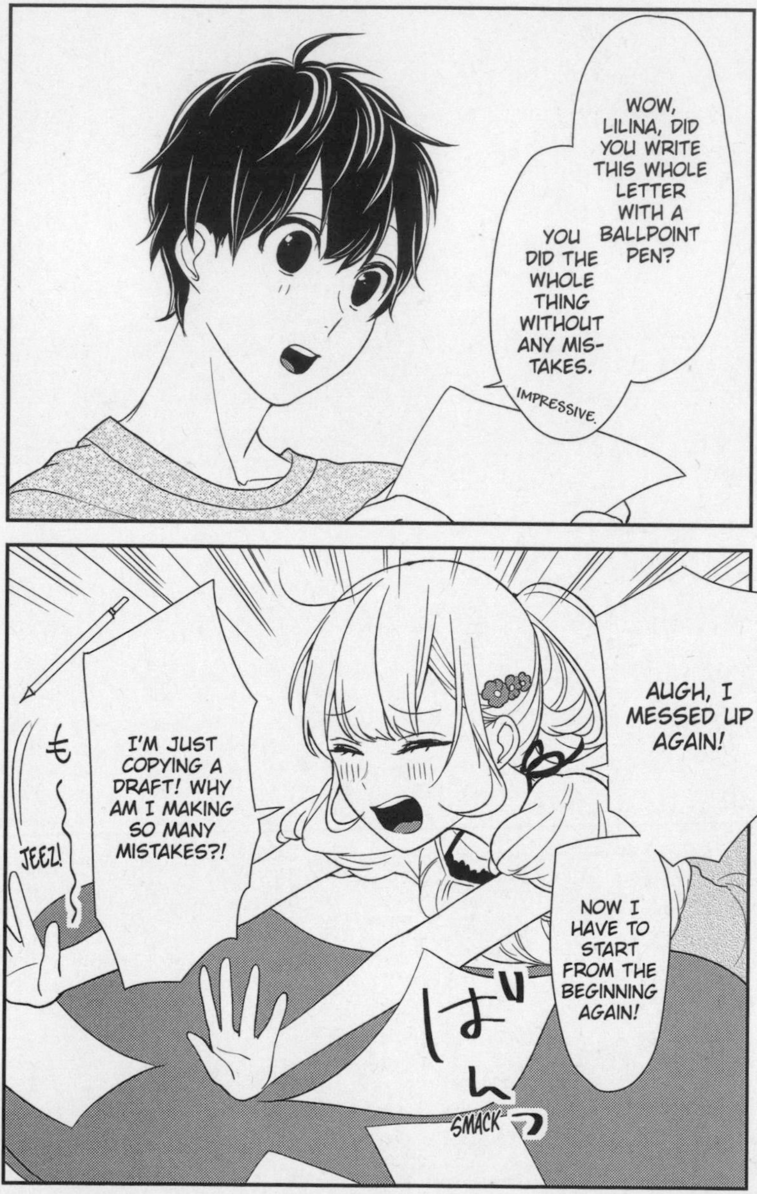
WOW, LILINA, DID YOU WRITE THIS WHOLE LETTER WITH A BALLPOINT PEN?
YOU DID THE WHOLE THING WITHOUT ANY MIS-TAKES.
IMPRESSIVE.
AUGH, I MESSED UP AGAIN!
I'M JUST COPYING A DRAFT! WHY AM I MAKING SO MANY MISTAKES?!
NOW I HAVE TO START FROM THE BEGINNING AGAIN!
もー
JEEZ!
ばんっ
SMACK

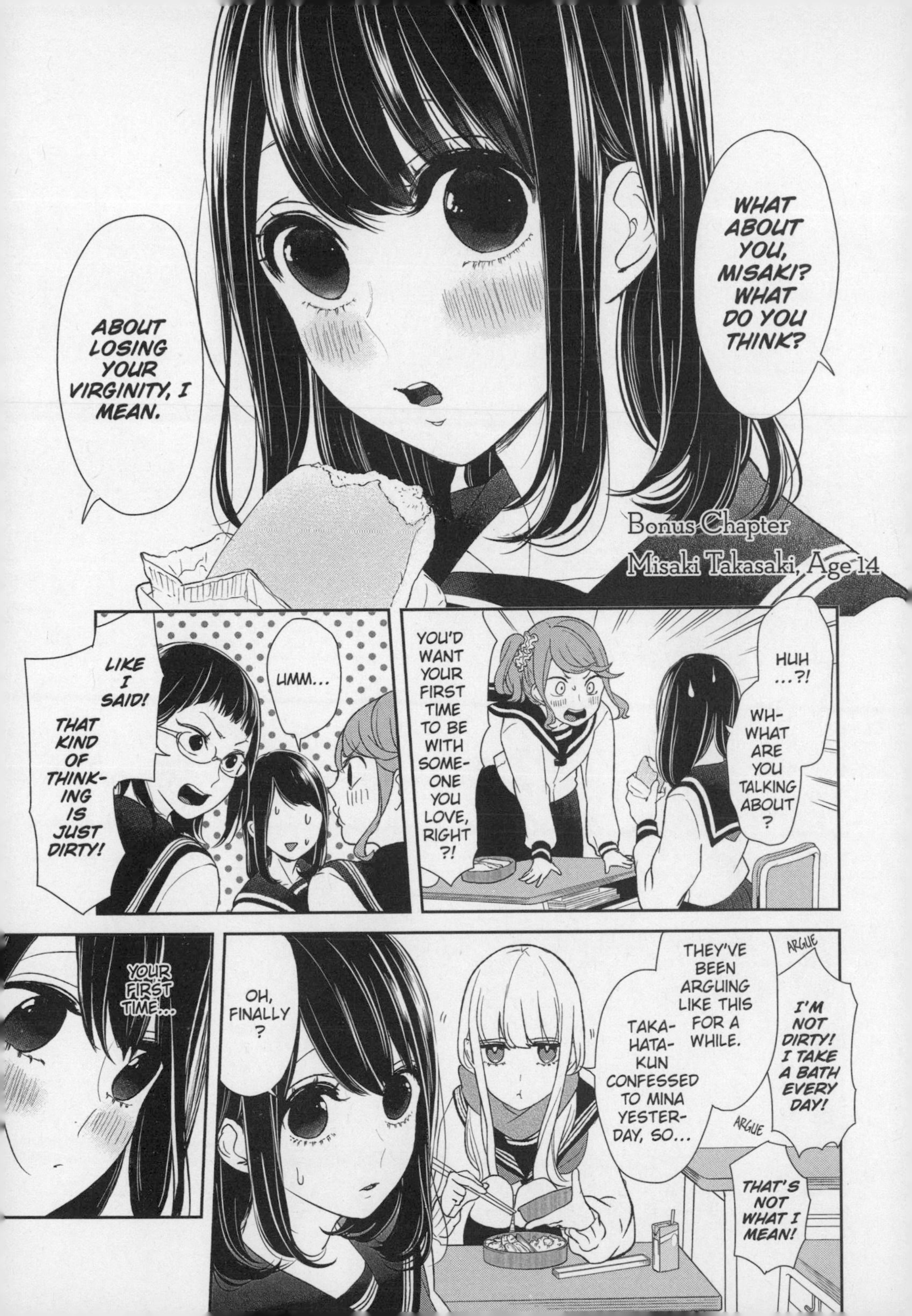
WHAT ABOUT YOU, MISAKI? WHAT DO YOU THINK?
ABOUT LOSING YOUR VIRGINITY, I MEAN.
Bonus Chapter
Misaki Takasaki, Age 14
HUH ...?!
WH-WHAT ARE YOU TALKING ABOUT?
YOU'D WANT YOUR FIRST TIME TO BE WITH SOME-ONE YOU LOVE, RIGHT?!
UMM...
LIKE I SAID! THAT KIND OF THINK-ING IS JUST DIRTY!
ARGUE
I'M NOT DIRTY! I TAKE A BATH EVERY DAY!
ARGUE
THAT'S NOT WHAT I MEAN!
THEY'VE BEEN ARGUING LIKE THIS FOR A WHILE.
TAKA-HATA-KUN CONFESSED TO MINA YESTER-DAY, SO...
OH, FINALLY?
YOUR FIRST TIME...

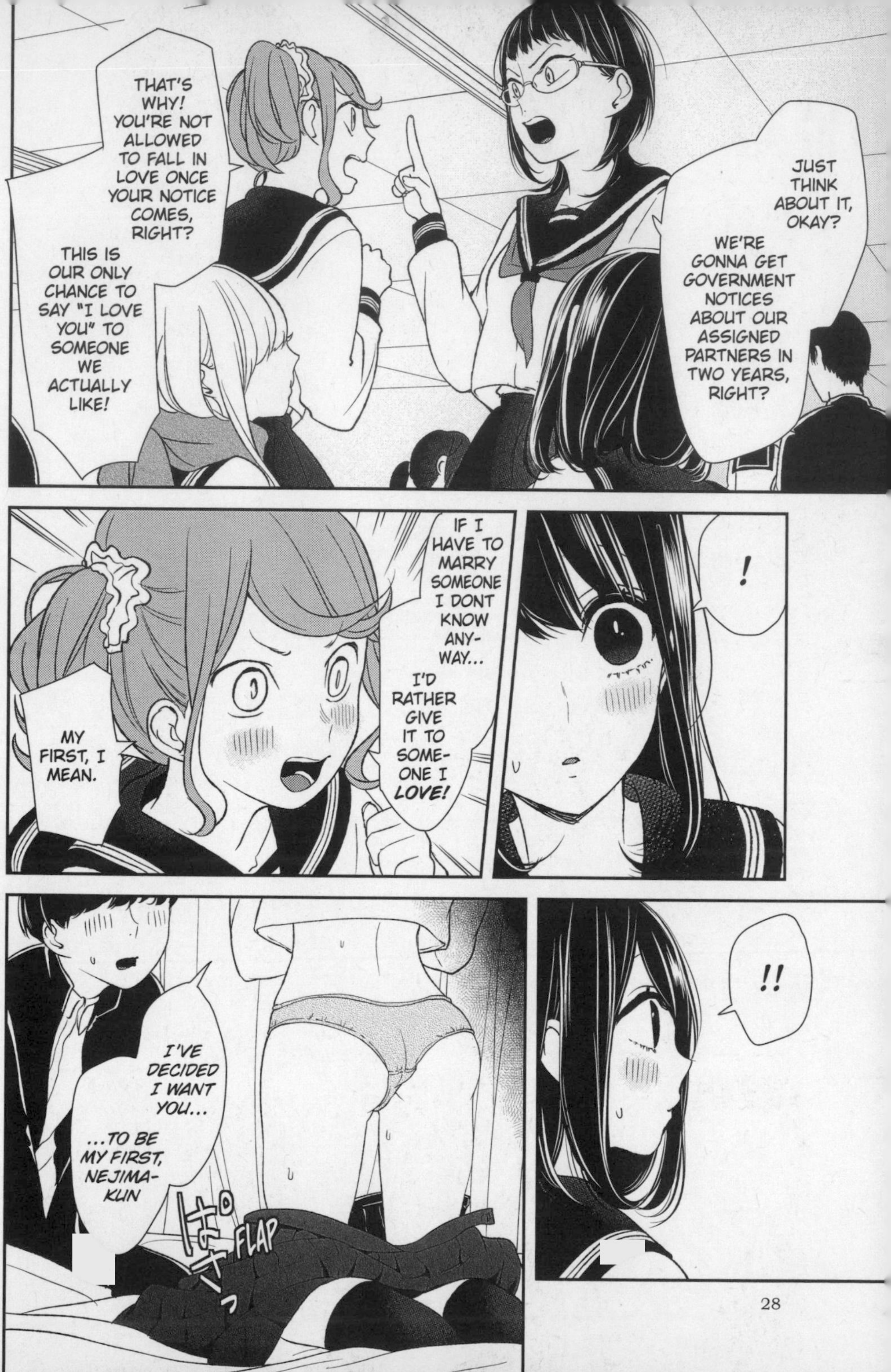
JUST THINK ABOUT IT, OKAY?
WE'RE GONNA GET GOVERNMENT NOTICES ABOUT OUR ASSIGNED PARTNERS IN TWO YEARS, RIGHT?
THAT'S WHY! YOU'RE NOT ALLOWED TO FALL IN LOVE ONCE YOUR NOTICE COMES, RIGHT?
THIS IS OUR ONLY CHANCE TO SAY "I LOVE YOU" TO SOMEONE WE ACTUALLY LIKE!
!
IF I HAVE TO MARRY SOMEONE I DONT KNOW ANY-WAY...
I'D RATHER GIVE IT TO SOME-ONE I *LOVE!*
MY FIRST, I MEAN.
!!
I'VE DECIDED I WANT YOU...
...TO BE MY FIRST, NEJIMA-KUN
FLAP

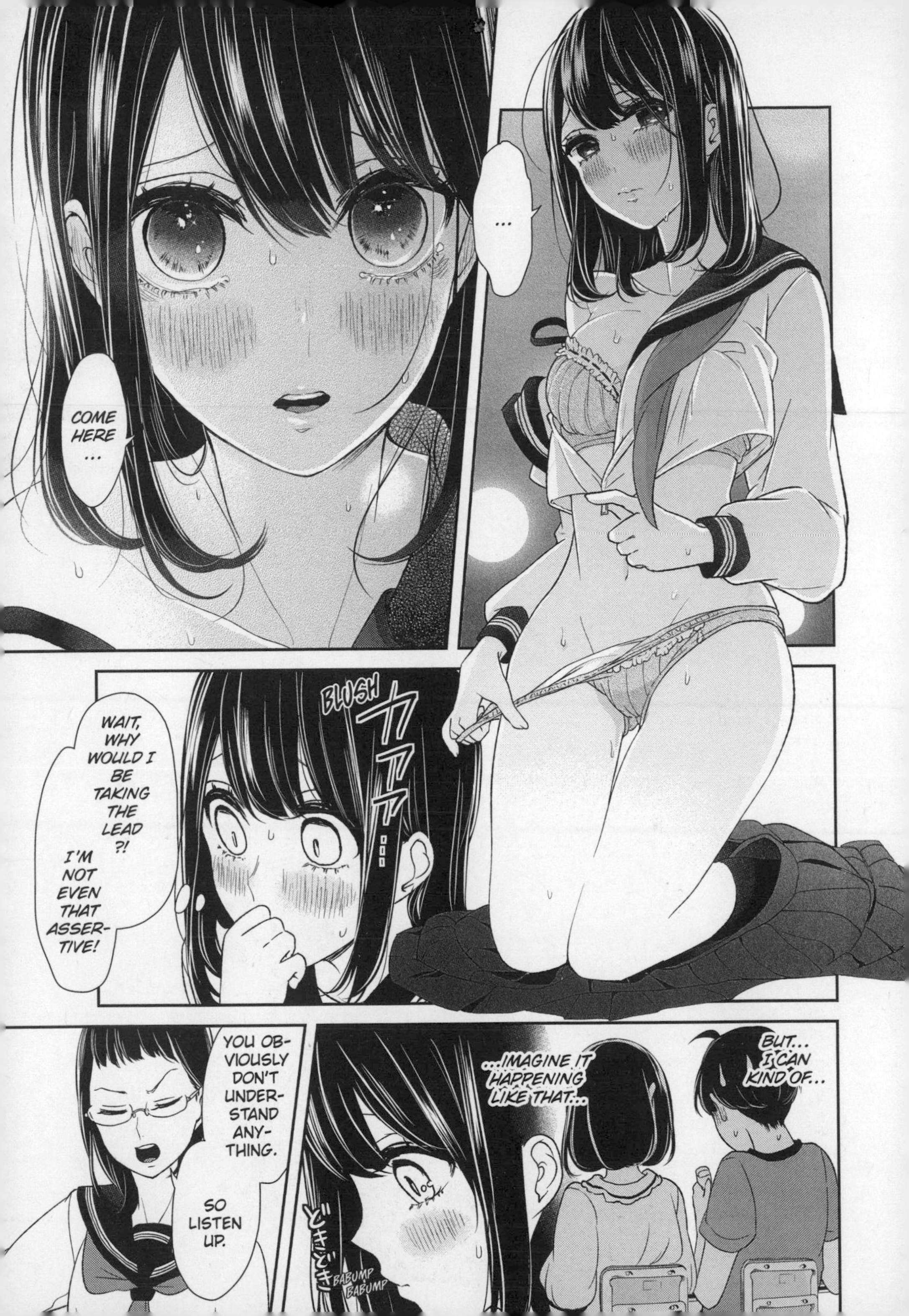
...
COME HERE...
BLUSH
WAIT, WHY WOULD I BE TAKING THE LEAD?!
I'M NOT EVEN THAT ASSERTIVE!
BUT... I CAN KIND OF...
...IMAGINE IT HAPPENING LIKE THAT...
BABUMP BABUMP
YOU OBVIOUSLY DON'T UNDERSTAND ANYTHING.
SO LISTEN UP.

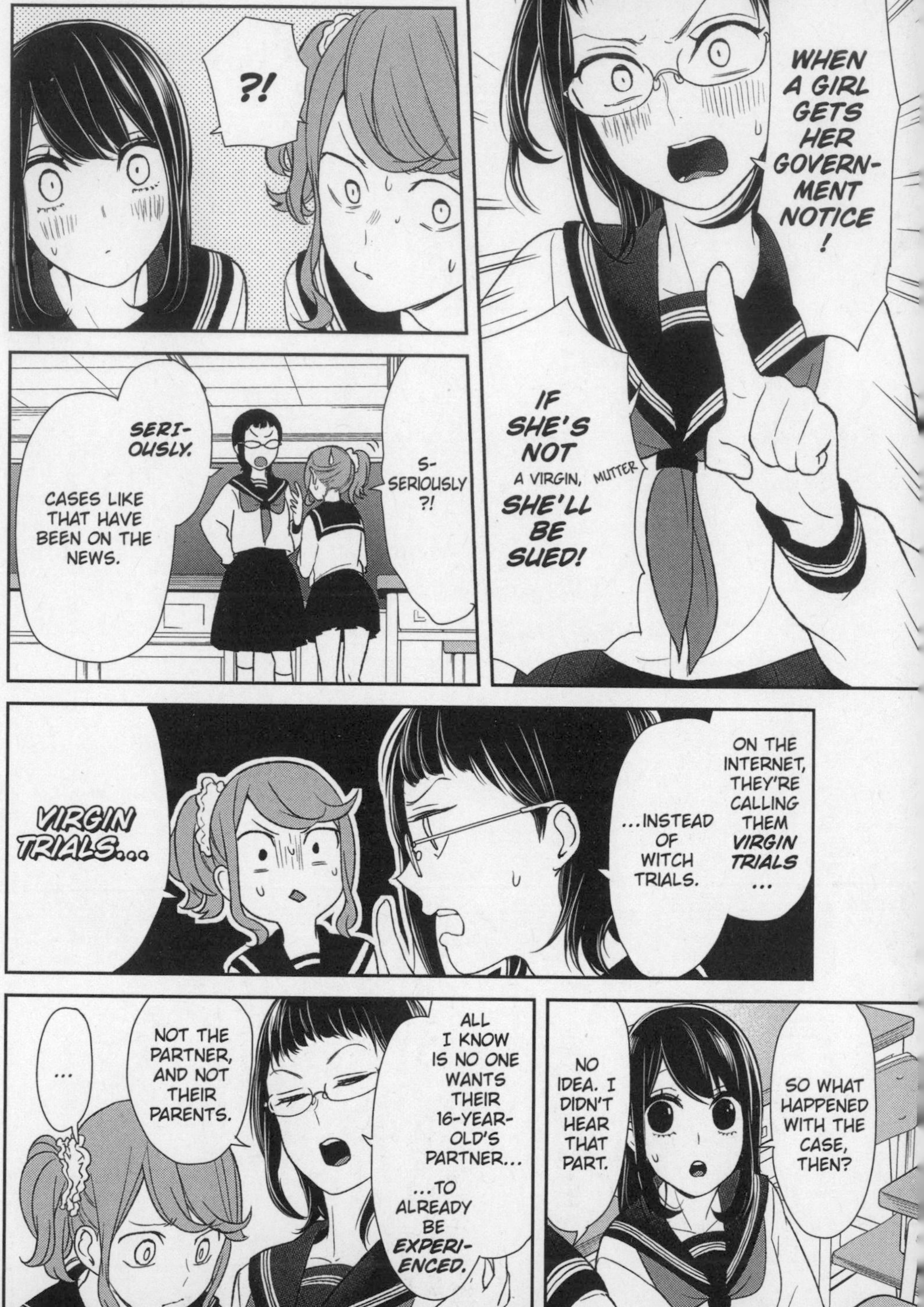
WHEN A GIRL GETS HER GOVERNMENT NOTICE!
IF SHE'S NOT A VIRGIN, SHE'LL BE SUED!
MUTTER
?!
S-SERIOUSLY?!
SERIOUSLY.
CASES LIKE THAT HAVE BEEN ON THE NEWS.
ON THE INTERNET, THEY'RE CALLING THEM VIRGIN TRIALS...
...INSTEAD OF WITCH TRIALS.
VIRGIN TRIALS...
SO WHAT HAPPENED WITH THE CASE, THEN?
NO IDEA. I DIDN'T HEAR THAT PART.
ALL I KNOW IS NO ONE WANTS THEIR 16-YEAR-OLD'S PARTNER...
...TO ALREADY BE EXPERIENCED.
NOT THE PARTNER, AND NOT THEIR PARENTS.
...

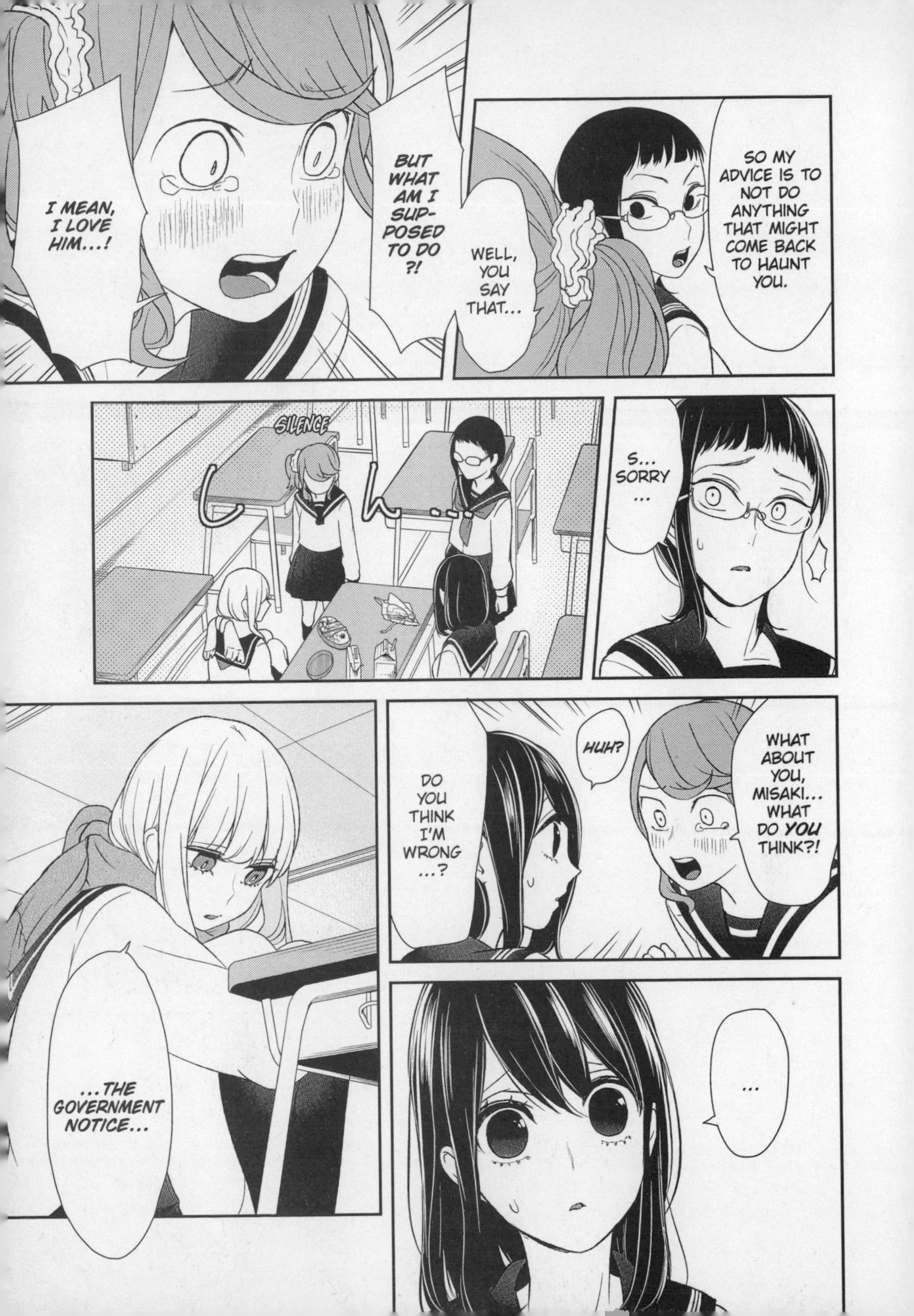
SO MY ADVICE IS TO NOT DO ANYTHING THAT MIGHT COME BACK TO HAUNT YOU.
WELL, YOU SAY THAT...
BUT WHAT AM I SUP-POSED TO DO ?!
I MEAN, I LOVE HIM...!
S... SORRY ...
SILENCE
しん...
WHAT ABOUT YOU, MISAKI... WHAT DO *YOU* THINK?!
HUH?
DO YOU THINK I'M WRONG ...?
...
...THE GOVERNMENT NOTICE...

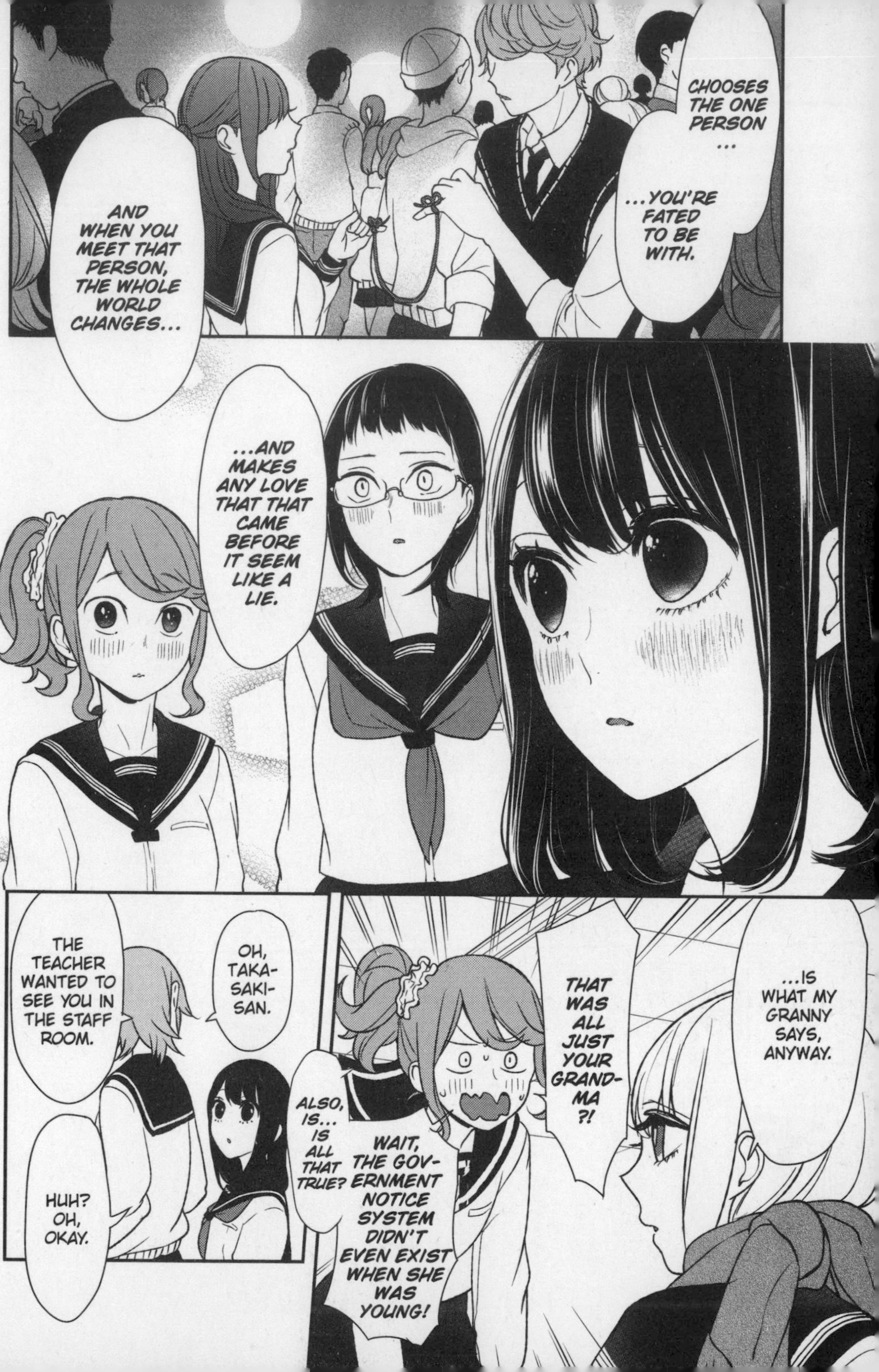
CHOOSES THE ONE PERSON ...
...YOU'RE FATED TO BE WITH.
AND WHEN YOU MEET THAT PERSON, THE WHOLE WORLD CHANGES...
...AND MAKES ANY LOVE THAT THAT CAME BEFORE IT SEEM LIKE A LIE.
...IS WHAT MY GRANNY SAYS, ANYWAY.
THAT WAS ALL JUST YOUR GRANDMA?!
WAIT, THE GOVERNMENT NOTICE SYSTEM DIDN'T EVEN EXIST WHEN SHE WAS YOUNG!
ALSO, IS... IS ALL THAT TRUE?
OH, TAKASAKI-SAN.
THE TEACHER WANTED TO SEE YOU IN THE STAFF ROOM.
HUH? OH, OKAY.

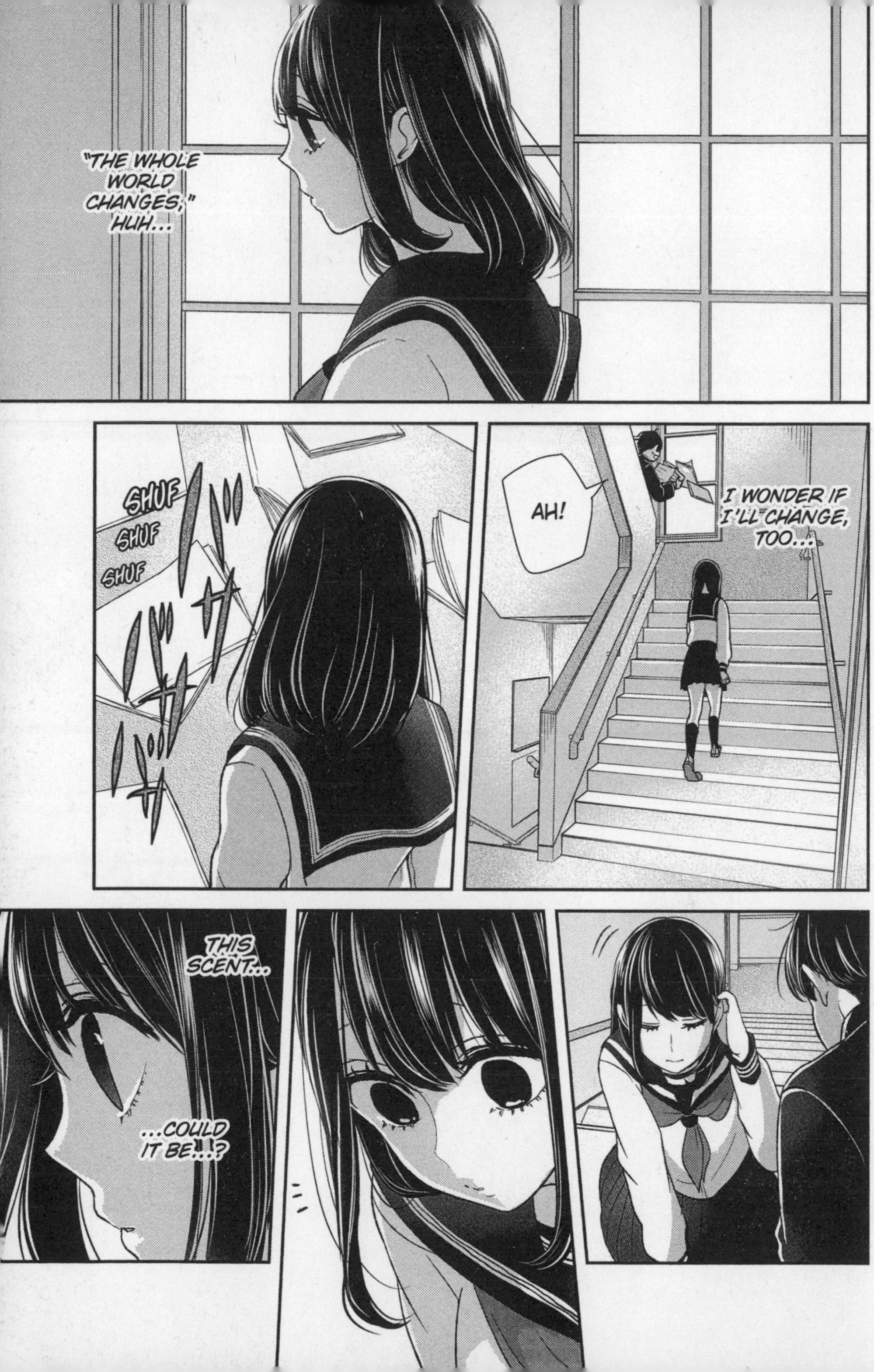
"THE WHOLE WORLD CHANGES," HUH...
I WONDER IF I'LL CHANGE, TOO...
AH!
SHUF
SHUF
SHUF
THIS SCENT...
...COULD IT BE...?

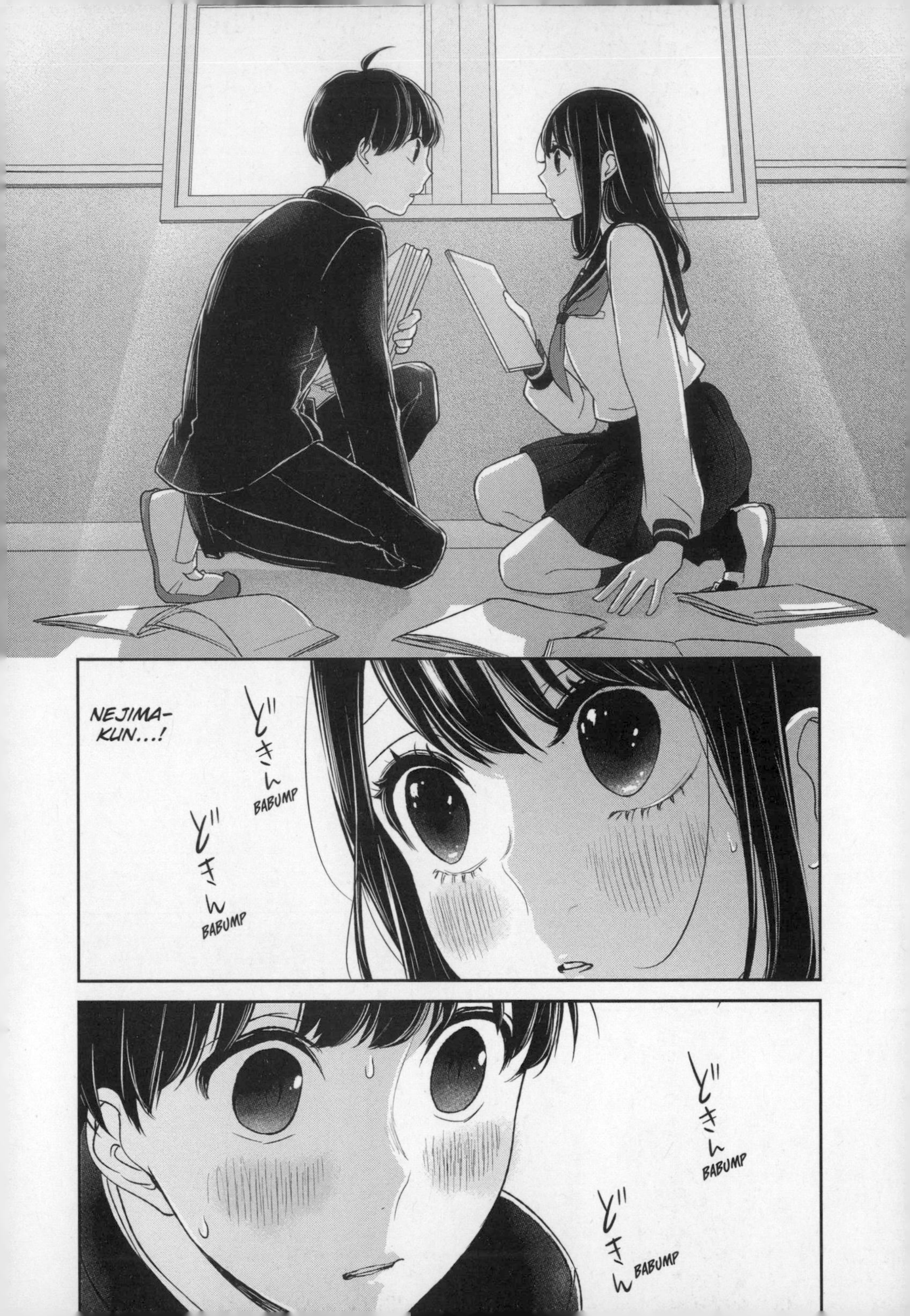
どきん
BABUMP
どきん
BABUMP
NEJIMA-KUN...!
どきん
BABUMP
どきん
BABUMP

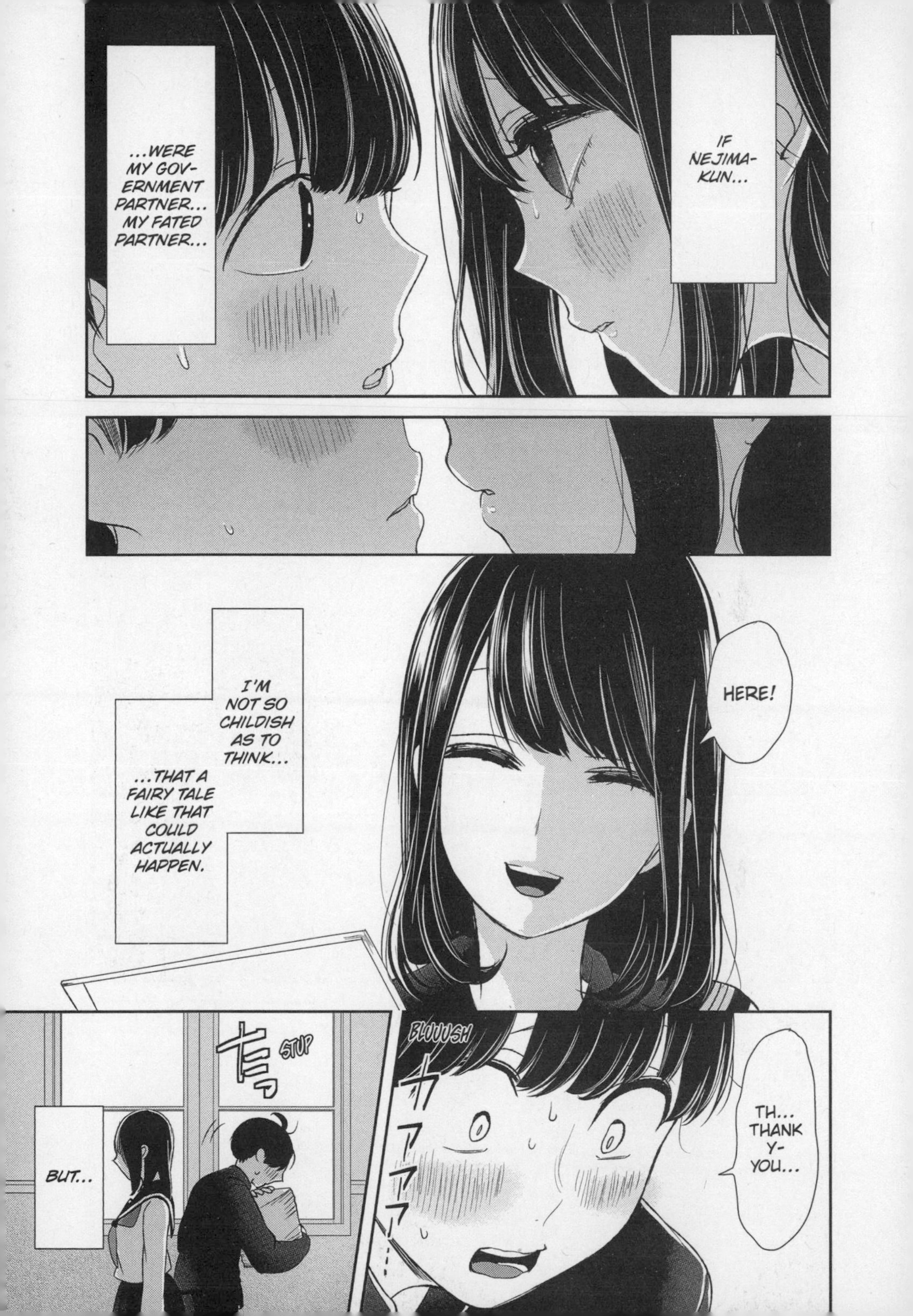
IF NEJIMA-KUN...
...WERE MY GOVERNMENT PARTNER... MY FATED PARTNER...
HERE!
I'M NOT SO CHILDISH AS TO THINK...
...THAT A FAIRY TALE LIKE THAT COULD ACTUALLY HAPPEN.
BLUUUSH
TH... THANK Y-YOU...
STUP
BUT...

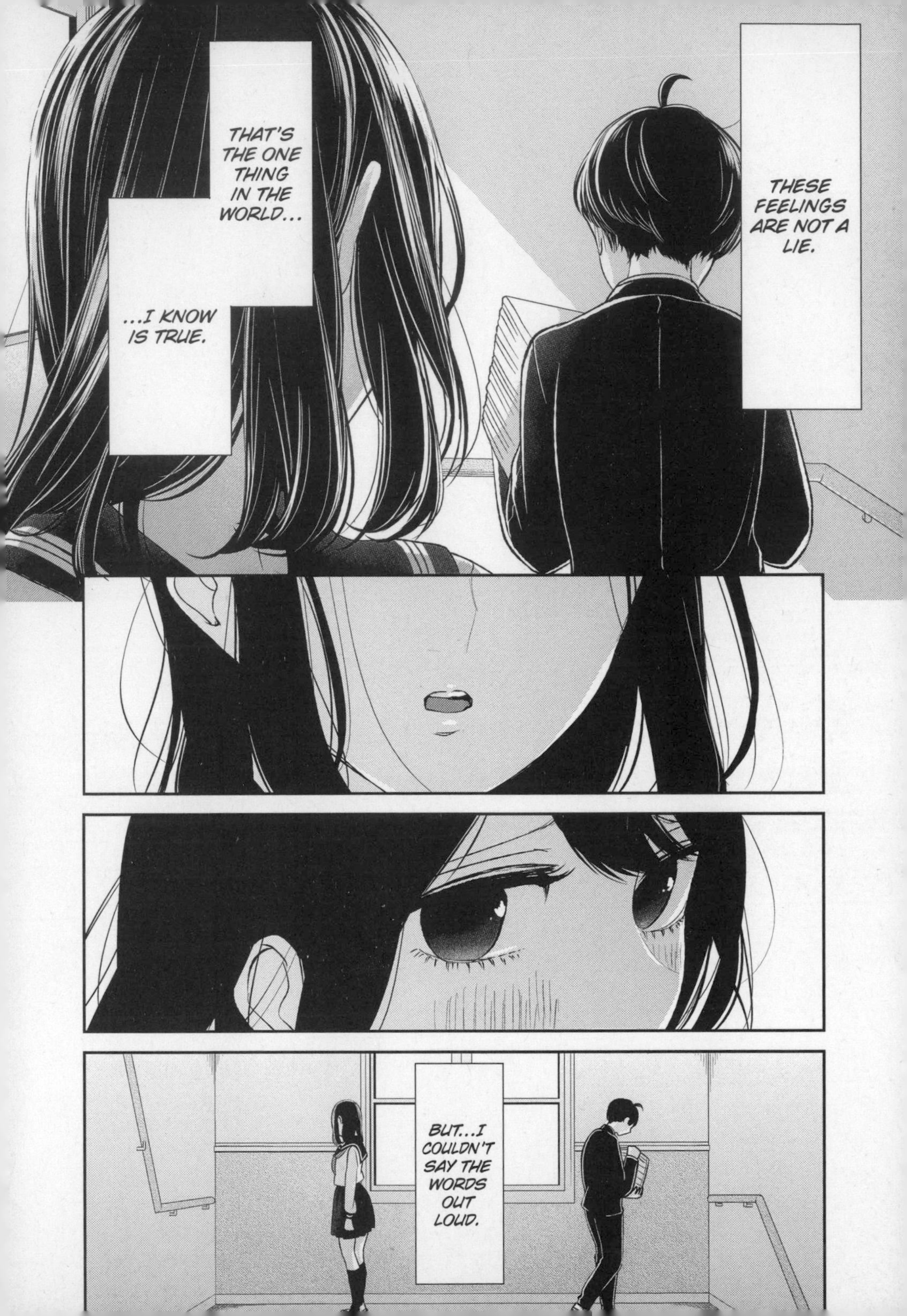
THESE FEELINGS ARE NOT A LIE.
THAT'S THE ONE THING IN THE WORLD...
...I KNOW IS TRUE.
BUT...I COULDN'T SAY THE WORDS OUT LOUD.

Chapter 16
Feelings Without Lies

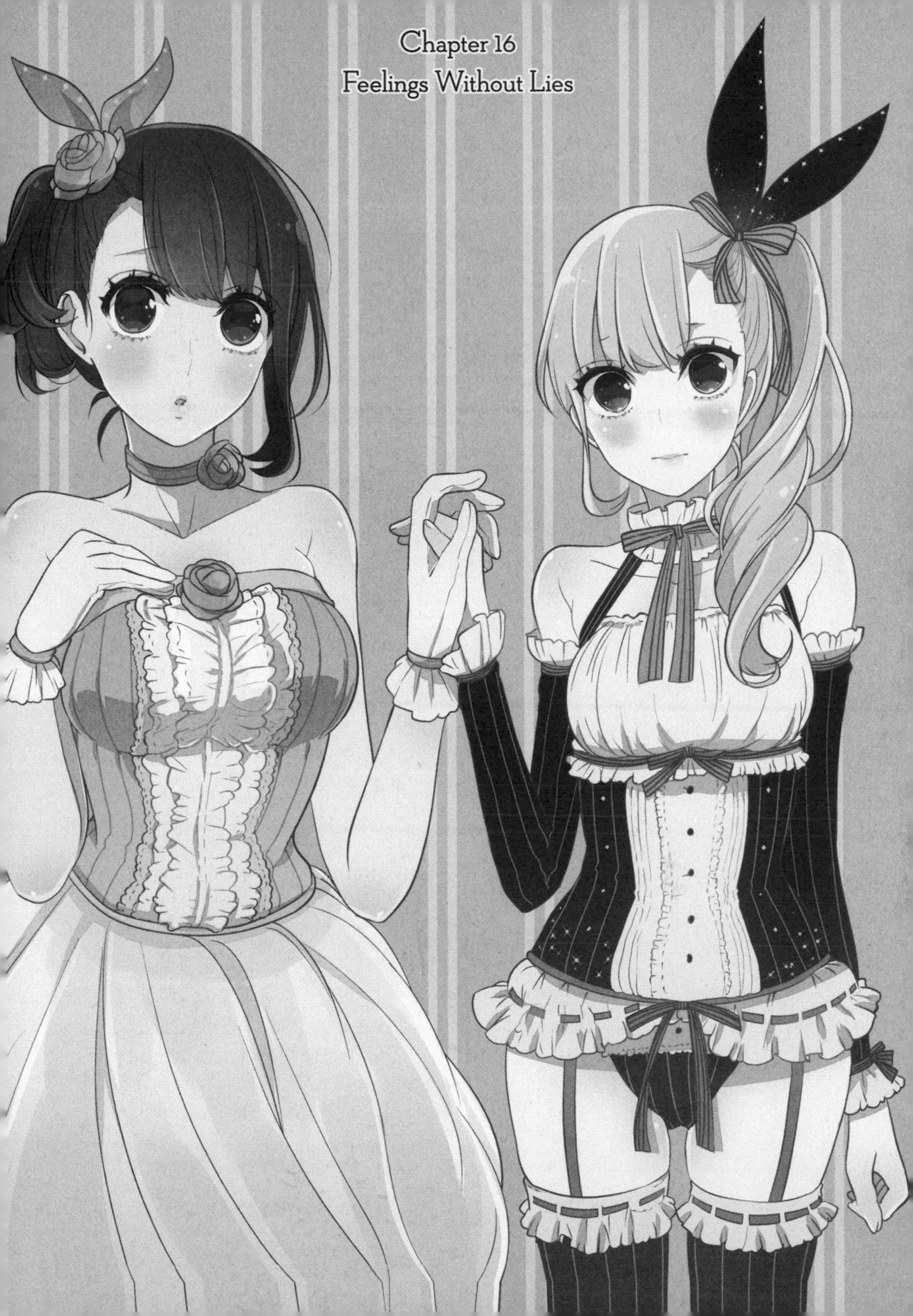

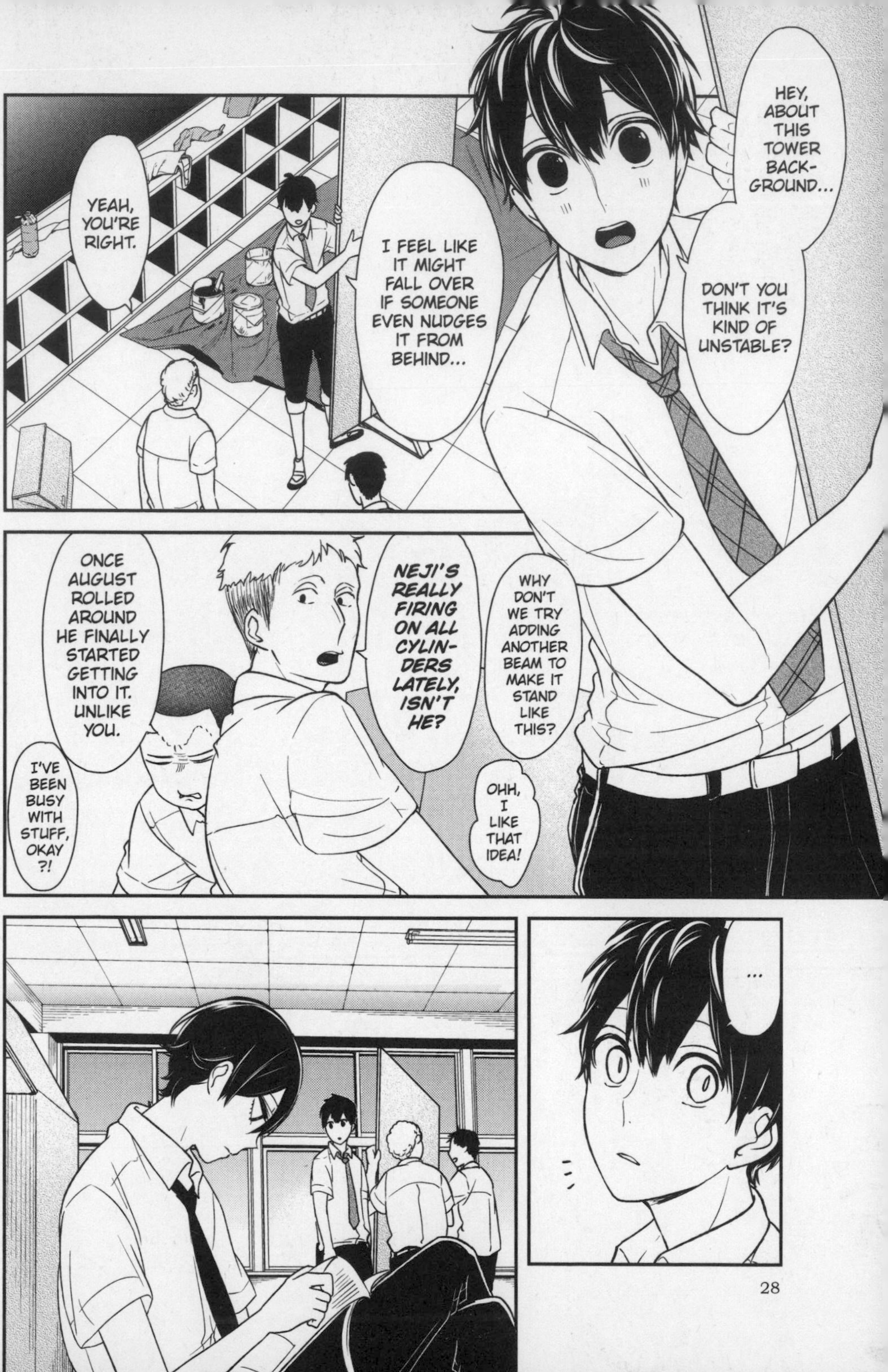
HEY, ABOUT THIS TOWER BACK-GROUND...
DON'T YOU THINK IT'S KIND OF UNSTABLE?
I FEEL LIKE IT MIGHT FALL OVER IF SOMEONE EVEN NUDGES IT FROM BEHIND...
YEAH, YOU'RE RIGHT.
WHY DON'T WE TRY ADDING ANOTHER BEAM TO MAKE IT STAND LIKE THIS?
OHH, I LIKE THAT IDEA!
NEJI'S REALLY FIRING ON ALL CYLIN-DERS LATELY, ISN'T HE?
ONCE AUGUST ROLLED AROUND HE FINALLY STARTED GETTING INTO IT. UNLIKE YOU.
I'VE BEEN BUSY WITH STUFF, OKAY?!
...

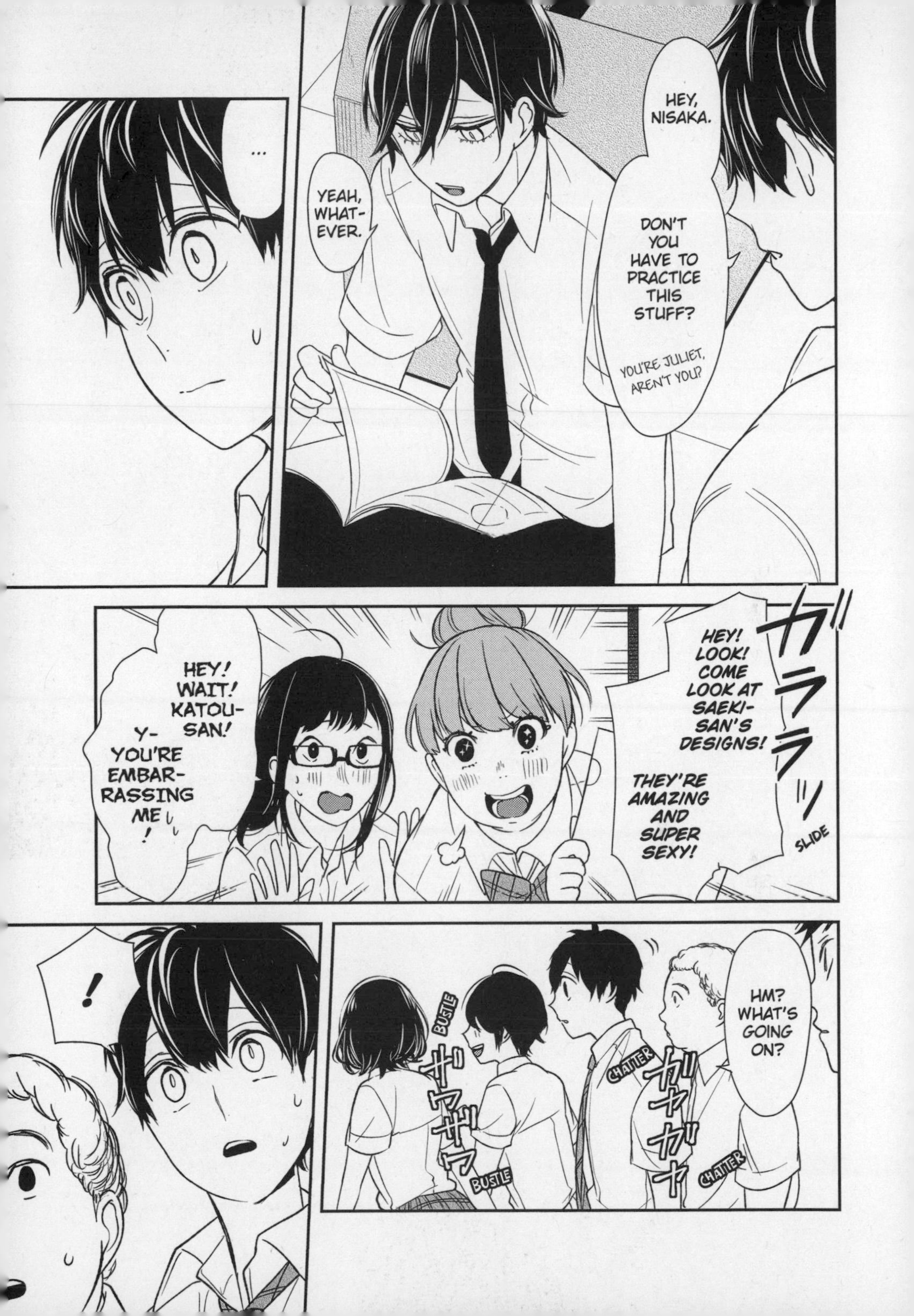
HEY, NISAKA.
DON'T YOU HAVE TO PRACTICE THIS STUFF?
YOU'RE JULIET, AREN'T YOU?
YEAH, WHATEVER.
...
ガラッ
SLIDE
HEY! LOOK! COME LOOK AT SAEKI-SAN'S DESIGNS!
THEY'RE AMAZING AND SUPER SEXY!
HEY! WAIT! KATOU-SAN! Y-YOU'RE EMBARRASSING ME!
HM? WHAT'S GOING ON?
ガヤガヤ
CHATTER
CHATTER
ザワザワ
BUSTLE
BUSTLE
!

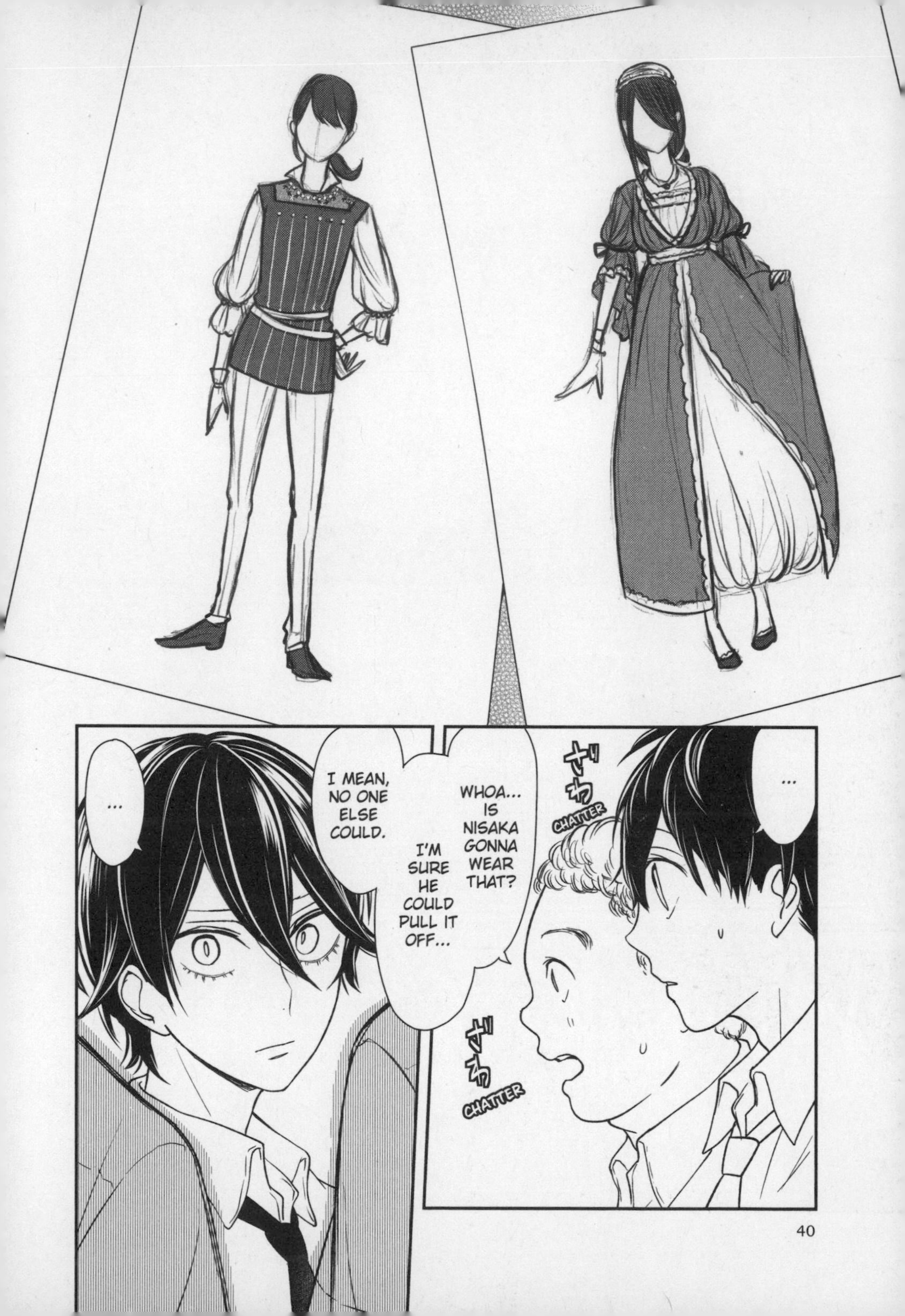
...
ざわ
CHATTER
WHOA... IS NISAKA GONNA WEAR THAT?
ざわ
CHATTER
I'M SURE HE COULD PULL IT OFF...
I MEAN, NO ONE ELSE COULD.
...

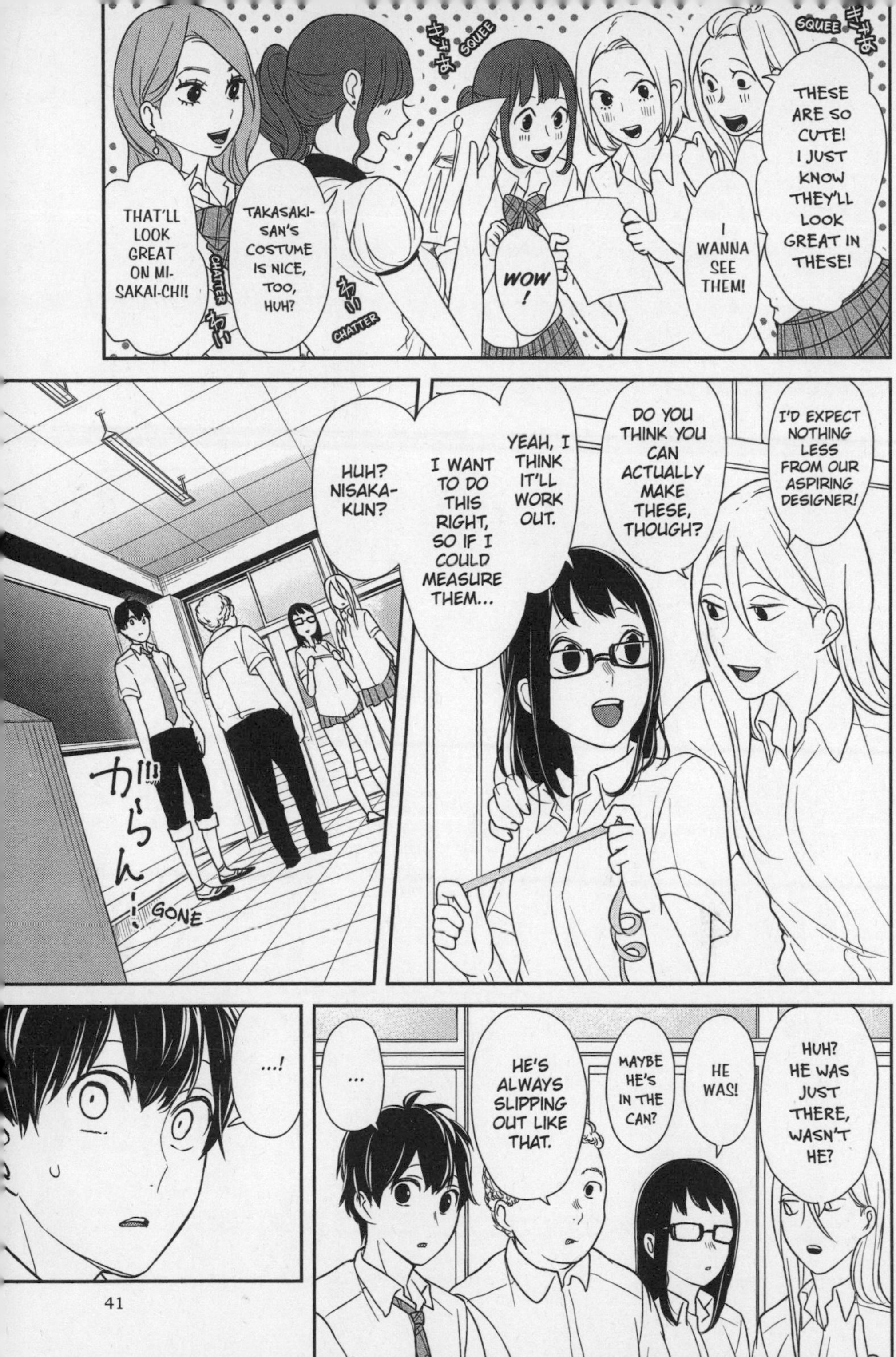
SQUEE
THESE ARE SO CUTE! I JUST KNOW THEY'LL LOOK GREAT IN THESE!
I WANNA SEE THEM!
WOW!
SQUEE
TAKASAKI-SAN'S COSTUME IS NICE, TOO, HUH?
CHATTER
THAT'LL LOOK GREAT ON MI-SAKAI-CHI!
CHATTER
I'D EXPECT NOTHING LESS FROM OUR ASPIRING DESIGNER!
DO YOU THINK YOU CAN ACTUALLY MAKE THESE, THOUGH?
YEAH, I THINK IT'LL WORK OUT.
I WANT TO DO THIS RIGHT, SO IF I COULD MEASURE THEM...
HUH? NISAKA-KUN?
GONE
HUH? HE WAS JUST THERE, WASN'T HE?
HE WAS!
MAYBE HE'S IN THE CAN?
HE'S ALWAYS SLIPPING OUT LIKE THAT.
...
...!

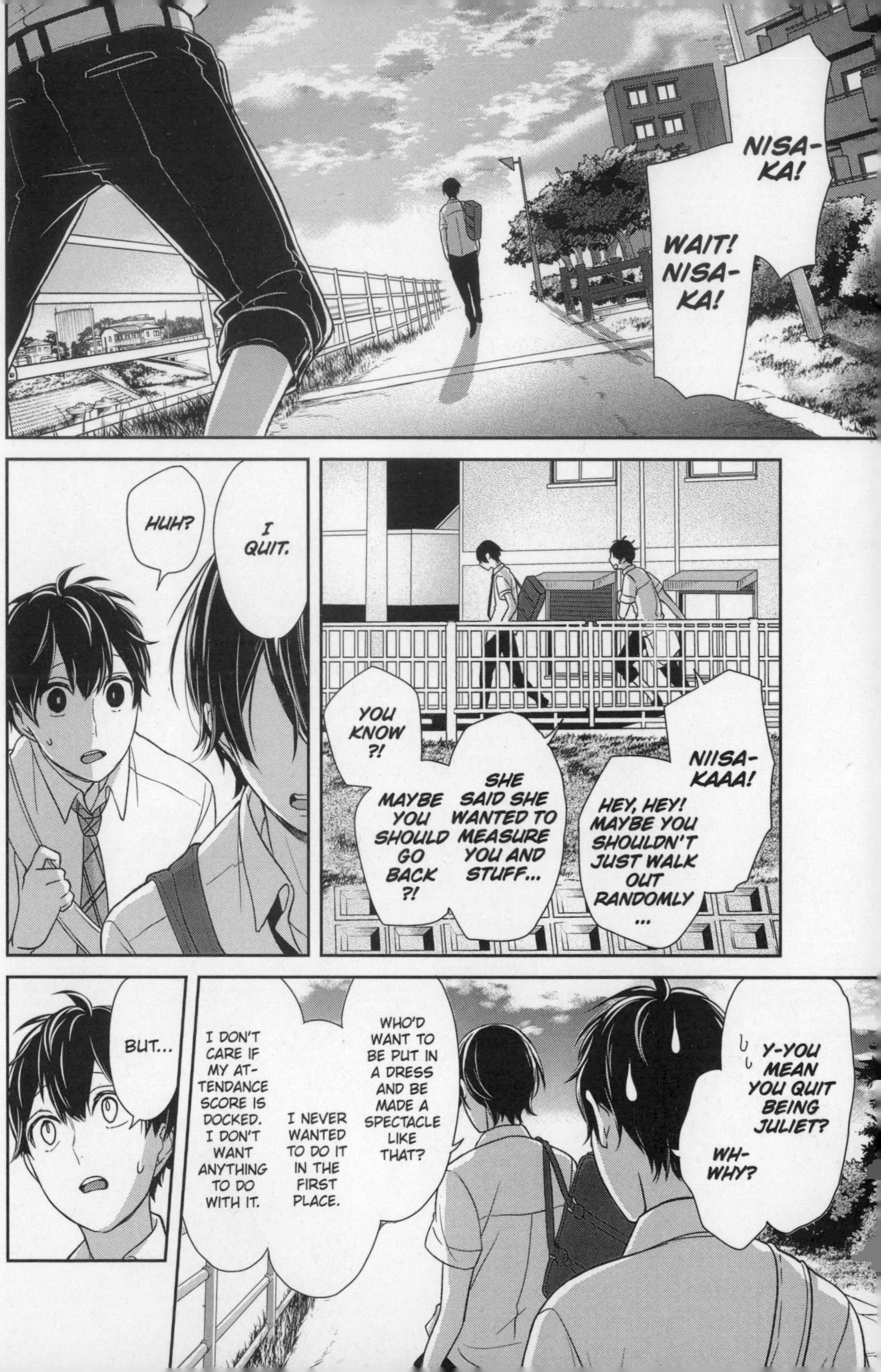
NISA-KA!
WAIT! NISA-KA!
NIISA-KAAA!
HEY, HEY! MAYBE YOU SHOULDN'T JUST WALK OUT RANDOMLY...
SHE SAID SHE WANTED TO MEASURE YOU AND STUFF...
YOU KNOW?!
MAYBE YOU SHOULD GO BACK?!
I QUIT.
HUH?
Y-YOU MEAN YOU QUIT BEING JULIET?
WH-WHY?
WHO'D WANT TO BE PUT IN A DRESS AND BE MADE A SPECTACLE LIKE THAT?
I NEVER WANTED TO DO IT IN THE FIRST PLACE.
I DON'T CARE IF MY AT-TENDANCE SCORE IS DOCKED. I DON'T WANT ANYTHING TO DO WITH IT.
BUT...

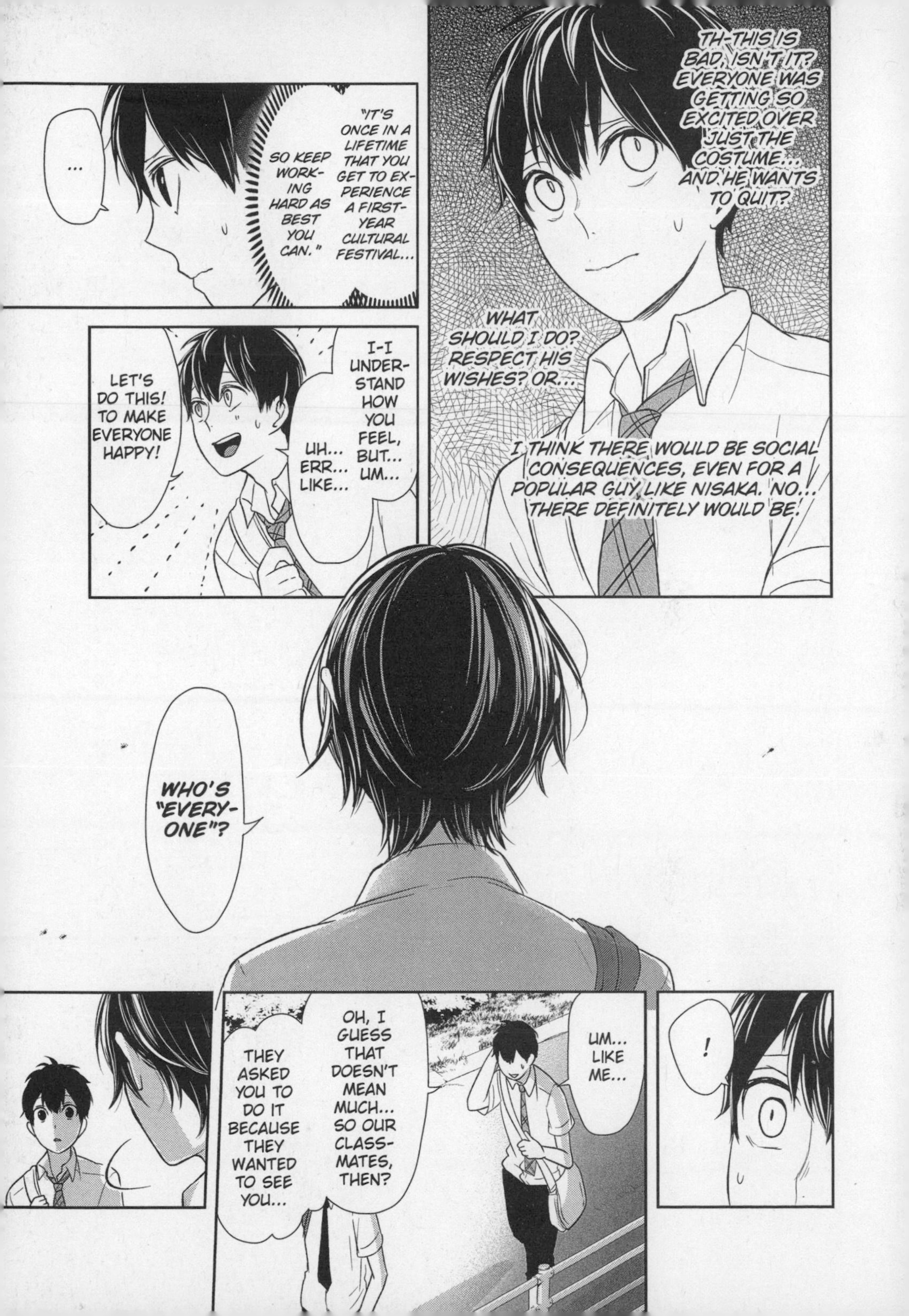
TH-THIS IS BAD, ISN'T IT? EVERYONE WAS GETTING SO EXCITED OVER JUST THE COSTUME... AND HE WANTS TO QUIT?
WHAT SHOULD I DO? RESPECT HIS WISHES? OR...
I THINK THERE WOULD BE SOCIAL CONSEQUENCES, EVEN FOR A POPULAR GUY LIKE NISAKA. NO... THERE DEFINITELY WOULD BE.
"IT'S ONCE IN A LIFETIME THAT YOU GET TO EXPERIENCE A FIRST-YEAR CULTURAL FESTIVAL...
SO KEEP WORKING HARD AS BEST YOU CAN."
...
I-I UNDERSTAND HOW YOU FEEL, BUT... UM...
UH... ERR... LIKE...
LET'S DO THIS! TO MAKE EVERYONE HAPPY!
WHO'S "EVERYONE"?
!
UM... LIKE ME...
OH, I GUESS THAT DOESN'T MEAN MUCH... SO OUR CLASSMATES, THEN?
THEY ASKED YOU TO DO IT BECAUSE THEY WANTED TO SEE YOU...

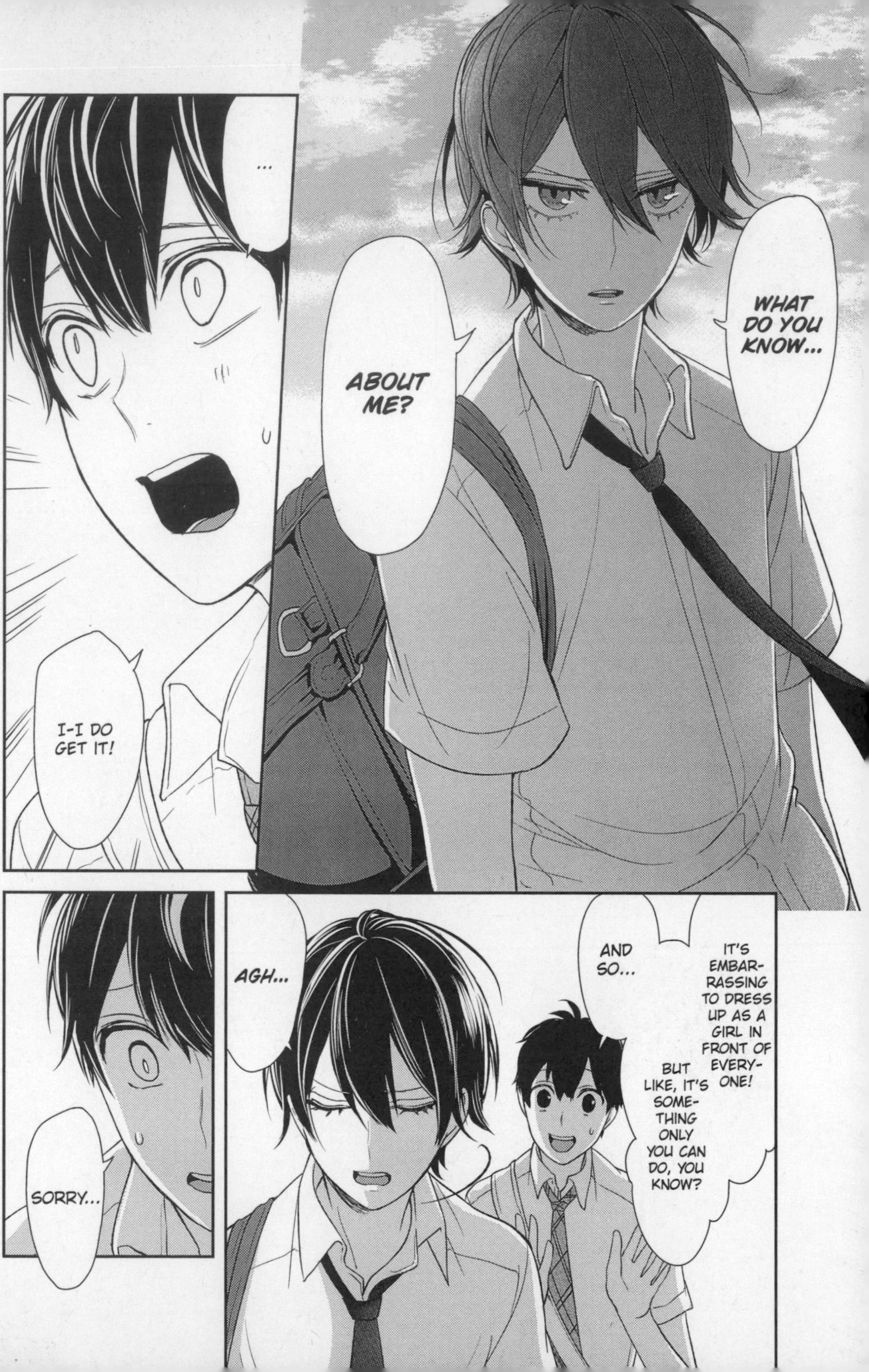
WHAT DO YOU KNOW...
ABOUT ME?
...
I-I DO GET IT!
AND SO...
IT'S EMBARRASSING TO DRESS UP AS A GIRL IN FRONT OF EVERYONE!
BUT LIKE, IT'S SOMETHING ONLY YOU CAN DO, YOU KNOW?
AGH...
SORRY...

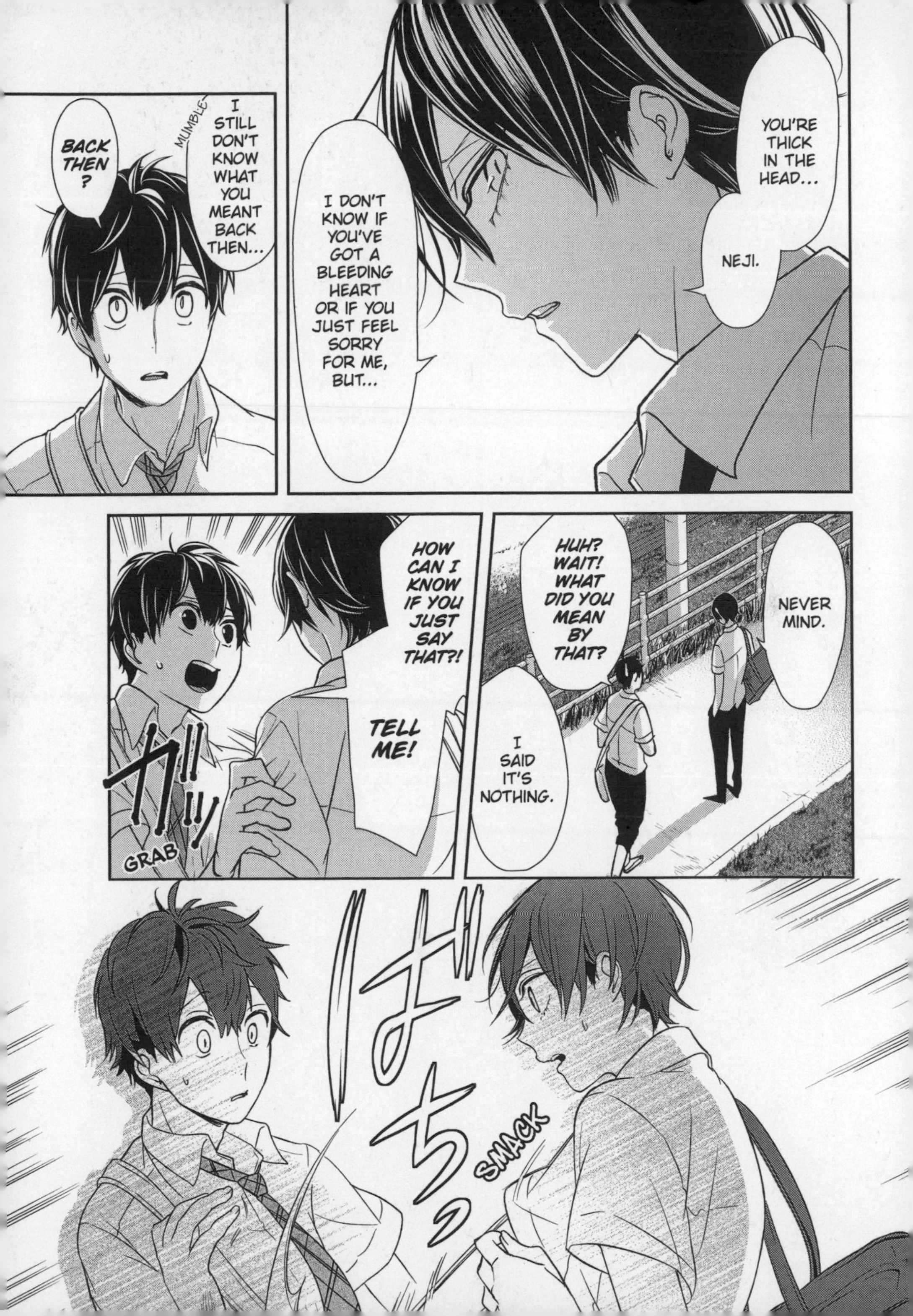
YOU'RE THICK IN THE HEAD...
NEJI.
I DON'T KNOW IF YOU'VE GOT A BLEEDING HEART OR IF YOU JUST FEEL SORRY FOR ME, BUT...
I STILL DON'T KNOW WHAT YOU MEANT BACK THEN...
MUMBLE
BACK THEN?
NEVER MIND.
HUH? WAIT! WHAT DID YOU MEAN BY THAT?
I SAID IT'S NOTHING.
HOW CAN I KNOW IF YOU JUST SAY THAT?!
TELL ME!
GRAB
SMACK

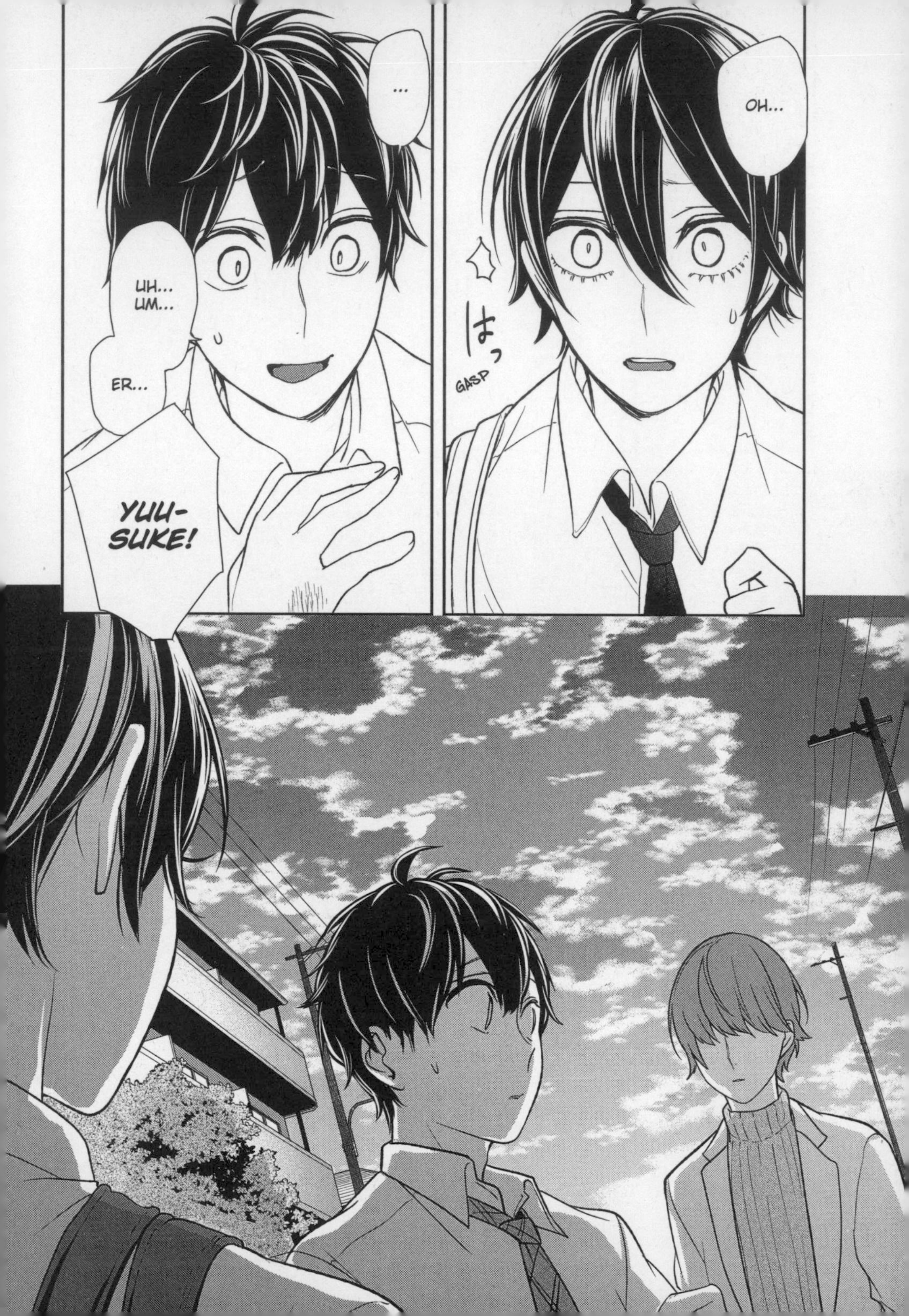
OH...
はっ
GASP
...
UH... UM...
ER...
YUU-SUKE!

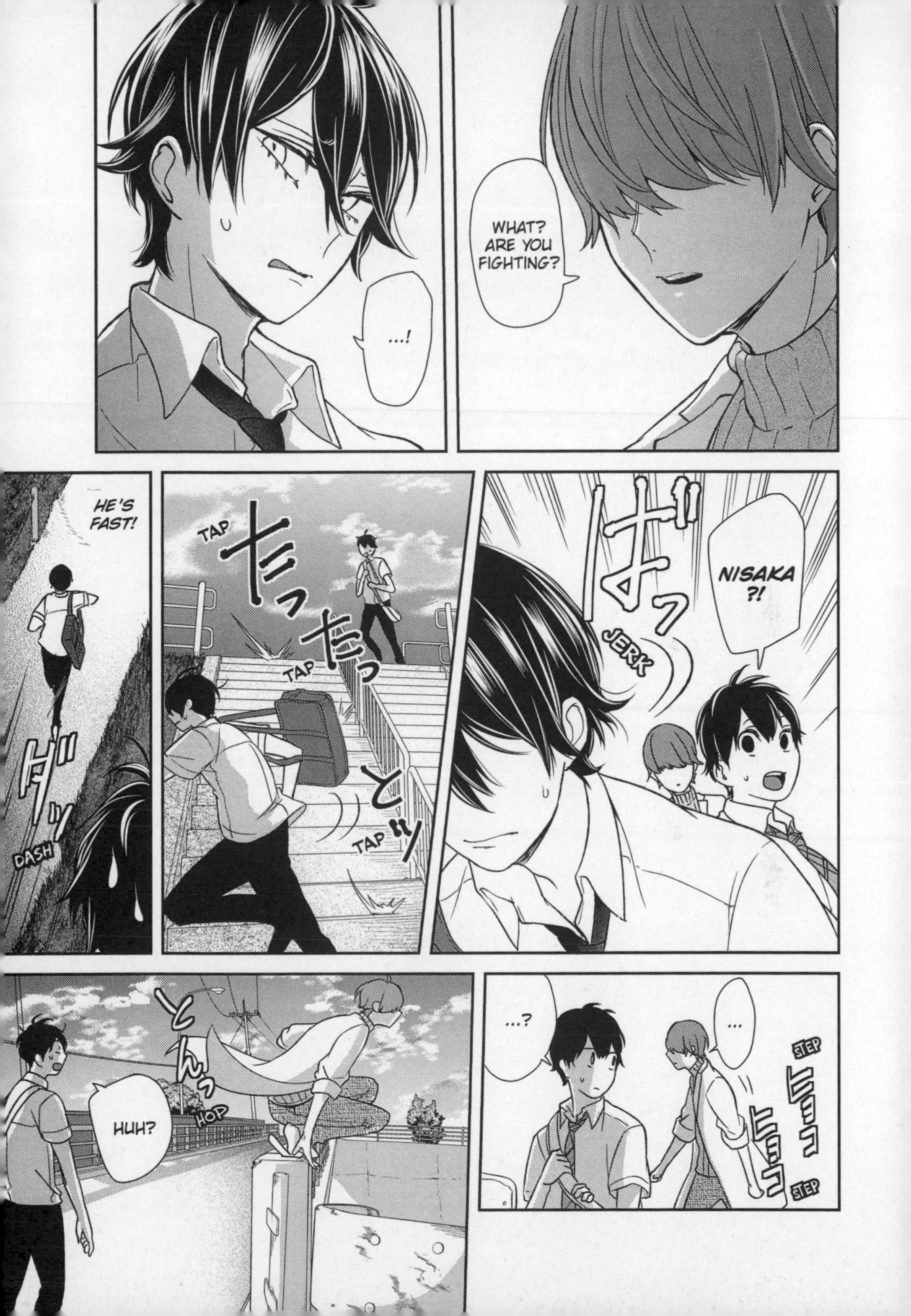
WHAT? ARE YOU FIGHTING?
...!
ばっ
JERK
NISAKA ?!
たっ
TAP
たっ
TAP
TAP
HE'S FAST!
ダッ
DASH
ヒョコ
STEP
ヒョコ
STEP
...
...?
とんっ
HOP
HUH?

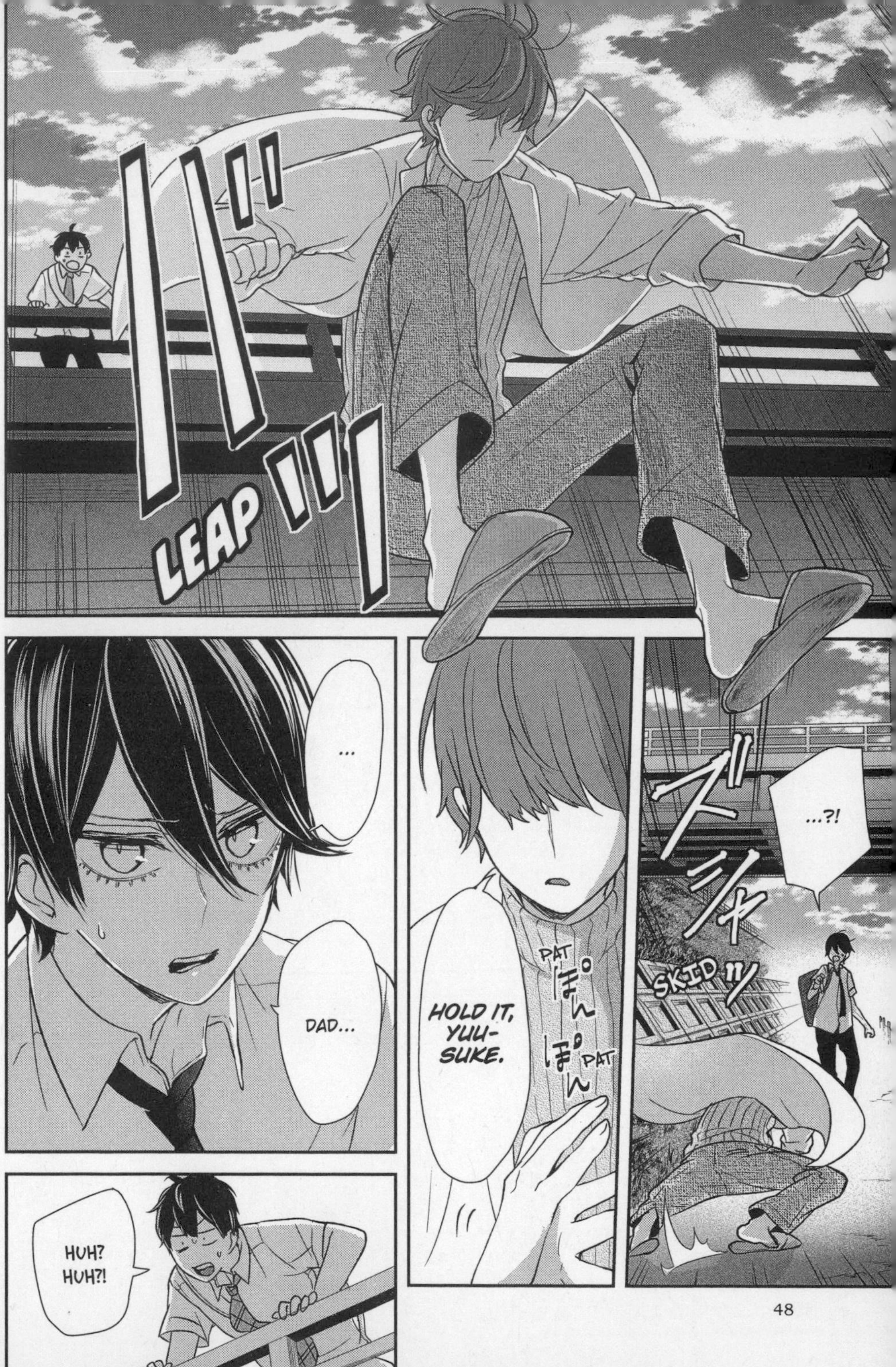
LEAP!!
...?!
ズシャ
SKID!!
HOLD IT, YUU-SUKE.
PAT
ぽん
PAT
ぽん
...
DAD...
HUH? HUH?!

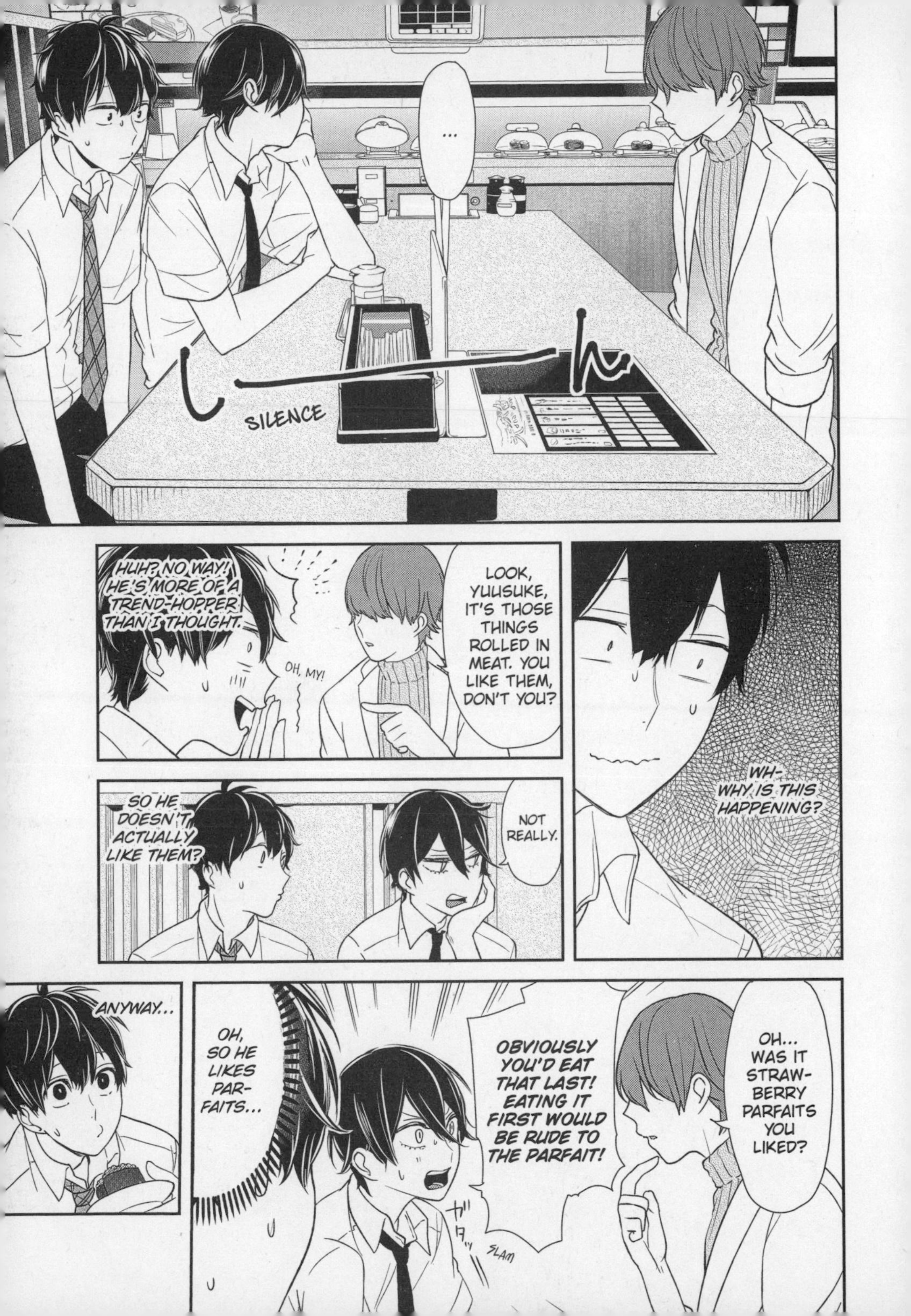
...
SILENCE
WH- WHY IS THIS HAPPENING?
LOOK, YUUSUKE, IT'S THOSE THINGS ROLLED IN MEAT. YOU LIKE THEM, DON'T YOU?
OH, MY!
HUH? NO WAY! HE'S MORE OF A TREND-HOPPER THAN I THOUGHT.
NOT REALLY.
SO HE DOESN'T ACTUALLY LIKE THEM?
OH... WAS IT STRAW-BERRY PARFAITS YOU LIKED?
OBVIOUSLY YOU'D EAT THAT LAST! EATING IT FIRST WOULD BE RUDE TO THE PARFAIT!
SLAM
OH, SO HE LIKES PAR-FAITS...
ANYWAY...

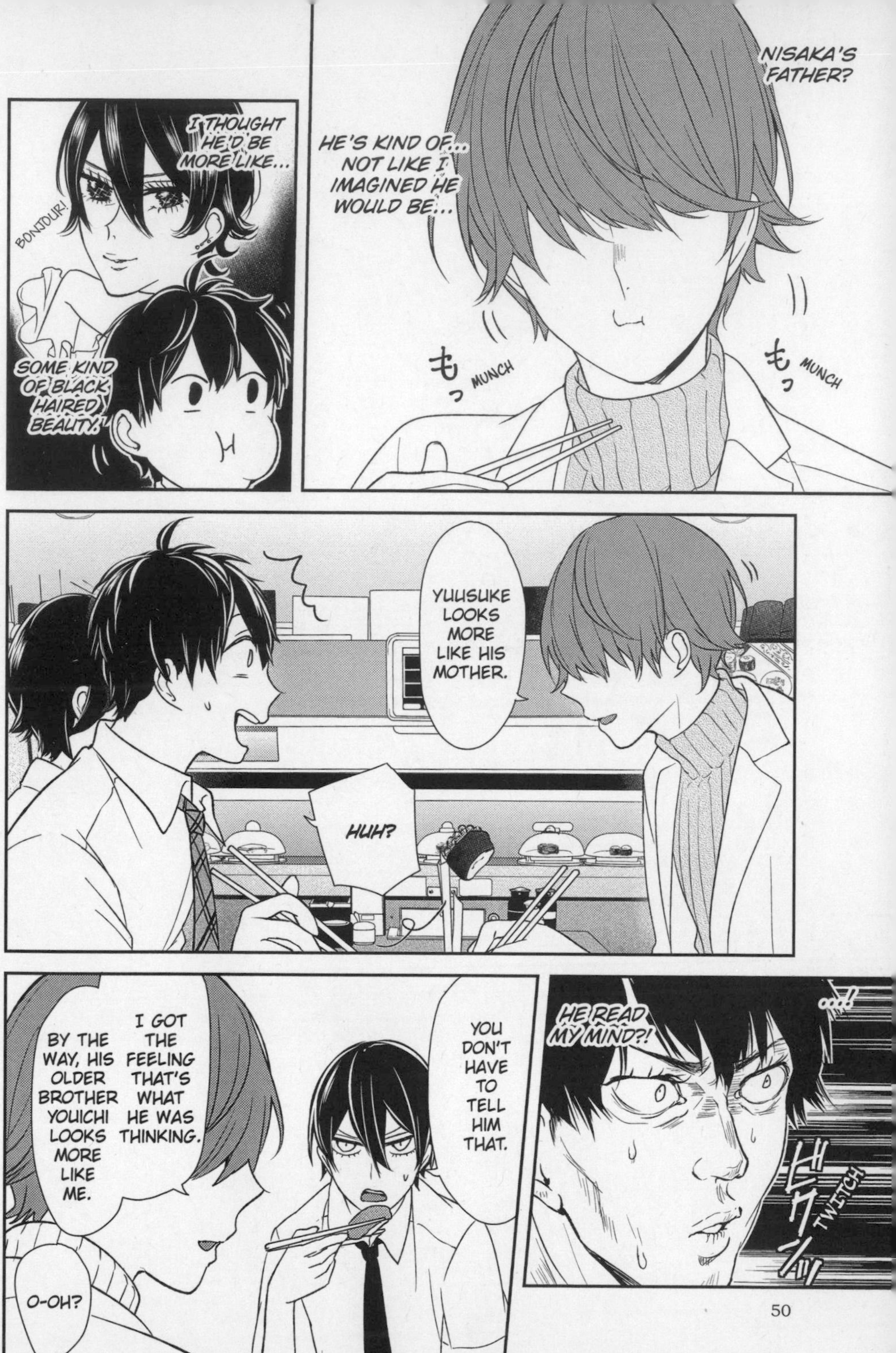
NISAKA'S FATHER?
HE'S KIND OF... NOT LIKE I IMAGINED HE WOULD BE...
MUNCH
MUNCH
I THOUGHT HE'D BE MORE LIKE...
BONJOUR!
SOME KIND OF BLACK HAIRED BEAUTY!
YUUSUKE LOOKS MORE LIKE HIS MOTHER.
HUH?
...!
HE READ MY MIND?!
TWITCH
YOU DON'T HAVE TO TELL HIM THAT.
I GOT THE FEELING THAT'S WHAT HE WAS THINKING.
BY THE WAY, HIS OLDER BROTHER YOUICHI LOOKS MORE LIKE ME.
O-OH?

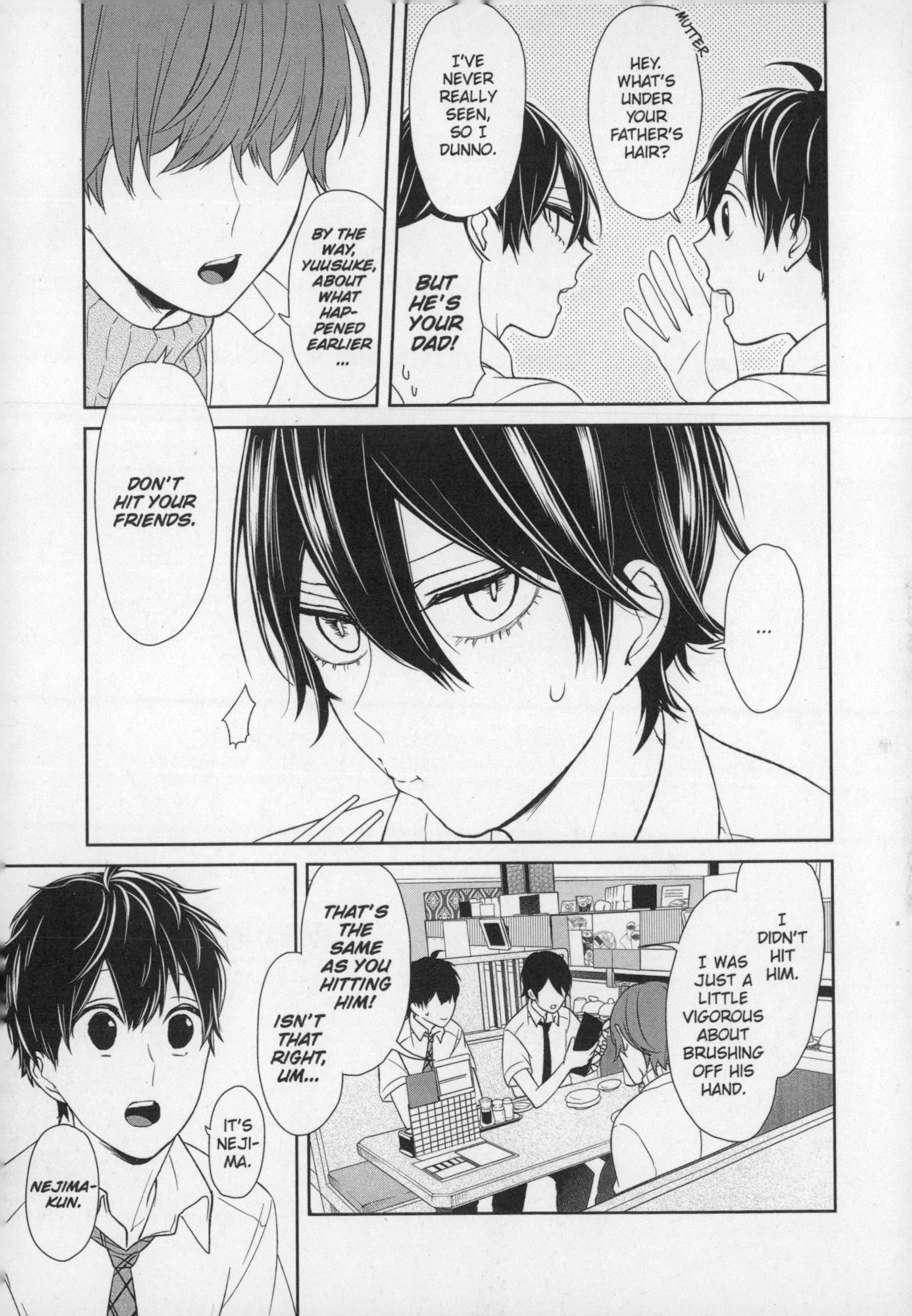
MUTTER
HEY. WHAT'S UNDER YOUR FATHER'S HAIR?
I'VE NEVER REALLY SEEN, SO I DUNNO.
BUT HE'S YOUR DAD!
BY THE WAY, YUUSUKE, ABOUT WHAT HAP-PENED EARLIER ...
DON'T HIT YOUR FRIENDS.
...
I DIDN'T HIT HIM.
I WAS JUST A LITTLE VIGOROUS ABOUT BRUSHING OFF HIS HAND.
THAT'S THE SAME AS YOU HITTING HIM!
ISN'T THAT RIGHT, UM...
IT'S NEJI-MA.
NEJIMA-KUN.

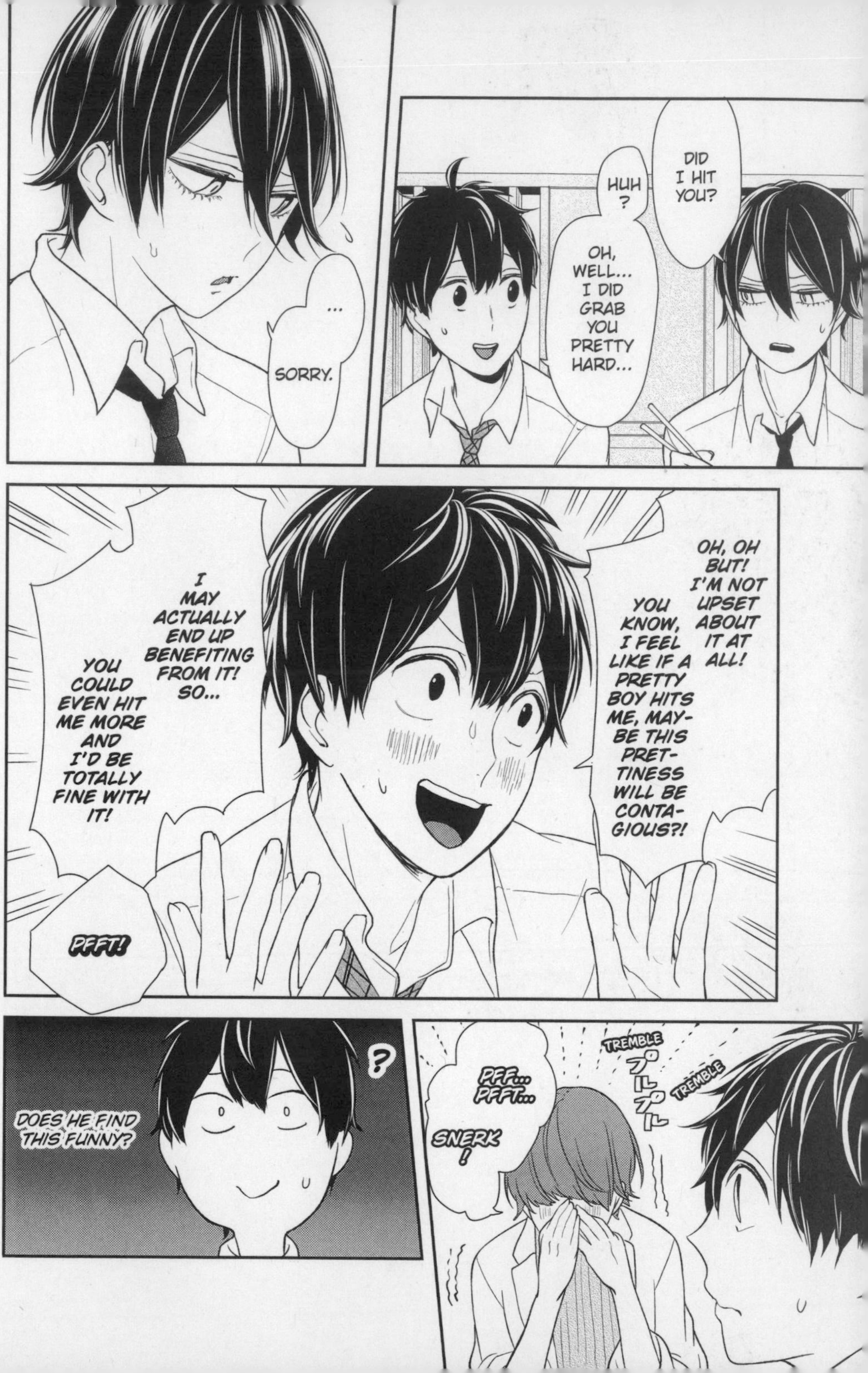
DID I HIT YOU?
HUH?
OH, WELL... I DID GRAB YOU PRETTY HARD...
... SORRY.
OH, OH BUT! I'M NOT UPSET ABOUT IT AT ALL!
YOU KNOW, I FEEL LIKE IF A PRETTY BOY HITS ME, MAY-BE THIS PRET-TINESS WILL BE CONTA-GIOUS?!
I MAY ACTUALLY END UP BENEFITING FROM IT! SO...
YOU COULD EVEN HIT ME MORE AND I'D BE TOTALLY FINE WITH IT!
PFFT!
TREMBLE
プルプル
TREMBLE
PFF... PFFT...
SNERK!
?
DOES HE FIND THIS FUNNY?

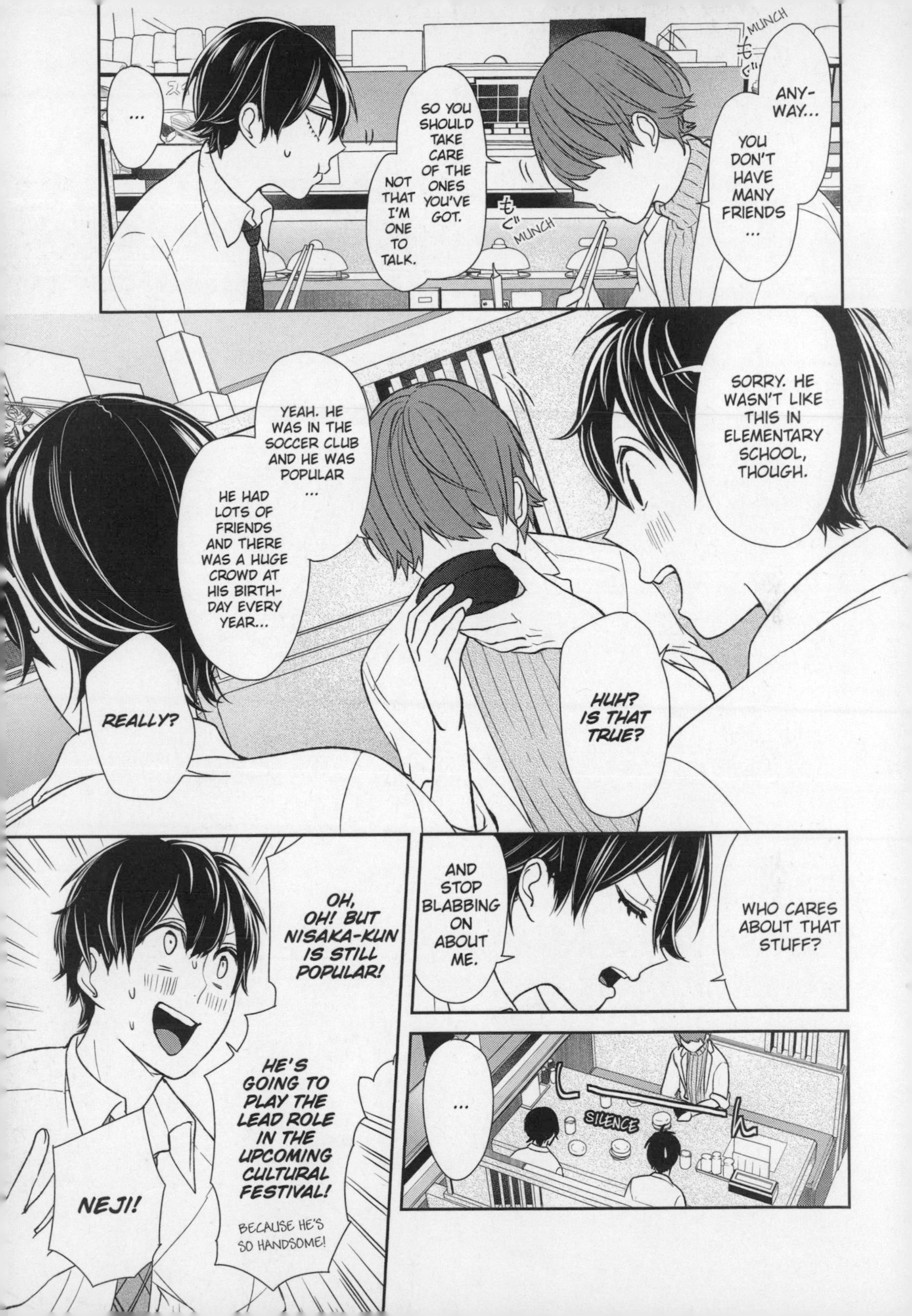
MUNCH
ANY-WAY...
YOU DON'T HAVE MANY FRIENDS ...
SO YOU SHOULD TAKE CARE OF THE ONES YOU'VE GOT.
NOT THAT I'M ONE TO TALK.
MUNCH
...
SORRY. HE WASN'T LIKE THIS IN ELEMENTARY SCHOOL, THOUGH.
YEAH. HE WAS IN THE SOCCER CLUB AND HE WAS POPULAR ...
HE HAD LOTS OF FRIENDS AND THERE WAS A HUGE CROWD AT HIS BIRTH-DAY EVERY YEAR...
HUH? IS THAT TRUE?
REALLY?
WHO CARES ABOUT THAT STUFF?
AND STOP BLABBING ON ABOUT ME.
SILENCE
...
OH, OH! BUT NISAKA-KUN IS STILL POPULAR!
HE'S GOING TO PLAY THE LEAD ROLE IN THE UPCOMING CULTURAL FESTIVAL!
BECAUSE HE'S SO HANDSOME!
NEJI!

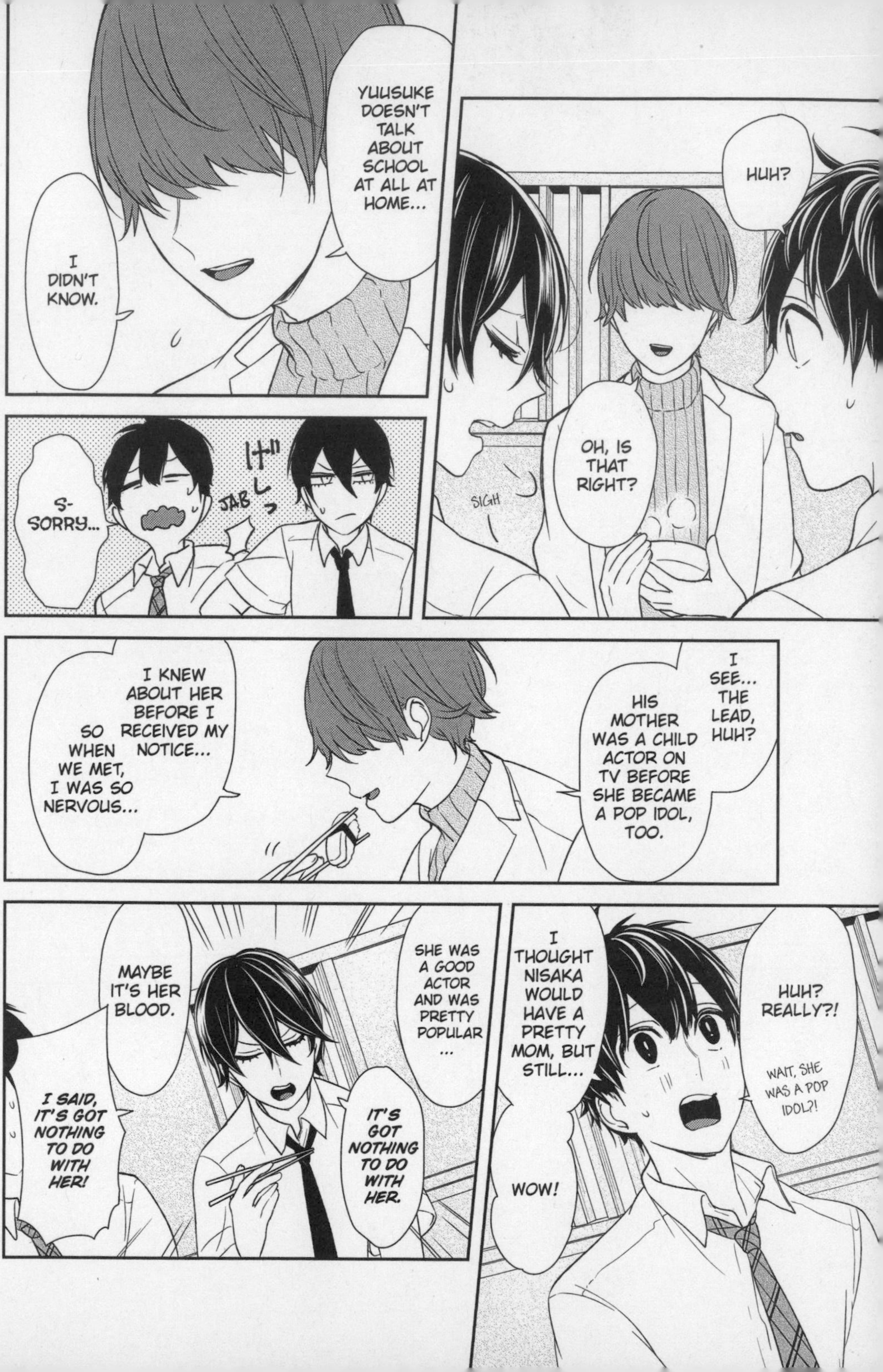
HUH?
OH, IS THAT RIGHT?
SIGH
YUUSUKE DOESN'T TALK ABOUT SCHOOL AT ALL AT HOME...
I DIDN'T KNOW.
げしっ
JAB
S-SORRY...
I SEE... THE LEAD, HUH?
HIS MOTHER WAS A CHILD ACTOR ON TV BEFORE SHE BECAME A POP IDOL, TOO.
I KNEW ABOUT HER BEFORE I RECEIVED MY NOTICE...
SO WHEN WE MET, I WAS SO NERVOUS...
HUH? REALLY?!
WAIT, SHE WAS A POP IDOL?!
I THOUGHT NISAKA WOULD HAVE A PRETTY MOM, BUT STILL...
WOW!
SHE WAS A GOOD ACTOR AND WAS PRETTY POPULAR...
MAYBE IT'S HER BLOOD.
IT'S GOT NOTHING TO DO WITH HER.
I SAID, IT'S GOT NOTHING TO DO WITH HER!

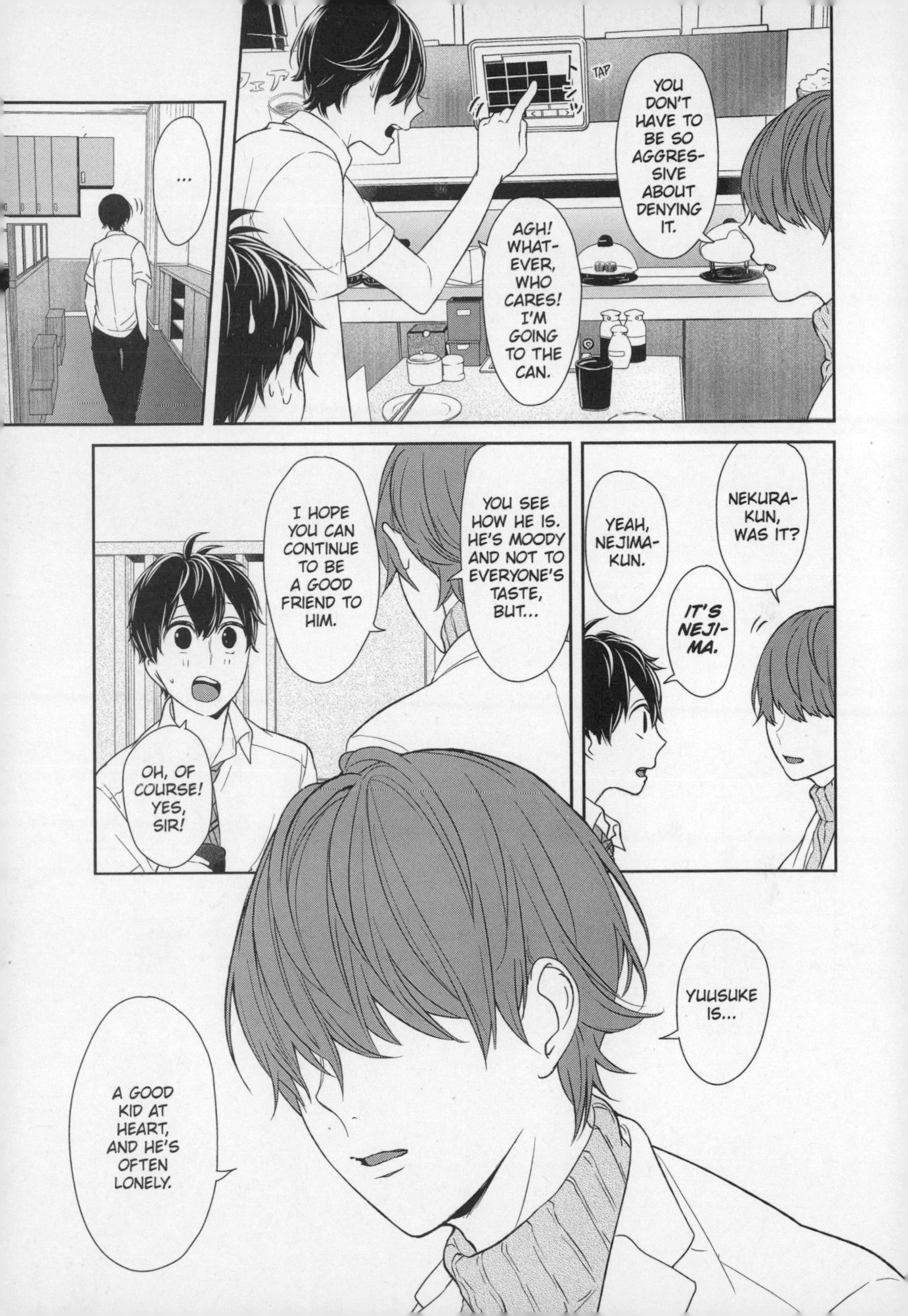
YOU DON'T HAVE TO BE SO AGGRESSIVE ABOUT DENYING IT.
TAP
AGH! WHATEVER, WHO CARES! I'M GOING TO THE CAN.
...
NEKURA-KUN, WAS IT?
YEAH, NEJIMA-KUN.
IT'S NEJIMA.
YOU SEE HOW HE IS. HE'S MOODY AND NOT TO EVERYONE'S TASTE, BUT...
I HOPE YOU CAN CONTINUE TO BE A GOOD FRIEND TO HIM.
OH, OF COURSE! YES, SIR!
YUUSUKE IS...
A GOOD KID AT HEART, AND HE'S OFTEN LONELY.

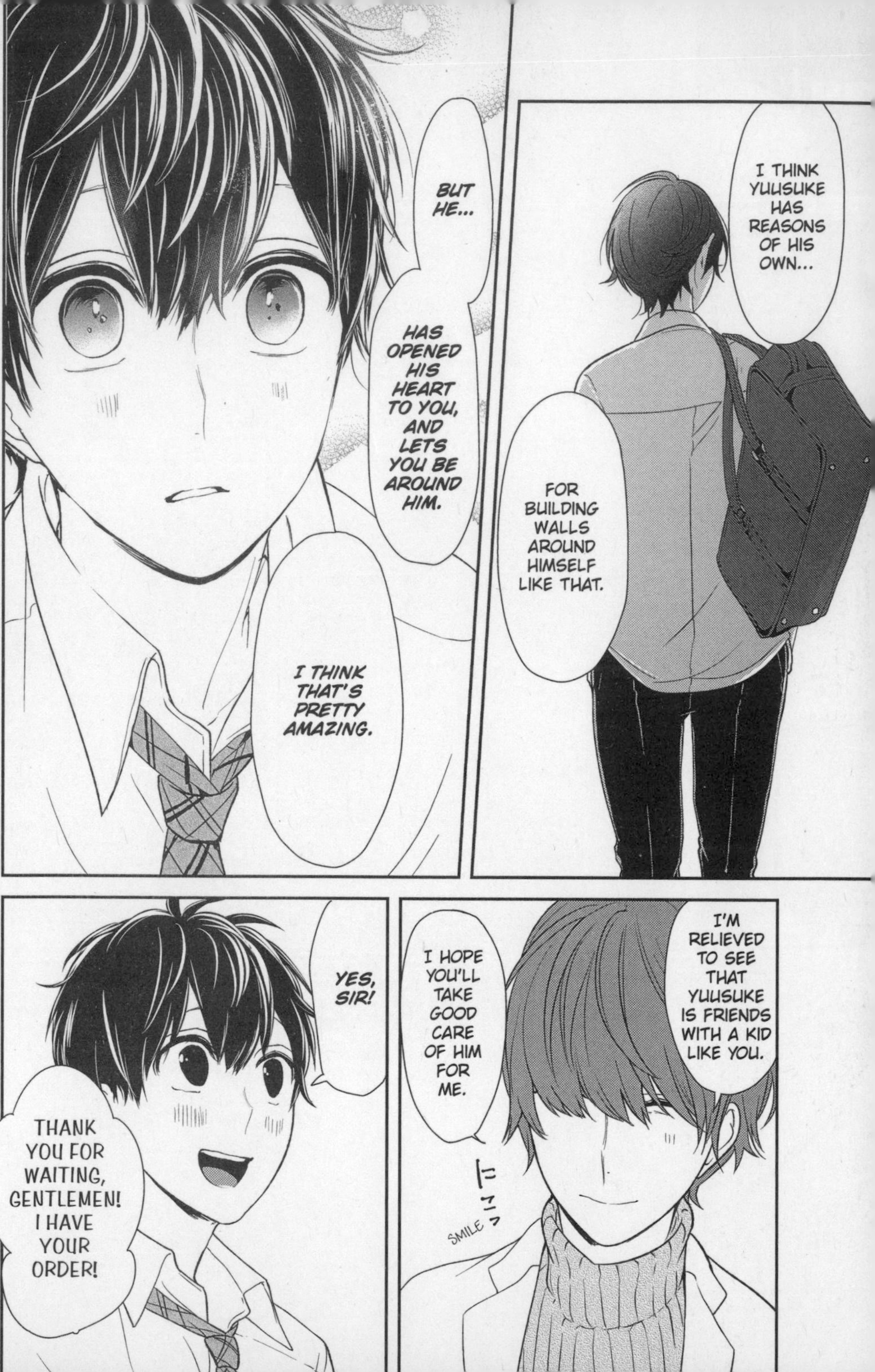
I THINK YUUSUKE HAS REASONS OF HIS OWN...
FOR BUILDING WALLS AROUND HIMSELF LIKE THAT.
BUT HE...
HAS OPENED HIS HEART TO YOU, AND LETS YOU BE AROUND HIM.
I THINK THAT'S PRETTY AMAZING.
I'M RELIEVED TO SEE THAT YUUSUKE IS FRIENDS WITH A KID LIKE YOU.
I HOPE YOU'LL TAKE GOOD CARE OF HIM FOR ME.
SMILE
YES, SIR!
THANK YOU FOR WAITING, GENTLEMEN! I HAVE YOUR ORDER!

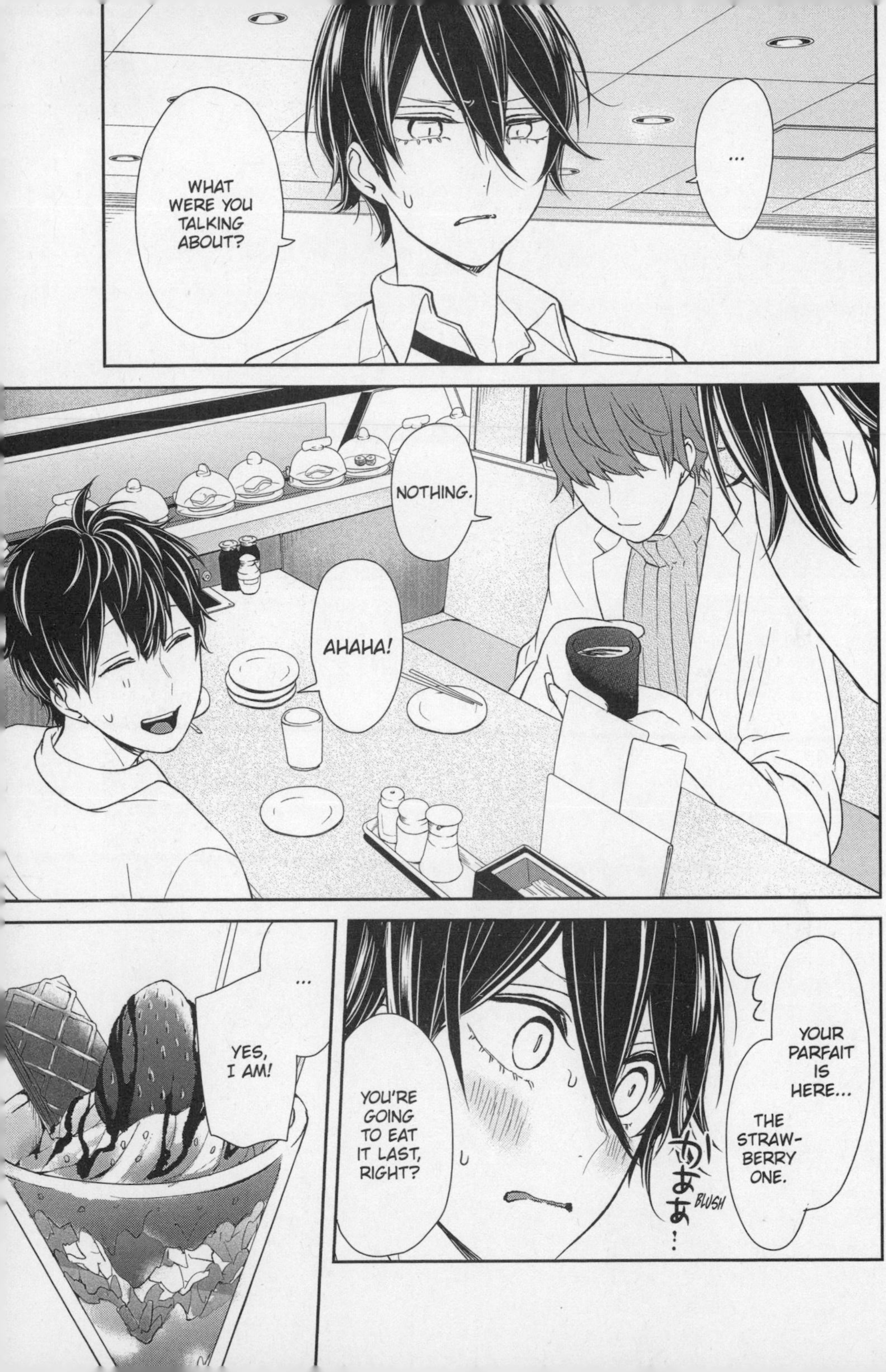
...
WHAT WERE YOU TALKING ABOUT?
NOTHING.
AHAHA!
YOUR PARFAIT IS HERE... THE STRAWBERRY ONE.
わぁぁ…
BLUSH
YOU'RE GOING TO EAT IT LAST, RIGHT?
...
YES, I AM!

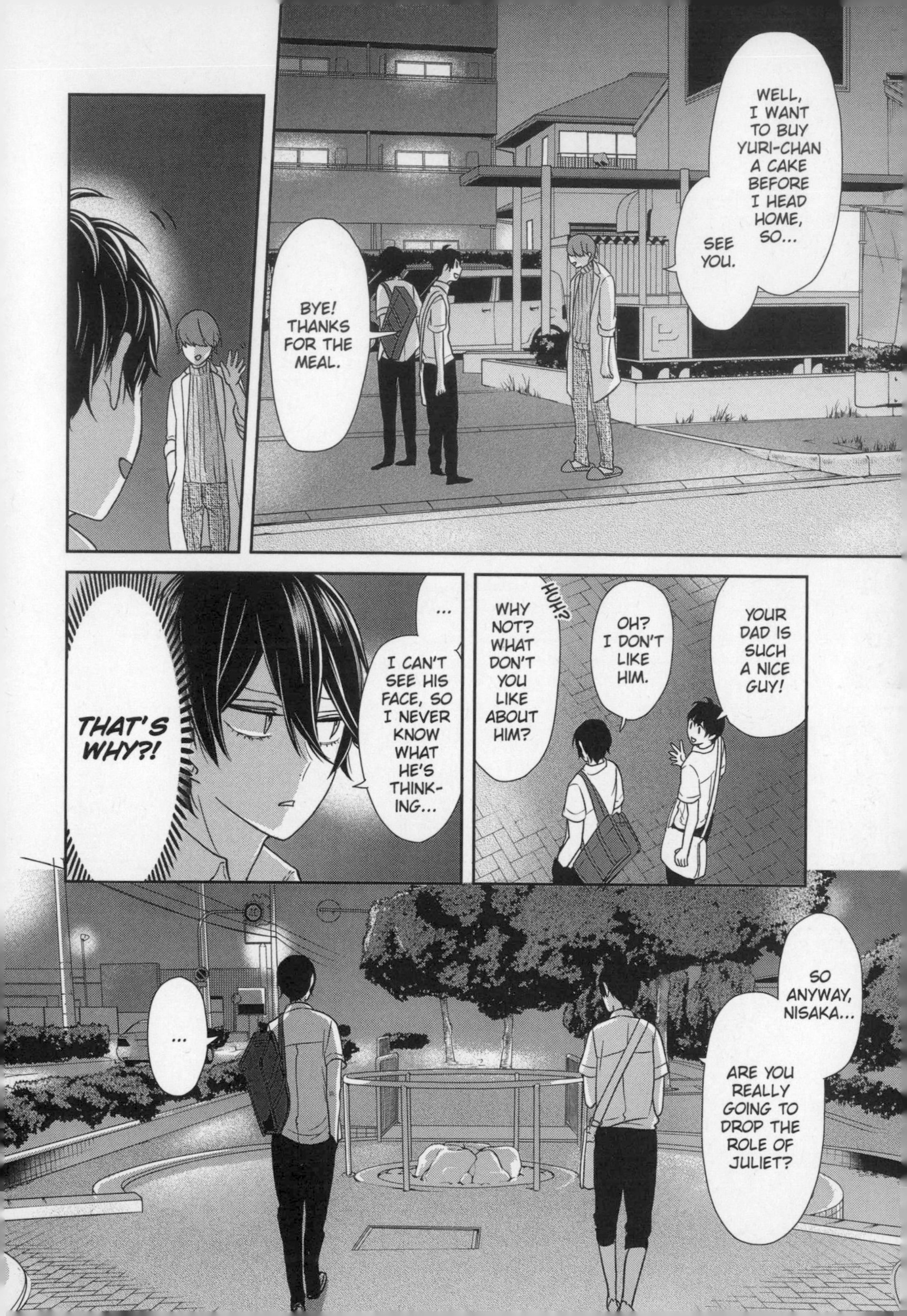

WELL, I WANT TO BUY YURI-CHAN A CAKE BEFORE I HEAD HOME, SO...
SEE YOU.
BYE! THANKS FOR THE MEAL.
YOUR DAD IS SUCH A NICE GUY!
OH? I DON'T LIKE HIM.
HUH?
WHY NOT? WHAT DON'T YOU LIKE ABOUT HIM?
...
I CAN'T SEE HIS FACE, SO I NEVER KNOW WHAT HE'S THINK-ING...
THAT'S WHY?!
SO ANYWAY, NISAKA...
ARE YOU REALLY GOING TO DROP THE ROLE OF JULIET?
...

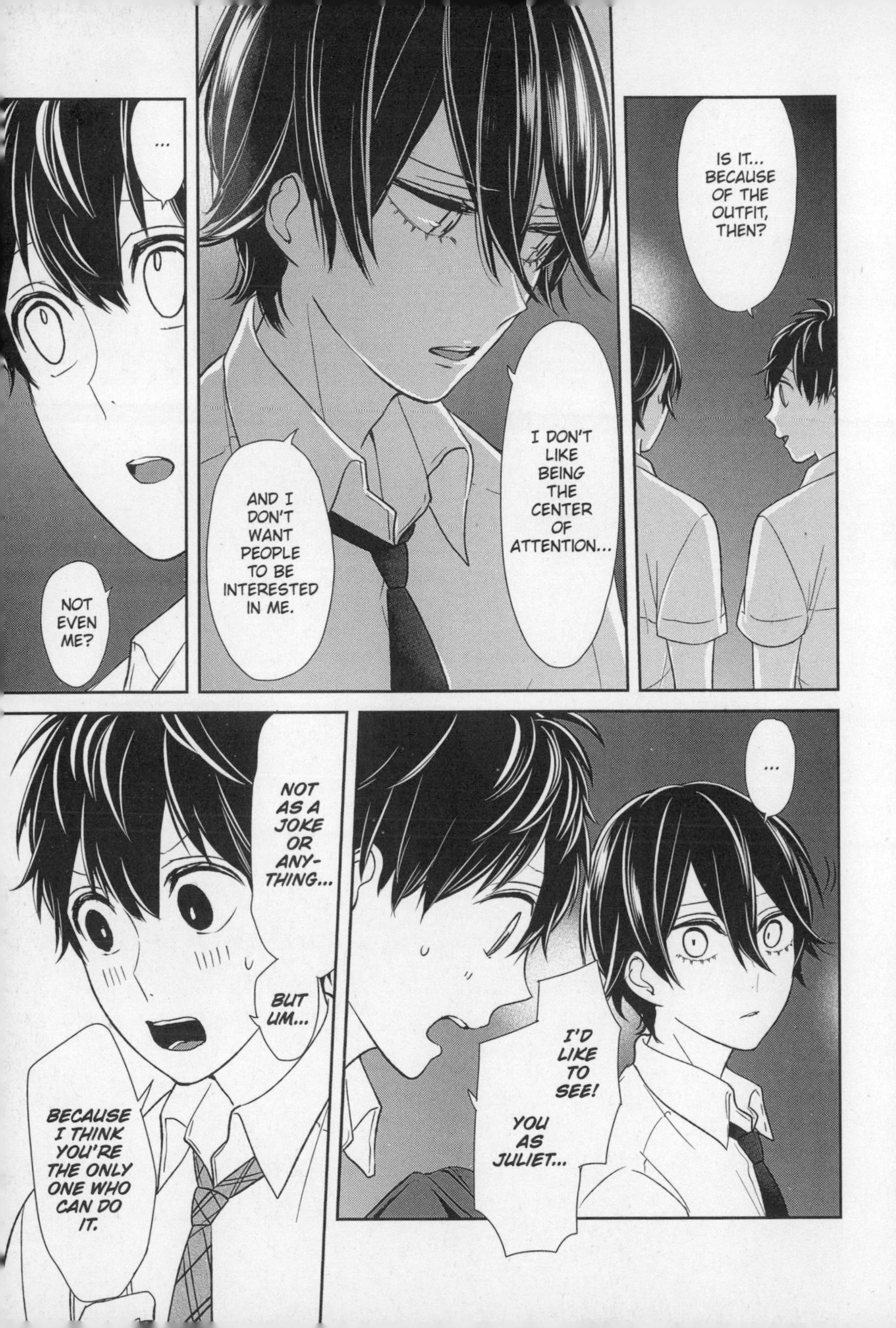
IS IT... BECAUSE OF THE OUTFIT, THEN?
I DON'T LIKE BEING THE CENTER OF ATTENTION...
AND I DON'T WANT PEOPLE TO BE INTERESTED IN ME.
...
NOT EVEN ME?
...
I'D LIKE TO SEE!
YOU AS JULIET...
NOT AS A JOKE OR ANY-THING...
BUT UM...
BECAUSE I THINK YOU'RE THE ONLY ONE WHO CAN DO IT.

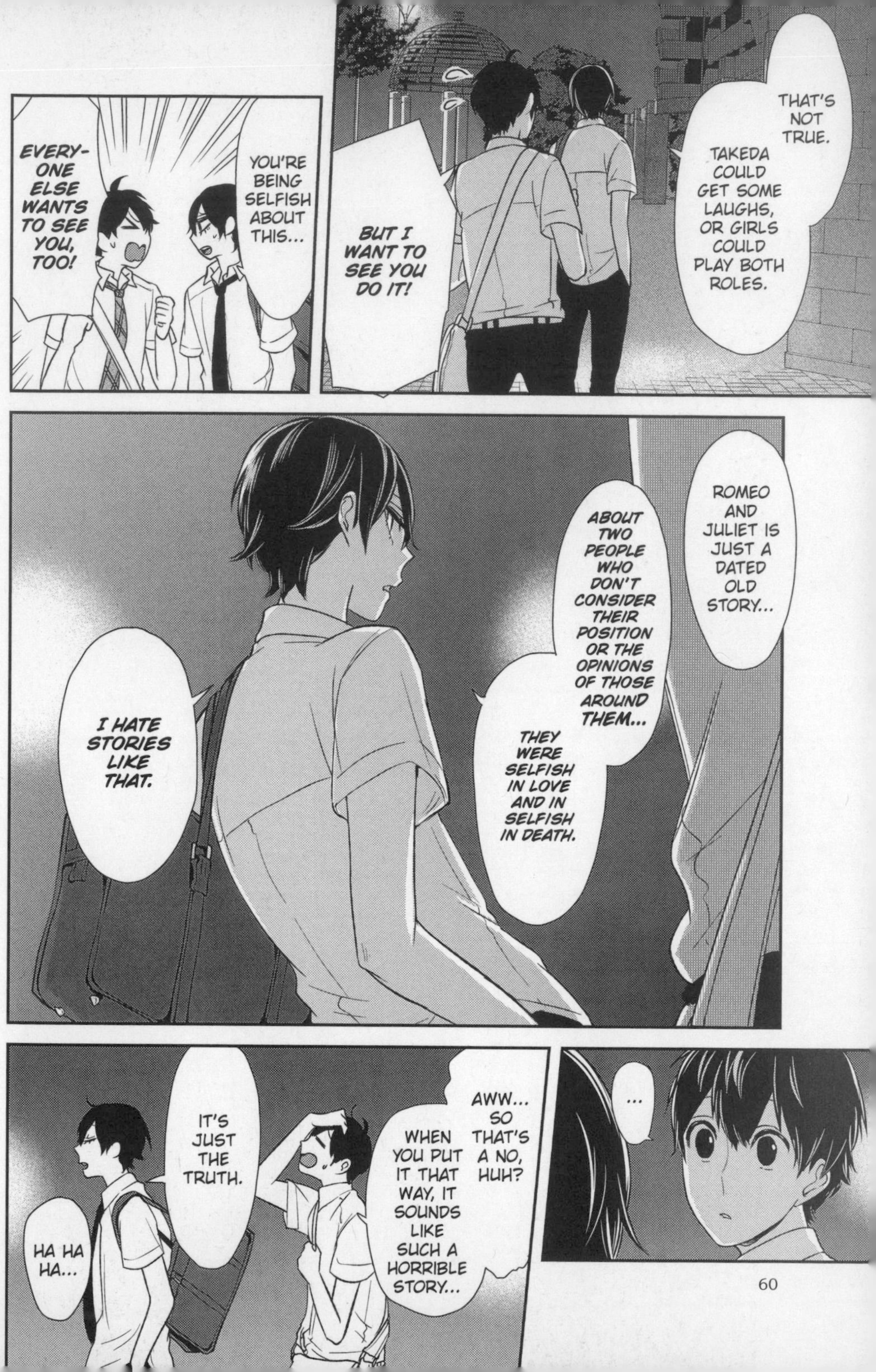
THAT'S NOT TRUE.
TAKEDA COULD GET SOME LAUGHS, OR GIRLS COULD PLAY BOTH ROLES.
BUT I WANT TO SEE YOU DO IT!
YOU'RE BEING SELFISH ABOUT THIS...
EVERY-ONE ELSE WANTS TO SEE YOU, TOO!
ROMEO AND JULIET IS JUST A DATED OLD STORY...
ABOUT TWO PEOPLE WHO DON'T CONSIDER THEIR POSITION OR THE OPINIONS OF THOSE AROUND THEM...
THEY WERE SELFISH IN LOVE AND IN SELFISH IN DEATH.
I HATE STORIES LIKE THAT.
...
AWW... SO THAT'S A NO, HUH?
WHEN YOU PUT IT THAT WAY, IT SOUNDS LIKE SUCH A HORRIBLE STORY...
IT'S JUST THE TRUTH.
HA HA HA...

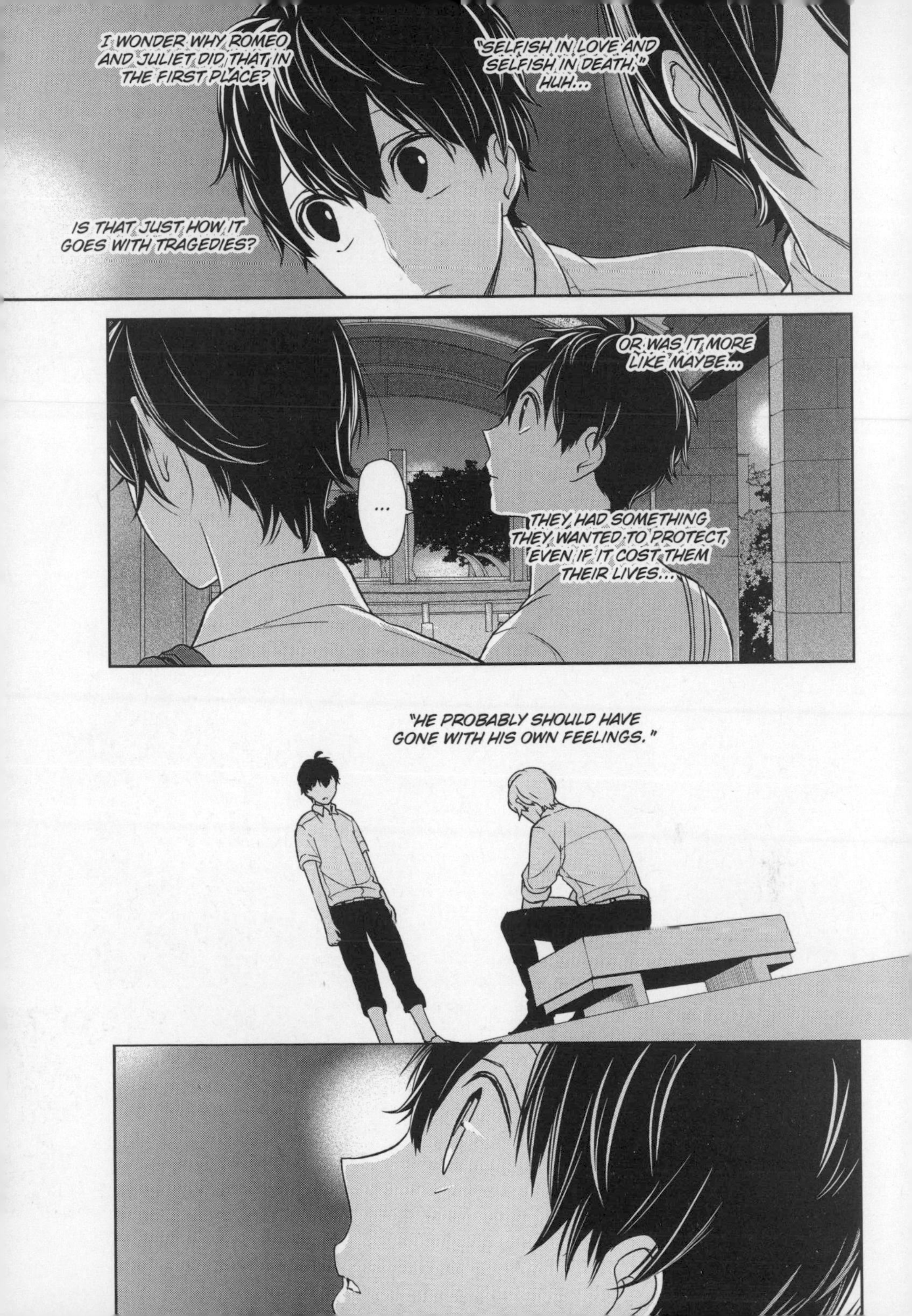
"SELFISH IN LOVE AND SELFISH IN DEATH," HUH...
I WONDER WHY ROMEO AND JULIET DID THAT IN THE FIRST PLACE?
IS THAT JUST HOW IT GOES WITH TRAGEDIES?
OR WAS IT MORE LIKE MAYBE...
THEY HAD SOMETHING THEY WANTED TO PROTECT, EVEN IF IT COST THEM THEIR LIVES...
...
"HE PROBABLY SHOULD HAVE GONE WITH HIS OWN FEELINGS."

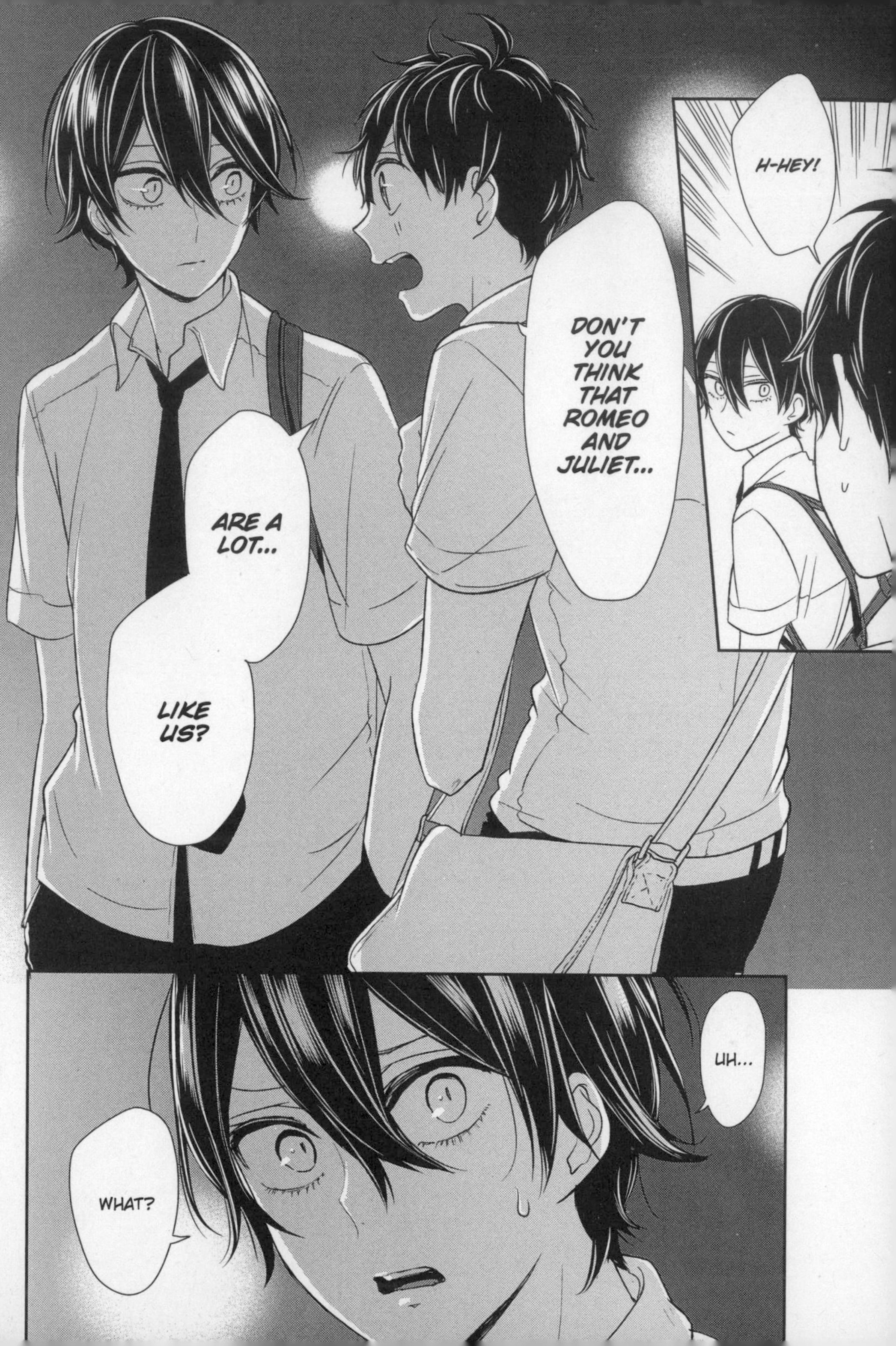
H-HEY!
DON'T YOU THINK THAT ROMEO AND JULIET...
ARE A LOT...
LIKE US?
UH...
WHAT?

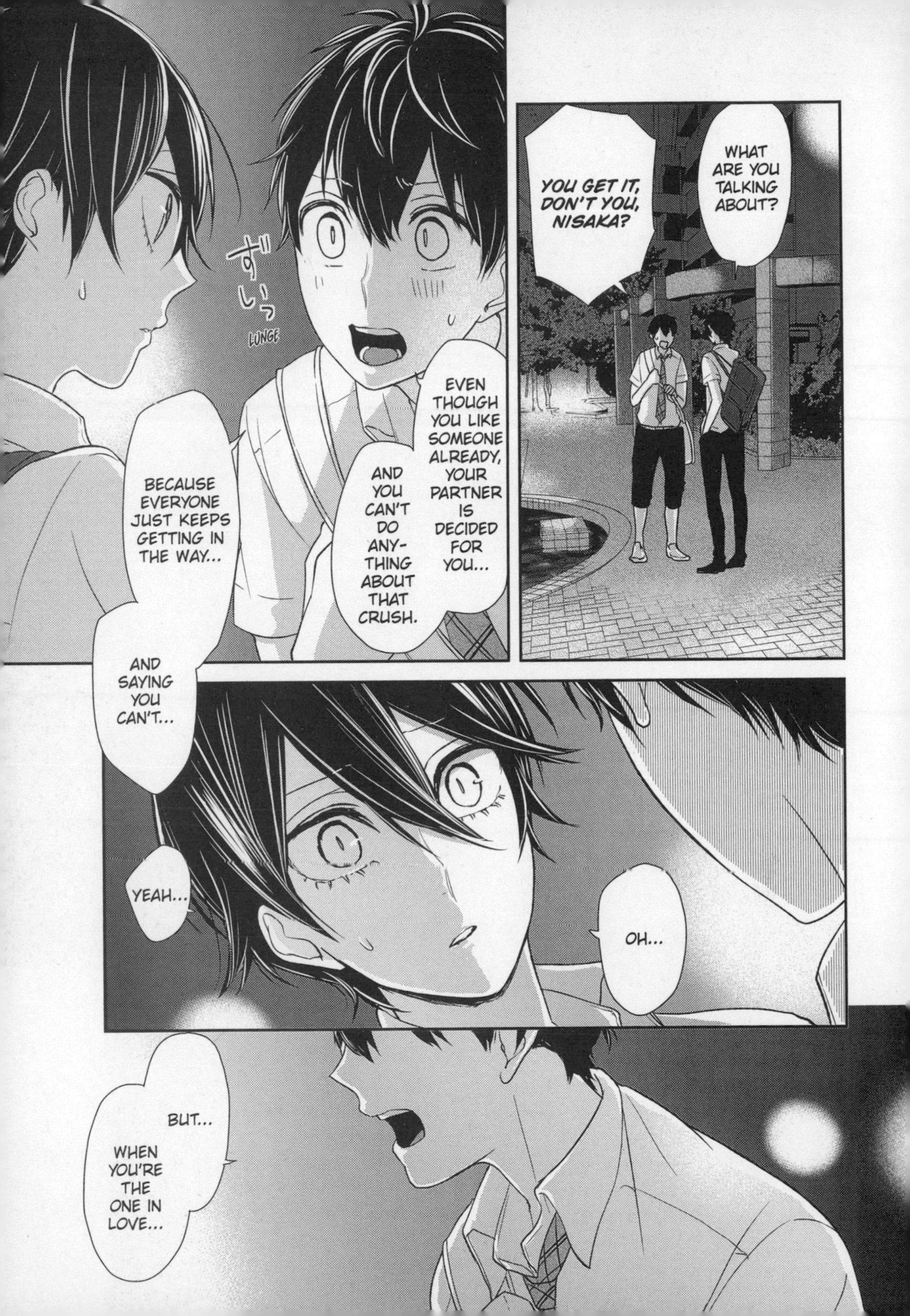
WHAT ARE YOU TALKING ABOUT?
YOU GET IT, DON'T YOU, NISAKA?
ずいっ
LUNGE
EVEN THOUGH YOU LIKE SOMEONE ALREADY, YOUR PARTNER IS DECIDED FOR YOU...
AND YOU CAN'T DO ANY-THING ABOUT THAT CRUSH.
BECAUSE EVERYONE JUST KEEPS GETTING IN THE WAY...
AND SAYING YOU CAN'T...
OH...
YEAH...
BUT... WHEN YOU'RE THE ONE IN LOVE...

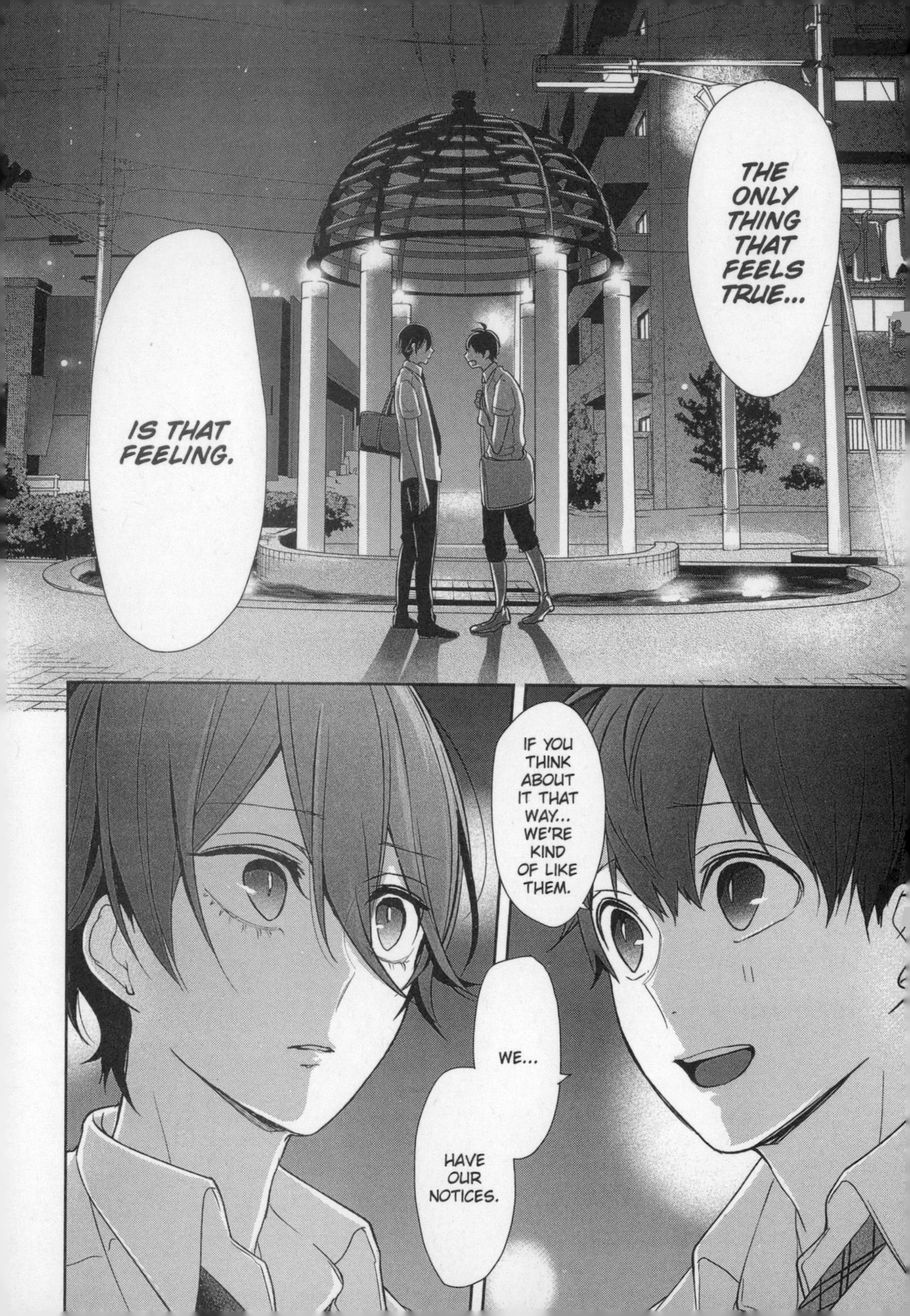
THE ONLY THING THAT FEELS TRUE...
IS THAT FEELING.
IF YOU THINK ABOUT IT THAT WAY... WE'RE KIND OF LIKE THEM.
WE...
HAVE OUR NOTICES.

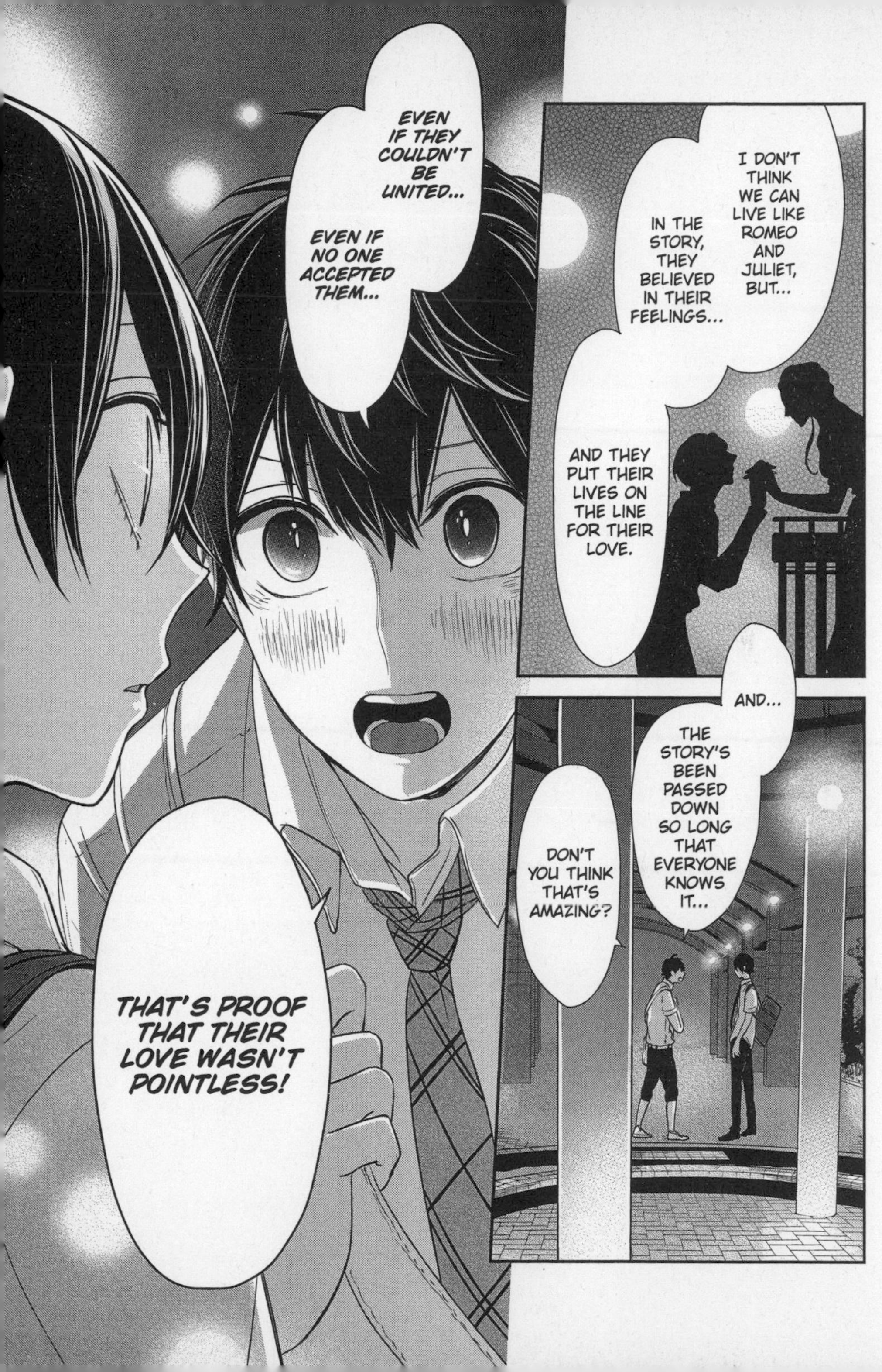
I DON'T THINK WE CAN LIVE LIKE ROMEO AND JULIET, BUT...
IN THE STORY, THEY BELIEVED IN THEIR FEELINGS...
AND THEY PUT THEIR LIVES ON THE LINE FOR THEIR LOVE.
AND...
THE STORY'S BEEN PASSED DOWN SO LONG THAT EVERYONE KNOWS IT...
DON'T YOU THINK THAT'S AMAZING?
EVEN IF THEY COULDN'T BE UNITED...
EVEN IF NO ONE ACCEPTED THEM...
THAT'S PROOF THAT THEIR LOVE WASN'T POINTLESS!

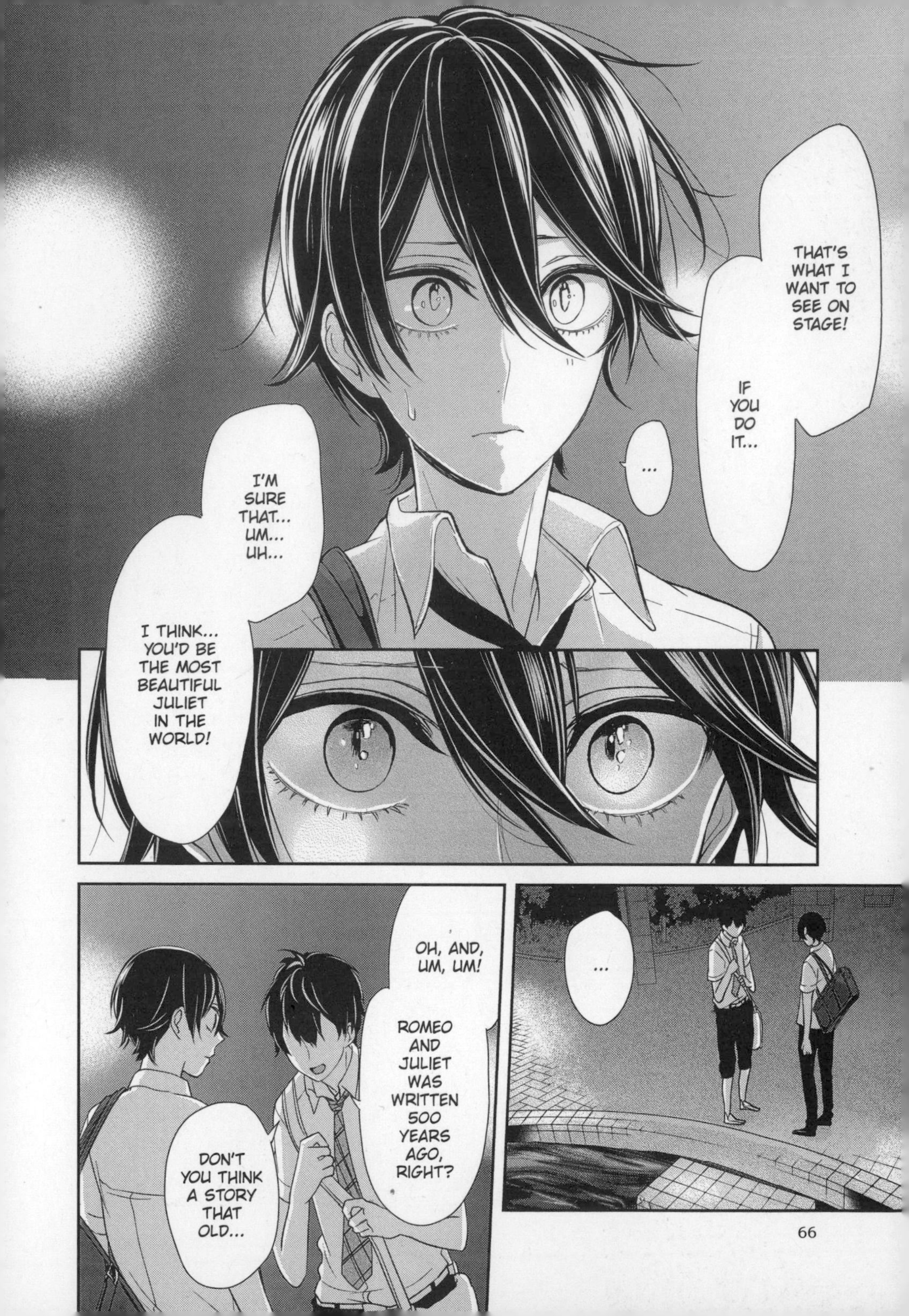
THAT'S WHAT I WANT TO SEE ON STAGE!
IF YOU DO IT...
...
I'M SURE THAT... UM... UH...
I THINK... YOU'D BE THE MOST BEAUTIFUL JULIET IN THE WORLD!
...
OH, AND, UM, UM!
ROMEO AND JULIET WAS WRITTEN 500 YEARS AGO, RIGHT?
DON'T YOU THINK A STORY THAT OLD...

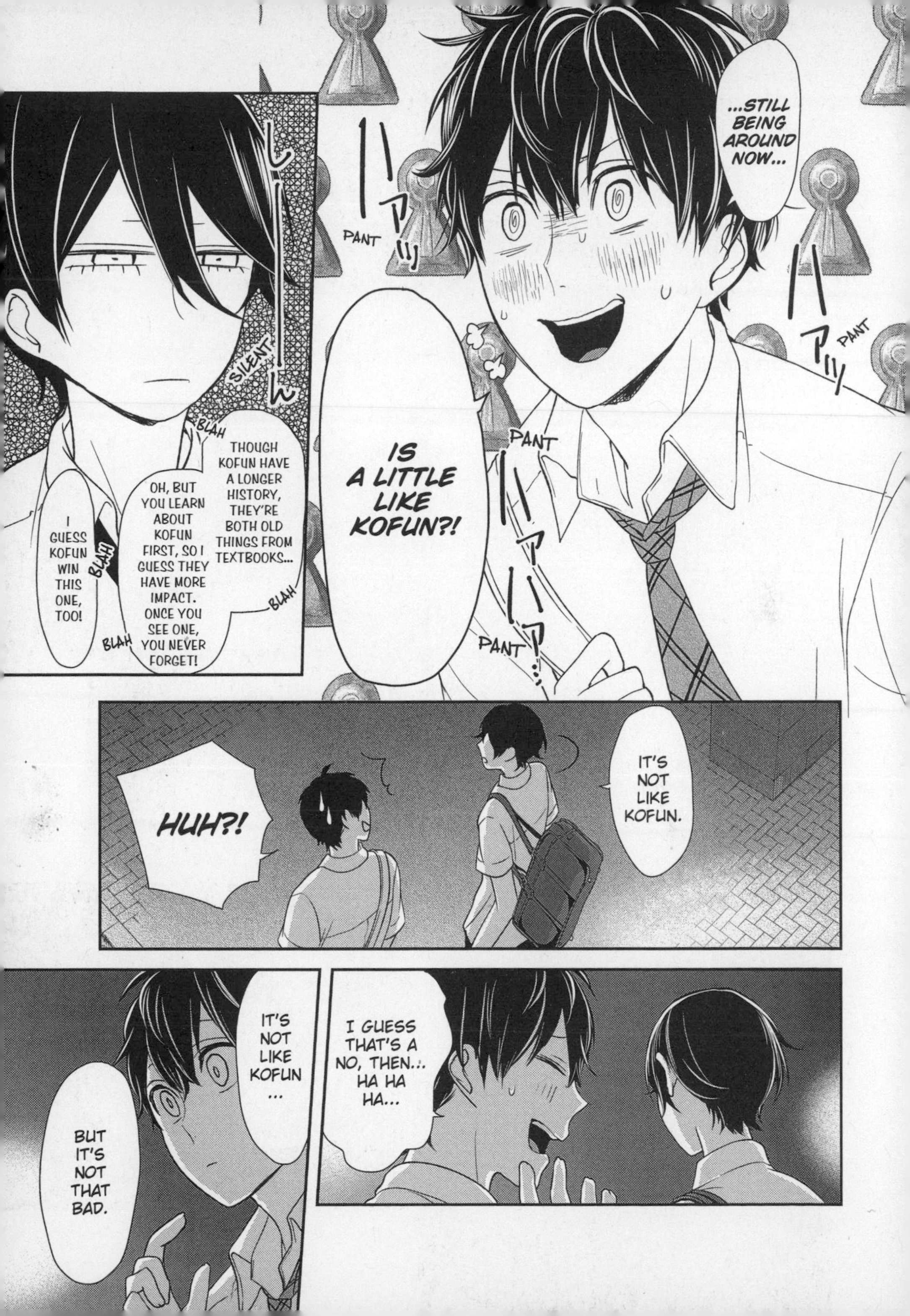
...STILL BEING AROUND NOW...
PANT
PANT
PANT
PANT
IS A LITTLE LIKE KOFUN?!
SILENT
BLAH
THOUGH KOFUN HAVE A LONGER HISTORY, THEY'RE BOTH OLD THINGS FROM TEXTBOOKS...
OH, BUT YOU LEARN ABOUT KOFUN FIRST, SO I GUESS THEY HAVE MORE IMPACT. ONCE YOU SEE ONE, YOU NEVER FORGET!
BLAH
BLAH
I GUESS KOFUN WIN THIS ONE, TOO!
BLAH
IT'S NOT LIKE KOFUN.
HUH?!
I GUESS THAT'S A NO, THEN... HA HA HA...
IT'S NOT LIKE KOFUN...
BUT IT'S NOT THAT BAD.

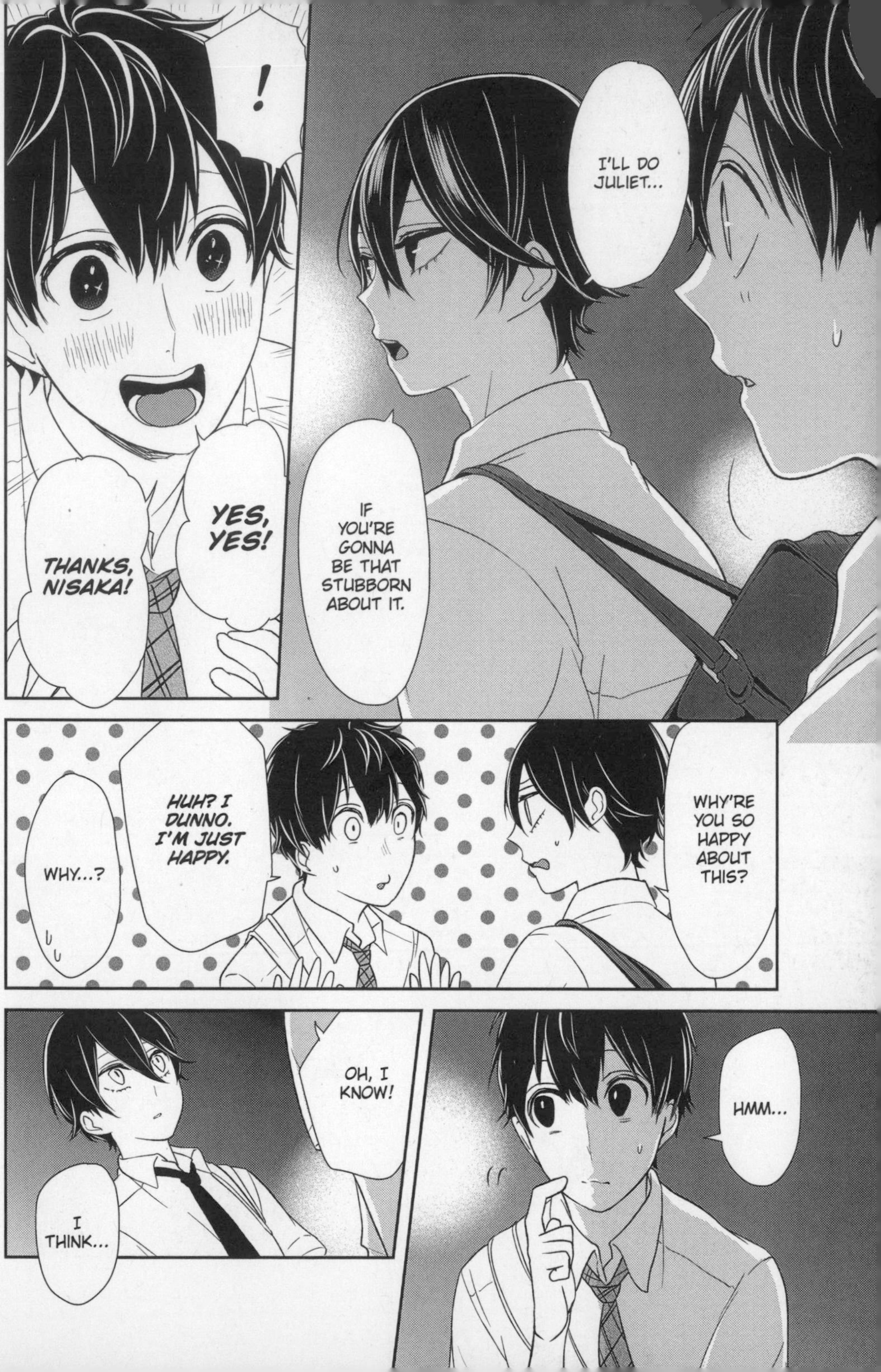
I'LL DO JULIET...
IF YOU'RE GONNA BE THAT STUBBORN ABOUT IT.
!
YES, YES!
THANKS, NISAKA!
WHY'RE YOU SO HAPPY ABOUT THIS?
HUH? I DUNNO. I'M JUST HAPPY.
WHY...?
HMM...
OH, I KNOW!
I THINK...

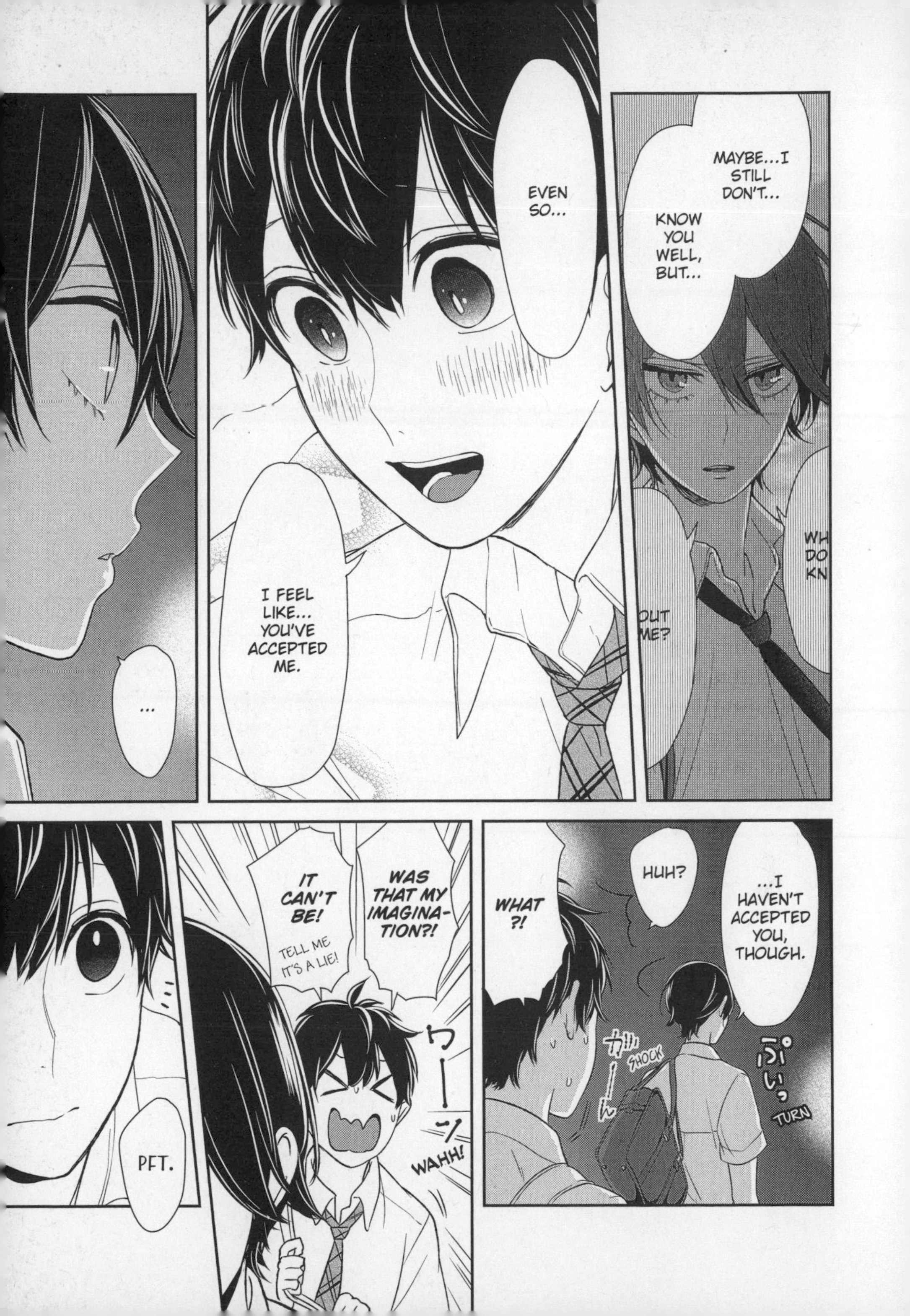
MAYBE...I STILL DON'T...
KNOW YOU WELL, BUT...
EVEN SO...
I FEEL LIKE... YOU'VE ACCEPTED ME.
...
...I HAVEN'T ACCEPTED YOU, THOUGH.
ぷいっ
TURN
HUH?
SHOCK
WHAT?!
WAS THAT MY IMAGINATION?!
IT CAN'T BE!
TELL ME IT'S A LIE!
WAHH!
PFT.

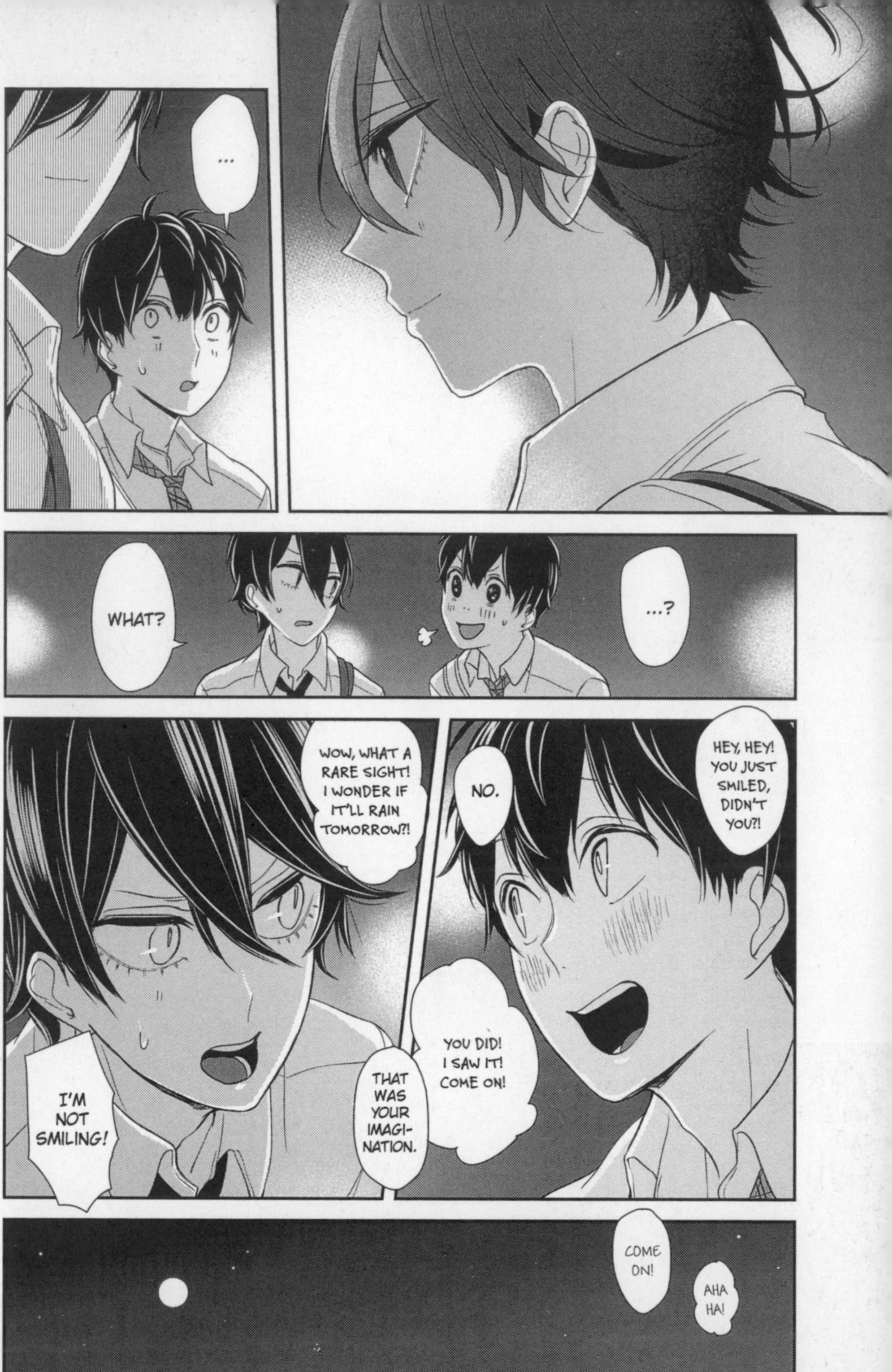
...
...?
WHAT?
HEY, HEY! YOU JUST SMILED, DIDN'T YOU?!
NO.
YOU DID! I SAW IT! COME ON!
WOW, WHAT A RARE SIGHT! I WONDER IF IT'LL RAIN TOMORROW?!
THAT WAS YOUR IMAGINATION.
I'M NOT SMILING!
COME ON!
AHA HA!

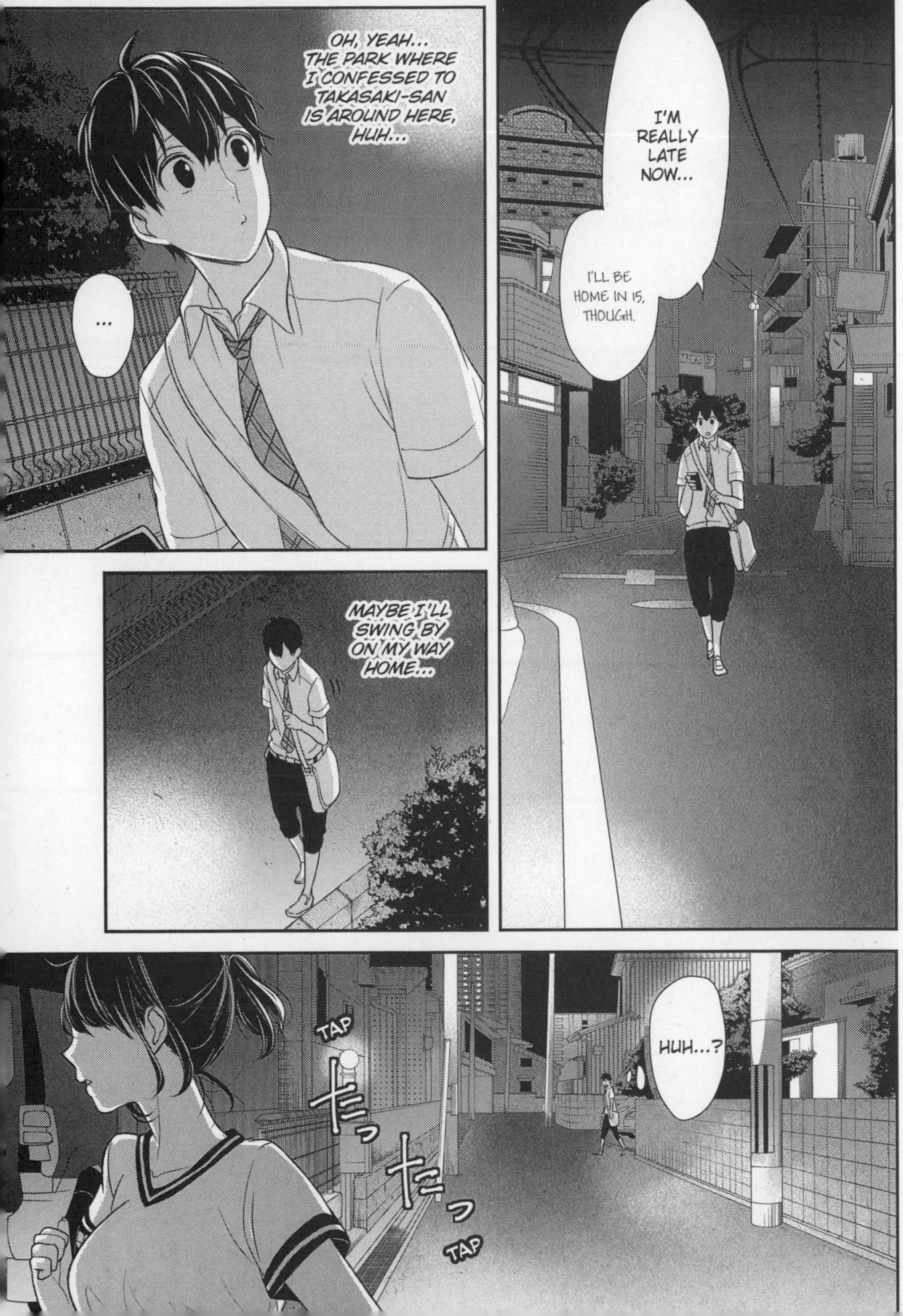
I'M REALLY LATE NOW...
I'LL BE HOME IN 15, THOUGH.
OH, YEAH... THE PARK WHERE I CONFESSED TO TAKASAKI-SAN IS AROUND HERE, HUH...
...
MAYBE I'LL SWING BY ON MY WAY HOME...
HUH...?
TAP
たっ
たっ
TAP

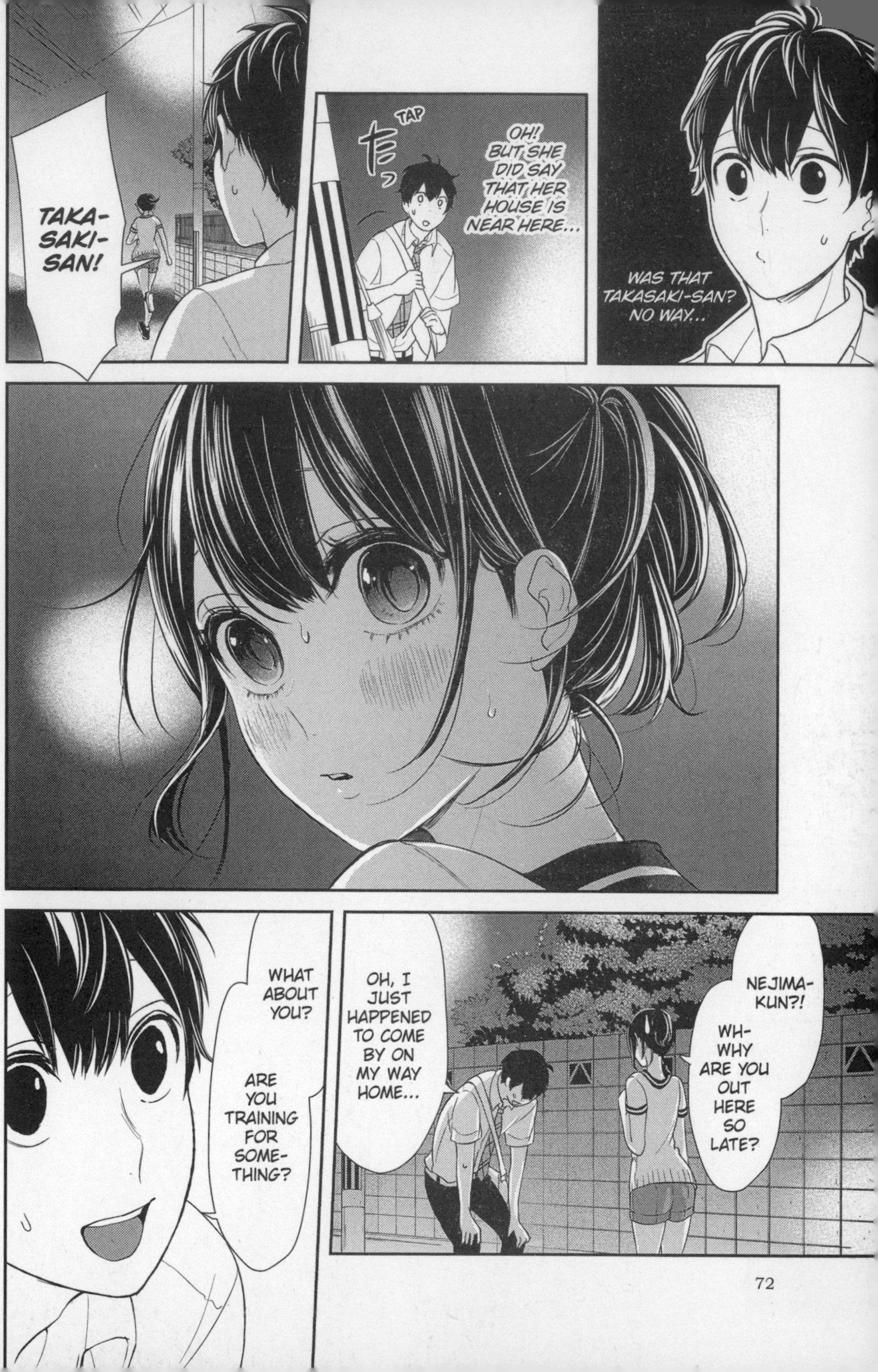
WAS THAT TAKASAKI-SAN? NO WAY...
たっ
TAP
OH! BUT SHE DID SAY THAT HER HOUSE IS NEAR HERE...
TAKA-SAKI-SAN!
NEJIMA-KUN?!
WH-WHY ARE YOU OUT HERE SO LATE?
OH, I JUST HAPPENED TO COME BY ON MY WAY HOME...
WHAT ABOUT YOU?
ARE YOU TRAINING FOR SOME-THING?

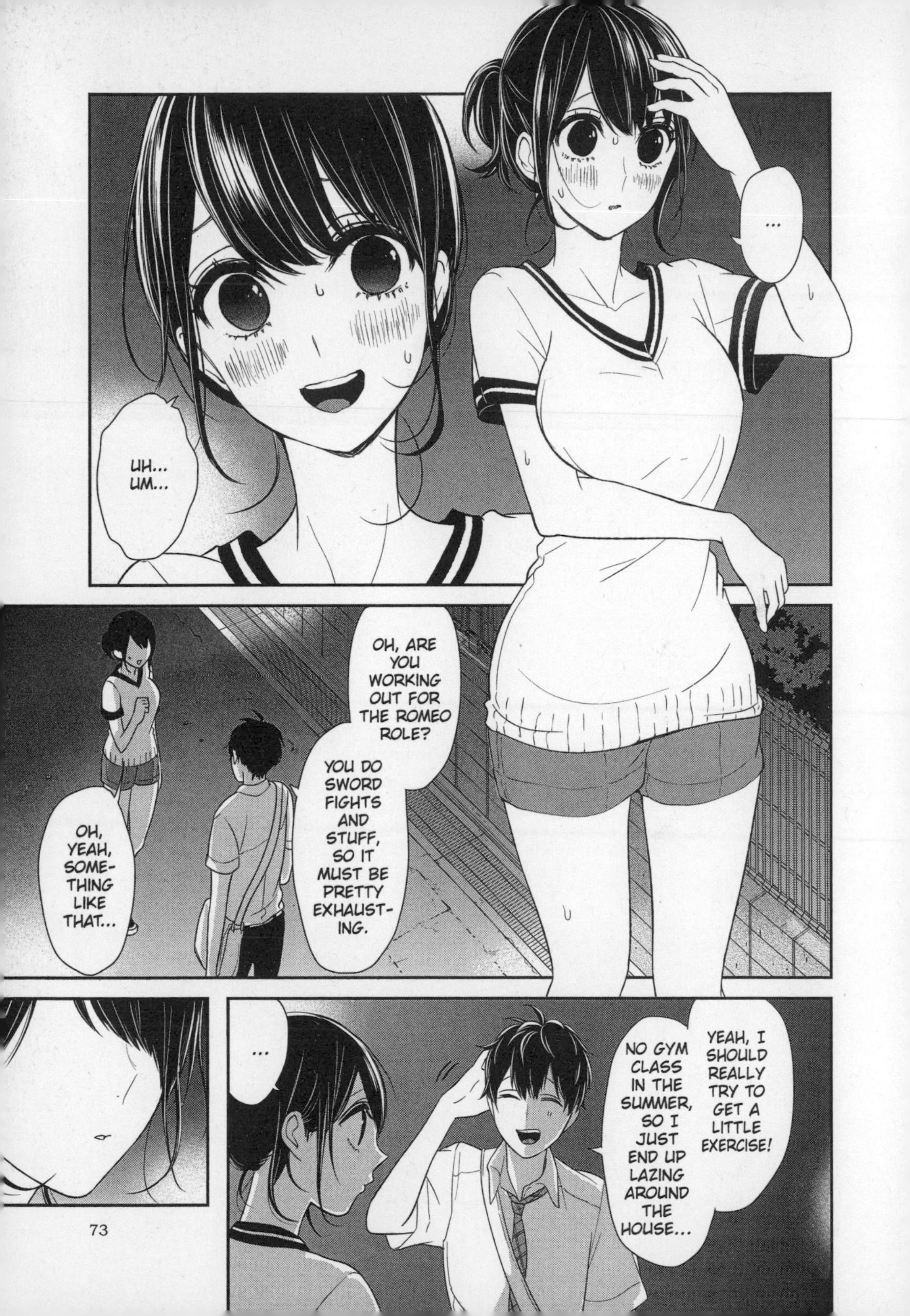
...
UH... UM...
OH, ARE YOU WORKING OUT FOR THE ROMEO ROLE?
YOU DO SWORD FIGHTS AND STUFF, SO IT MUST BE PRETTY EXHAUST-ING.
OH, YEAH, SOME-THING LIKE THAT...
YEAH, I SHOULD REALLY TRY TO GET A LITTLE EXERCISE!
NO GYM CLASS IN THE SUMMER, SO I JUST END UP LAZING AROUND THE HOUSE...
...

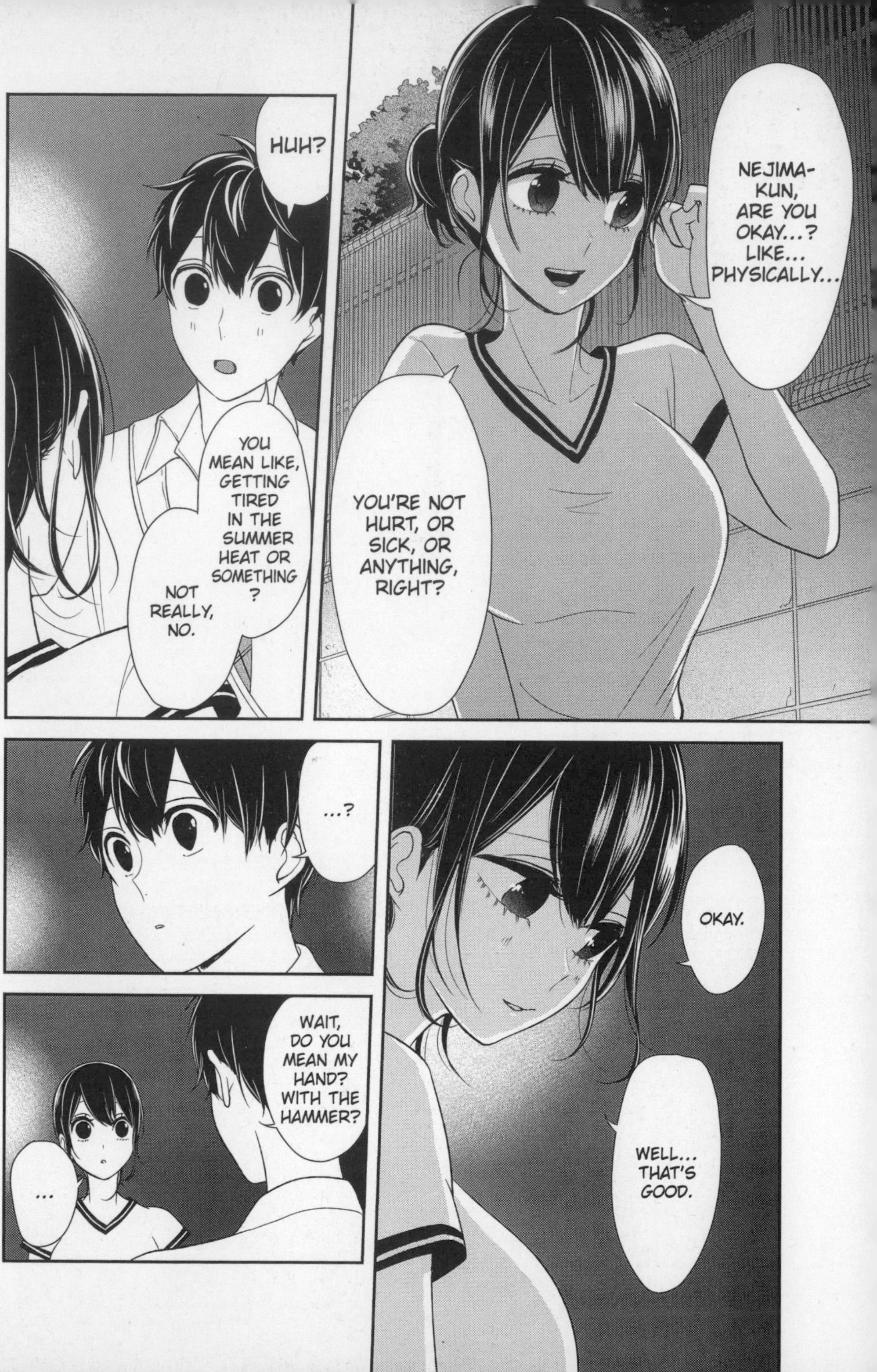
NEJIMA-KUN, ARE YOU OKAY...? LIKE... PHYSICALLY...
YOU'RE NOT HURT, OR SICK, OR ANYTHING, RIGHT?
HUH?
YOU MEAN LIKE, GETTING TIRED IN THE SUMMER HEAT OR SOMETHING?
NOT REALLY, NO.
OKAY.
WELL... THAT'S GOOD.
...?
WAIT, DO YOU MEAN MY HAND? WITH THE HAMMER?
...

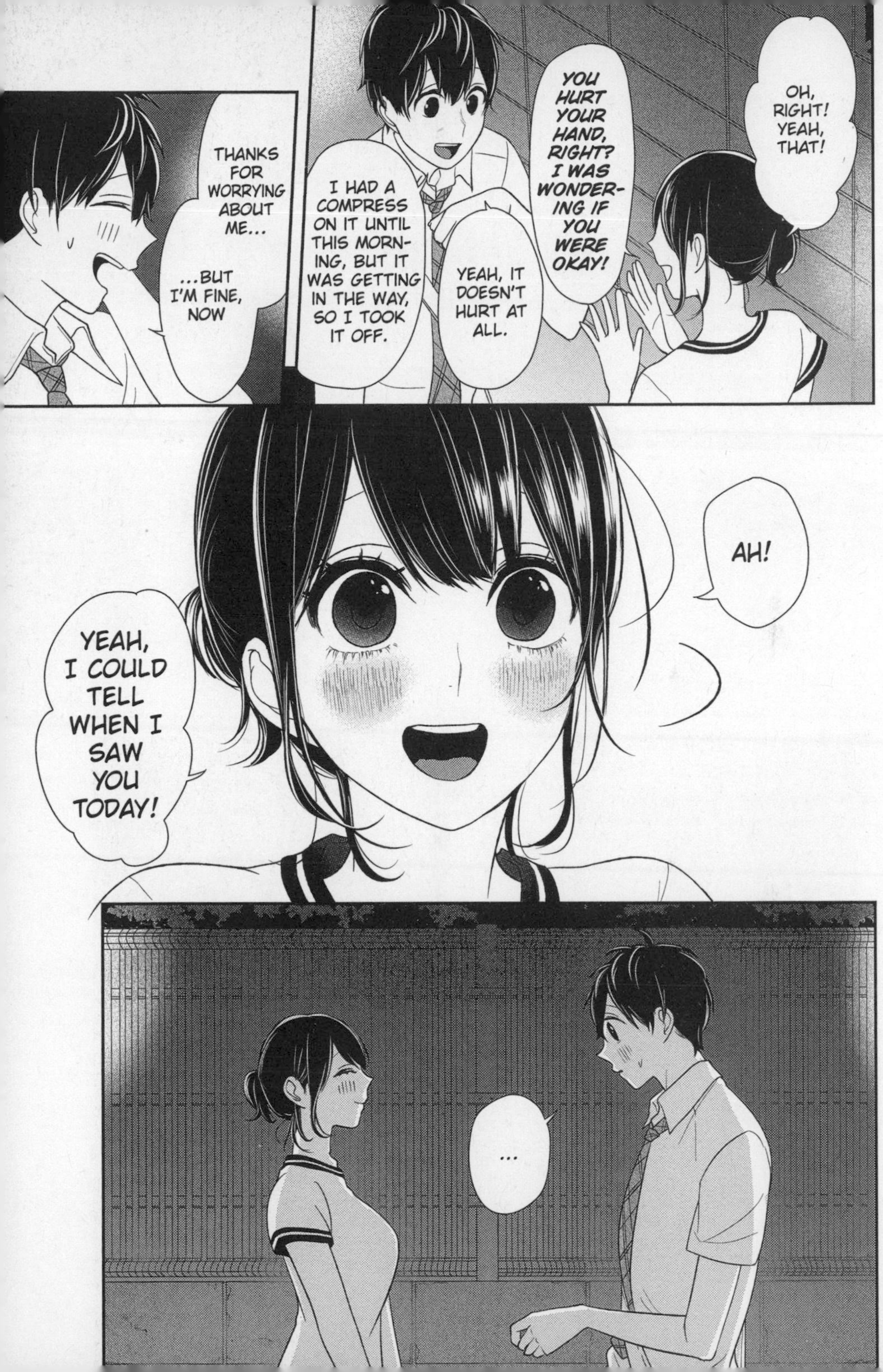
OH, RIGHT! YEAH, THAT!
YOU HURT YOUR HAND, RIGHT? I WAS WONDER-ING IF YOU WERE OKAY!
YEAH, IT DOESN'T HURT AT ALL.
I HAD A COMPRESS ON IT UNTIL THIS MORN-ING, BUT IT WAS GETTING IN THE WAY, SO I TOOK IT OFF.
THANKS FOR WORRYING ABOUT ME...
...BUT I'M FINE, NOW
AH!
YEAH, I COULD TELL WHEN I SAW YOU TODAY!
...

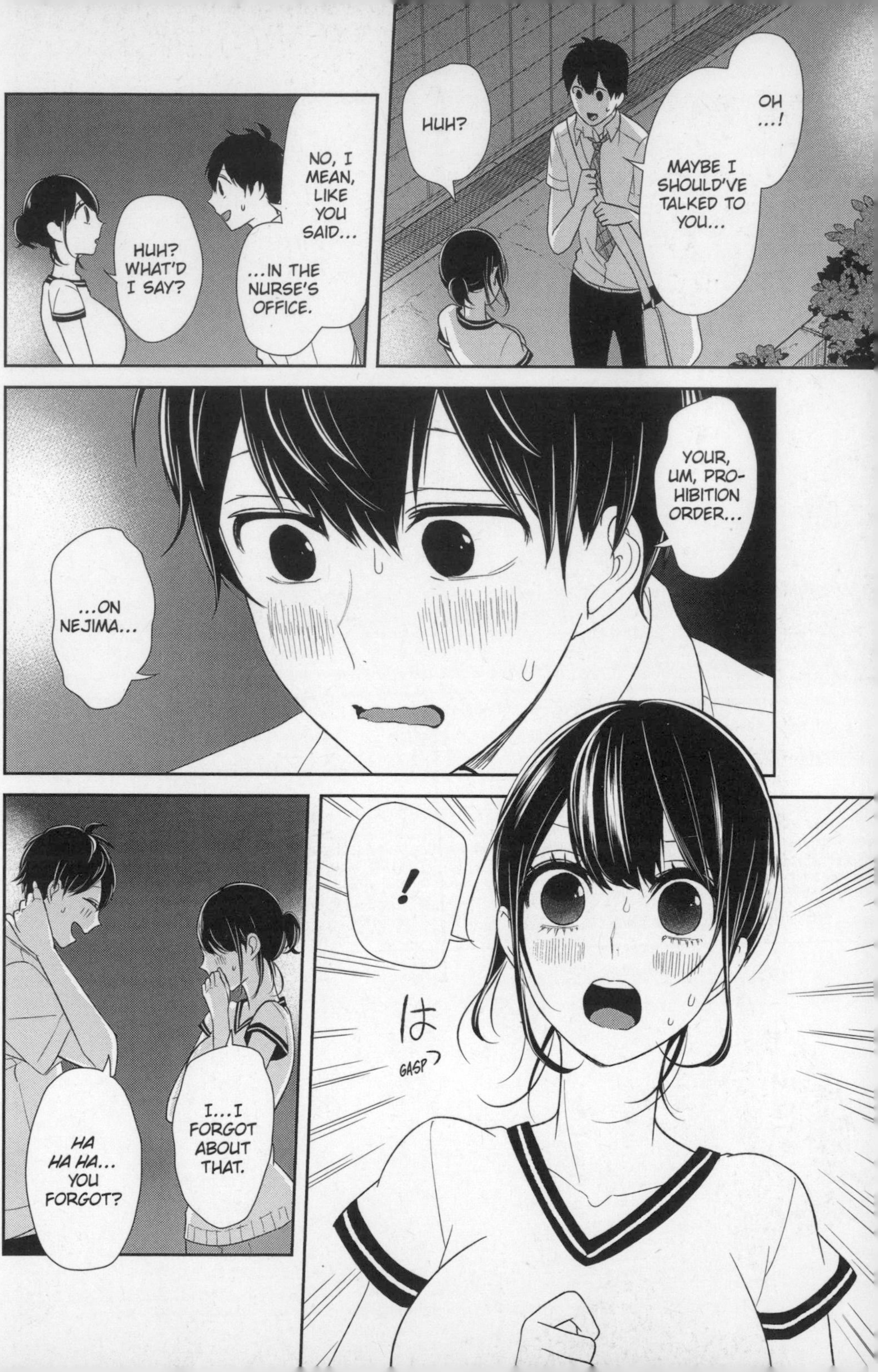
OH ...!
MAYBE I SHOULD'VE TALKED TO YOU...
HUH?
NO, I MEAN, LIKE YOU SAID...
...IN THE NURSE'S OFFICE.
HUH? WHAT'D I SAY?
YOUR, UM, PRO-HIBITION ORDER...
...ON NEJIMA...
!
は
GASP
I...I FORGOT ABOUT THAT.
HA HA HA... YOU FORGOT?

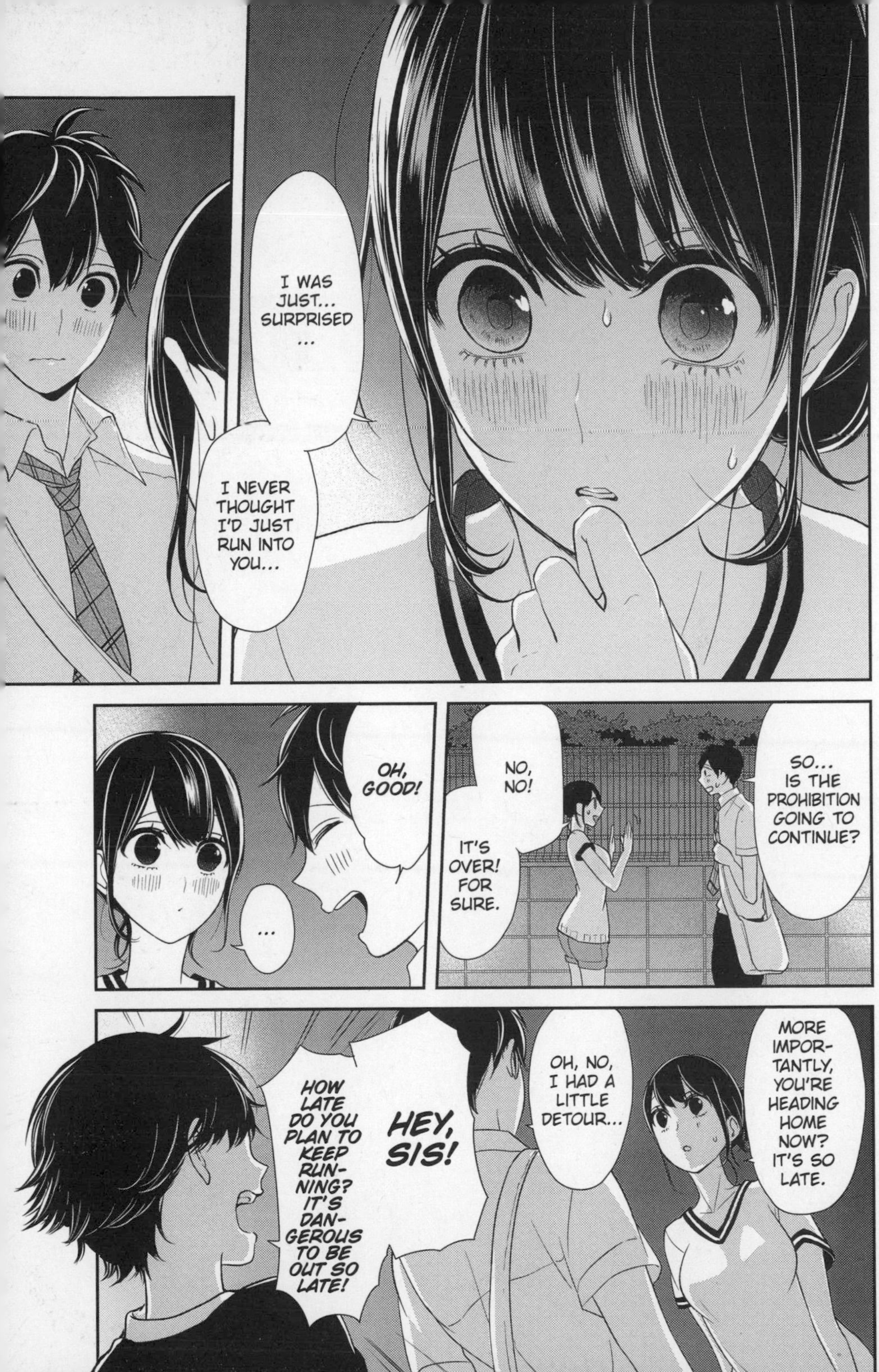
I WAS JUST... SURPRISED...
I NEVER THOUGHT I'D JUST RUN INTO YOU...
SO... IS THE PROHIBITION GOING TO CONTINUE?
NO, NO!
IT'S OVER! FOR SURE.
OH, GOOD!
...
MORE IMPORTANTLY, YOU'RE HEADING HOME NOW? IT'S SO LATE.
OH, NO, I HAD A LITTLE DETOUR...
HEY, SIS!
HOW LATE DO YOU PLAN TO KEEP RUNNING? IT'S DANGEROUS TO BE OUT SO LATE!

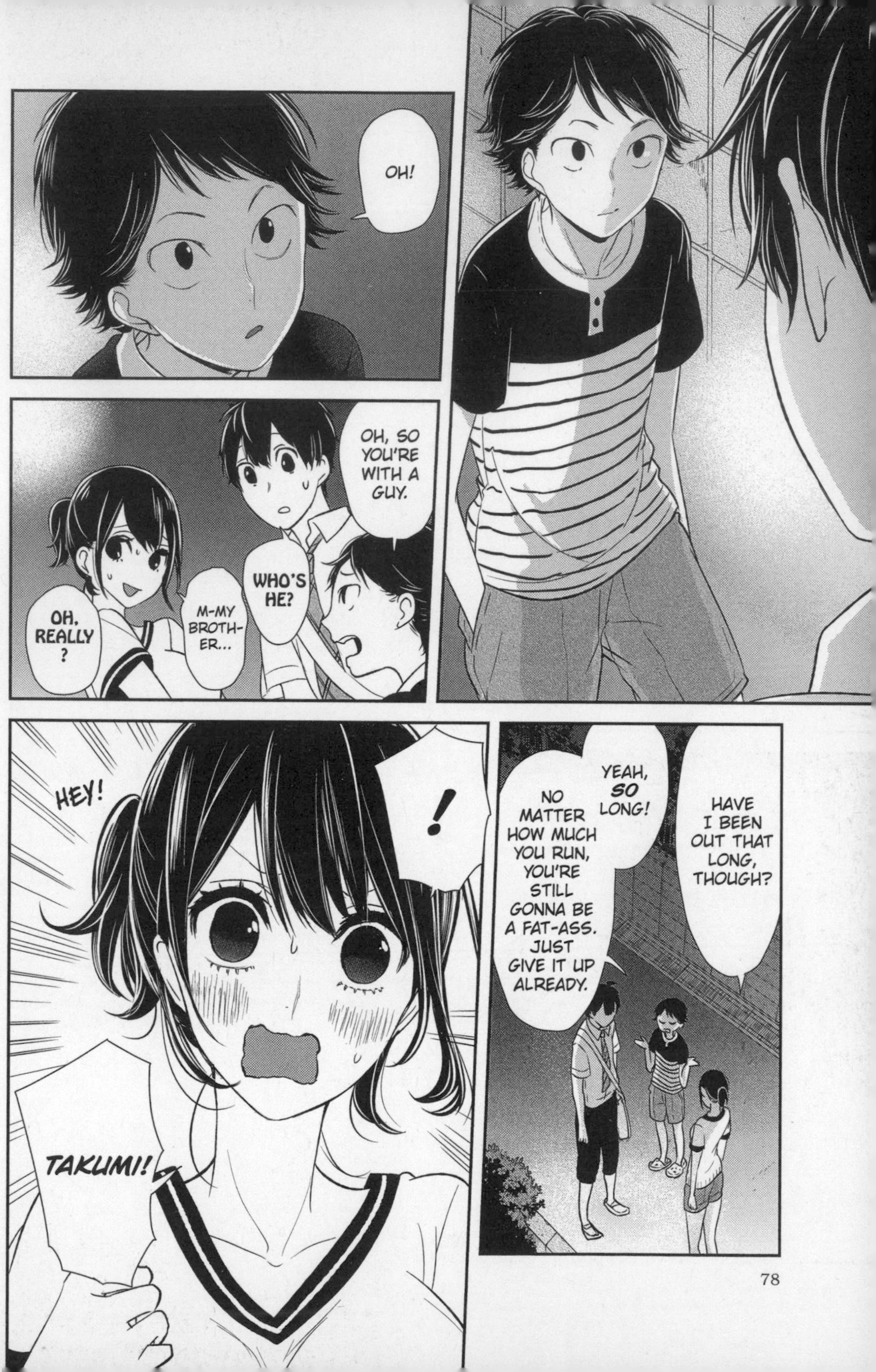
OH!
OH, SO YOU'RE WITH A GUY.
WHO'S HE?
M-MY BROTHER...
OH, REALLY?
HAVE I BEEN OUT THAT LONG, THOUGH?
YEAH, SO LONG!
NO MATTER HOW MUCH YOU RUN, YOU'RE STILL GONNA BE A FAT-ASS. JUST GIVE IT UP ALREADY.
!
HEY!
TAKUMI!

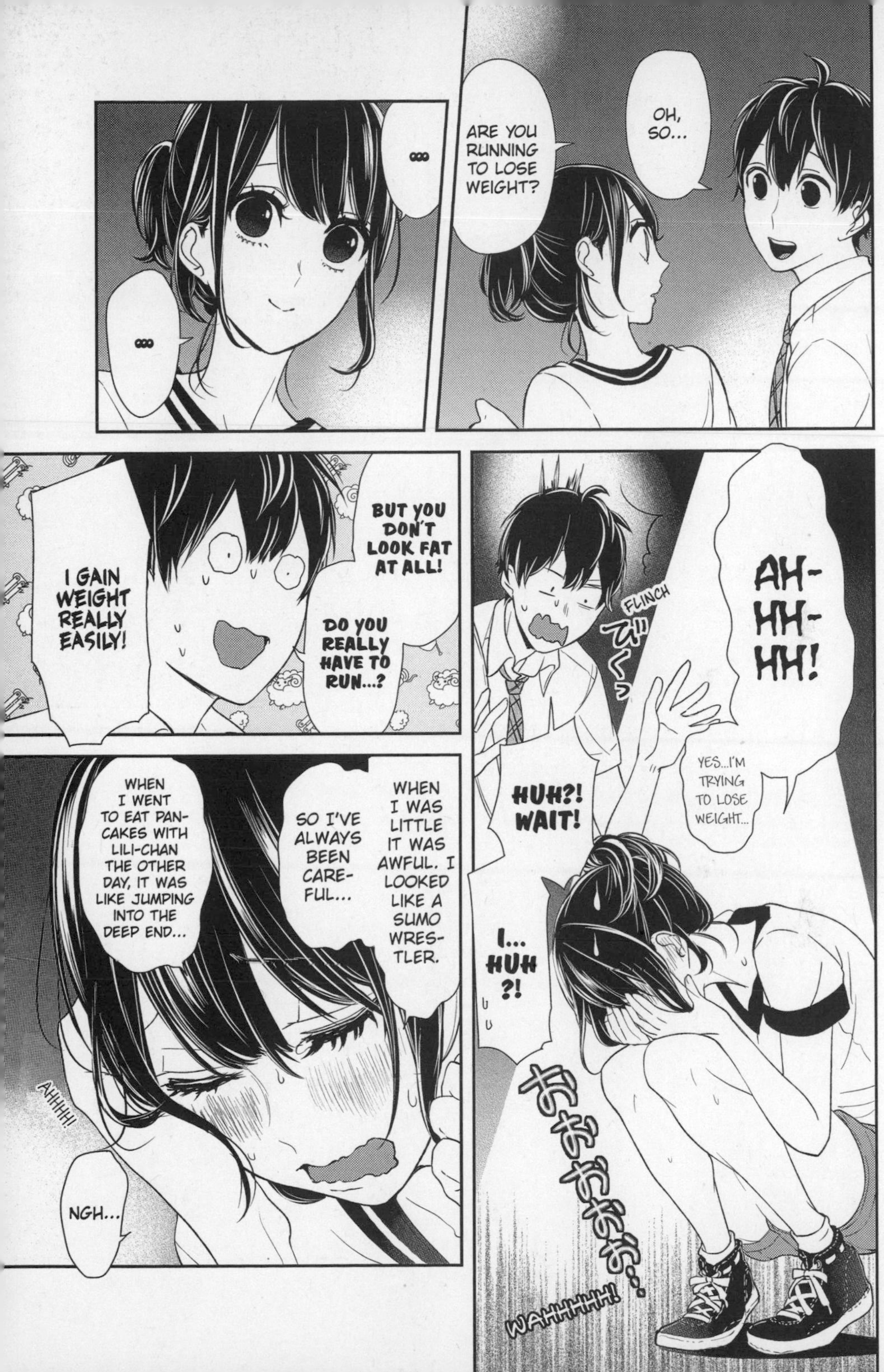
OH, SO...
ARE YOU RUNNING TO LOSE WEIGHT?
...
...
AH-HH-HH!
FLINCH
びくっ
YES...I'M TRYING TO LOSE WEIGHT...
HUH?! WAIT!
I... HUH?!
おおおおお...
WAHHHHH!
BUT YOU DON'T LOOK FAT AT ALL!
DO YOU REALLY HAVE TO RUN...?
I GAIN WEIGHT REALLY EASILY!
WHEN I WAS LITTLE IT WAS AWFUL. I LOOKED LIKE A SUMO WRESTLER.
SO I'VE ALWAYS BEEN CAREFUL...
WHEN I WENT TO EAT PANCAKES WITH LILI-CHAN THE OTHER DAY, IT WAS LIKE JUMPING INTO THE DEEP END...
AHHHH!
NGH...

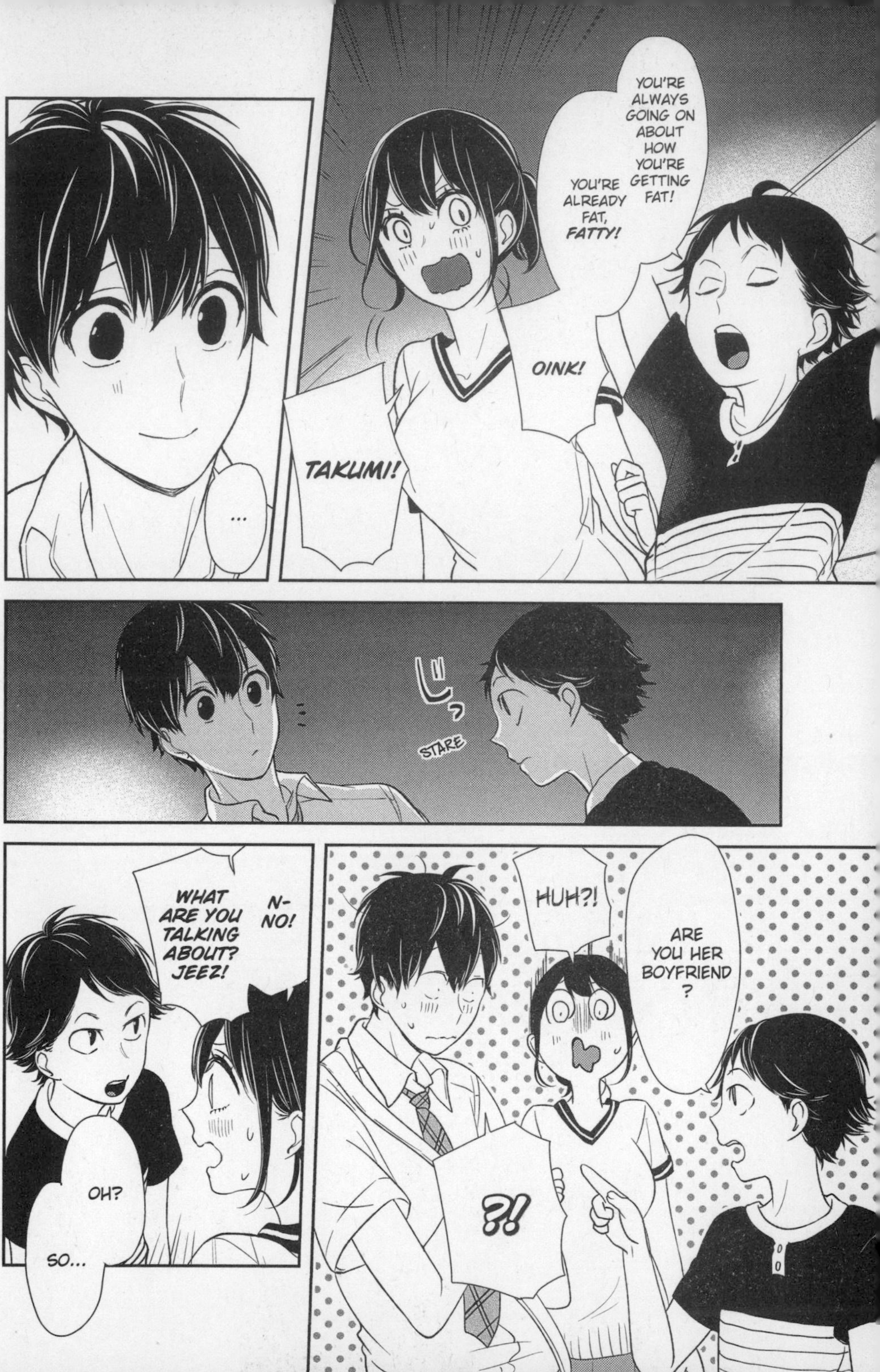
YOU'RE ALWAYS GOING ON ABOUT HOW YOU'RE GETTING FAT!
YOU'RE ALREADY FAT, FATTY!
OINK!
TAKUMI!
...
じっ
STARE
ARE YOU HER BOYFRIEND ?
HUH?!
?!
N-NO!
WHAT ARE YOU TALKING ABOUT? JEEZ!
OH?
SO...

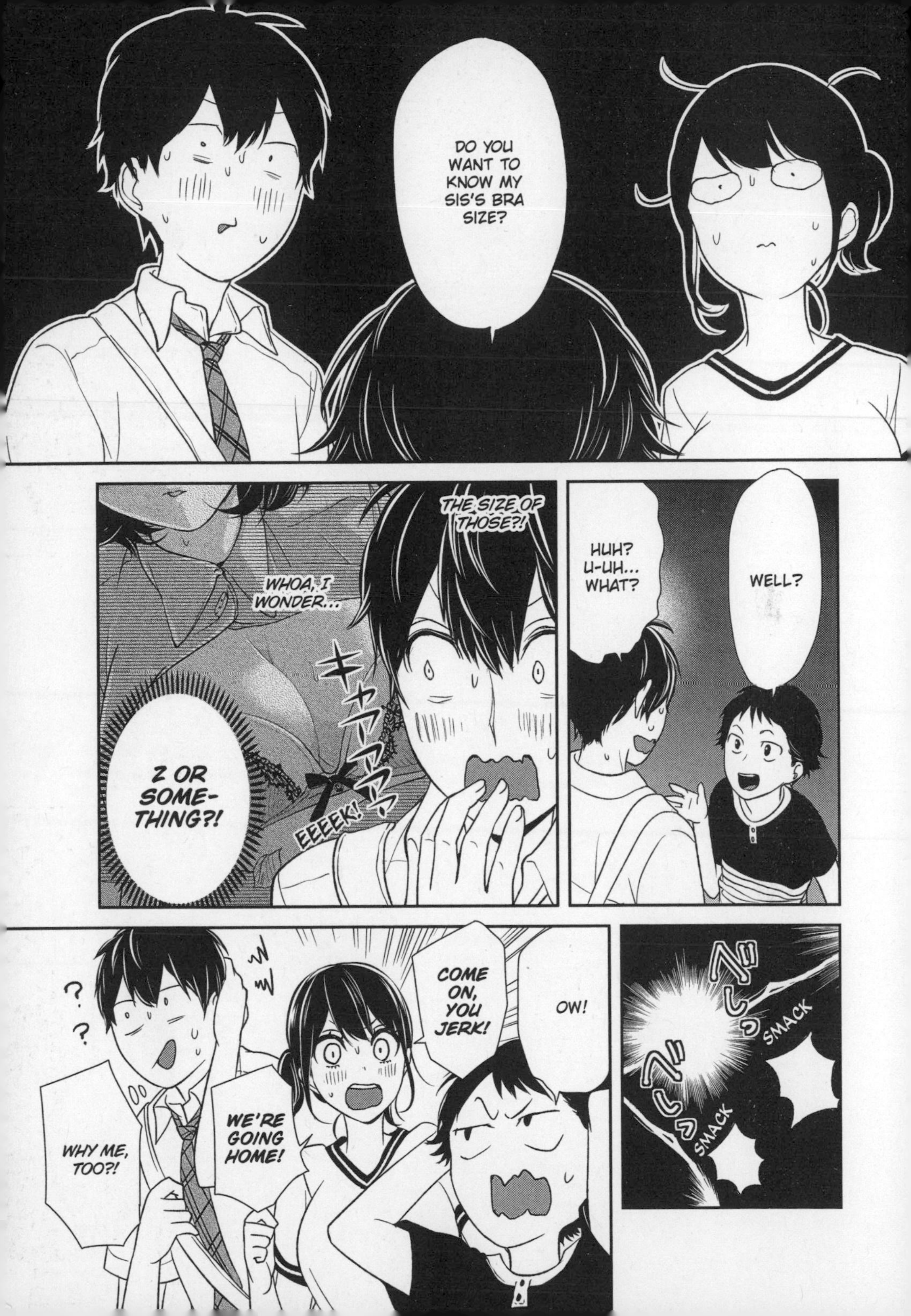
DO YOU WANT TO KNOW MY SIS'S BRA SIZE?
WELL?
HUH? U-UH... WHAT?
THE SIZE OF THOSE?!
WHOA, I WONDER...
EEEEK!
Z OR SOME-THING?!
SMACK
SMACK
OW!
COME ON, YOU JERK!
WE'RE GOING HOME!
WHY ME, TOO?!

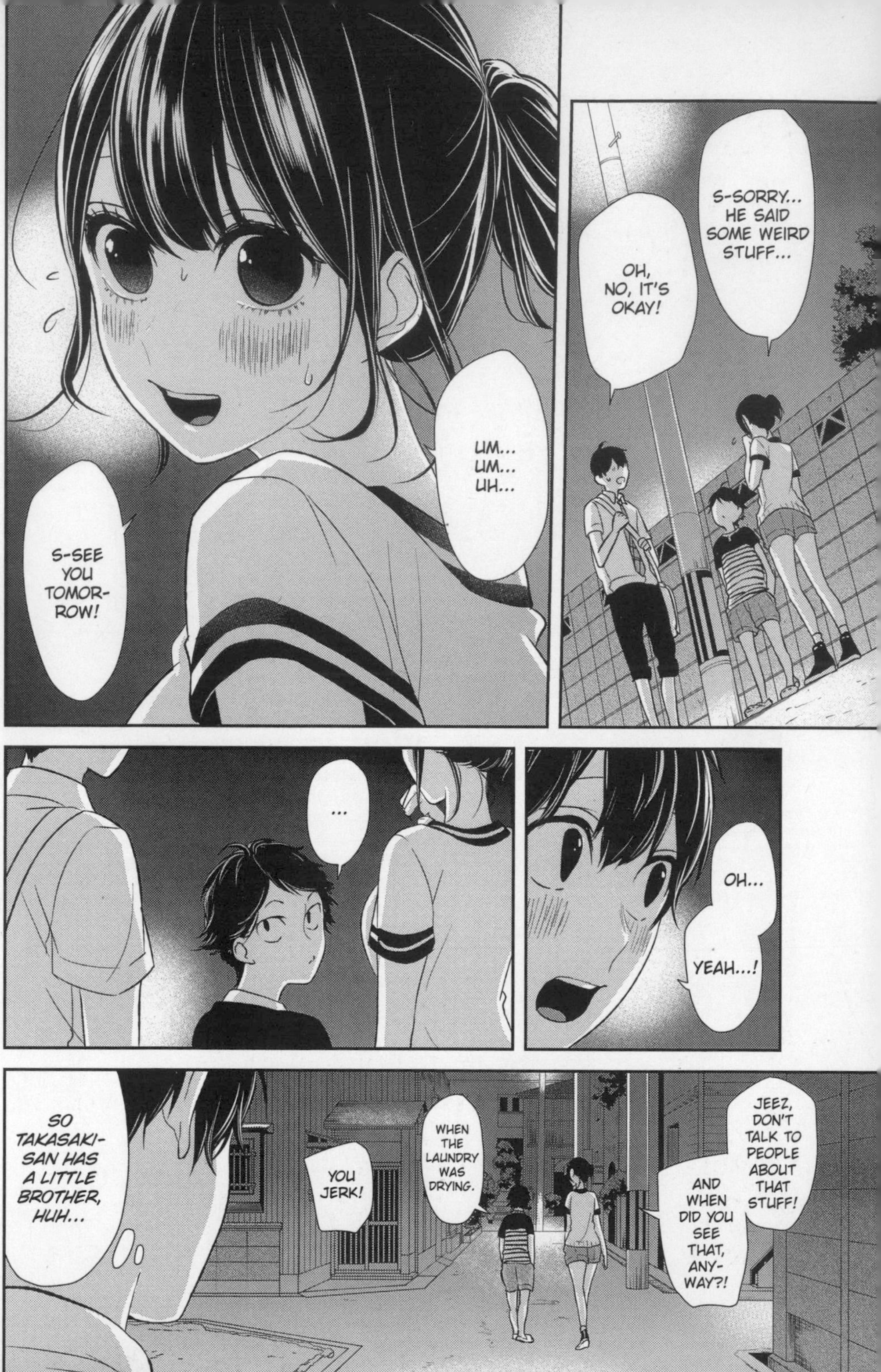
S-SORRY... HE SAID SOME WEIRD STUFF...
OH, NO, IT'S OKAY!
UM... UM... UH...
S-SEE YOU TOMORROW!
OH...
YEAH...!
...
JEEZ, DON'T TALK TO PEOPLE ABOUT THAT STUFF!
AND WHEN DID YOU SEE THAT, ANYWAY?!
WHEN THE LAUNDRY WAS DRYING.
YOU JERK!
SO TAKASAKI-SAN HAS A LITTLE BROTHER, HUH...

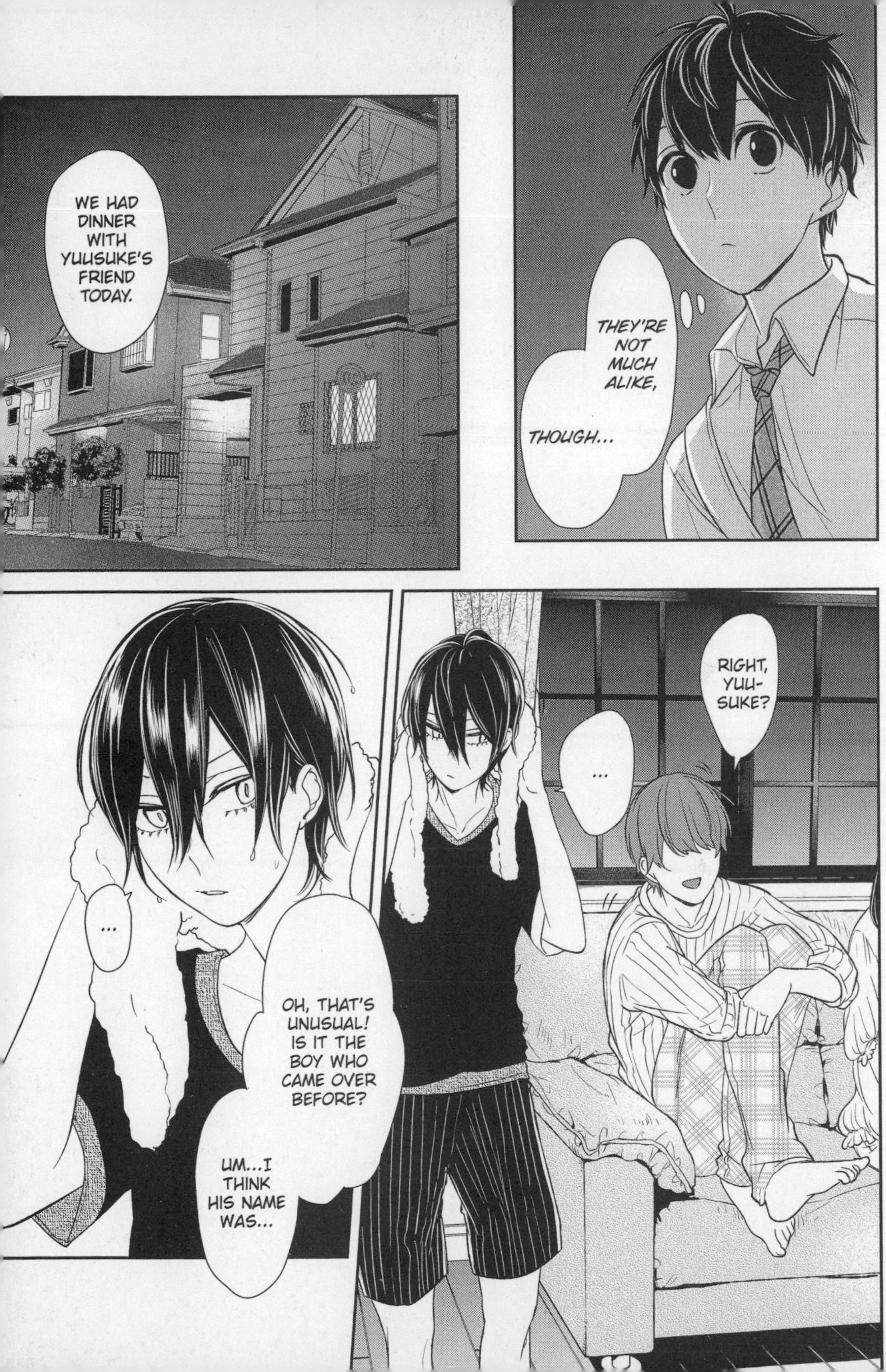
THEY'RE NOT MUCH ALIKE,
THOUGH...
WE HAD DINNER WITH YUUSUKE'S FRIEND TODAY.
RIGHT, YUU-SUKE?
...
...
OH, THAT'S UNUSUAL! IS IT THE BOY WHO CAME OVER BEFORE?
UM...I THINK HIS NAME WAS...

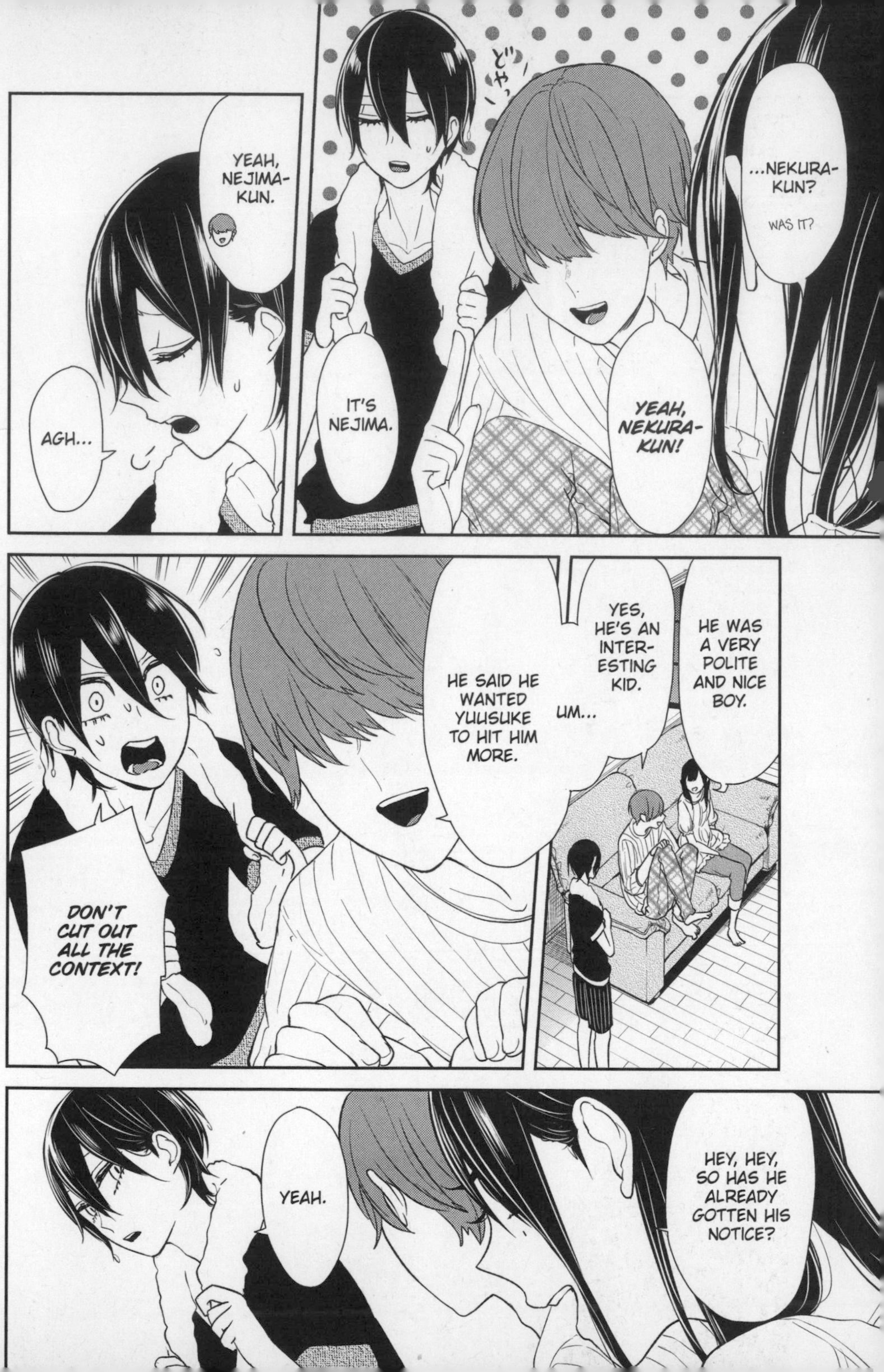

...NEKURA-KUN?
WAS IT?
YEAH, NEKURA-KUN!
どやっ
IT'S NEJIMA.
YEAH, NEJIMA-KUN.
AGH...
HE WAS A VERY POLITE AND NICE BOY.
YES, HE'S AN INTERESTING KID.
UM...
HE SAID HE WANTED YUUSUKE TO HIT HIM MORE.
DON'T CUT OUT ALL THE CONTEXT!
HEY, HEY, SO HAS HE ALREADY GOTTEN HIS NOTICE?
YEAH.

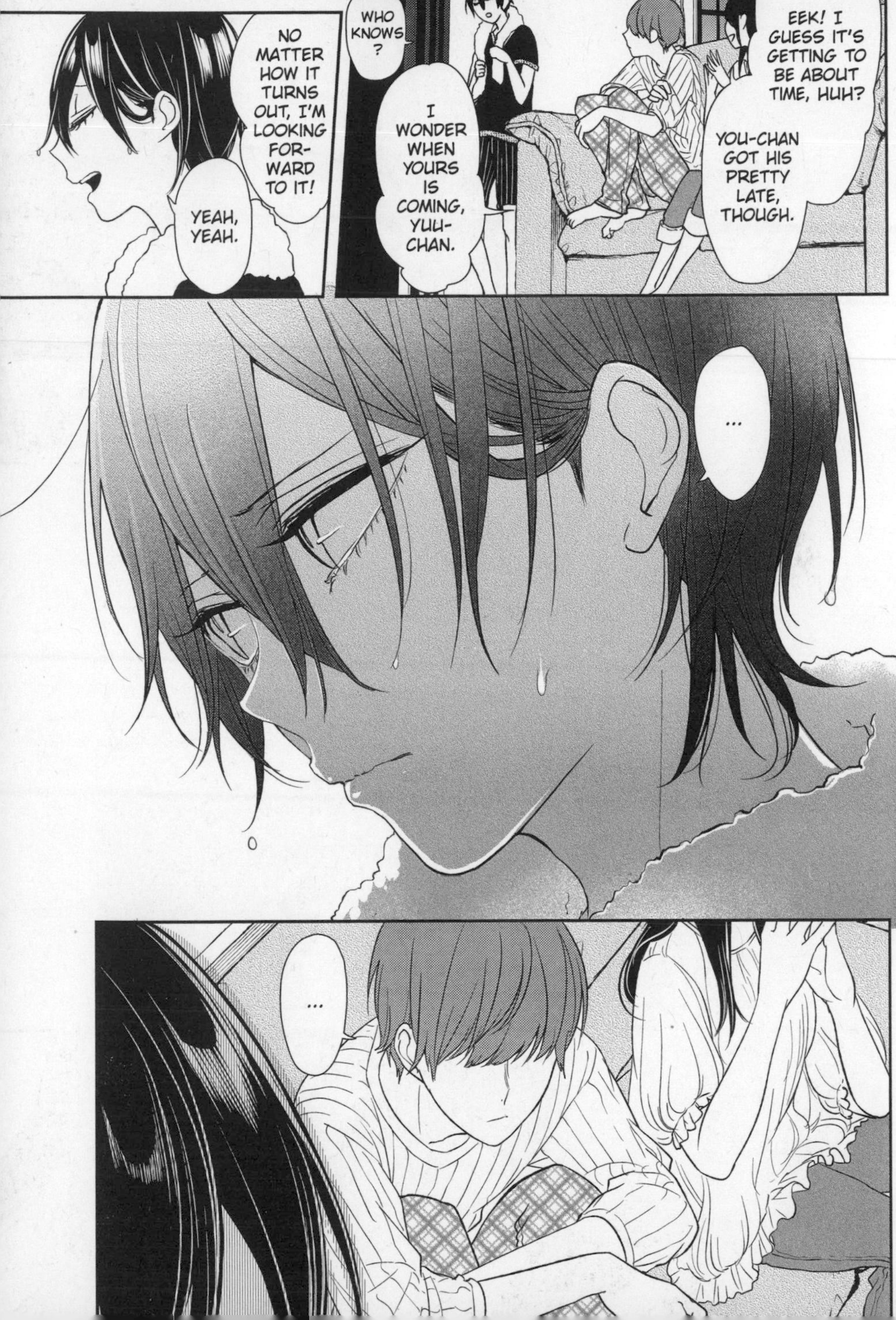
EEK! I GUESS IT'S GETTING TO BE ABOUT TIME, HUH?
YOU-CHAN GOT HIS PRETTY LATE, THOUGH.
WHO KNOWS?
I WONDER WHEN YOURS IS COMING, YUU-CHAN.
NO MATTER HOW IT TURNS OUT, I'M LOOKING FOR-WARD TO IT!
YEAH, YEAH.
...
...

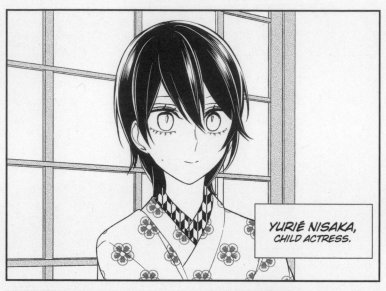

YURIÉ NISAKA, CHILD ACTRESS.
MAN, HE REALLY LOOKS LIKE HIS MOM WHEN SHE WAS A KID.
WHAT'RE YOU LOOKING AT?!
TCH!
HE'LL BE FURIOUS IF I SAY IT, THOUGH...
JEEZ, GUESS THIS IS HIS REBELLIOUS PHASE.

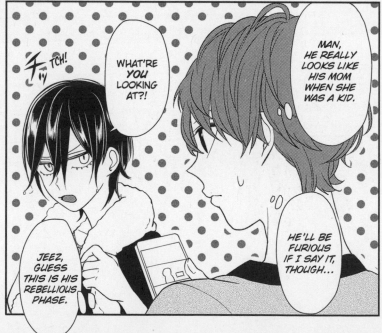

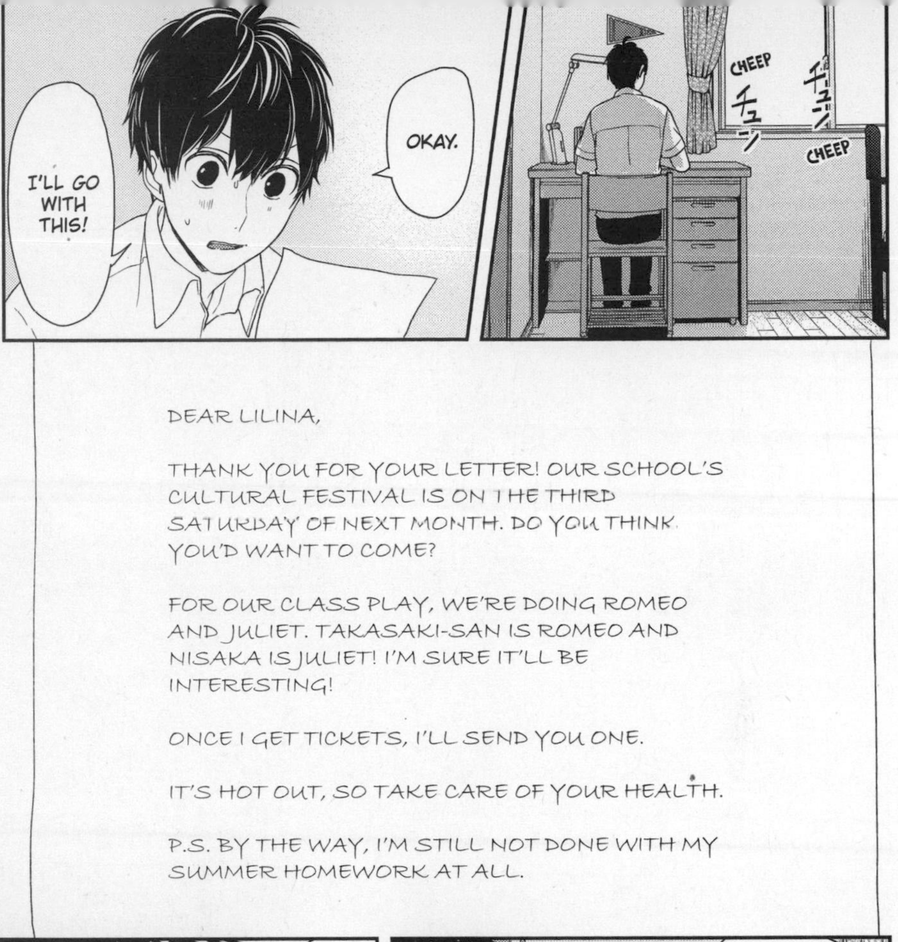
CHEEP
CHEEP
OKAY.
I'LL GO WITH THIS!
DEAR LILINA,
THANK YOU FOR YOUR LETTER! OUR SCHOOL'S CULTURAL FESTIVAL IS ON THE THIRD SATURDAY OF NEXT MONTH. DO YOU THINK YOU'D WANT TO COME?
FOR OUR CLASS PLAY, WE'RE DOING ROMEO AND JULIET. TAKASAKI-SAN IS ROMEO AND NISAKA IS JULIET! I'M SURE IT'LL BE INTERESTING!
ONCE I GET TICKETS, I'LL SEND YOU ONE.
IT'S HOT OUT, SO TAKE CARE OF YOUR HEALTH.
P.S. BY THE WAY, I'M STILL NOT DONE WITH MY SUMMER HOMEWORK AT ALL.
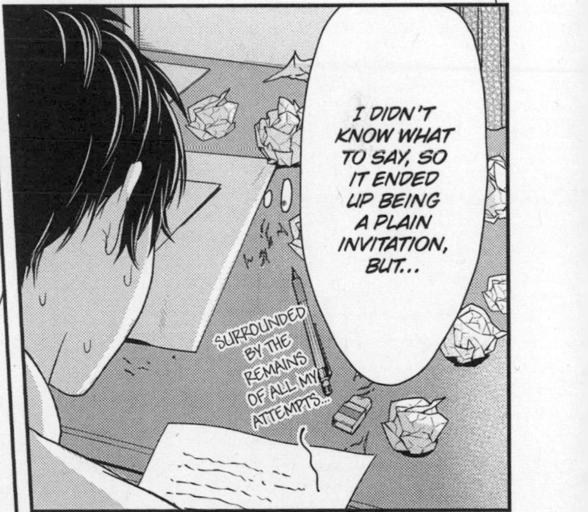
I DIDN'T KNOW WHAT TO SAY, SO IT ENDED UP BEING A PLAIN INVITATION, BUT...
SURROUNDED BY THE REMAINS OF ALL MY ATTEMPTS...
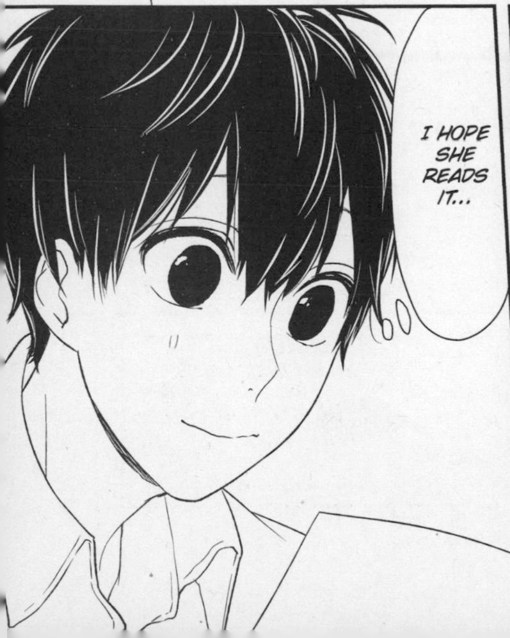
I HOPE SHE READS IT...

Chapter 17
The Philosophy of Love

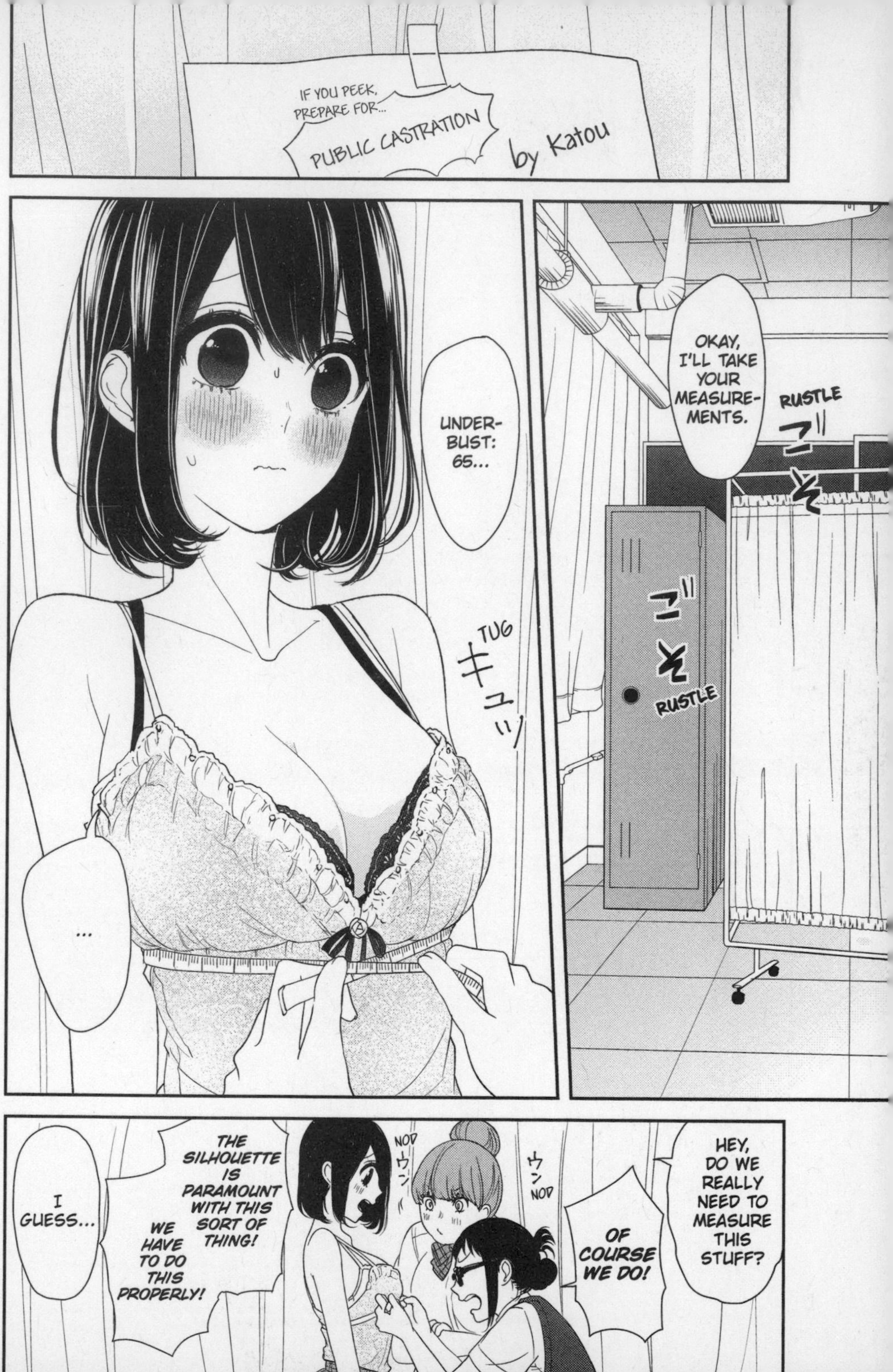
IF YOU PEEK, PREPARE FOR...
PUBLIC CASTRATION
by Katou
OKAY, I'LL TAKE YOUR MEASUREMENTS.
RUSTLE ゴソ
ゴソ RUSTLE
UNDER-BUST: 65...
TUG キュッ
...
HEY, DO WE REALLY NEED TO MEASURE THIS STUFF?
OF COURSE WE DO!
ウン NOD
NOD ウン
THE SILHOUETTE IS PARAMOUNT WITH THIS SORT OF THING!
WE HAVE TO DO THIS PROPERLY!
I GUESS...

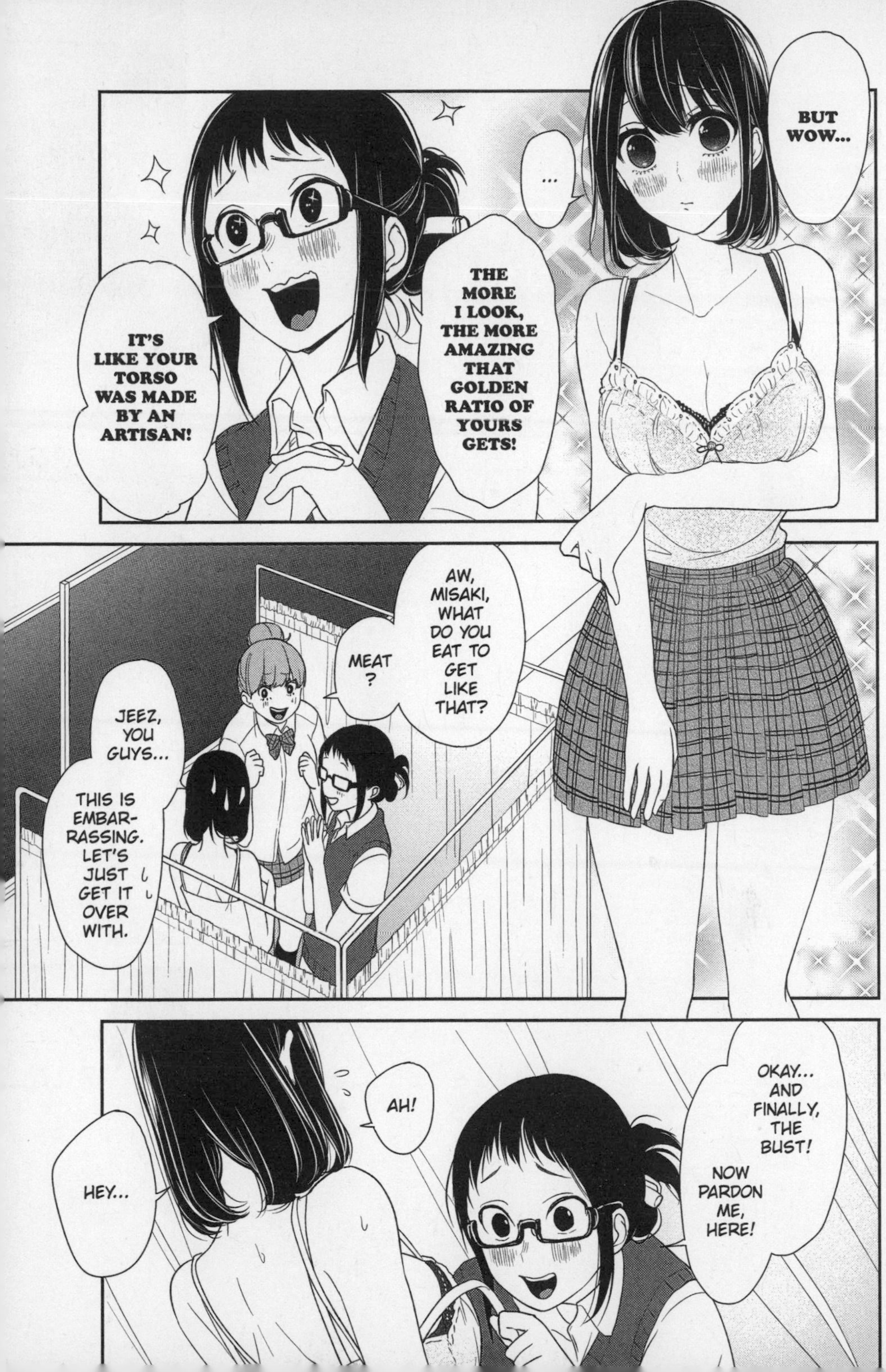
BUT WOW...
...
THE MORE I LOOK, THE MORE AMAZING THAT GOLDEN RATIO OF YOURS GETS!
IT'S LIKE YOUR TORSO WAS MADE BY AN ARTISAN!
AW, MISAKI, WHAT DO YOU EAT TO GET LIKE THAT?
MEAT?
JEEZ, YOU GUYS...
THIS IS EMBARRASSING. LET'S JUST GET IT OVER WITH.
OKAY... AND FINALLY, THE BUST!
NOW PARDON ME, HERE!
AH!
HEY...

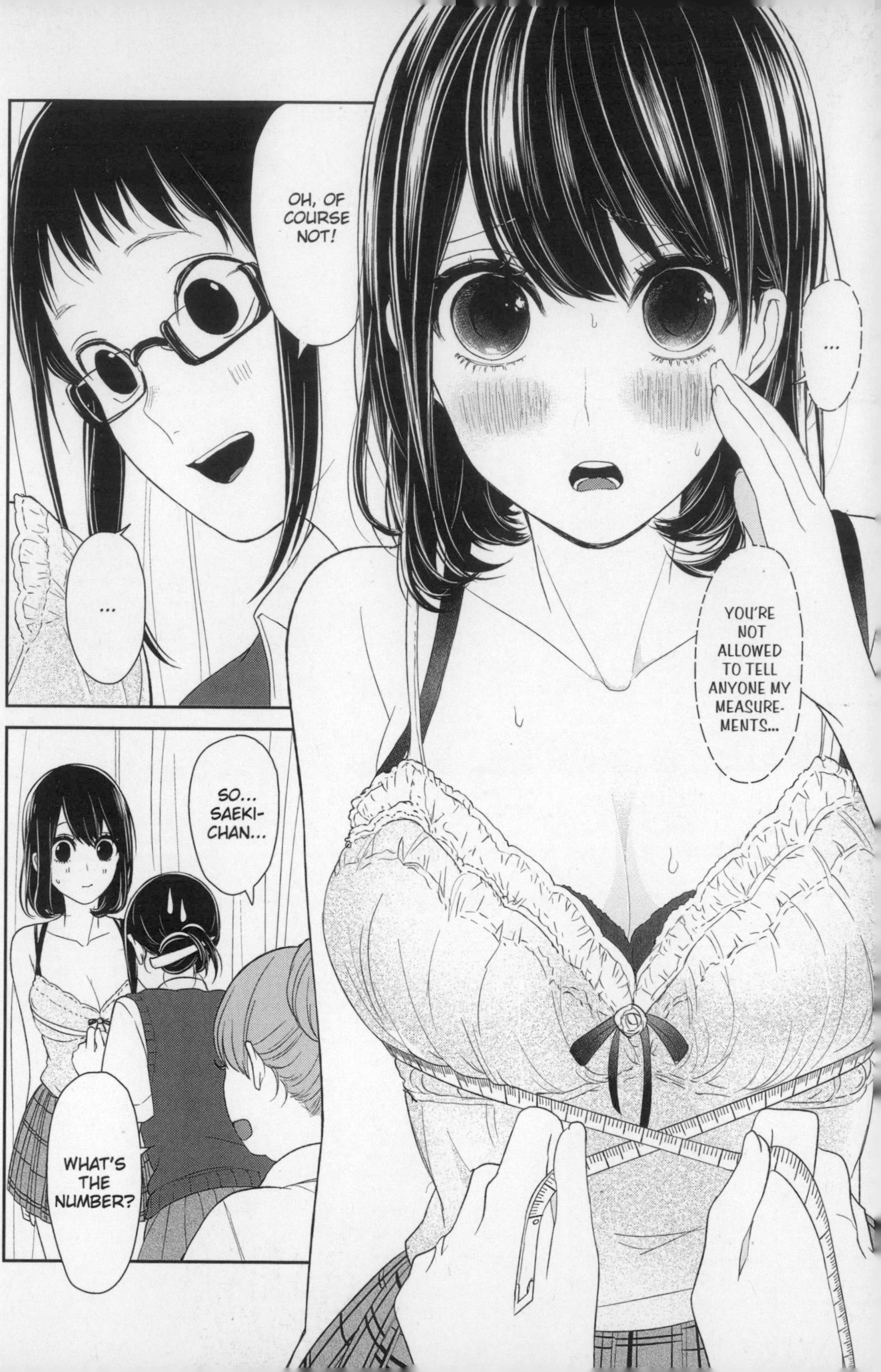
...
YOU'RE NOT ALLOWED TO TELL ANYONE MY MEASUREMENTS...
OH, OF COURSE NOT!
...
SO... SAEKI-CHAN...
WHAT'S THE NUMBER?

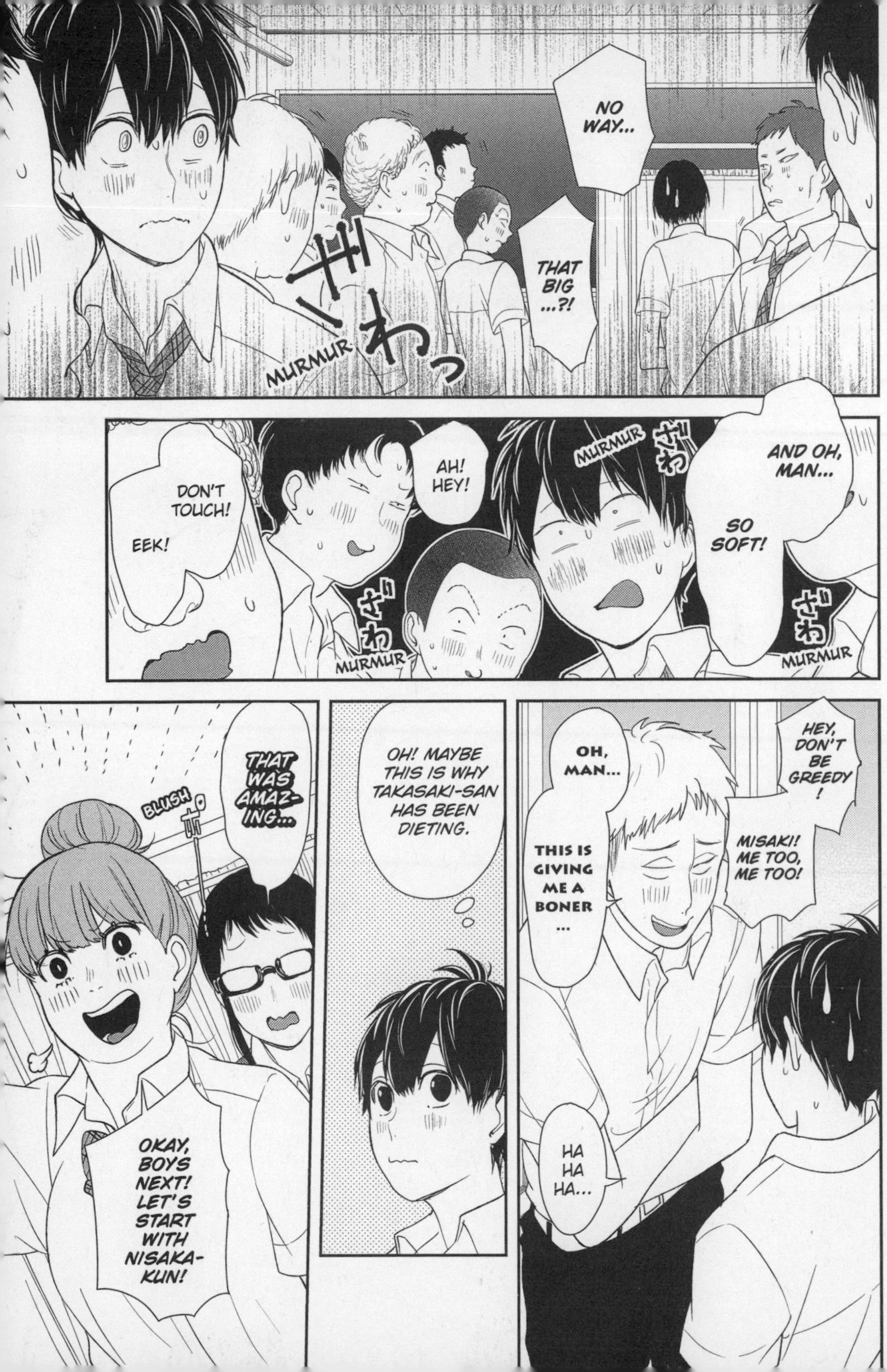
NO WAY...
THAT BIG ...?!
ざわっ
MURMUR
AND OH, MAN...
SO SOFT!
ざわ
MURMUR
ざわ
MURMUR
AH! HEY!
ざわ
MURMUR
DON'T TOUCH!
EEK!
HEY, DON'T BE GREEDY!
MISAKI! ME TOO, ME TOO!
OH, MAN...
THIS IS GIVING ME A BONER ...
HA HA HA...
OH! MAYBE THIS IS WHY TAKASAKI-SAN HAS BEEN DIETING.
THAT WAS AMAZING...
BLUSH
OKAY, BOYS NEXT! LET'S START WITH NISAKA-KUN!

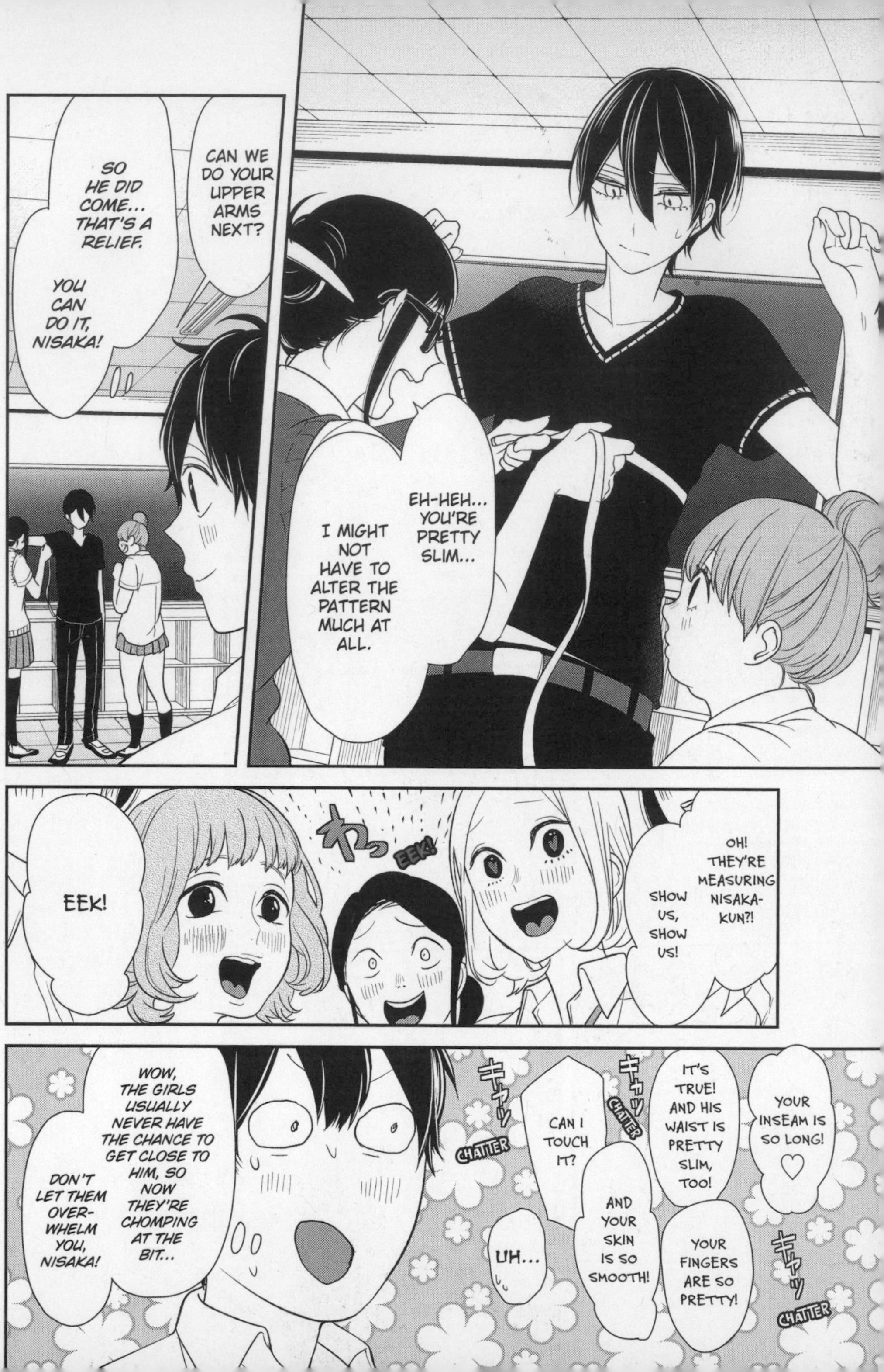
EH-HEH... YOU'RE PRETTY SLIM...
I MIGHT NOT HAVE TO ALTER THE PATTERN MUCH AT ALL.
CAN WE DO YOUR UPPER ARMS NEXT?
SO HE DID COME... THAT'S A RELIEF.
YOU CAN DO IT, NISAKA!
OH! THEY'RE MEASURING NISAKA-KUN?!
SHOW US, SHOW US!
わっ EEK!
EEK!
YOUR INSEAM IS SO LONG! ♥
キャッ CHATTER
IT'S TRUE! AND HIS WAIST IS PRETTY SLIM, TOO!
キャッ CHATTER
CAN I TOUCH IT?
キャッ CHATTER
YOUR FINGERS ARE SO PRETTY!
AND YOUR SKIN IS SO SMOOTH!
UH...
WOW, THE GIRLS USUALLY NEVER HAVE THE CHANCE TO GET CLOSE TO HIM, SO NOW THEY'RE CHOMPING AT THE BIT...
DON'T LET THEM OVER-WHELM YOU, NISAKA!

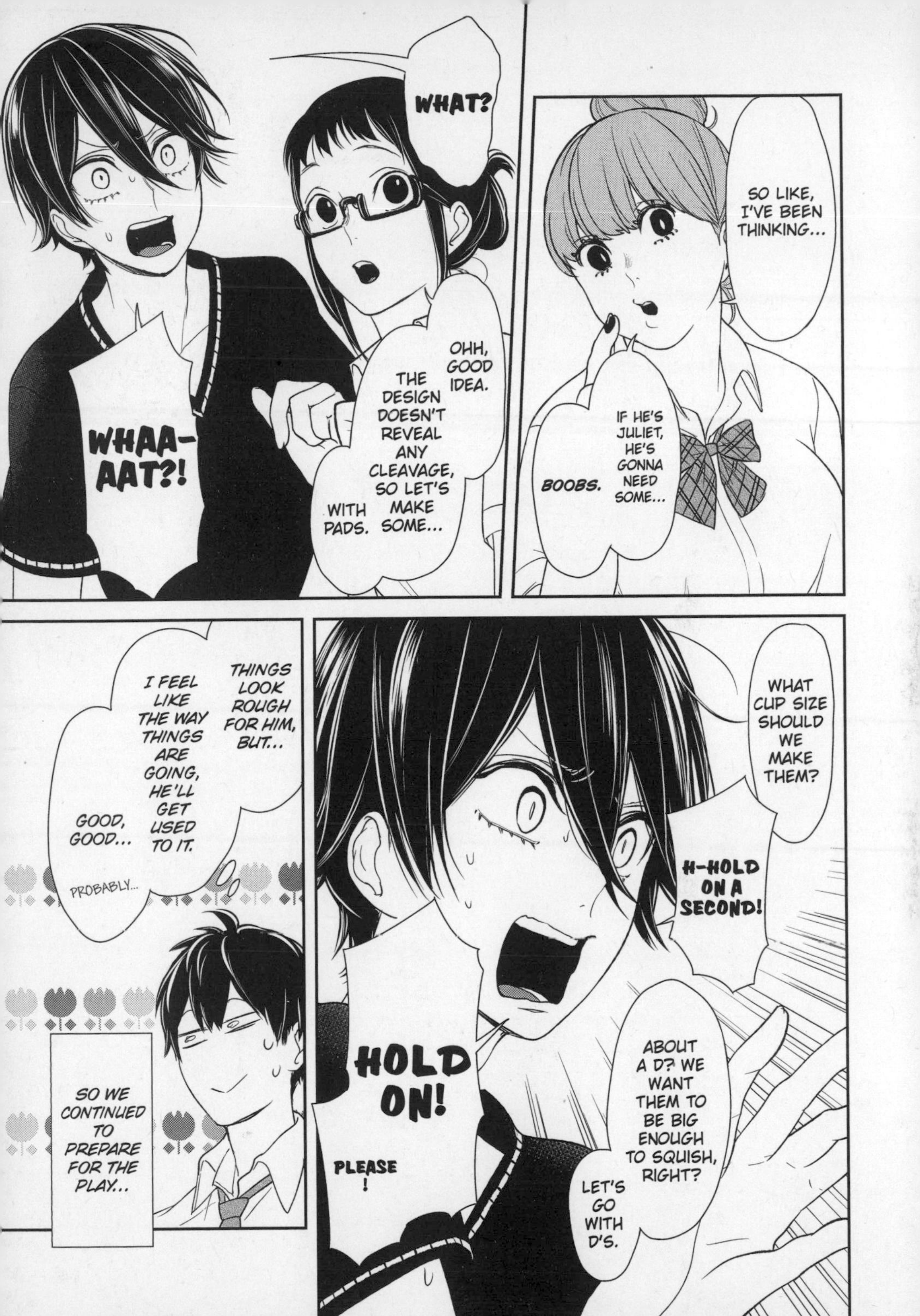
SO LIKE, I'VE BEEN THINKING...
IF HE'S JULIET, HE'S GONNA NEED SOME...
BOOBS.
WHAT?
OHH, GOOD IDEA.
THE DESIGN DOESN'T REVEAL ANY CLEAVAGE, SO LET'S MAKE SOME...
WITH PADS.
WHAA-AAT?!
WHAT CUP SIZE SHOULD WE MAKE THEM?
H-HOLD ON A SECOND!
ABOUT A D? WE WANT THEM TO BE BIG ENOUGH TO SQUISH, RIGHT?
LET'S GO WITH D'S.
HOLD ON!
PLEASE!
THINGS LOOK ROUGH FOR HIM, BUT...
I FEEL LIKE THE WAY THINGS ARE GOING, HE'LL GET USED TO IT.
GOOD, GOOD...
PROBABLY...
SO WE CONTINUED TO PREPARE FOR THE PLAY...

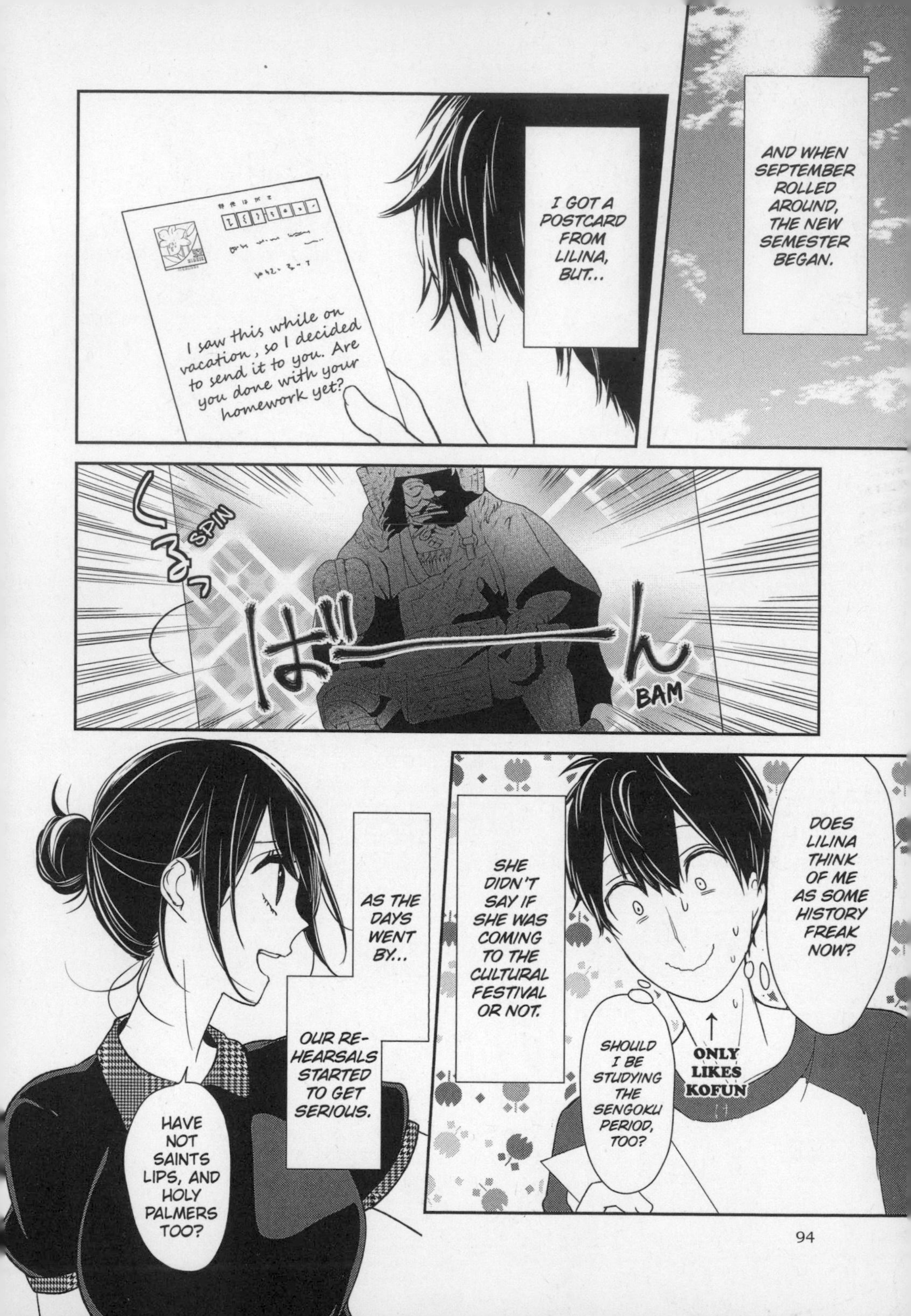
AND WHEN SEPTEMBER ROLLED AROUND, THE NEW SEMESTER BEGAN.
I GOT A POSTCARD FROM LILINA, BUT...
I saw this while on vacation, so I decided to send it to you. Are you done with your homework yet?
SPIN
BAM
DOES LILINA THINK OF ME AS SOME HISTORY FREAK NOW?
SHE DIDN'T SAY IF SHE WAS COMING TO THE CULTURAL FESTIVAL OR NOT.
SHOULD I BE STUDYING THE SENGOKU PERIOD, TOO?
ONLY LIKES KOFUN
AS THE DAYS WENT BY...
OUR RE-HEARSALS STARTED TO GET SERIOUS.
HAVE NOT SAINTS LIPS, AND HOLY PALMERS TOO?

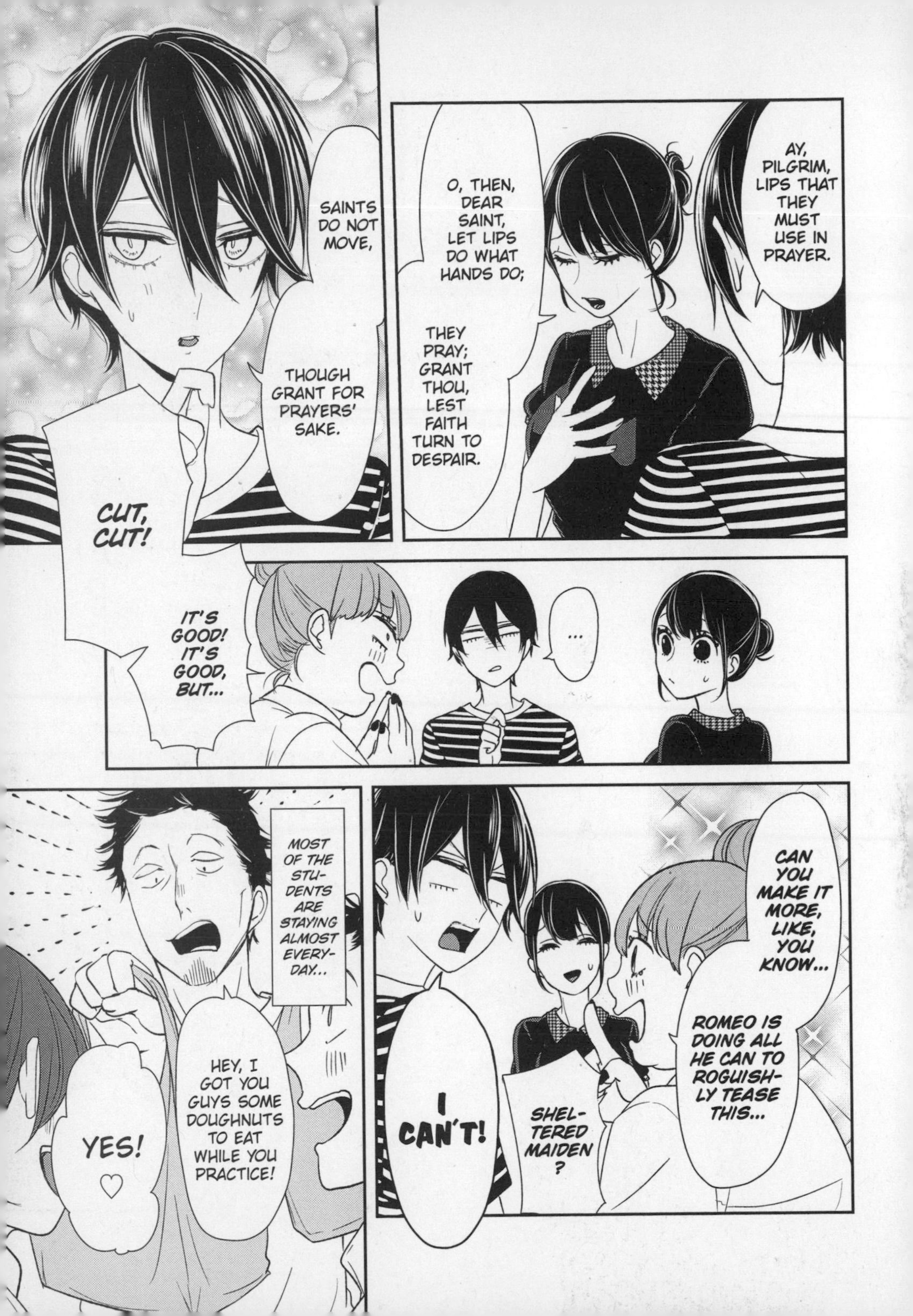
AY, PILGRIM, LIPS THAT THEY MUST USE IN PRAYER.
O, THEN, DEAR SAINT, LET LIPS DO WHAT HANDS DO;
THEY PRAY; GRANT THOU, LEST FAITH TURN TO DESPAIR.
SAINTS DO NOT MOVE,
THOUGH GRANT FOR PRAYERS' SAKE.
CUT, CUT!
...
IT'S GOOD! IT'S GOOD, BUT...
CAN YOU MAKE IT MORE, LIKE, YOU KNOW...
ROMEO IS DOING ALL HE CAN TO ROGUISHLY TEASE THIS...
SHELTERED MAIDEN?
I CAN'T!
MOST OF THE STUDENTS ARE STAYING ALMOST EVERYDAY...
HEY, I GOT YOU GUYS SOME DOUGHNUTS TO EAT WHILE YOU PRACTICE!
YES! ♡

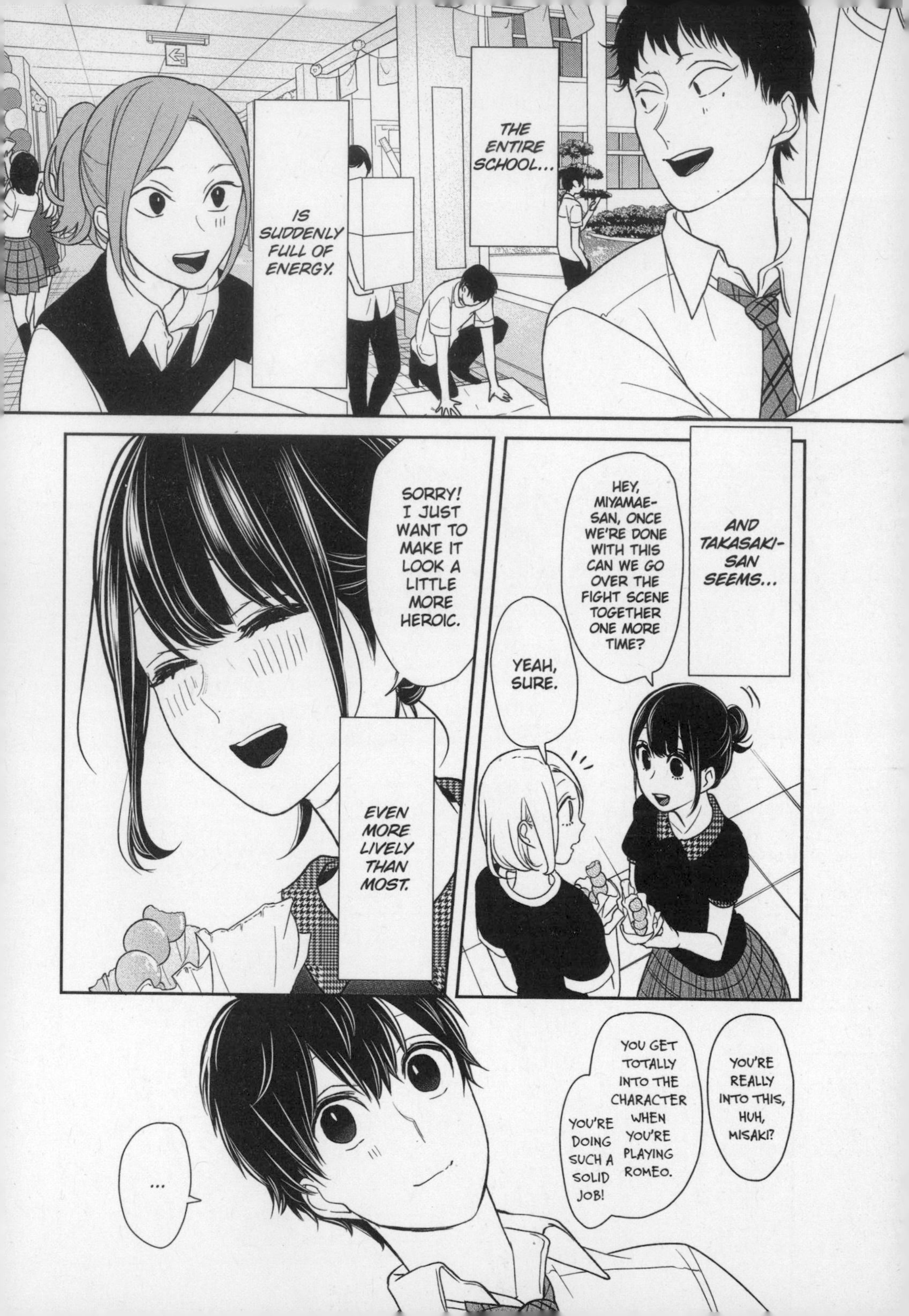
THE ENTIRE SCHOOL...
IS SUDDENLY FULL OF ENERGY.
AND TAKASAKI-SAN SEEMS...
HEY, MIYAMAE-SAN, ONCE WE'RE DONE WITH THIS CAN WE GO OVER THE FIGHT SCENE TOGETHER ONE MORE TIME?
YEAH, SURE.
SORRY! I JUST WANT TO MAKE IT LOOK A LITTLE MORE HEROIC.
EVEN MORE LIVELY THAN MOST.
YOU'RE REALLY INTO THIS, HUH, MISAKI?
YOU GET TOTALLY INTO THE CHARACTER WHEN YOU'RE PLAYING ROMEO.
YOU'RE DOING SUCH A SOLID JOB!
...

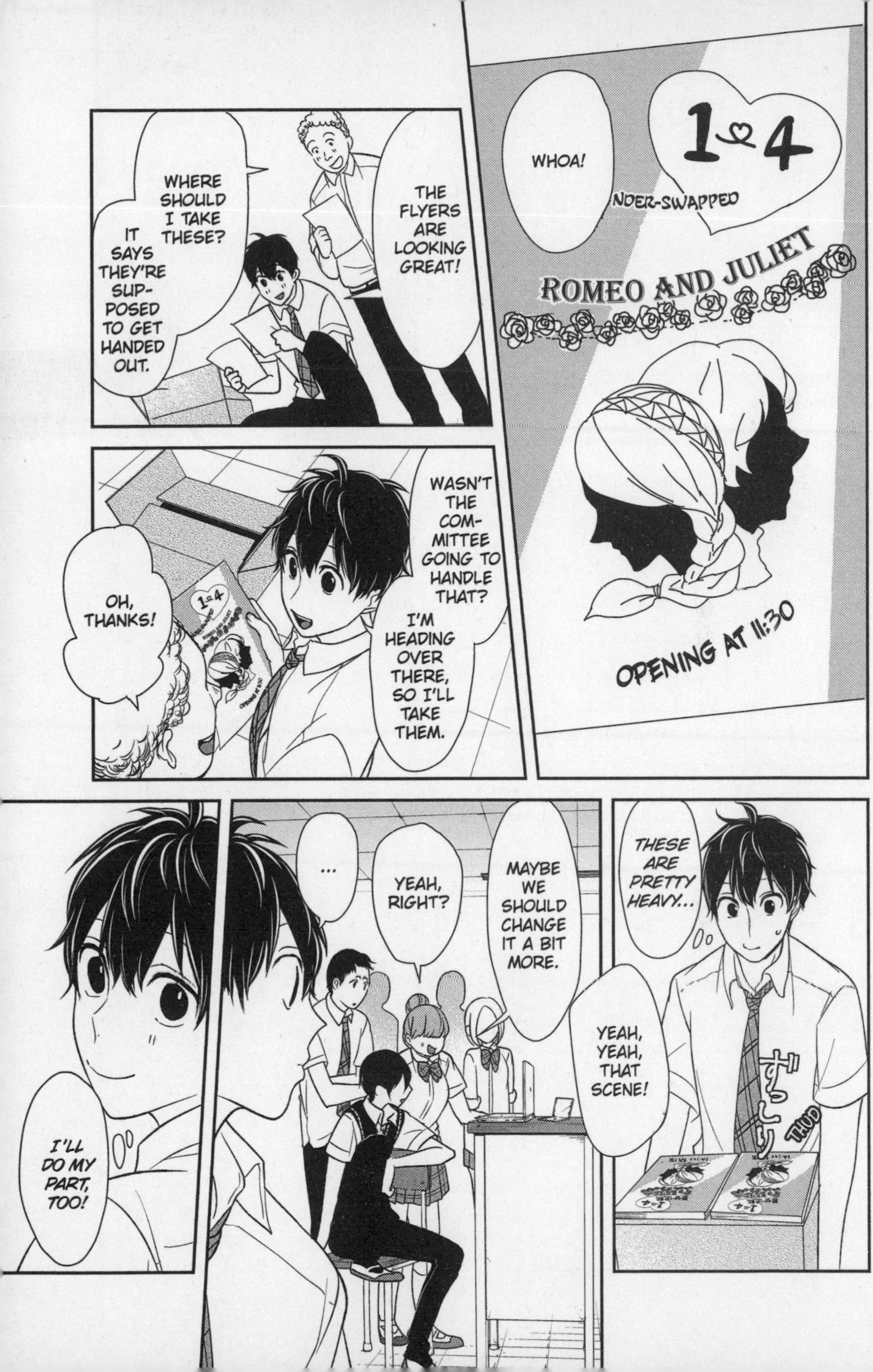
WHOA!
1♡4
NDER-SWAPPED
ROMEO AND JULIET
OPENING AT 11:30
THE FLYERS ARE LOOKING GREAT!
WHERE SHOULD I TAKE THESE?
IT SAYS THEY'RE SUP-POSED TO GET HANDED OUT.
WASN'T THE COM-MITTEE GOING TO HANDLE THAT?
I'M HEADING OVER THERE, SO I'LL TAKE THEM.
OH, THANKS!
THESE ARE PRETTY HEAVY...
ずしり
THUD
YEAH, YEAH, THAT SCENE!
MAYBE WE SHOULD CHANGE IT A BIT MORE.
YEAH, RIGHT?
...
I'LL DO MY PART, TOO!

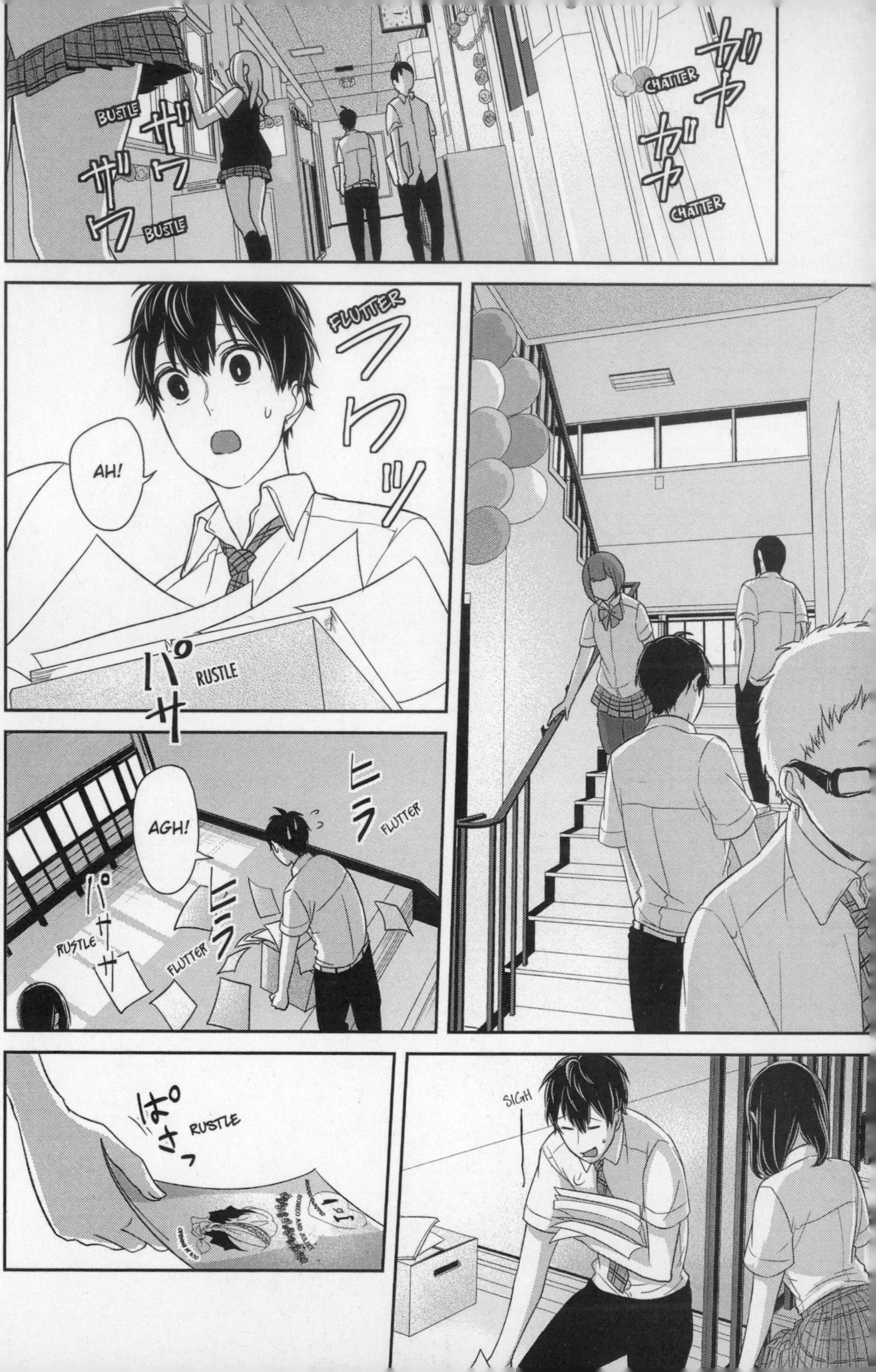
ガヤ
CHATTER
ガヤ
CHATTER
ザワ
BUSTLE
ザワ
BUSTLE
フワッ
FLUTTER
AH!
パサ
RUSTLE
ヒラ
FLUTTER
AGH!
ヒラ
FLUTTER
パサ
RUSTLE
SIGH
ぱさっ
RUSTLE

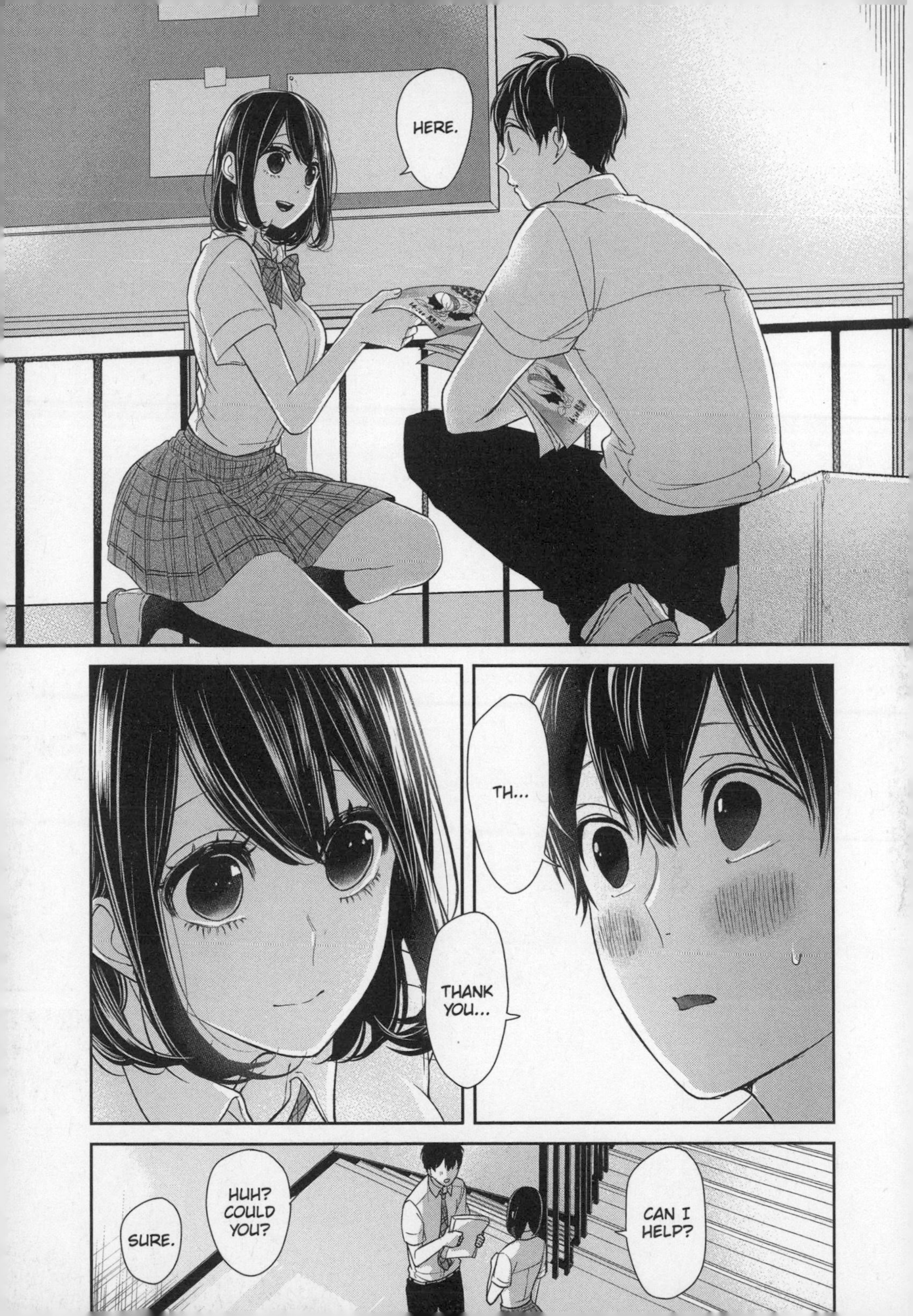
HERE.
TH...
THANK YOU...
CAN I HELP?
HUH? COULD YOU?
SURE.

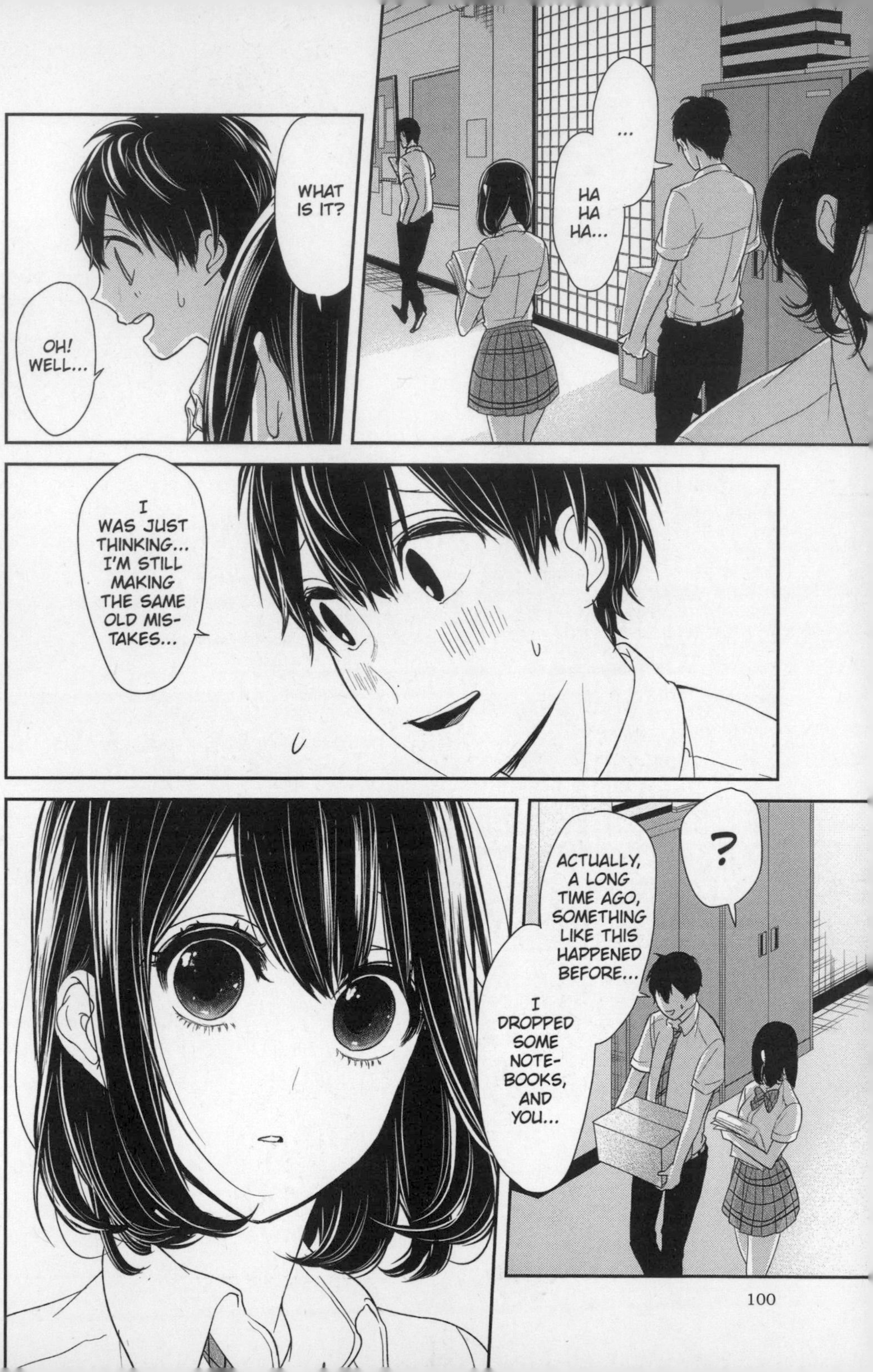
...
HA HA HA...
WHAT IS IT?
OH! WELL...
I WAS JUST THINKING... I'M STILL MAKING THE SAME OLD MIS-TAKES...
?
ACTUALLY, A LONG TIME AGO, SOMETHING LIKE THIS HAPPENED BEFORE...
I DROPPED SOME NOTE-BOOKS, AND YOU...

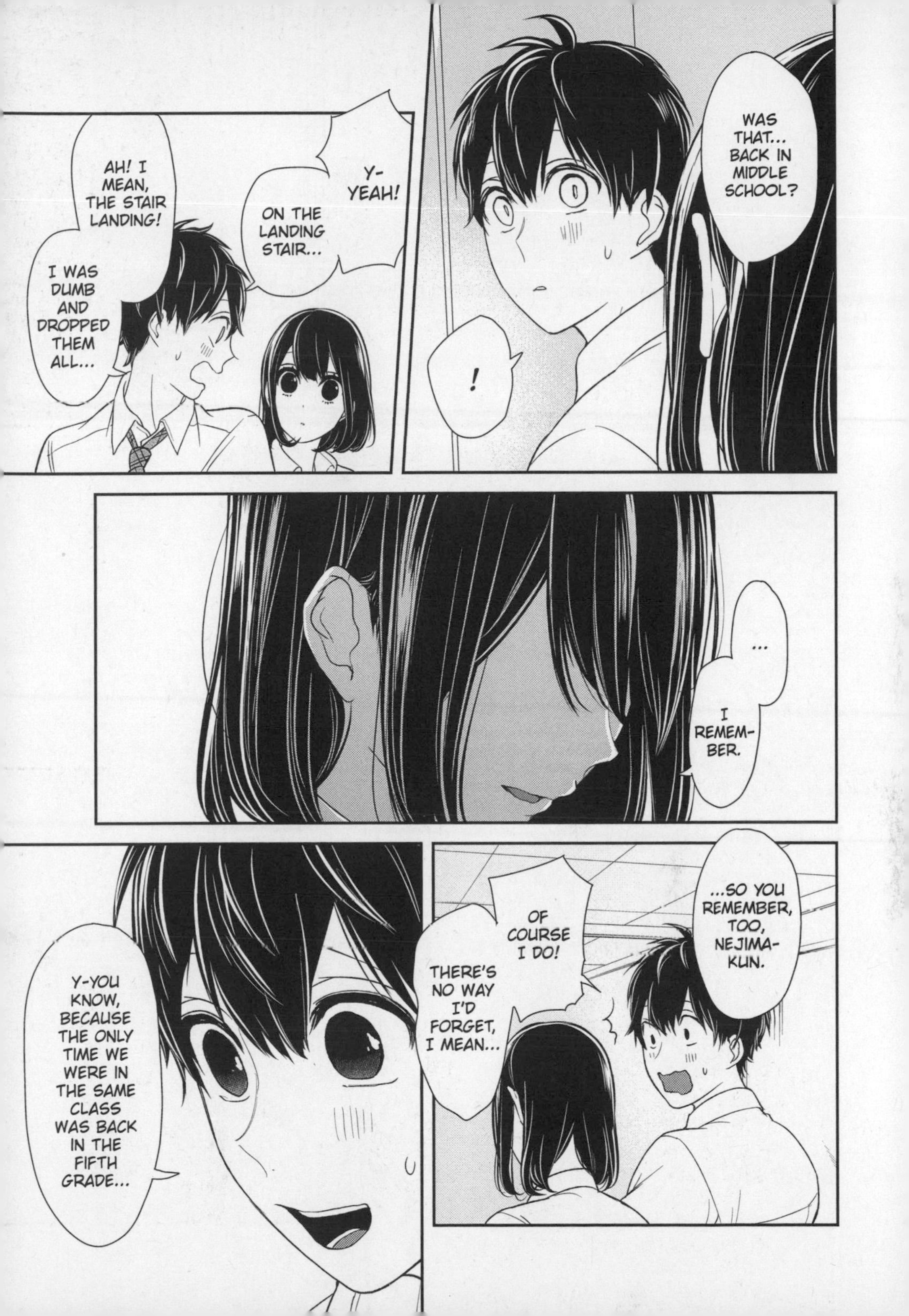
WAS THAT... BACK IN MIDDLE SCHOOL?
!
Y-YEAH!
ON THE LANDING STAIR...
AH! I MEAN, THE STAIR LANDING!
I WAS DUMB AND DROPPED THEM ALL...
...
I REMEMBER.
...SO YOU REMEMBER, TOO, NEJIMA-KUN.
OF COURSE I DO!
THERE'S NO WAY I'D FORGET, I MEAN...
Y-YOU KNOW, BECAUSE THE ONLY TIME WE WERE IN THE SAME CLASS WAS BACK IN THE FIFTH GRADE...

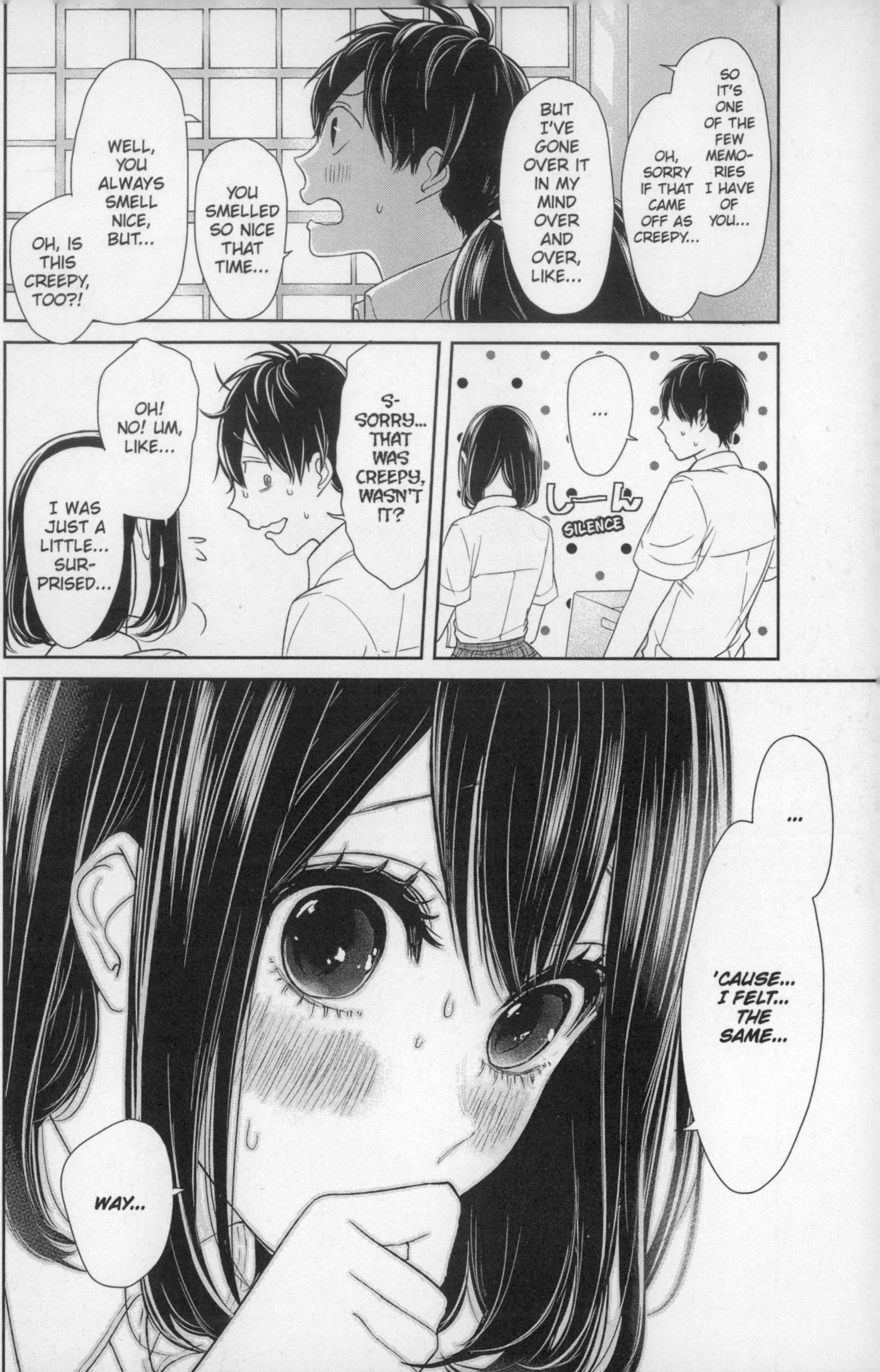
SO IT'S ONE OF THE FEW MEMORIES I HAVE OF YOU...
OH, SORRY IF THAT CAME OFF AS CREEPY...
BUT I'VE GONE OVER IT IN MY MIND OVER AND OVER, LIKE...
YOU SMELLED SO NICE THAT TIME...
WELL, YOU ALWAYS SMELL NICE, BUT...
OH, IS THIS CREEPY, TOO?!
...
SILENCE
S-SORRY... THAT WAS CREEPY, WASN'T IT?
OH! NO! UM, LIKE...
I WAS JUST A LITTLE... SURPRISED...
...
'CAUSE... I FELT... THE SAME...
WAY...

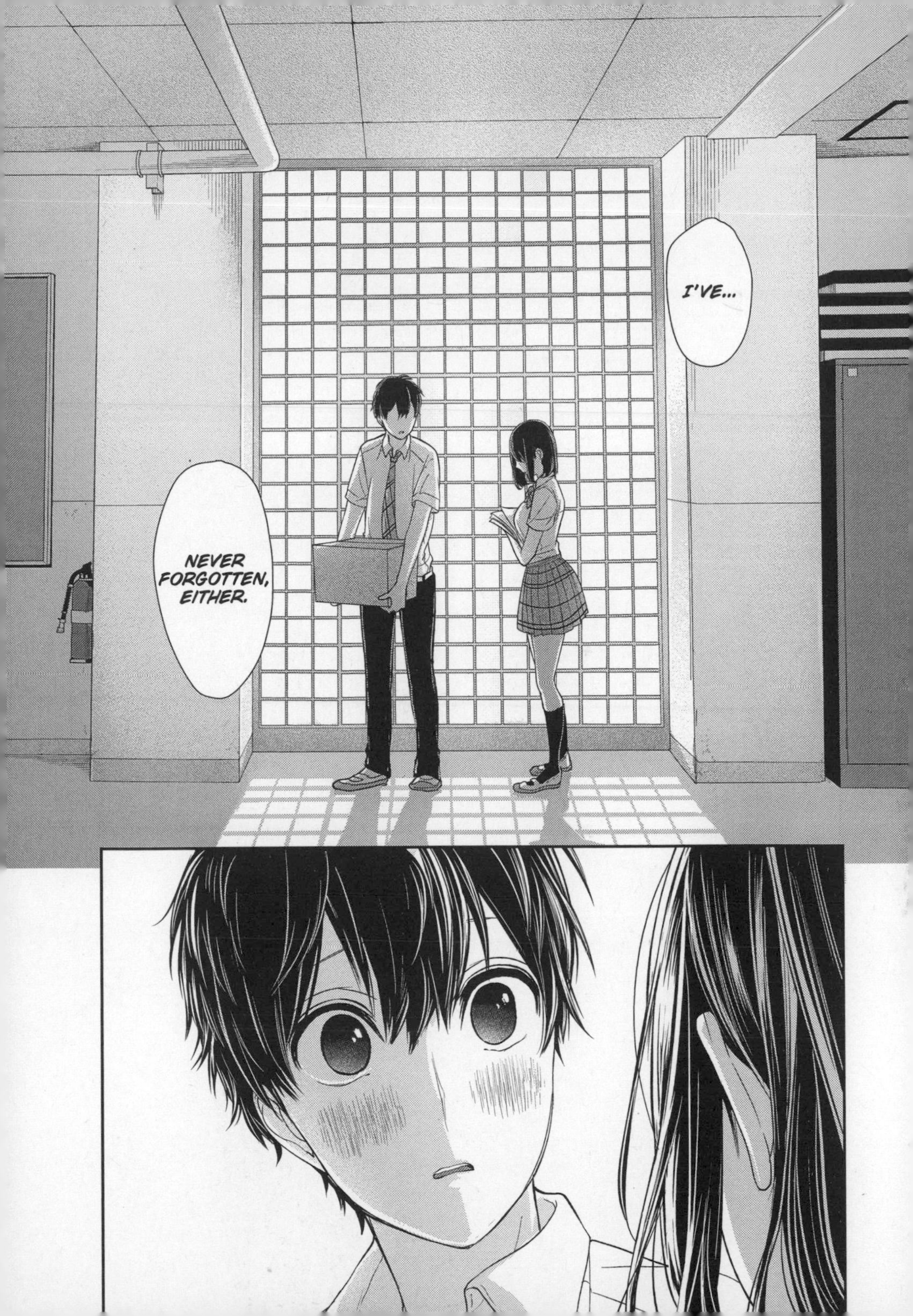
I'VE...
NEVER FORGOTTEN, EITHER.

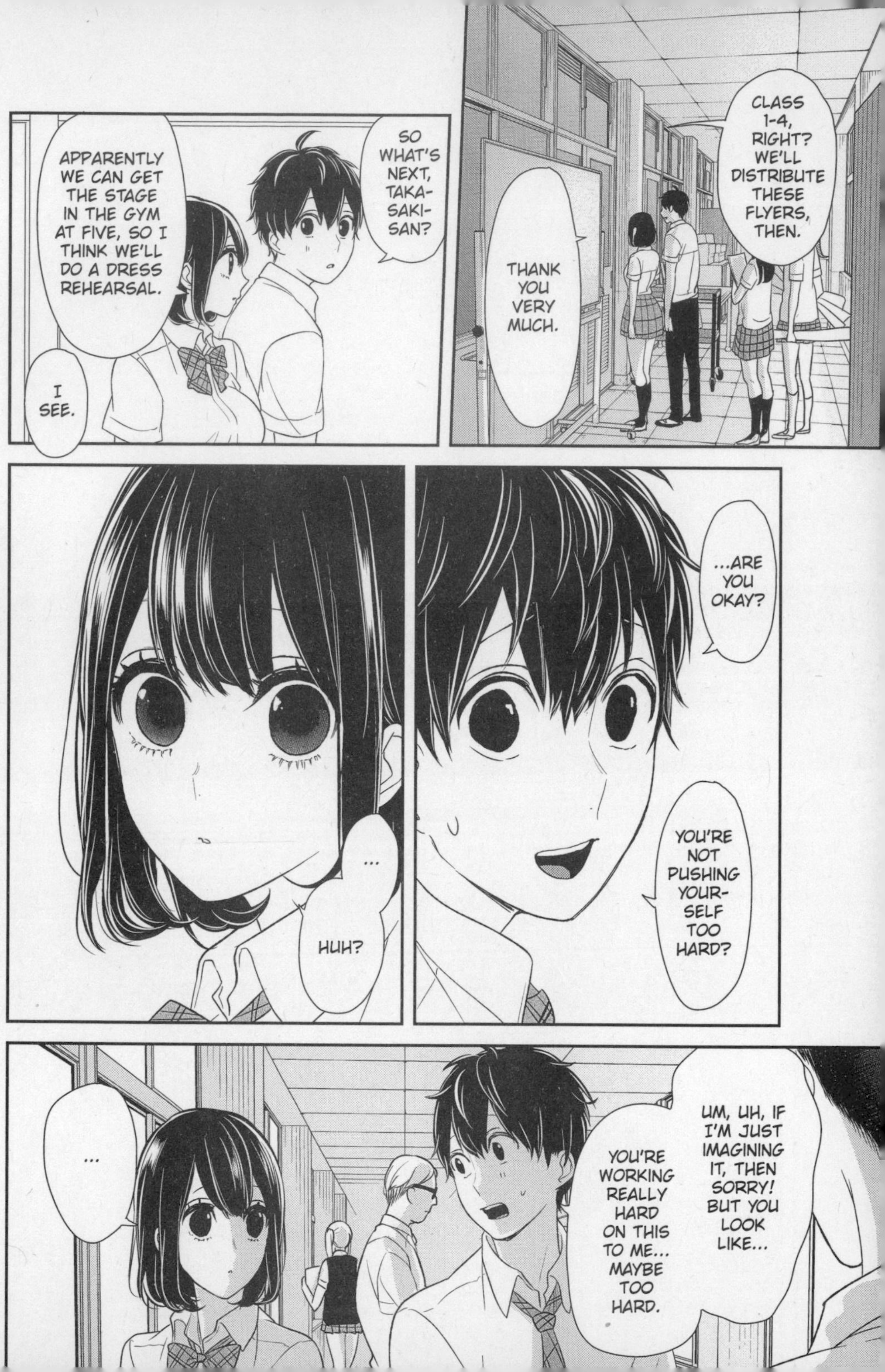
CLASS 1-4, RIGHT? WE'LL DISTRIBUTE THESE FLYERS, THEN.
THANK YOU VERY MUCH.
SO WHAT'S NEXT, TAKA-SAKI-SAN?
APPARENTLY WE CAN GET THE STAGE IN THE GYM AT FIVE, SO I THINK WE'LL DO A DRESS REHEARSAL.
I SEE.
...ARE YOU OKAY?
YOU'RE NOT PUSHING YOUR-SELF TOO HARD?
...
HUH?
UM, UH, IF I'M JUST IMAGINING IT, THEN SORRY! BUT YOU LOOK LIKE...
YOU'RE WORKING REALLY HARD ON THIS TO ME... MAYBE TOO HARD.
...

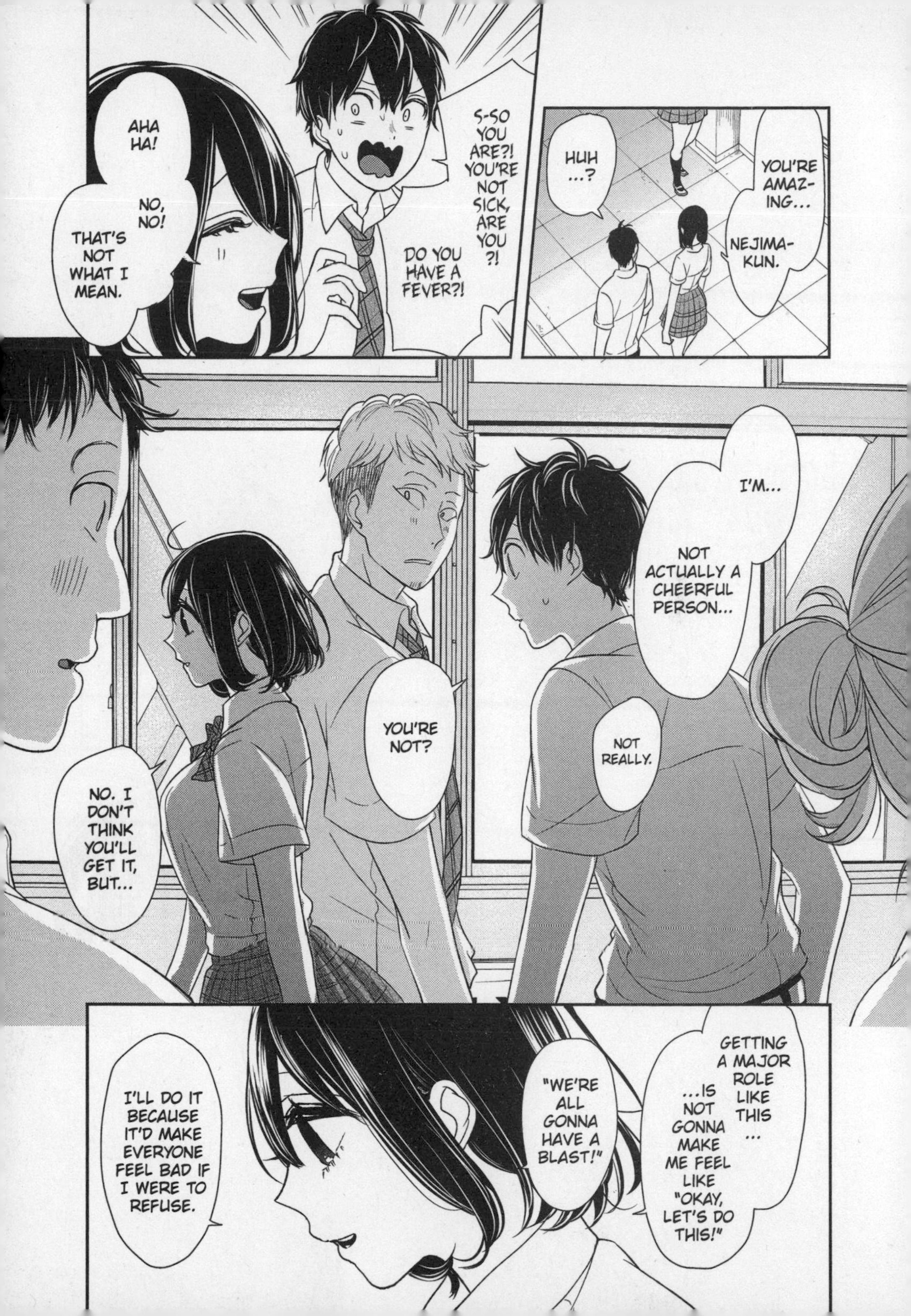
YOU'RE AMAZING...
NEJIMA-KUN.
HUH ...?
S-SO YOU ARE?! YOU'RE NOT SICK, ARE YOU?!
DO YOU HAVE A FEVER?!
AHA HA!
NO, NO! THAT'S NOT WHAT I MEAN.
I'M...
NOT ACTUALLY A CHEERFUL PERSON...
YOU'RE NOT?
NOT REALLY.
NO. I DON'T THINK YOU'LL GET IT, BUT...
GETTING A MAJOR ROLE LIKE THIS ...
...IS NOT GONNA MAKE ME FEEL LIKE "OKAY, LET'S DO THIS!"
"WE'RE ALL GONNA HAVE A BLAST!"
I'LL DO IT BECAUSE IT'D MAKE EVERYONE FEEL BAD IF I WERE TO REFUSE.

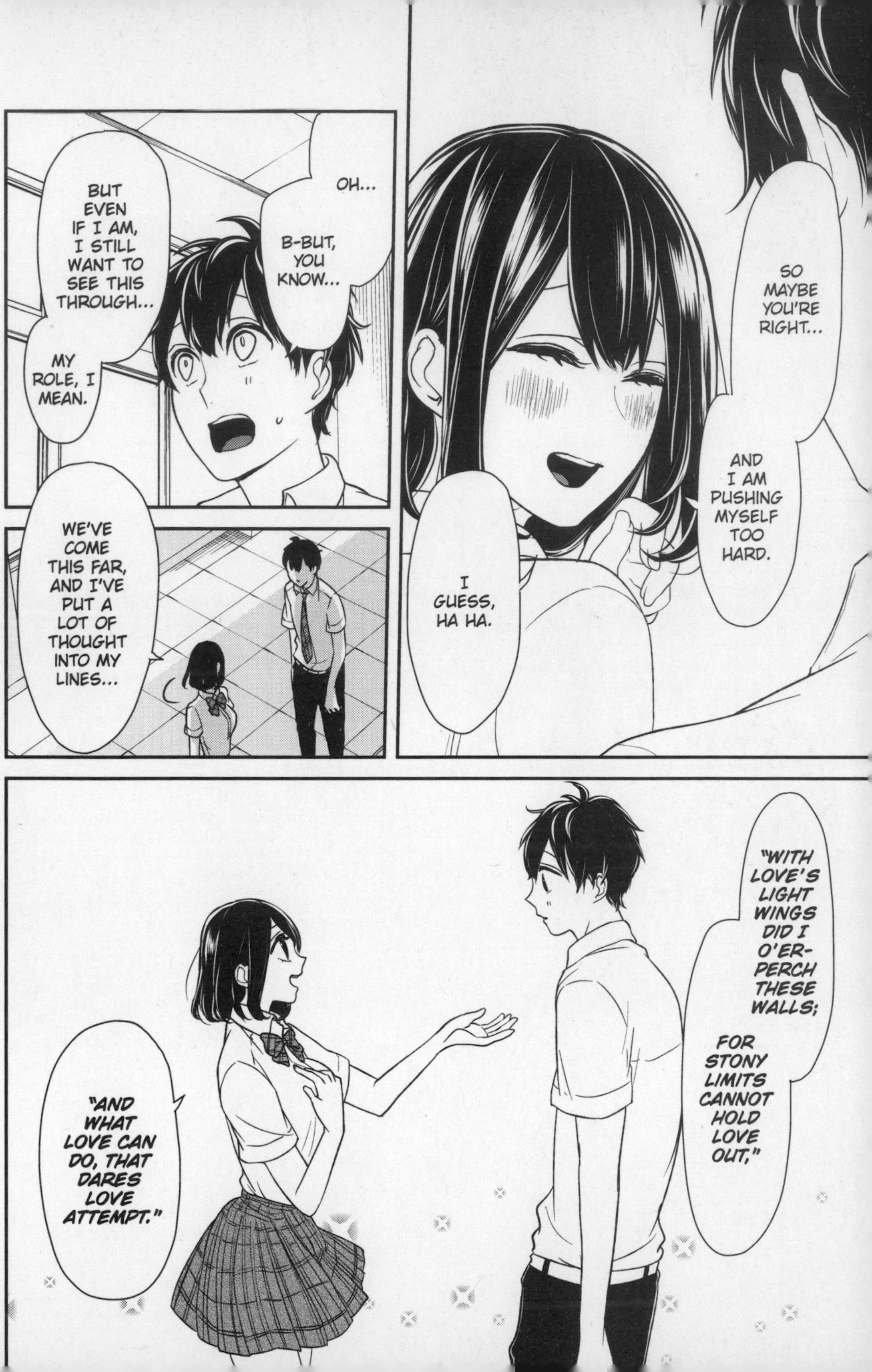
SO MAYBE YOU'RE RIGHT...
AND I AM PUSHING MYSELF TOO HARD.
I GUESS, HA HA.
OH...
B-BUT, YOU KNOW...
BUT EVEN IF I AM, I STILL WANT TO SEE THIS THROUGH...
MY ROLE, I MEAN.
WE'VE COME THIS FAR, AND I'VE PUT A LOT OF THOUGHT INTO MY LINES...
"WITH LOVE'S LIGHT WINGS DID I O'ER-PERCH THESE WALLS;
FOR STONY LIMITS CANNOT HOLD LOVE OUT,"
"AND WHAT LOVE CAN DO, THAT DARES LOVE ATTEMPT."

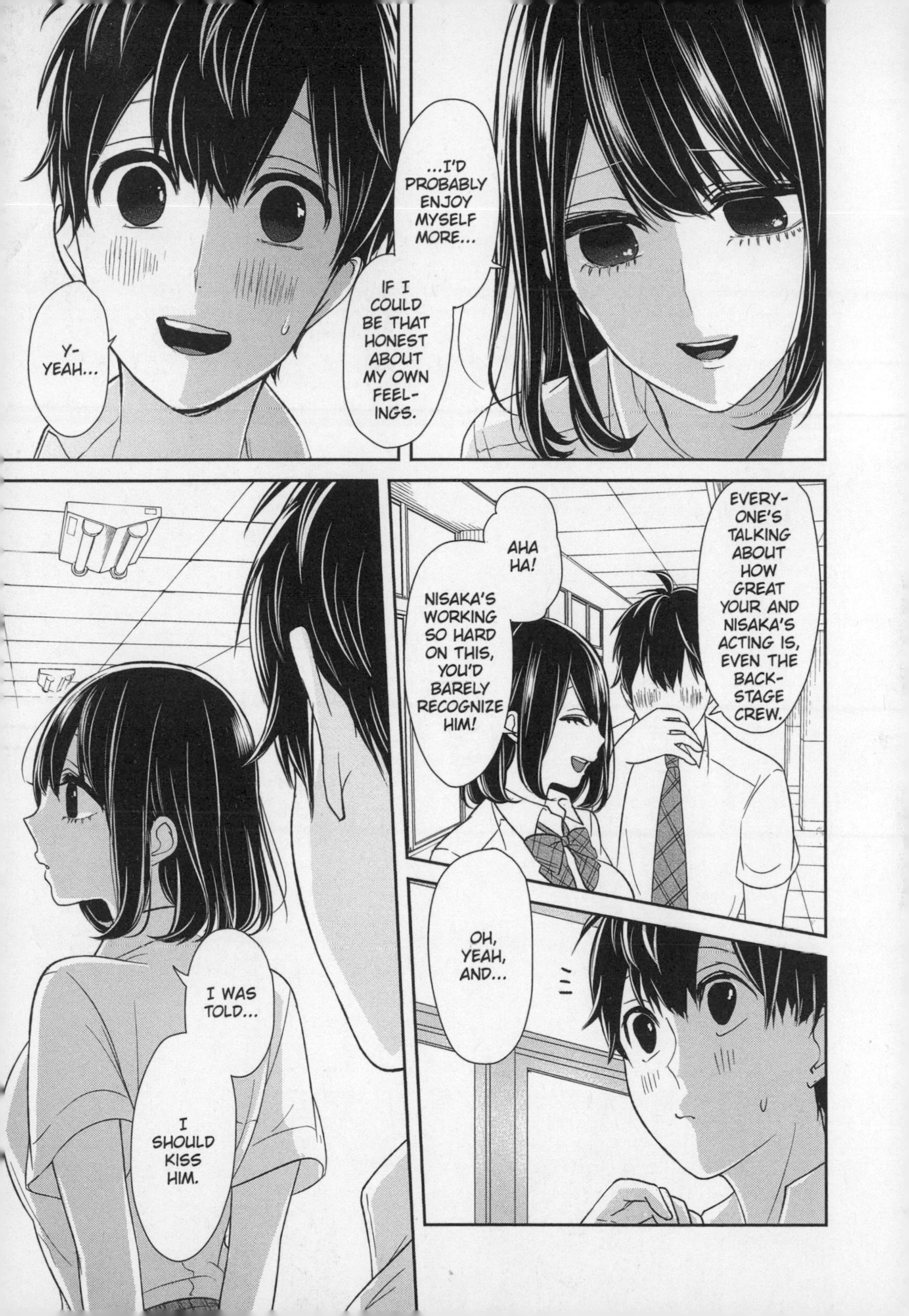
...I'D PROBABLY ENJOY MYSELF MORE...
IF I COULD BE THAT HONEST ABOUT MY OWN FEELINGS.
Y-YEAH...
EVERYONE'S TALKING ABOUT HOW GREAT YOUR AND NISAKA'S ACTING IS, EVEN THE BACKSTAGE CREW.
AHA HA!
NISAKA'S WORKING SO HARD ON THIS, YOU'D BARELY RECOGNIZE HIM!
OH, YEAH, AND...
I WAS TOLD...
I SHOULD KISS HIM.

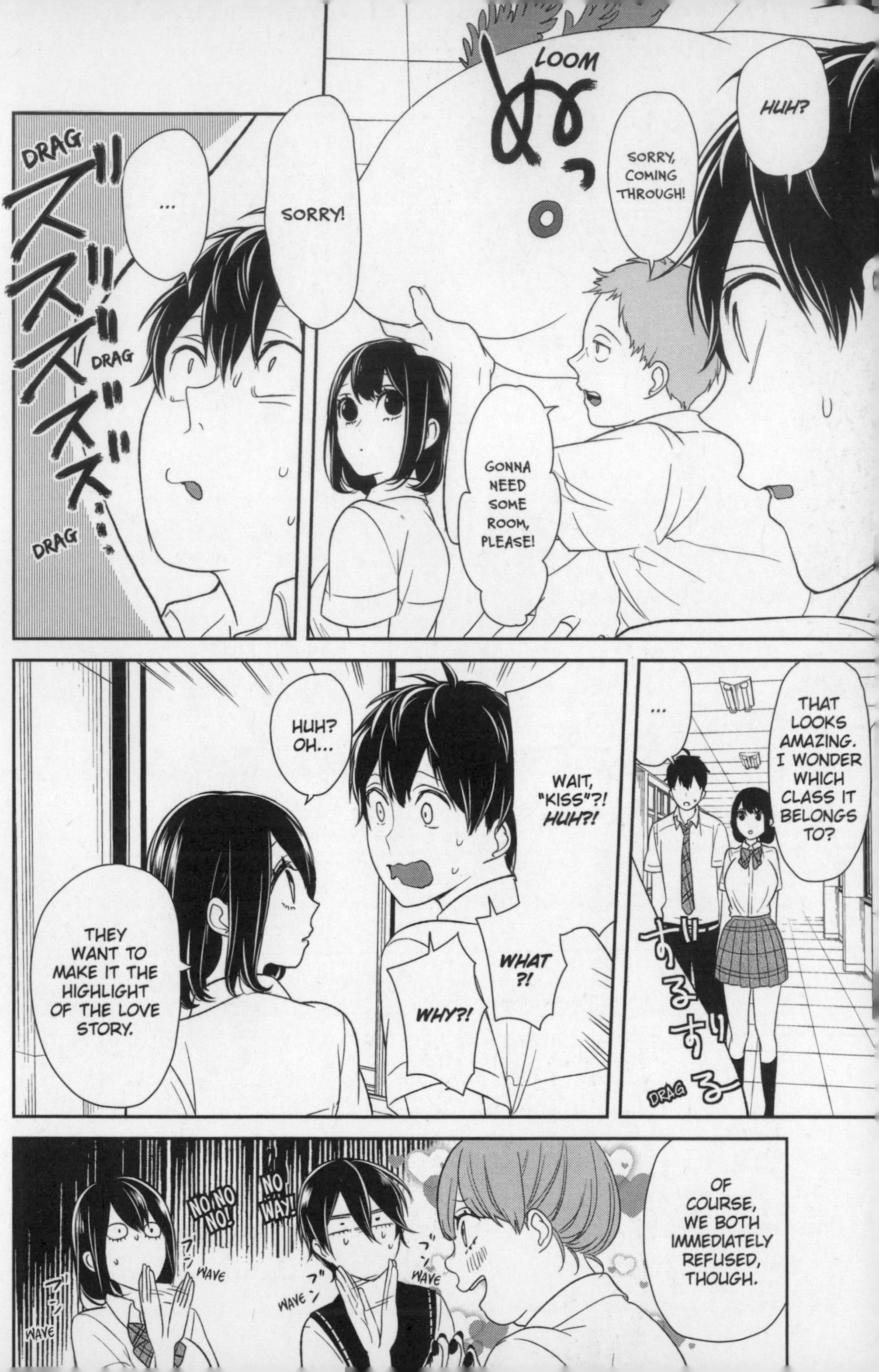
HUH?
SORRY, COMING THROUGH!
LOOM
ぬっ
GONNA NEED SOME ROOM, PLEASE!
SORRY!
...
DRAG
DRAG
DRAG
THAT LOOKS AMAZING. I WONDER WHICH CLASS IT BELONGS TO?
...
DRAG
HUH? OH...
WAIT, "KISS"?! HUH?!
WHAT?!
WHY?!
THEY WANT TO MAKE IT THE HIGHLIGHT OF THE LOVE STORY.
OF COURSE, WE BOTH IMMEDIATELY REFUSED, THOUGH.
NO WAY!
WAVE
WAVE
NO NO NO!
WAVE
WAVE

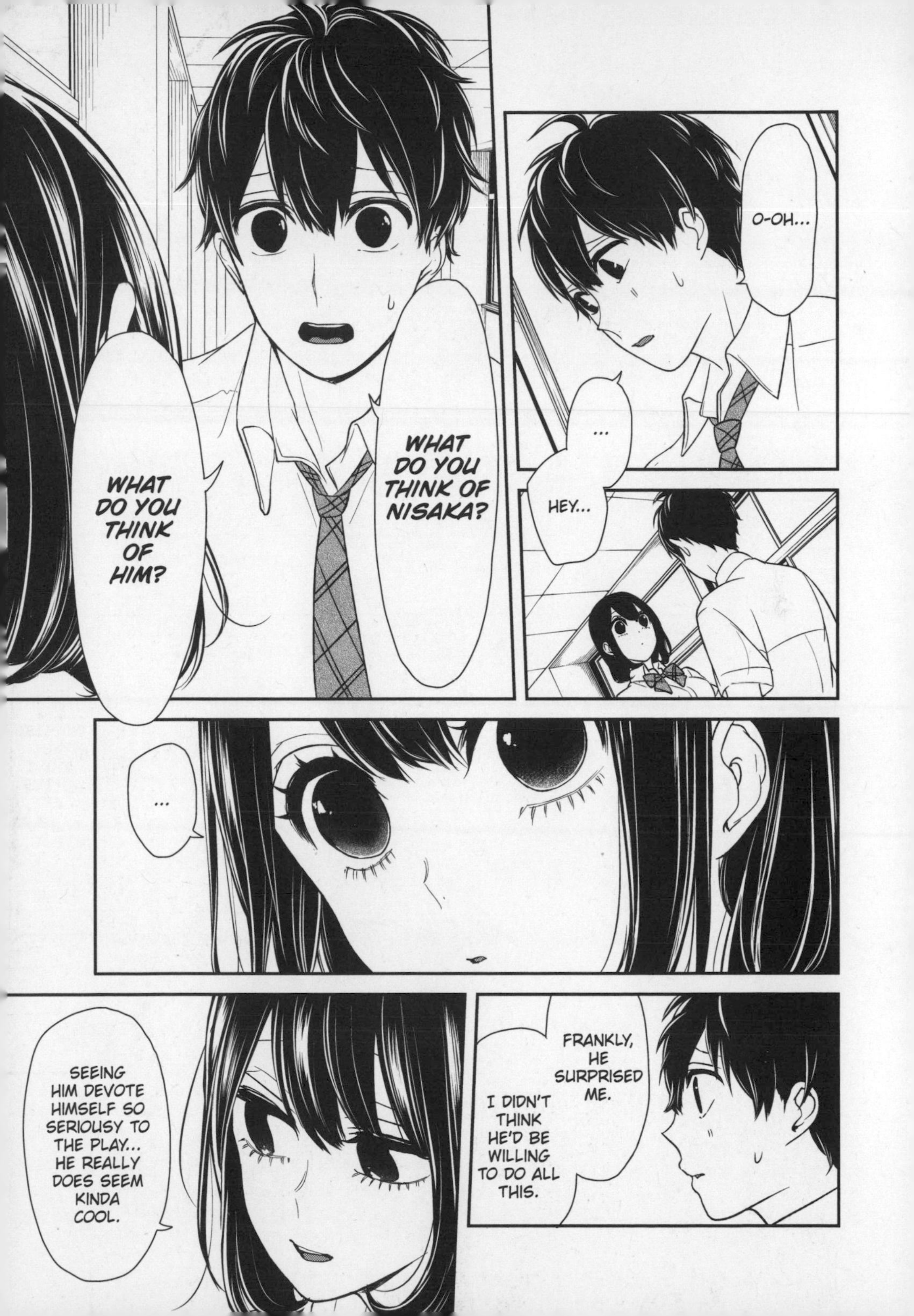
O-OH...
...
HEY...
WHAT DO YOU THINK OF NISAKA?
WHAT DO YOU THINK OF HIM?
...
FRANKLY, HE SURPRISED ME.
I DIDN'T THINK HE'D BE WILLING TO DO ALL THIS.
SEEING HIM DEVOTE HIMSELF SO SERIOUSY TO THE PLAY... HE REALLY DOES SEEM KINDA COOL.

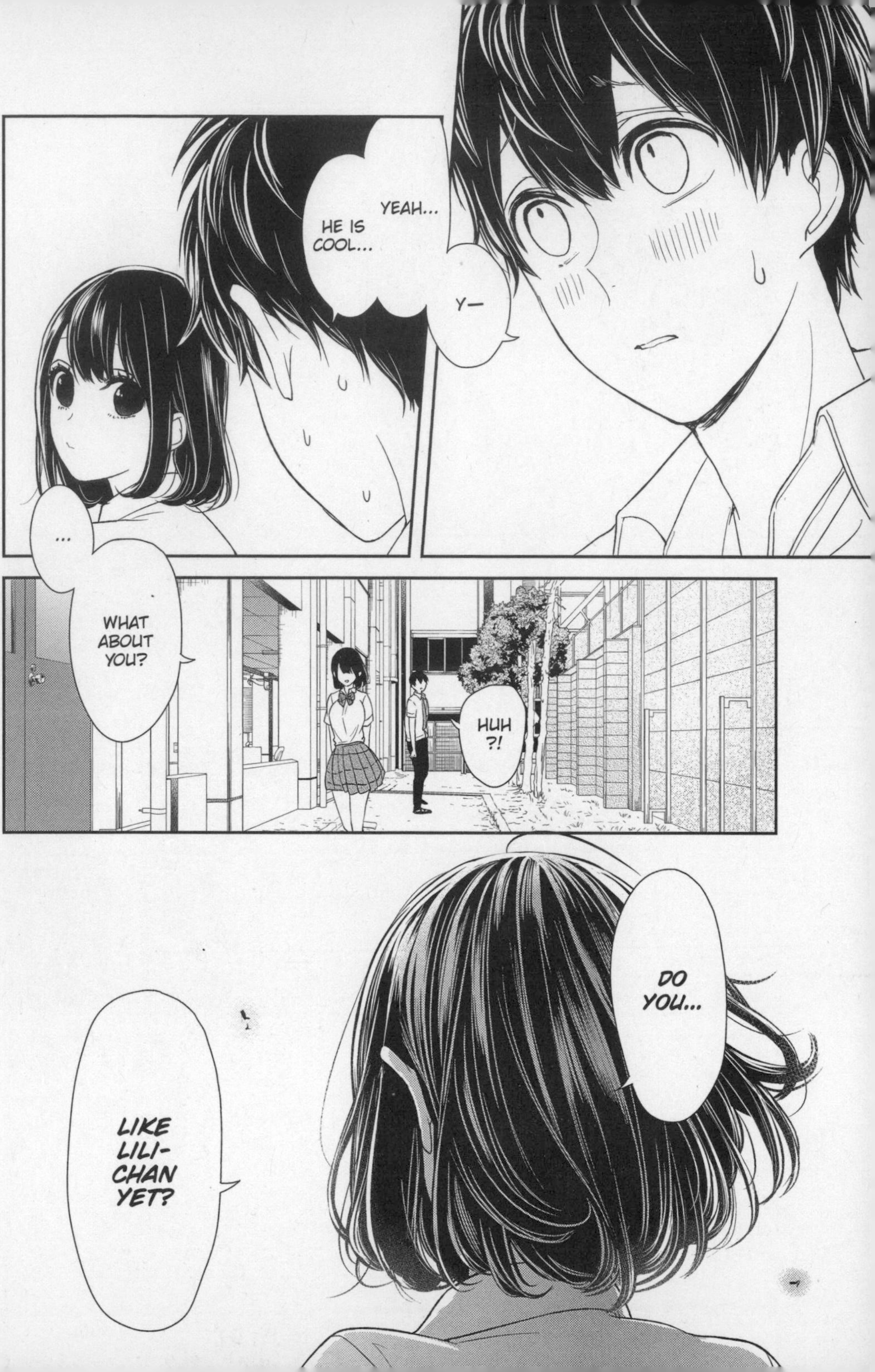
Y—
YEAH... HE IS COOL...
...
WHAT ABOUT YOU?
HUH?!
DO YOU...
LIKE LILI-CHAN YET?

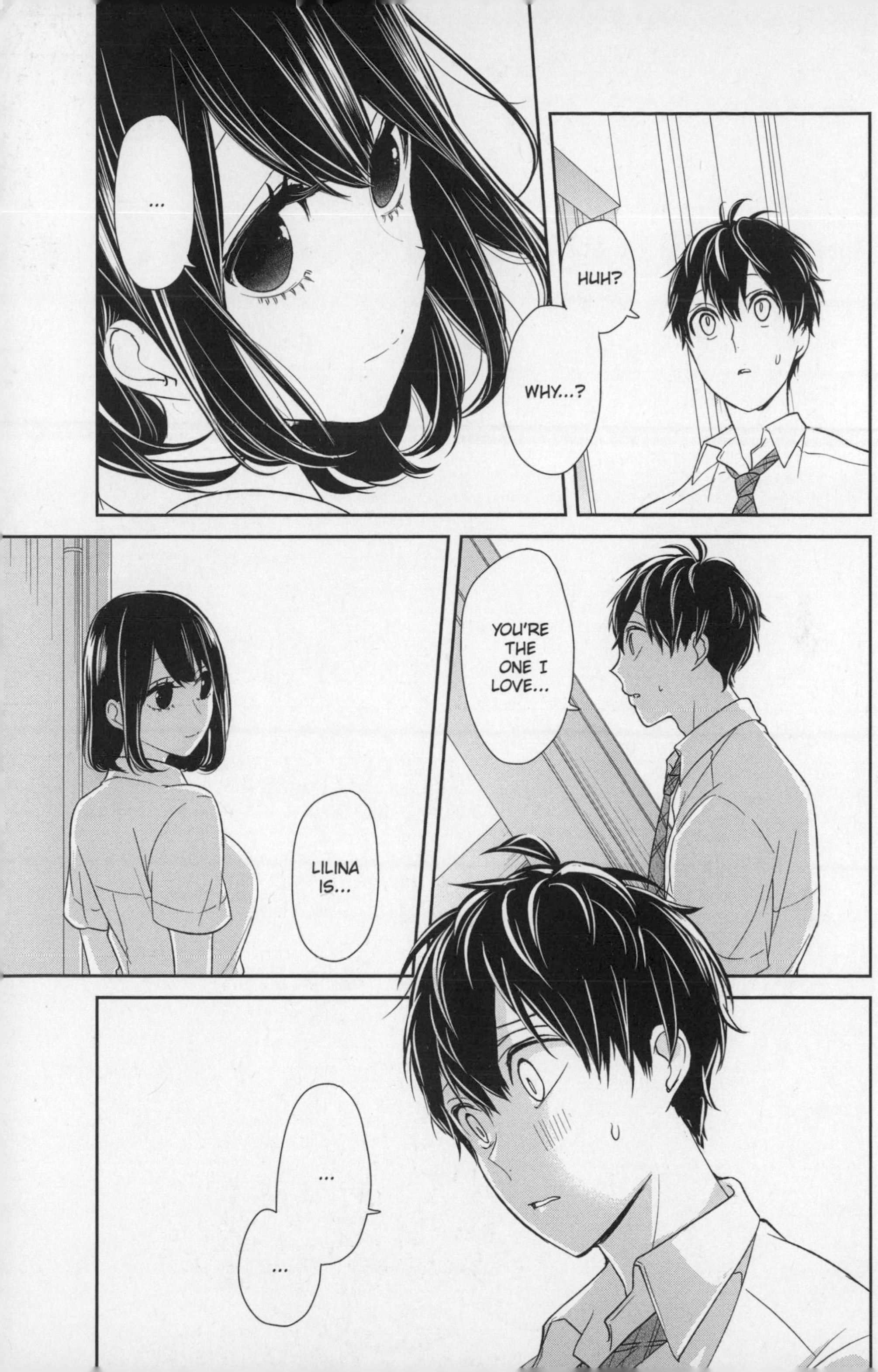
HUH?
WHY...?
...
YOU'RE THE ONE I LOVE...
LILINA IS...
...
...

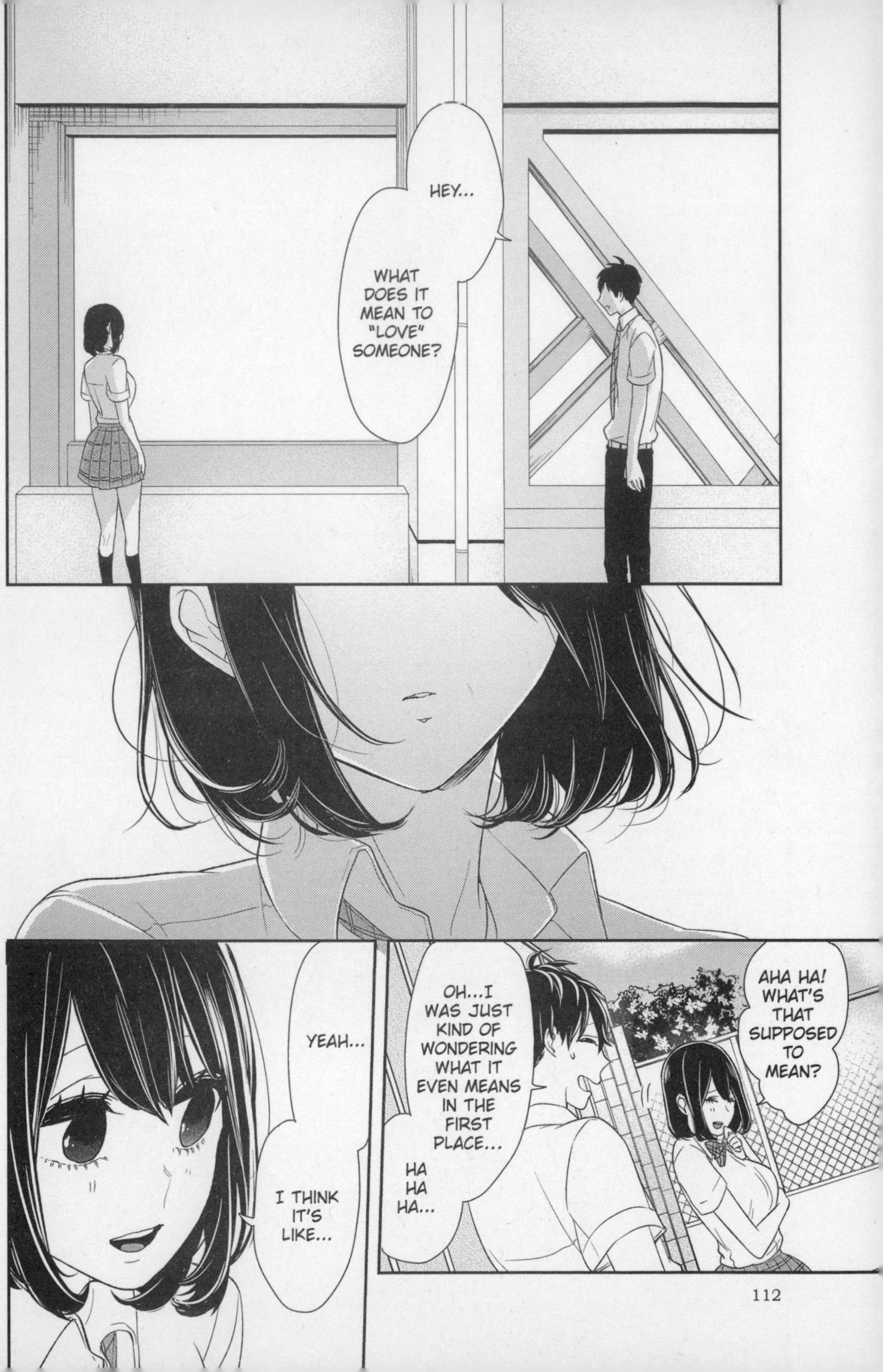
HEY...
WHAT DOES IT MEAN TO "LOVE" SOMEONE?
AHA HA! WHAT'S THAT SUPPOSED TO MEAN?
OH...I WAS JUST KIND OF WONDERING WHAT IT EVEN MEANS IN THE FIRST PLACE...
HA HA HA...
YEAH...
I THINK IT'S LIKE...

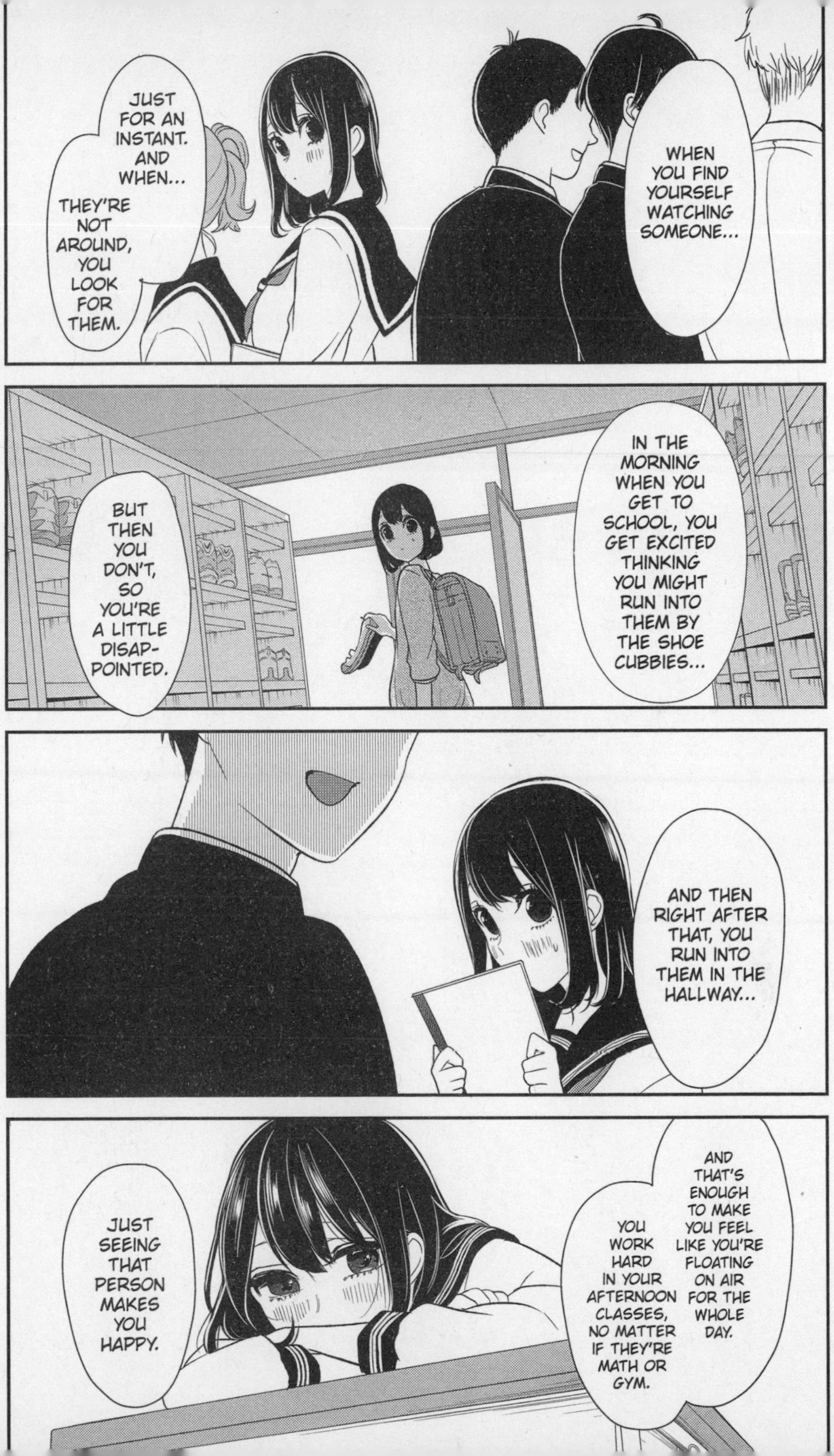
WHEN YOU FIND YOURSELF WATCHING SOMEONE...
JUST FOR AN INSTANT. AND WHEN...
THEY'RE NOT AROUND, YOU LOOK FOR THEM.
IN THE MORNING WHEN YOU GET TO SCHOOL, YOU GET EXCITED THINKING YOU MIGHT RUN INTO THEM BY THE SHOE CUBBIES...
BUT THEN YOU DON'T, SO YOU'RE A LITTLE DISAP-POINTED.
AND THEN RIGHT AFTER THAT, YOU RUN INTO THEM IN THE HALLWAY...
AND THAT'S ENOUGH TO MAKE YOU FEEL LIKE YOU'RE FLOATING ON AIR FOR THE WHOLE DAY.
YOU WORK HARD IN YOUR AFTERNOON CLASSES, NO MATTER IF THEY'RE MATH OR GYM.
JUST SEEING THAT PERSON MAKES YOU HAPPY.

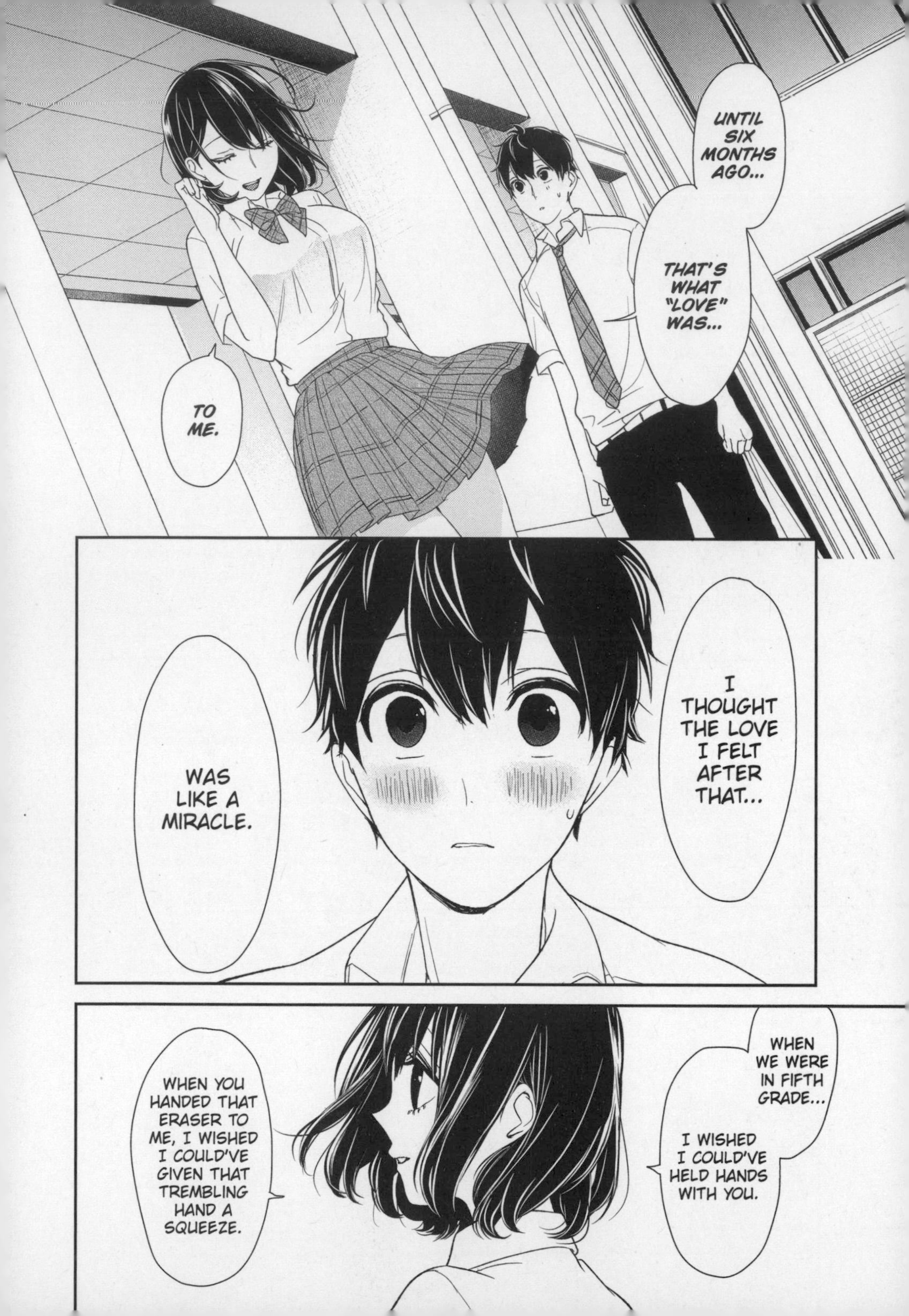
UNTIL SIX MONTHS AGO...
THAT'S WHAT "LOVE" WAS...
TO ME.
I THOUGHT THE LOVE I FELT AFTER THAT...
WAS LIKE A MIRACLE.
WHEN WE WERE IN FIFTH GRADE...
I WISHED I COULD'VE HELD HANDS WITH YOU.
WHEN YOU HANDED THAT ERASER TO ME, I WISHED I COULD'VE GIVEN THAT TREMBLING HAND A SQUEEZE.

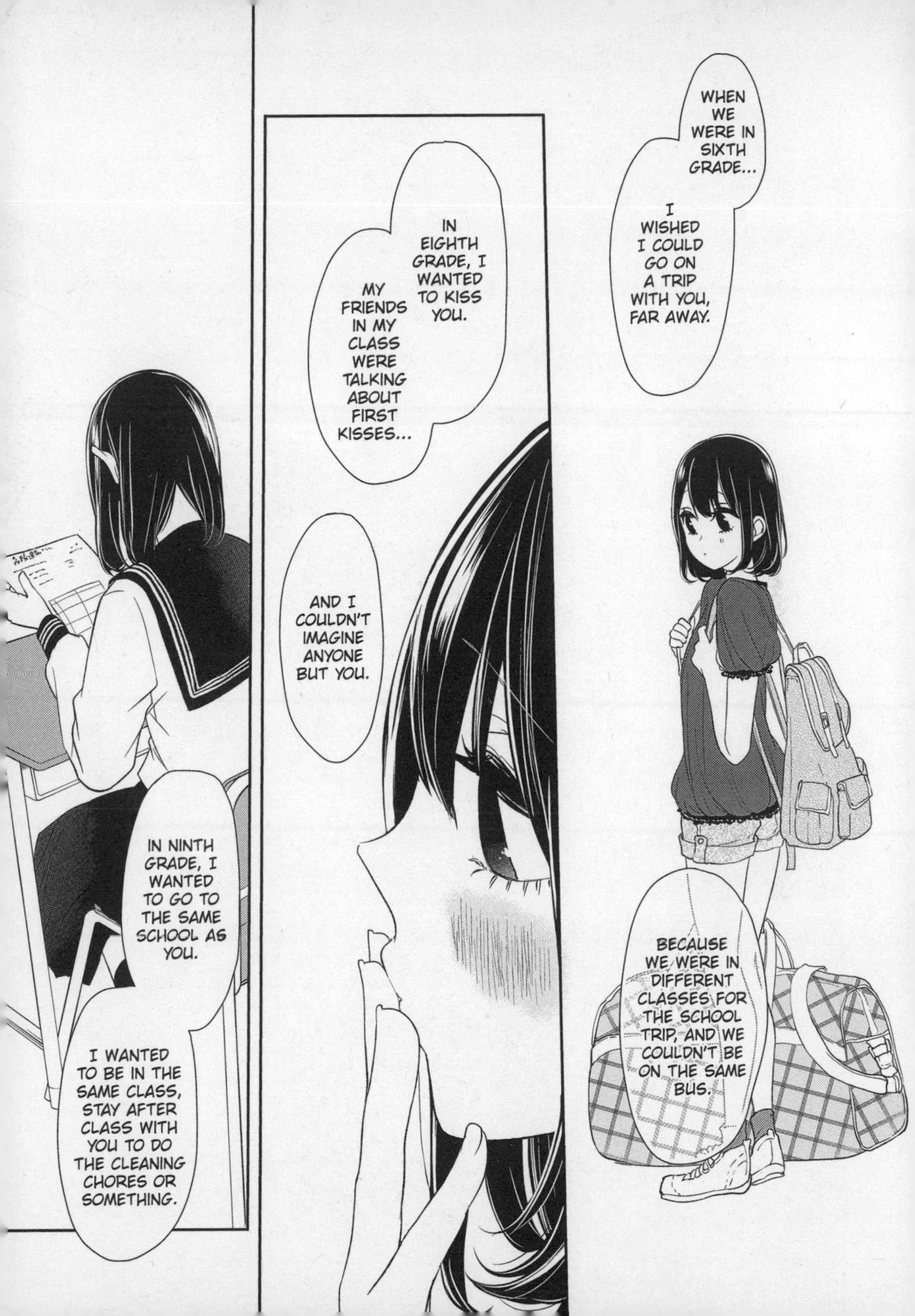
WHEN WE WERE IN SIXTH GRADE...
I WISHED I COULD GO ON A TRIP WITH YOU, FAR AWAY.
BECAUSE WE WERE IN DIFFERENT CLASSES FOR THE SCHOOL TRIP, AND WE COULDN'T BE ON THE SAME BUS.
IN EIGHTH GRADE, I WANTED TO KISS YOU.
MY FRIENDS IN MY CLASS WERE TALKING ABOUT FIRST KISSES...
AND I COULDN'T IMAGINE ANYONE BUT YOU.
IN NINTH GRADE, I WANTED TO GO TO THE SAME SCHOOL AS YOU.
I WANTED TO BE IN THE SAME CLASS, STAY AFTER CLASS WITH YOU TO DO THE CLEANING CHORES OR SOMETHING.

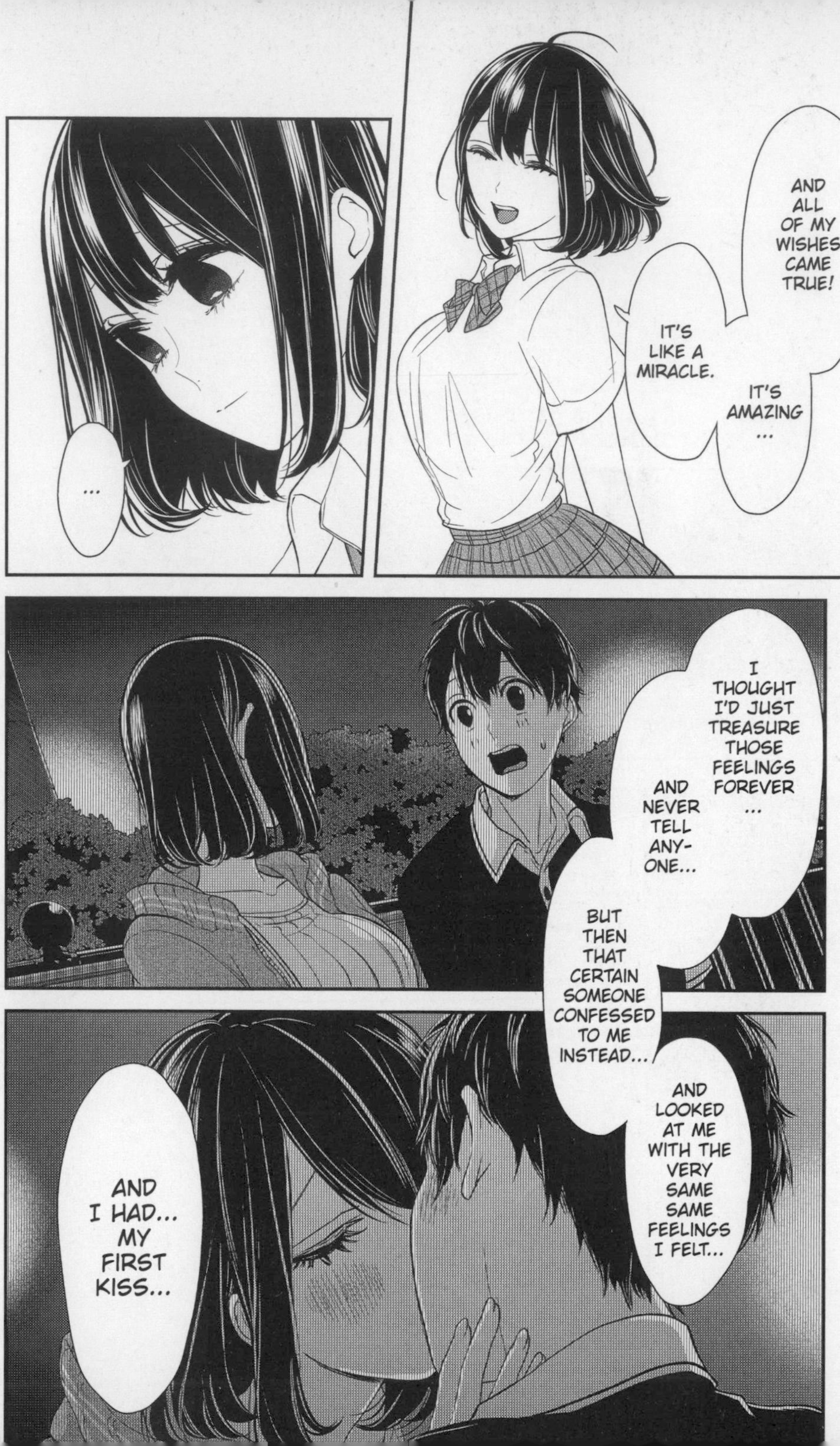
AND ALL OF MY WISHES CAME TRUE!
IT'S LIKE A MIRACLE.
IT'S AMAZING...
...
I THOUGHT I'D JUST TREASURE THOSE FEELINGS FOREVER...
AND NEVER TELL ANY-ONE...
BUT THEN THAT CERTAIN SOMEONE CONFESSED TO ME INSTEAD...
AND LOOKED AT ME WITH THE VERY SAME SAME FEELINGS I FELT...
AND I HAD... MY FIRST KISS...

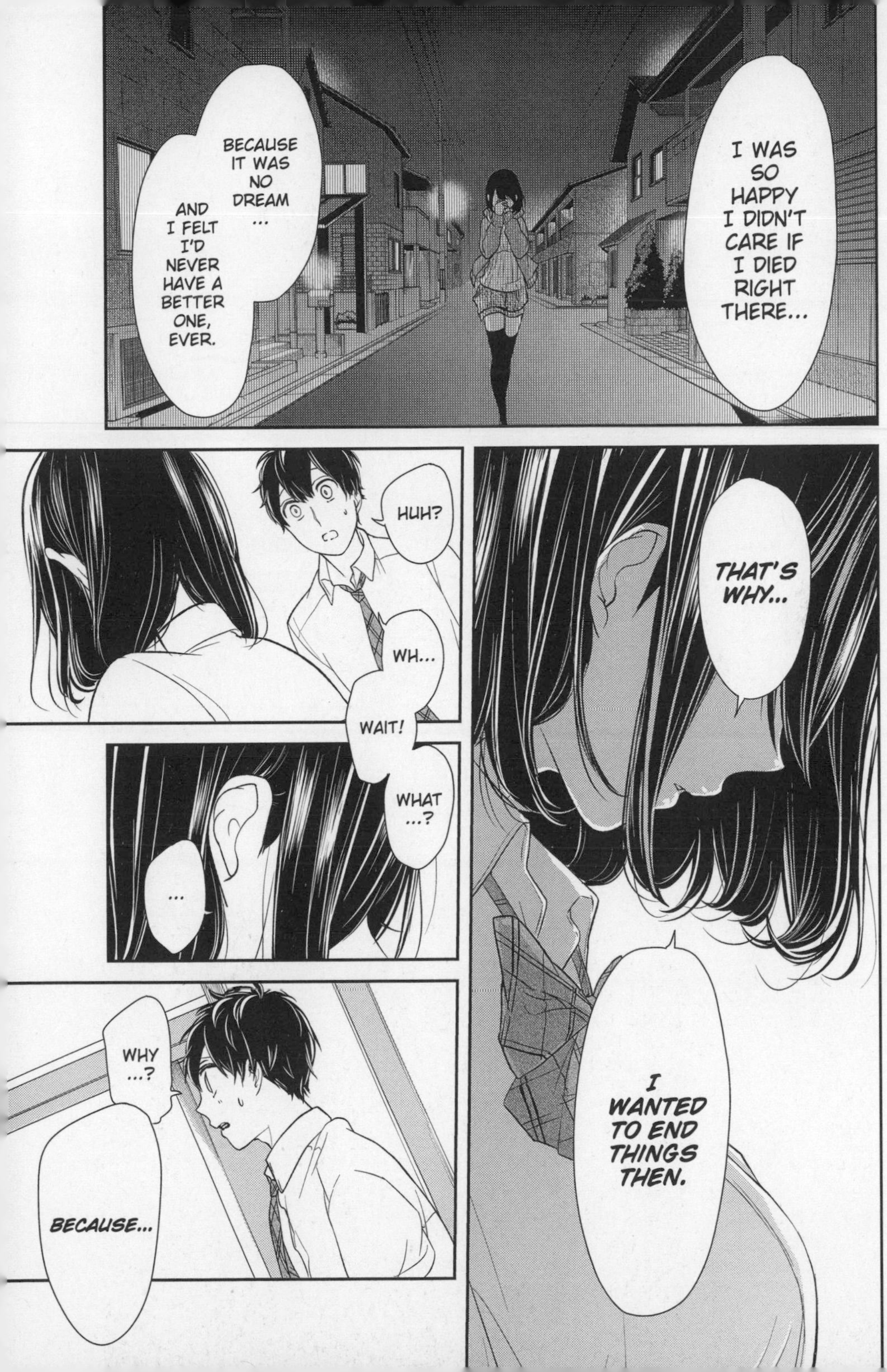
I WAS SO HAPPY I DIDN'T CARE IF I DIED RIGHT THERE...
BECAUSE IT WAS NO DREAM...
AND I FELT I'D NEVER HAVE A BETTER ONE, EVER.
THAT'S WHY...
I WANTED TO END THINGS THEN.
HUH?
WH...
WAIT!
WHAT...?
...
WHY...?
BECAUSE...

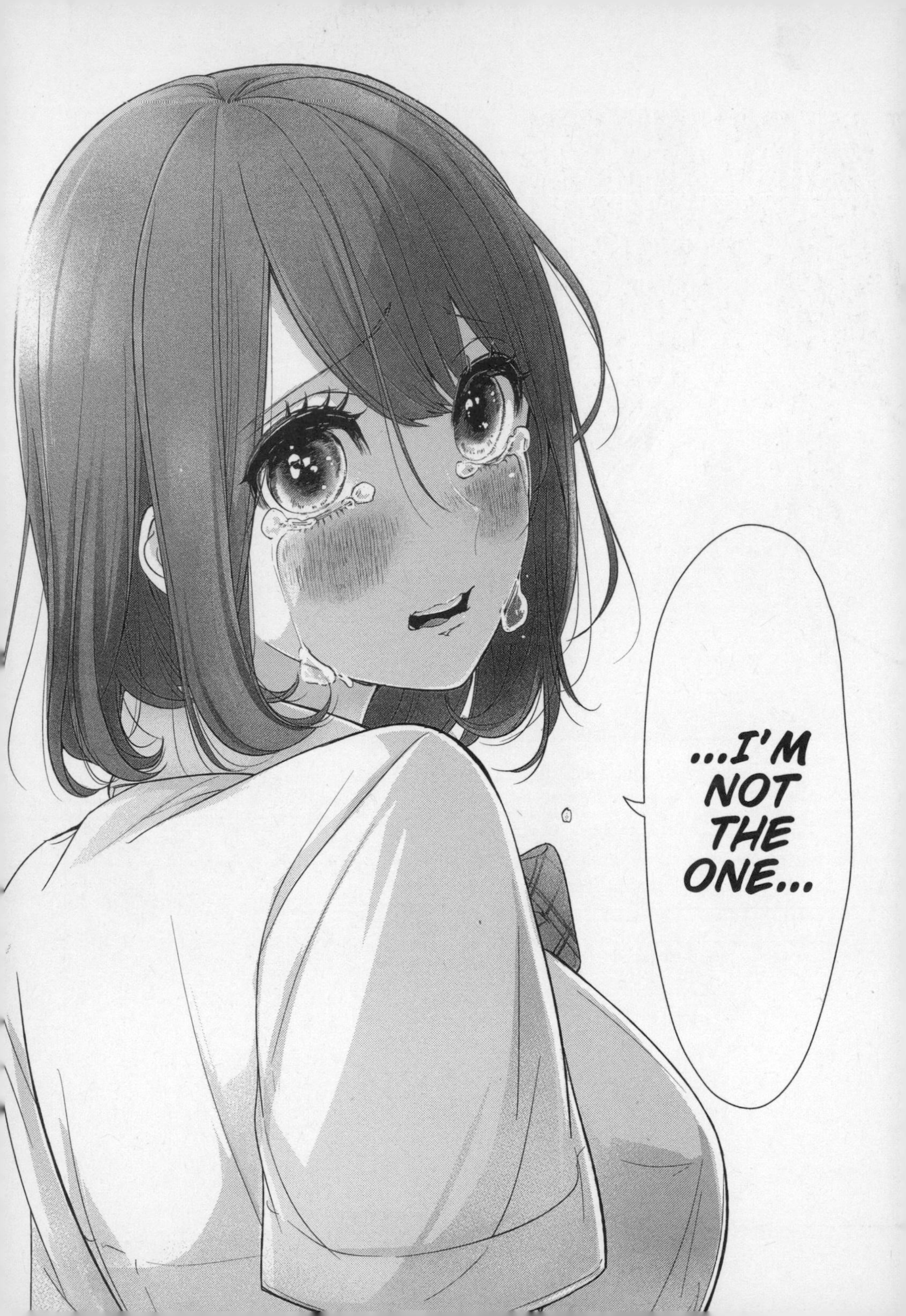
...I'M NOT THE ONE...

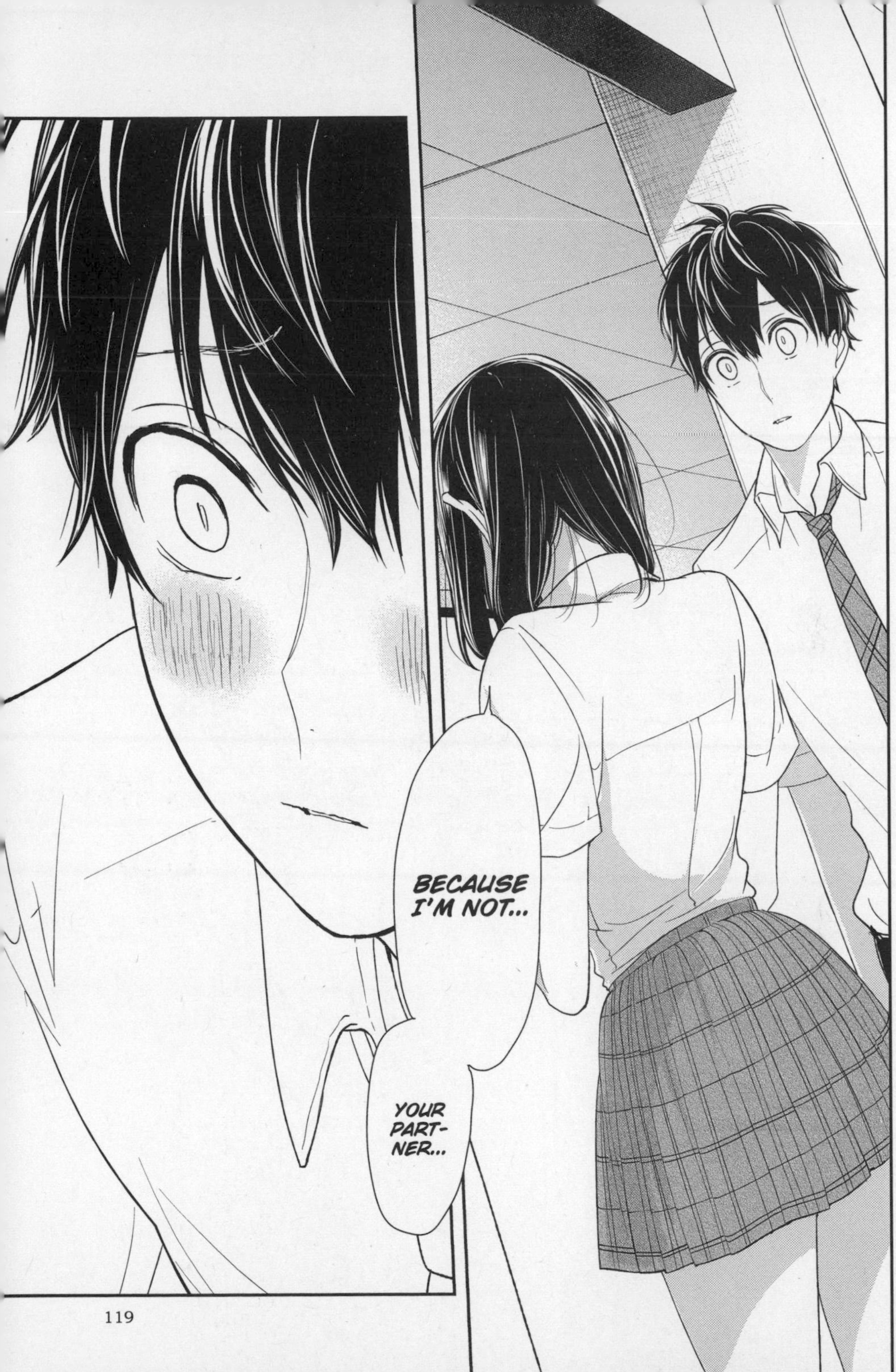
BECAUSE I'M NOT...
YOUR PART-NER...

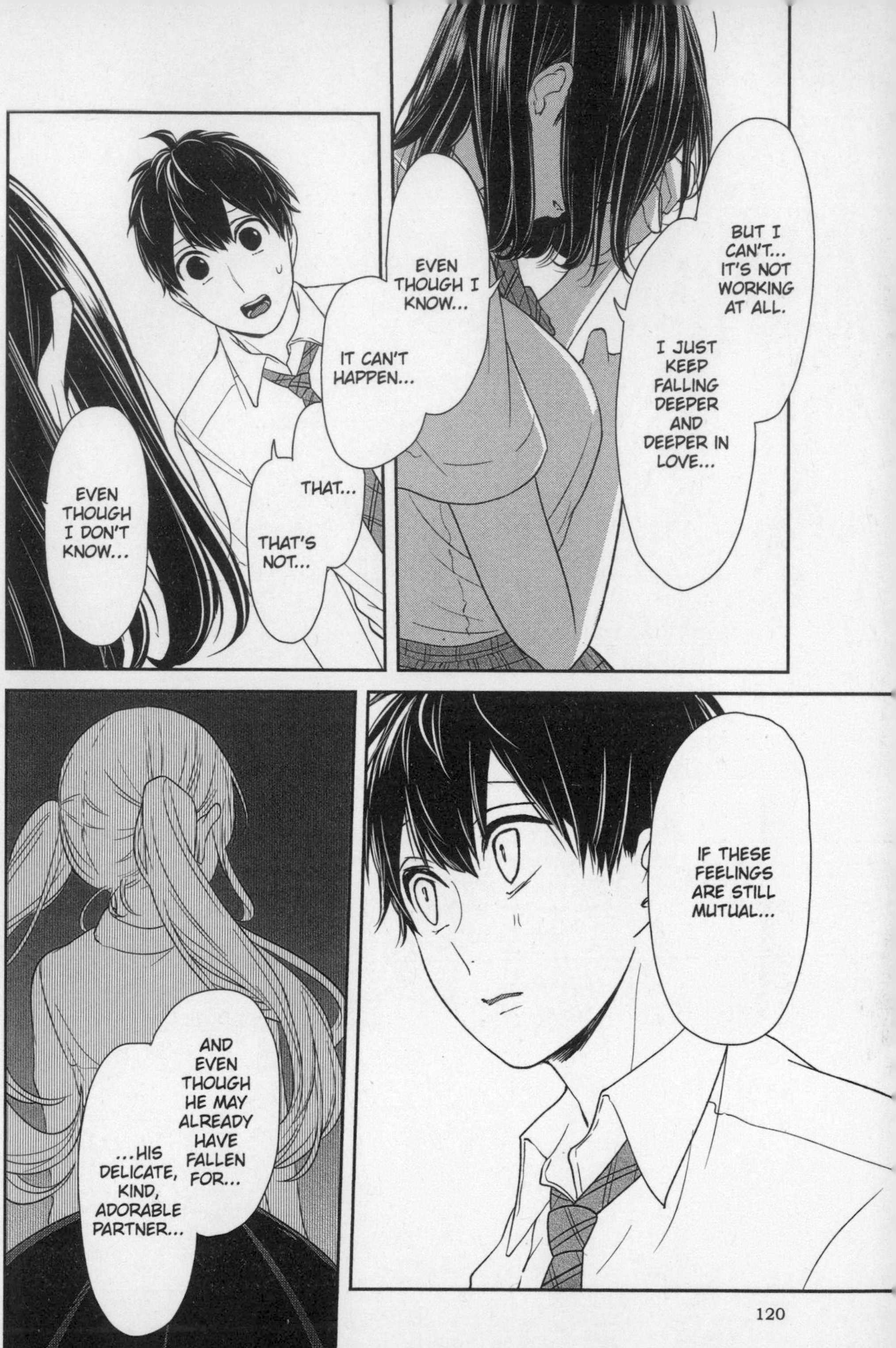
BUT I CAN'T... IT'S NOT WORKING AT ALL.
I JUST KEEP FALLING DEEPER AND DEEPER IN LOVE...
EVEN THOUGH I KNOW...
IT CAN'T HAPPEN...
THAT...
THAT'S NOT...
EVEN THOUGH I DON'T KNOW...
IF THESE FEELINGS ARE STILL MUTUAL...
AND EVEN THOUGH HE MAY ALREADY HAVE FALLEN FOR...
...HIS DELICATE, KIND, ADORABLE PARTNER...

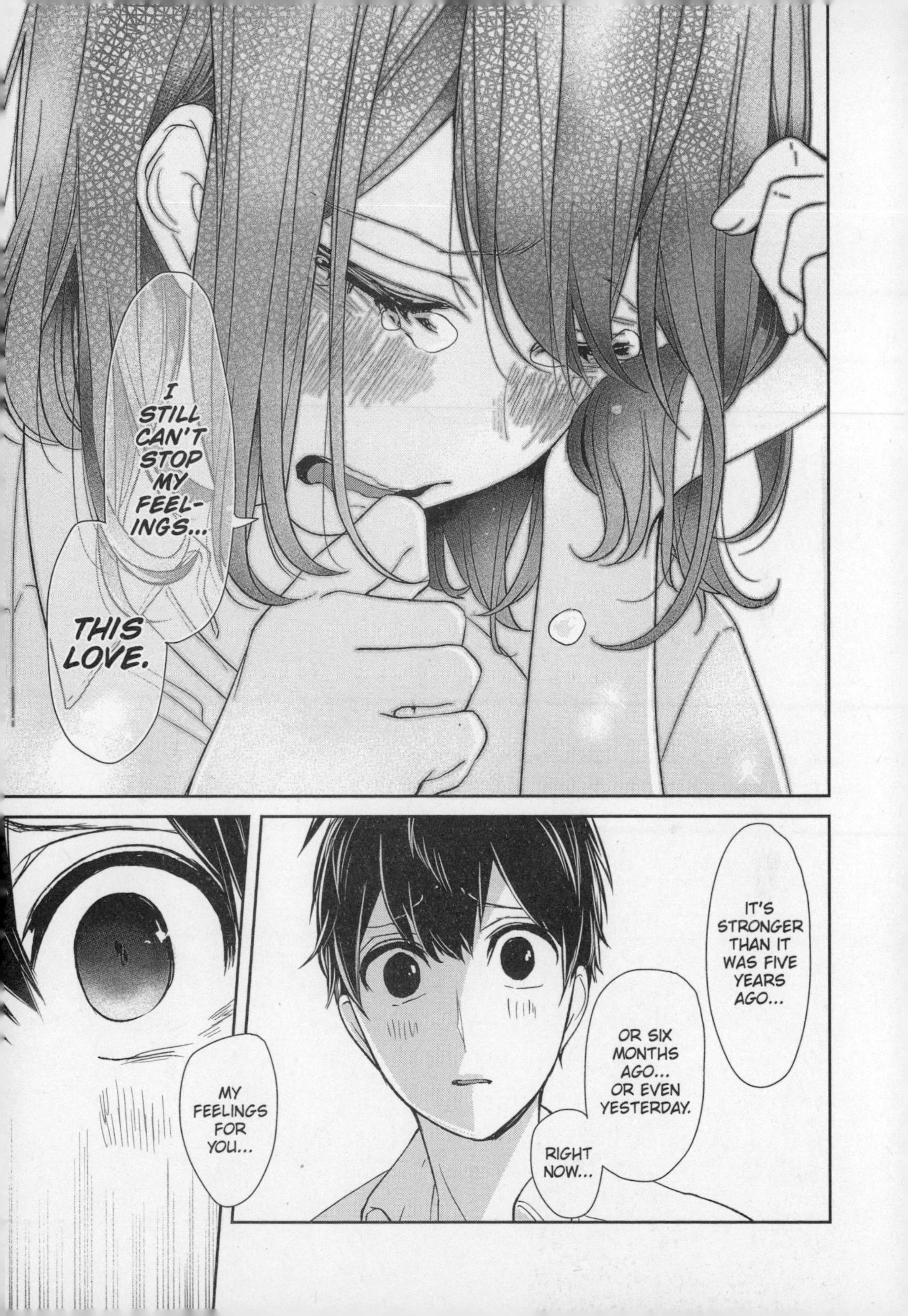
I STILL CAN'T STOP MY FEEL-INGS...
THIS LOVE.
IT'S STRONGER THAN IT WAS FIVE YEARS AGO...
OR SIX MONTHS AGO... OR EVEN YESTERDAY.
RIGHT NOW...
MY FEELINGS FOR YOU...

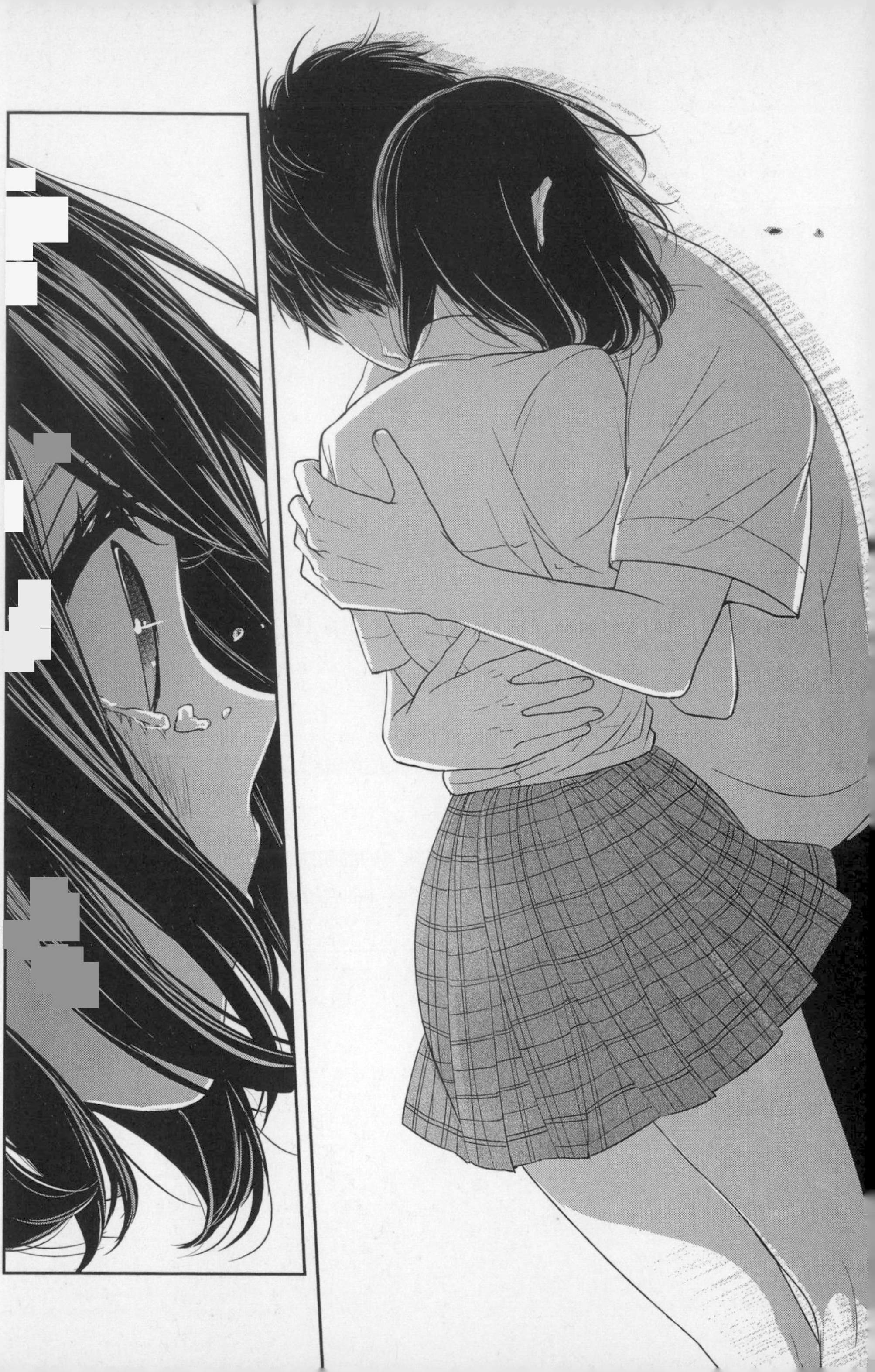

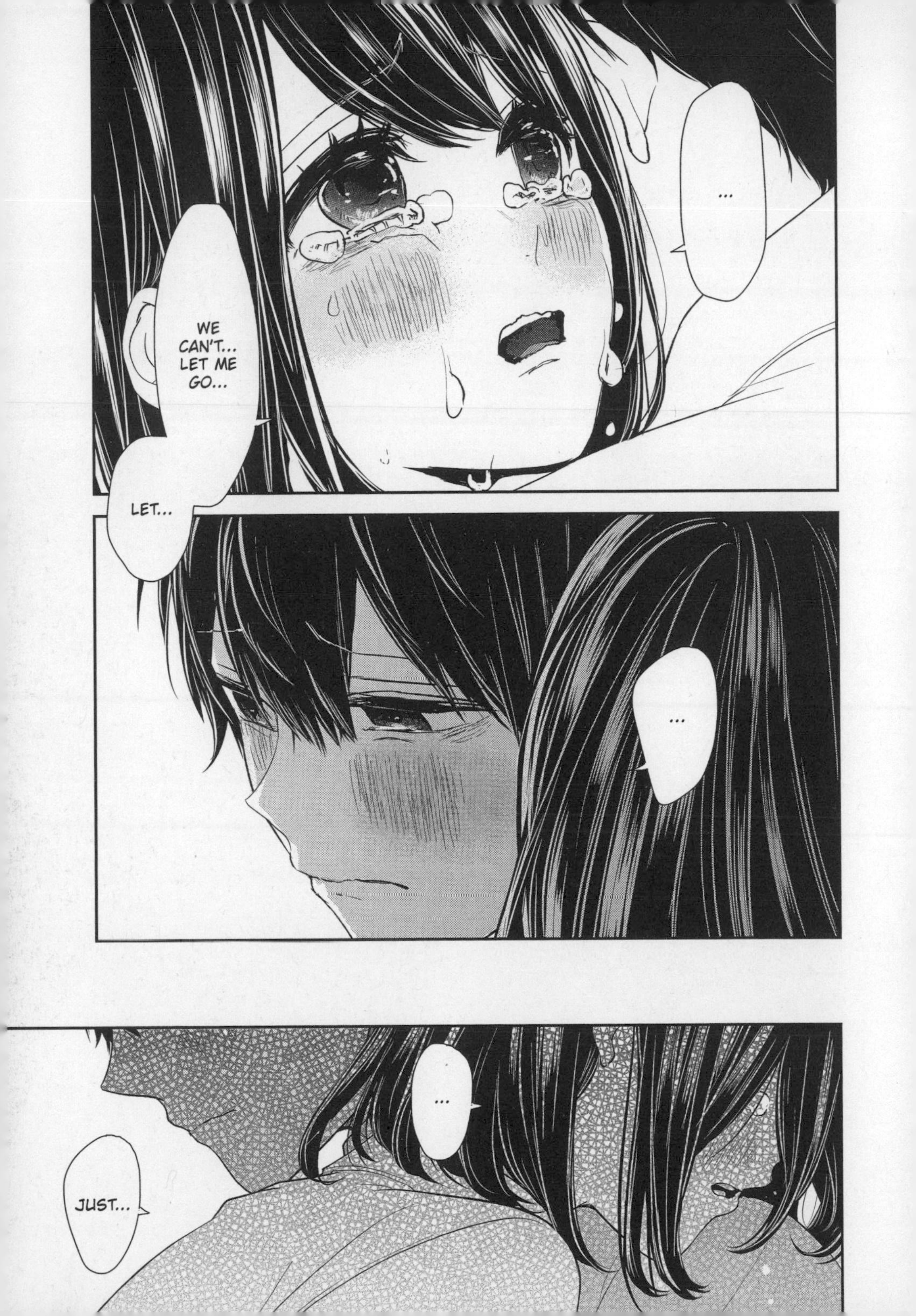
...
WE CAN'T... LET ME GO...
LET...
...
...
JUST...

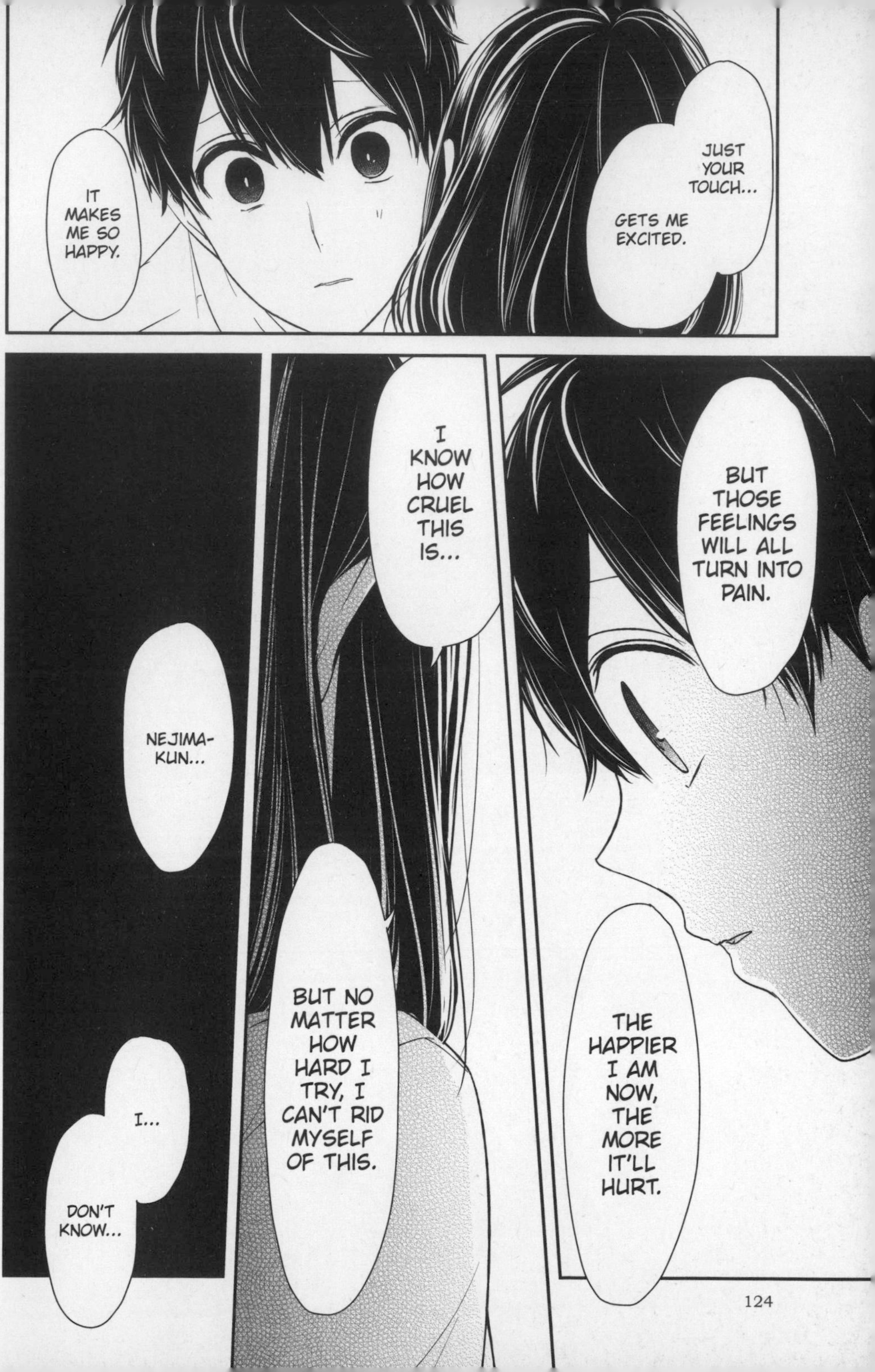
JUST YOUR TOUCH...
GETS ME EXCITED.
IT MAKES ME SO HAPPY.
BUT THOSE FEELINGS WILL ALL TURN INTO PAIN.
THE HAPPIER I AM NOW, THE MORE IT'LL HURT.
I KNOW HOW CRUEL THIS IS...
BUT NO MATTER HOW HARD I TRY, I CAN'T RID MYSELF OF THIS.
NEJIMA-KUN...
I...
DON'T KNOW...

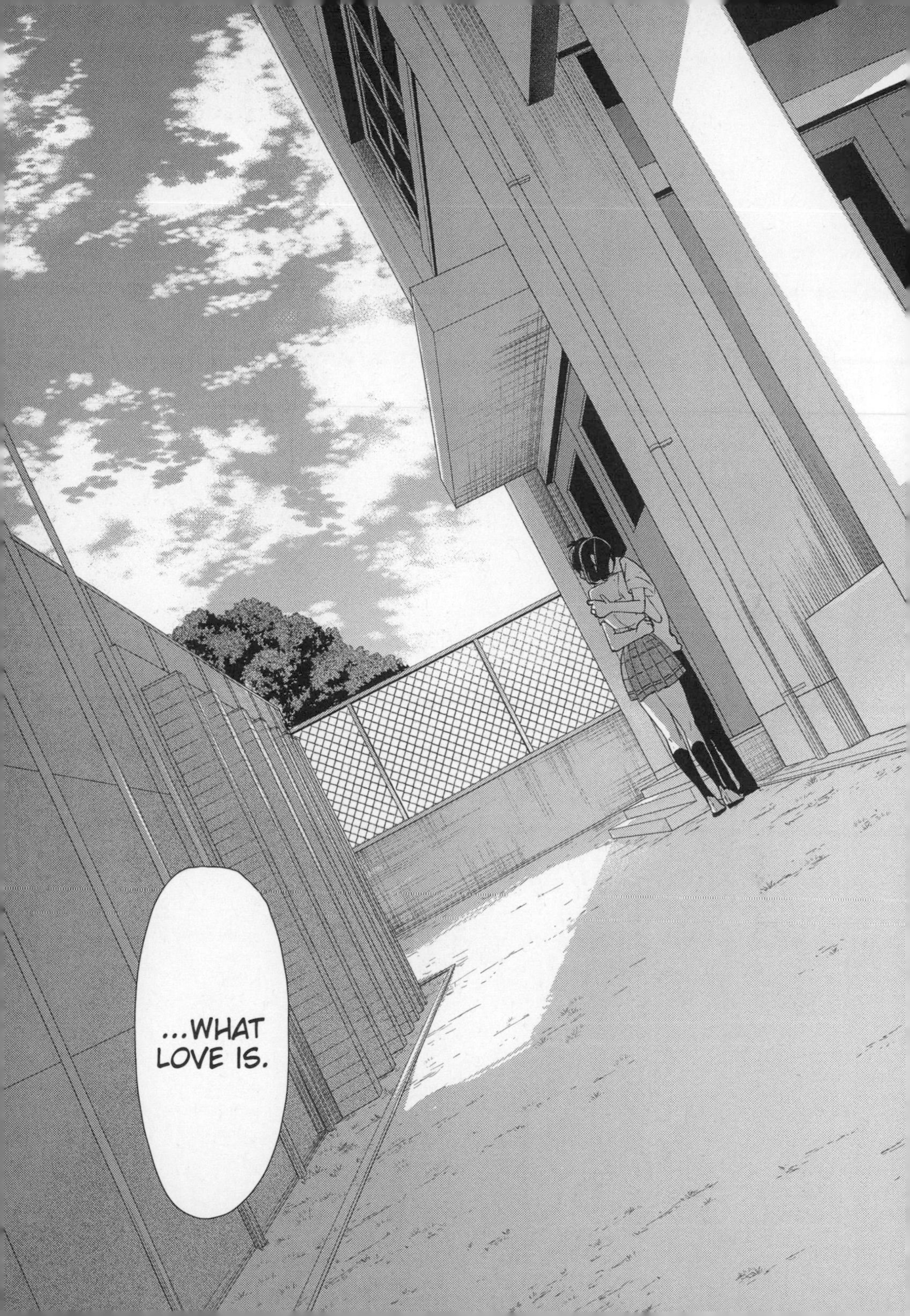
...WHAT LOVE IS.

Love&Lies

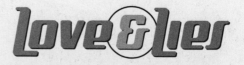

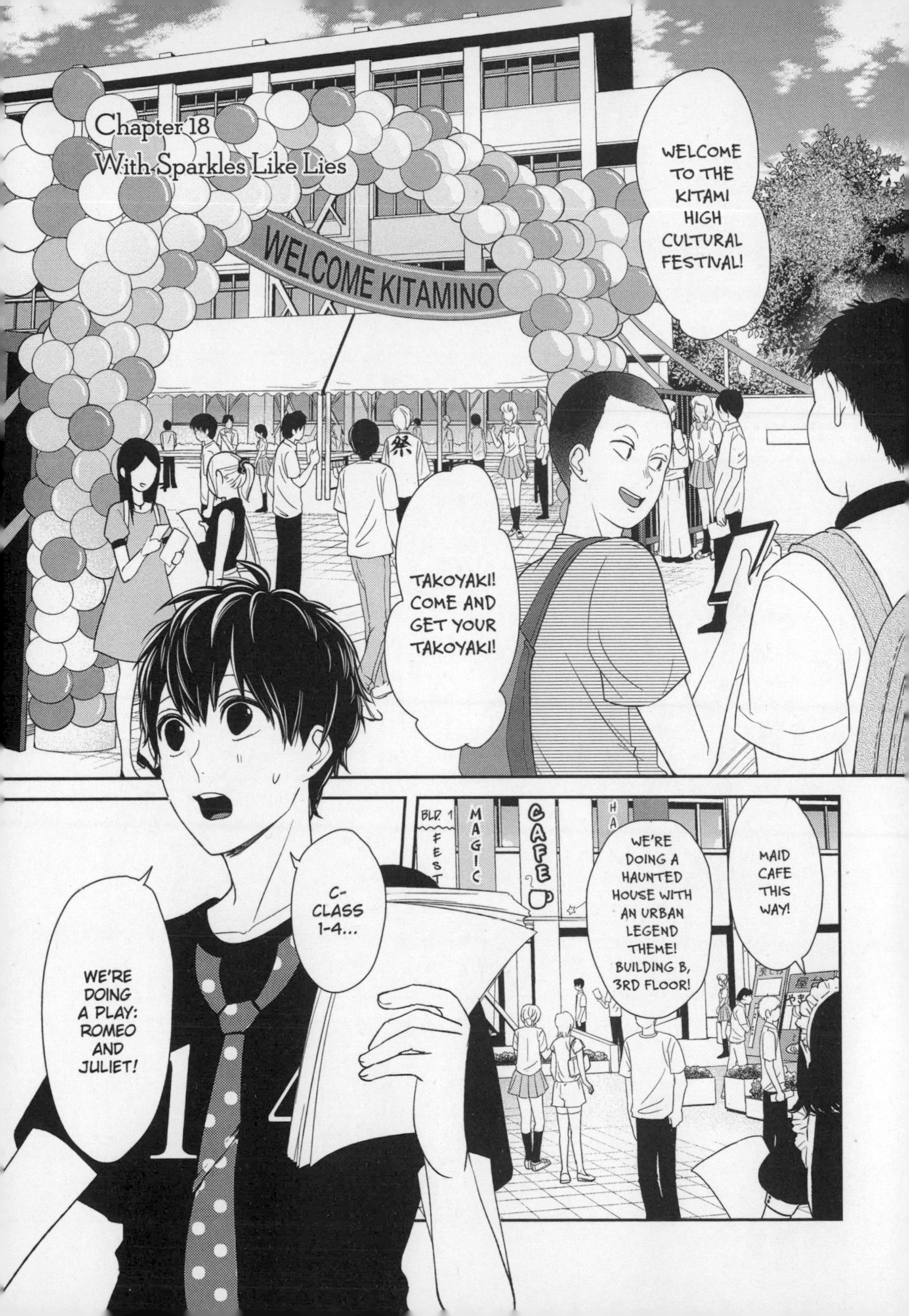
Chapter 18
With Sparkles Like Lies
WELCOME TO THE KITAMI HIGH CULTURAL FESTIVAL!
WELCOME KITAMINO
TAKOYAKI! COME AND GET YOUR TAKOYAKI!
MAID CAFE THIS WAY!
CAFE
WE'RE DOING A HAUNTED HOUSE WITH AN URBAN LEGEND THEME! BUILDING B, 3RD FLOOR!
MAGIC
BLD. 1
C- CLASS 1-4...
WE'RE DOING A PLAY: ROMEO AND JULIET!

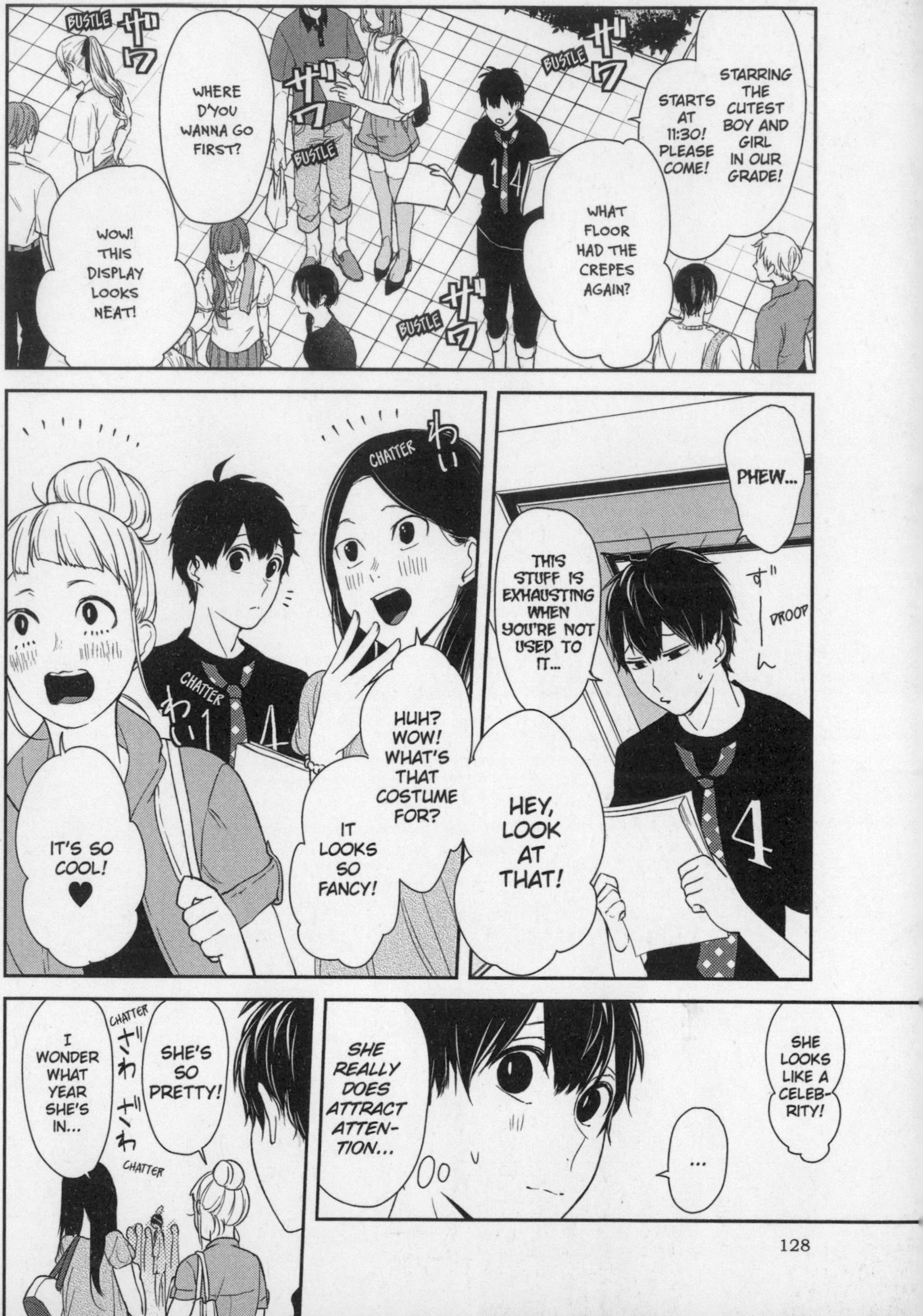
STARRING THE CUTEST BOY AND GIRL IN OUR GRADE!
STARTS AT 11:30! PLEASE COME!
BUSTLE
WHERE D'YOU WANNA GO FIRST?
BUSTLE
BUSTLE
WHAT FLOOR HAD THE CREPES AGAIN?
WOW! THIS DISPLAY LOOKS NEAT!
BUSTLE
PHEW...
THIS STUFF IS EXHAUSTING WHEN YOU'RE NOT USED TO IT...
DROOP
CHATTER
HEY, LOOK AT THAT!
HUH? WOW! WHAT'S THAT COSTUME FOR?
IT LOOKS SO FANCY!
IT'S SO COOL! ♥
CHATTER
SHE LOOKS LIKE A CELEBRITY!
...
SHE REALLY DOES ATTRACT ATTEN- TION...
SHE'S SO PRETTY!
CHATTER
I WONDER WHAT YEAR SHE'S IN...
CHATTER

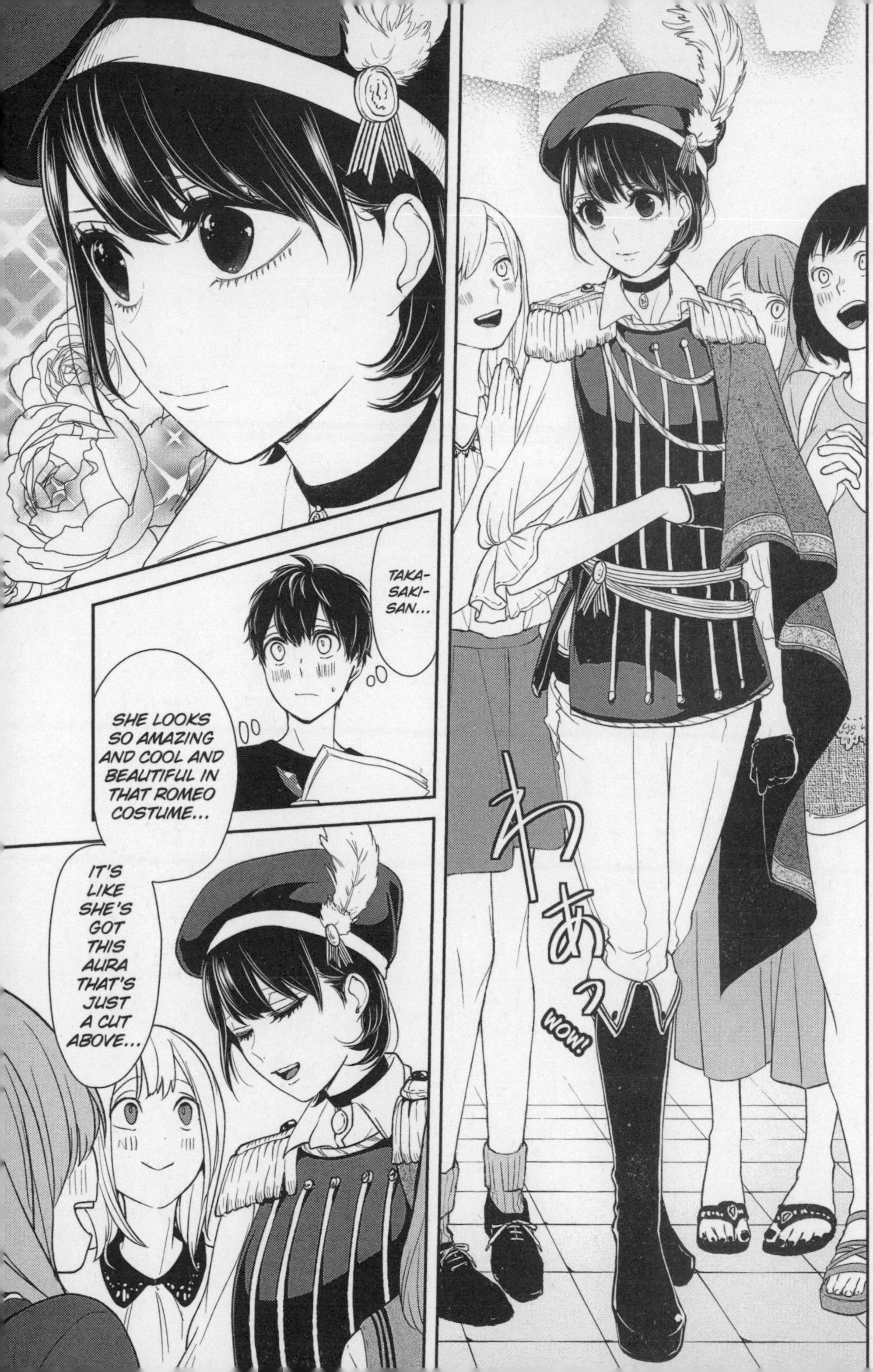
わあっ
WOW!
TAKA-SAKI-SAN…
SHE LOOKS SO AMAZING AND COOL AND BEAUTIFUL IN THAT ROMEO COSTUME…
IT'S LIKE SHE'S GOT THIS AURA THAT'S JUST A CUT ABOVE…

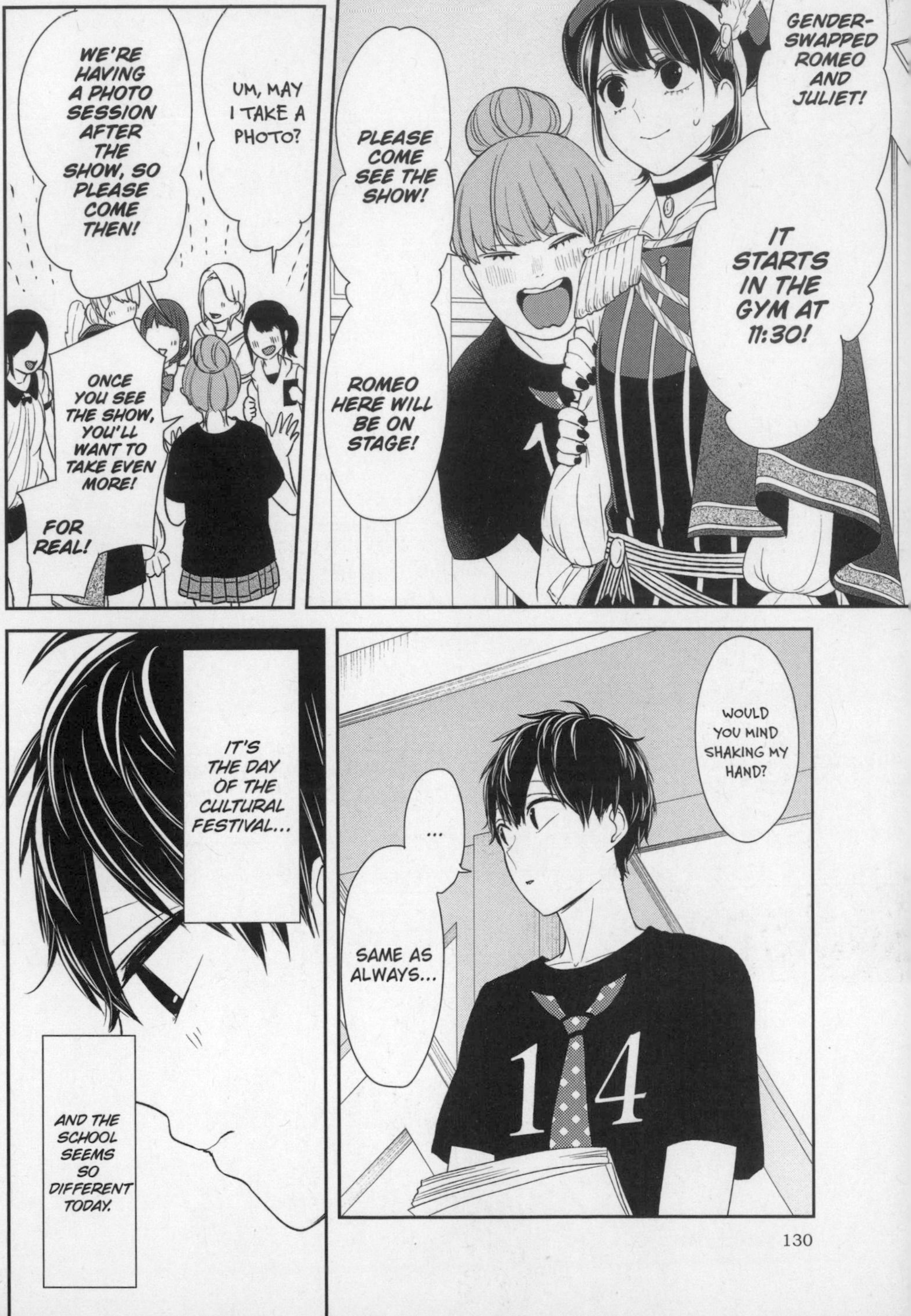
GENDER-SWAPPED ROMEO AND JULIET!
IT STARTS IN THE GYM AT 11:30!
PLEASE COME SEE THE SHOW!
ROMEO HERE WILL BE ON STAGE!
UM, MAY I TAKE A PHOTO?
WE'RE HAVING A PHOTO SESSION AFTER THE SHOW, SO PLEASE COME THEN!
ONCE YOU SEE THE SHOW, YOU'LL WANT TO TAKE EVEN MORE!
FOR REAL!
WOULD YOU MIND SHAKING MY HAND?
...
SAME AS ALWAYS...
IT'S THE DAY OF THE CULTURAL FESTIVAL...
AND THE SCHOOL SEEMS SO DIFFERENT TODAY.

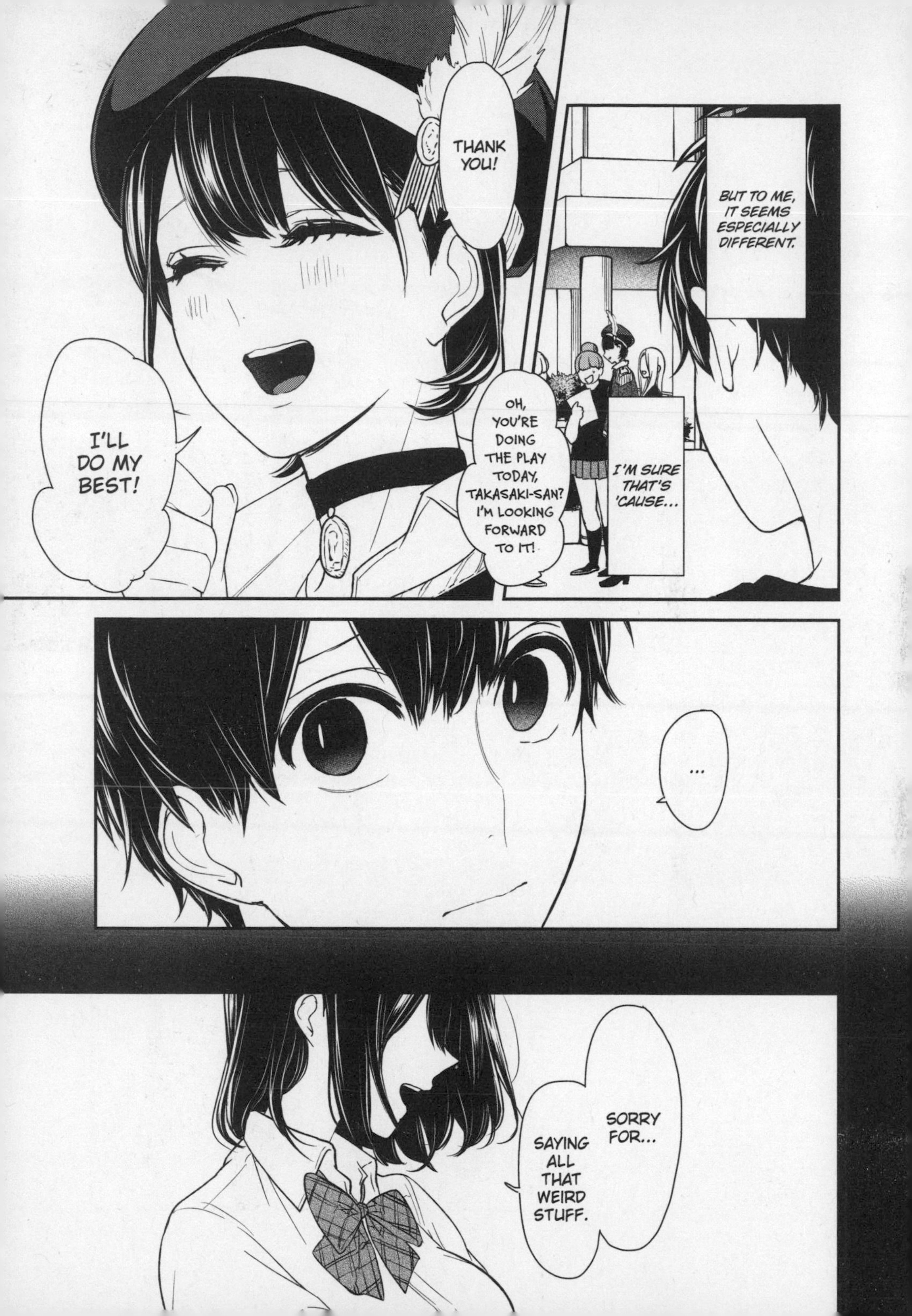
BUT TO ME, IT SEEMS ESPECIALLY DIFFERENT.
I'M SURE THAT'S 'CAUSE...
OH, YOU'RE DOING THE PLAY TODAY, TAKASAKI-SAN? I'M LOOKING FORWARD TO IT!
THANK YOU!
I'LL DO MY BEST!
...
SORRY FOR...
SAYING ALL THAT WEIRD STUFF.

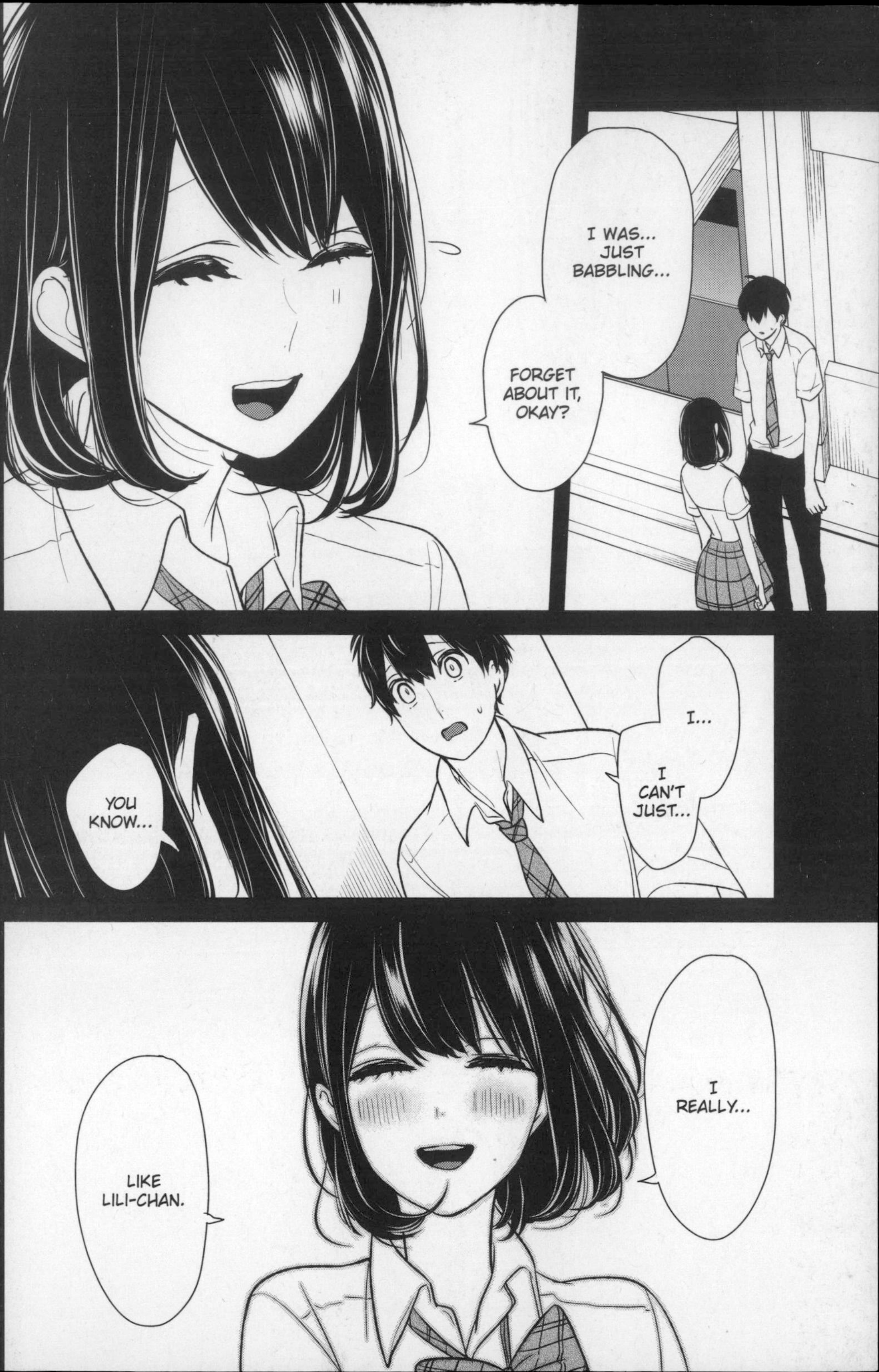
I WAS... JUST BABBLING...
FORGET ABOUT IT, OKAY?
I...
I CAN'T JUST...
YOU KNOW...
I REALLY...
LIKE LILI-CHAN.

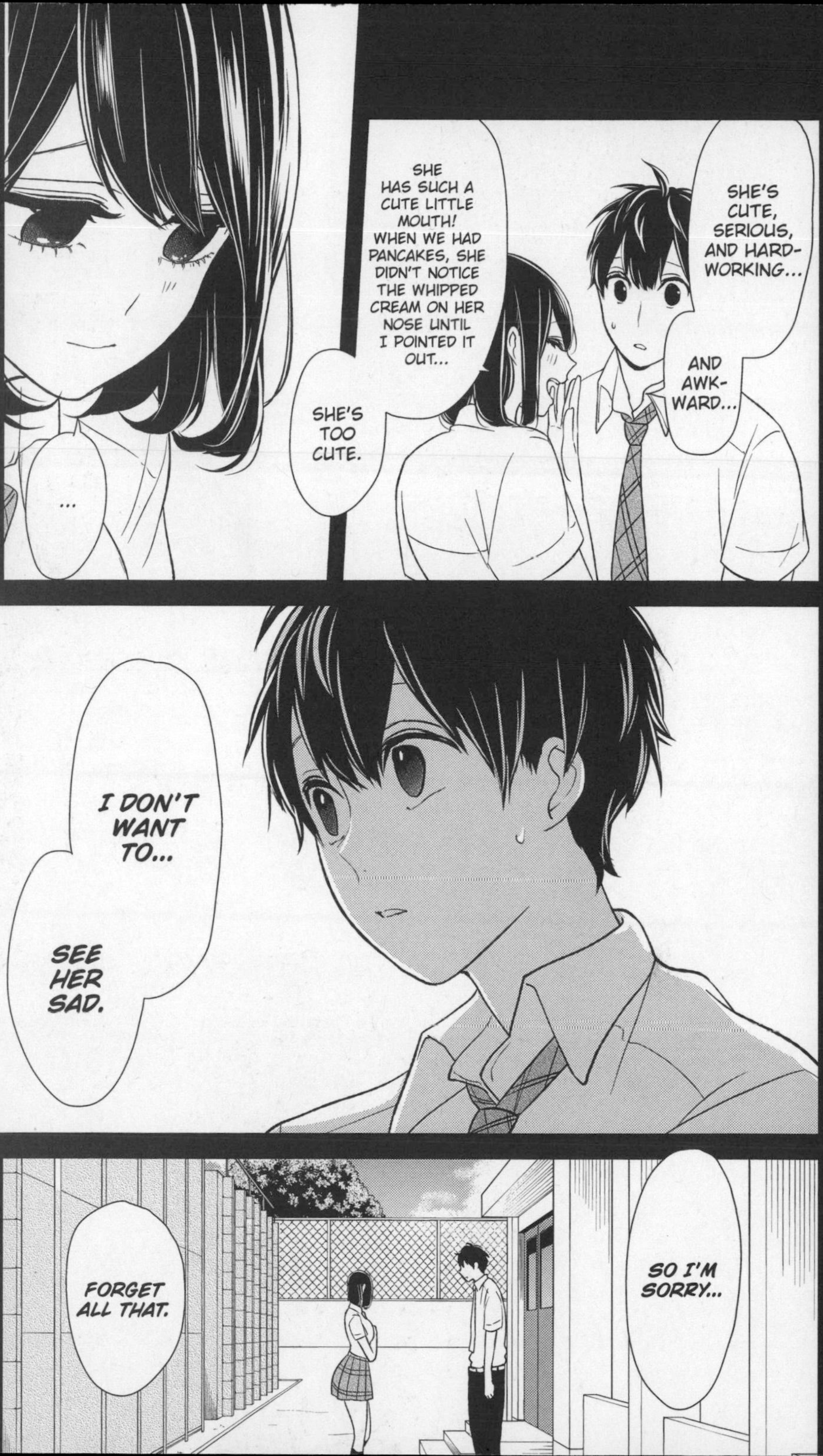
SHE'S CUTE, SERIOUS, AND HARD-WORKING...
AND AWKWARD...
SHE HAS SUCH A CUTE LITTLE MOUTH! WHEN WE HAD PANCAKES, SHE DIDN'T NOTICE THE WHIPPED CREAM ON HER NOSE UNTIL I POINTED IT OUT...
SHE'S TOO CUTE.
...
I DON'T WANT TO...
SEE HER SAD.
SO I'M SORRY...
FORGET ALL THAT.

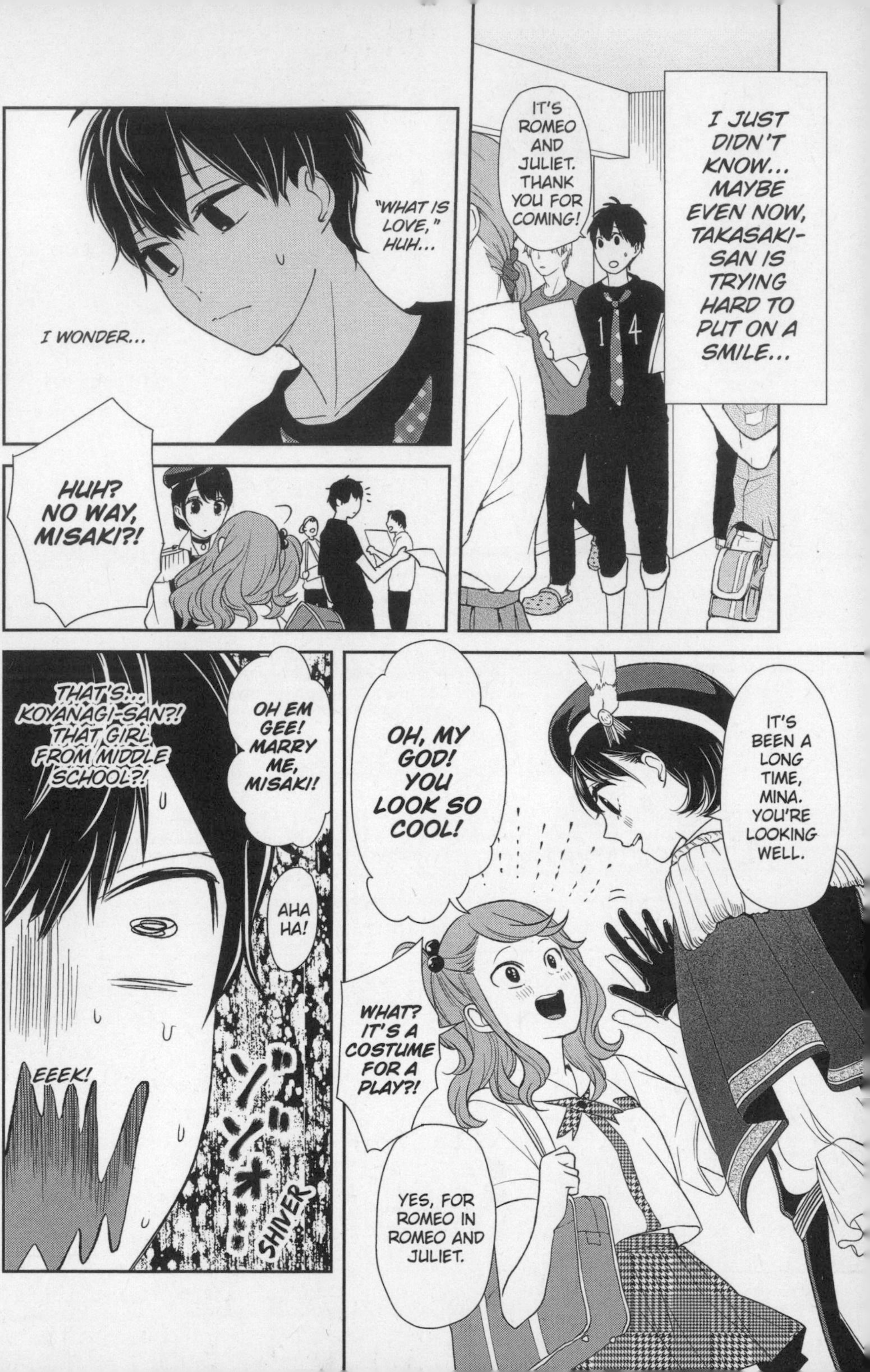
I JUST DIDN'T KNOW... MAYBE EVEN NOW, TAKASAKI-SAN IS TRYING HARD TO PUT ON A SMILE...
IT'S ROMEO AND JULIET. THANK YOU FOR COMING!
"WHAT IS LOVE," HUH...
I WONDER...
HUH? NO WAY, MISAKI?!
IT'S BEEN A LONG TIME, MINA. YOU'RE LOOKING WELL.
OH, MY GOD! YOU LOOK SO COOL!
WHAT? IT'S A COSTUME FOR A PLAY?!
YES, FOR ROMEO IN ROMEO AND JULIET.
OH EM GEE! MARRY ME, MISAKI!
THAT'S... KOYANAGI-SAN?! THAT GIRL FROM MIDDLE SCHOOL?!
AHA HA!
EEEK!
SHIVER

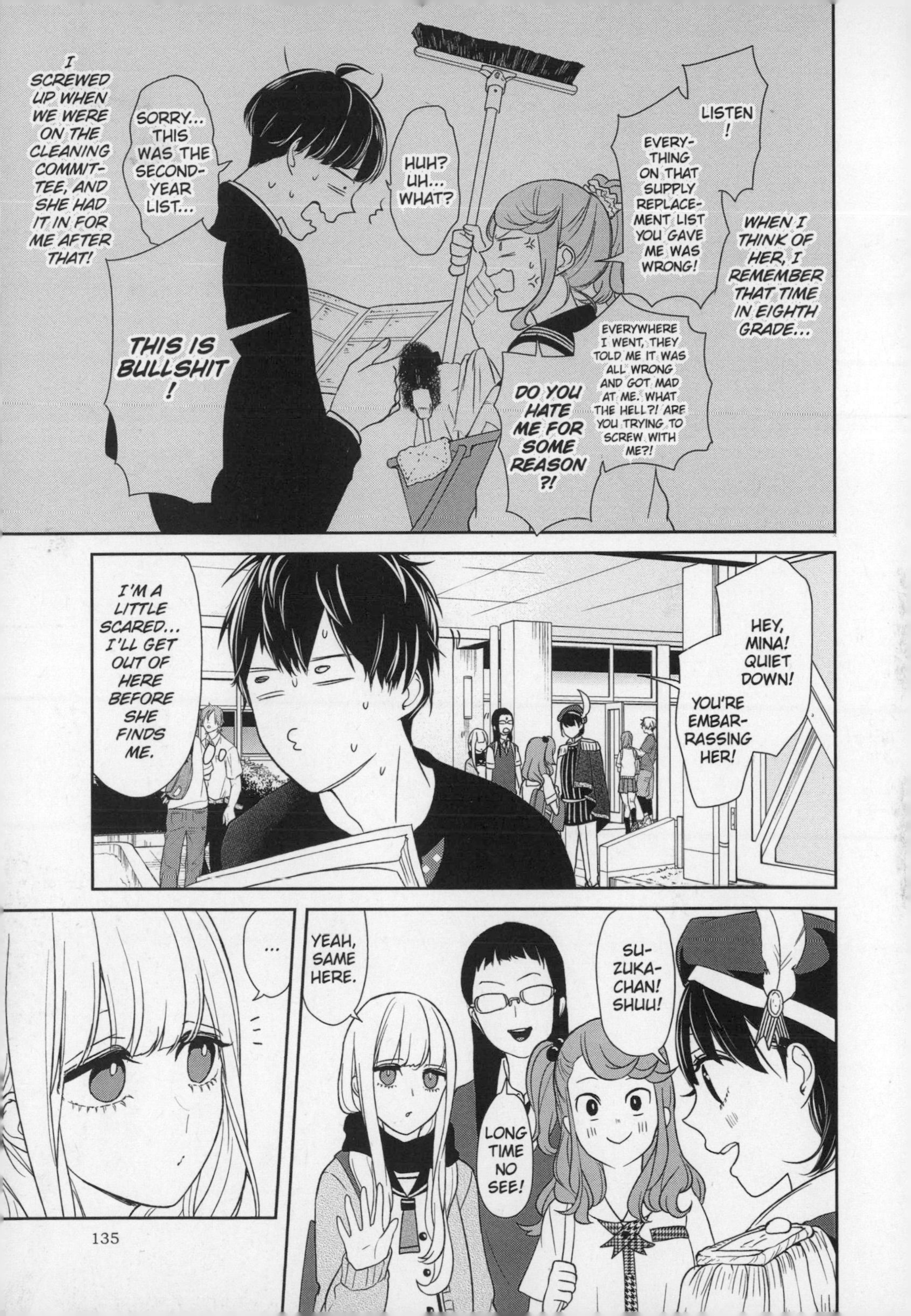
WHEN I THINK OF HER, I REMEMBER THAT TIME IN EIGHTH GRADE...
LISTEN!
EVERYTHING ON THAT SUPPLY REPLACEMENT LIST YOU GAVE ME WAS WRONG!
HUH? UH... WHAT?
SORRY... THIS WAS THE SECOND-YEAR LIST...
I SCREWED UP WHEN WE WERE ON THE CLEANING COMMITTEE, AND SHE HAD IT IN FOR ME AFTER THAT!
EVERYWHERE I WENT, THEY TOLD ME IT WAS ALL WRONG AND GOT MAD AT ME. WHAT THE HELL?! ARE YOU TRYING TO SCREW WITH ME?!
DO YOU HATE ME FOR SOME REASON?!
THIS IS BULLSHIT!
HEY, MINA! QUIET DOWN!
YOU'RE EMBARRASSING HER!
I'M A LITTLE SCARED... I'LL GET OUT OF HERE BEFORE SHE FINDS ME.
SUZUKA-CHAN! SHUU!
LONG TIME NO SEE!
YEAH, SAME HERE.
...

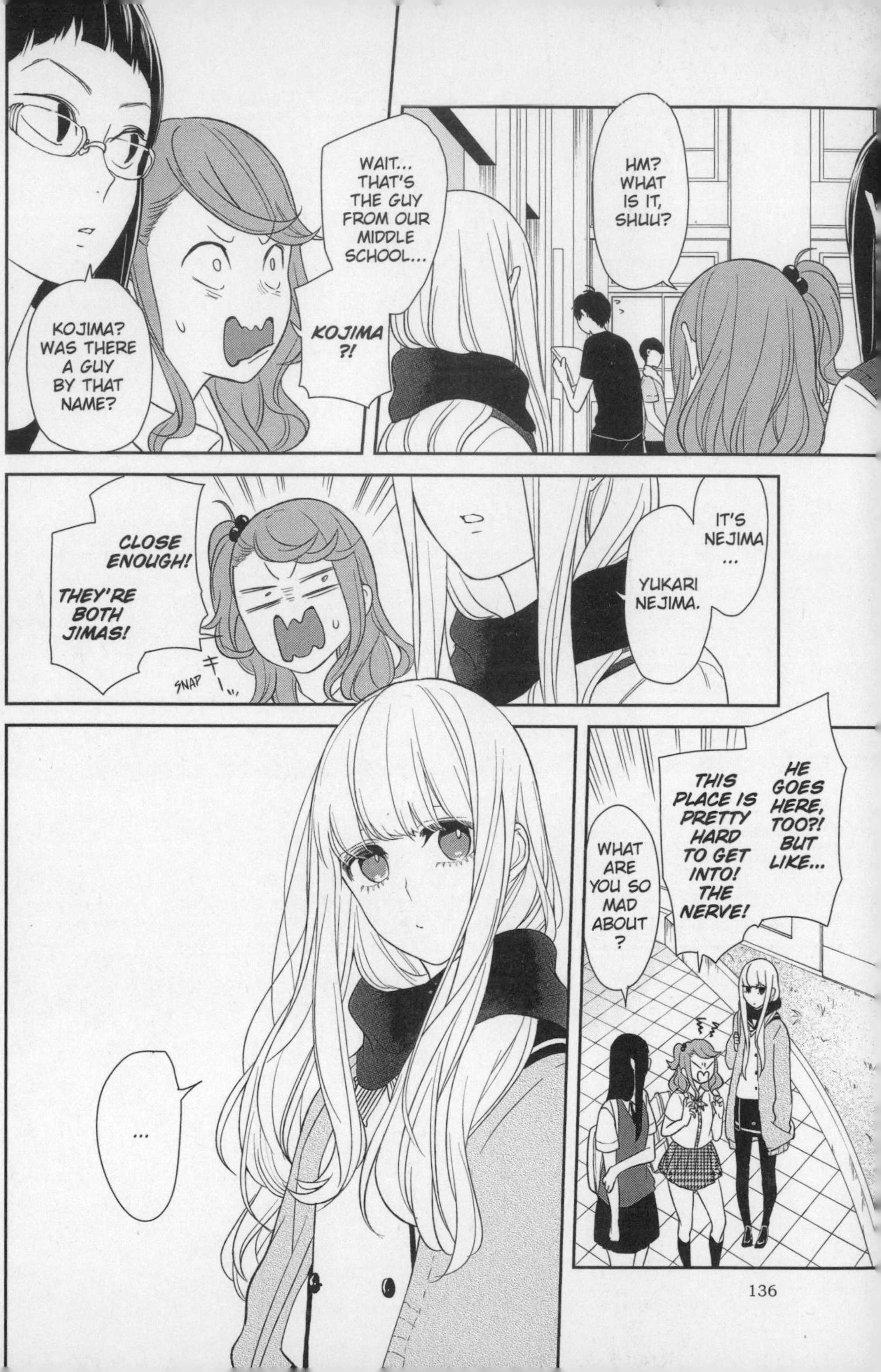
HM? WHAT IS IT, SHUU?
WAIT... THAT'S THE GUY FROM OUR MIDDLE SCHOOL...
KOJIMA ?!
KOJIMA? WAS THERE A GUY BY THAT NAME?
IT'S NEJIMA ...
YUKARI NEJIMA.
CLOSE ENOUGH!
THEY'RE BOTH JIMAS!
SNAP
HE GOES HERE, TOO?! BUT LIKE...
THIS PLACE IS PRETTY HARD TO GET INTO! THE NERVE!
WHAT ARE YOU SO MAD ABOUT ?
...

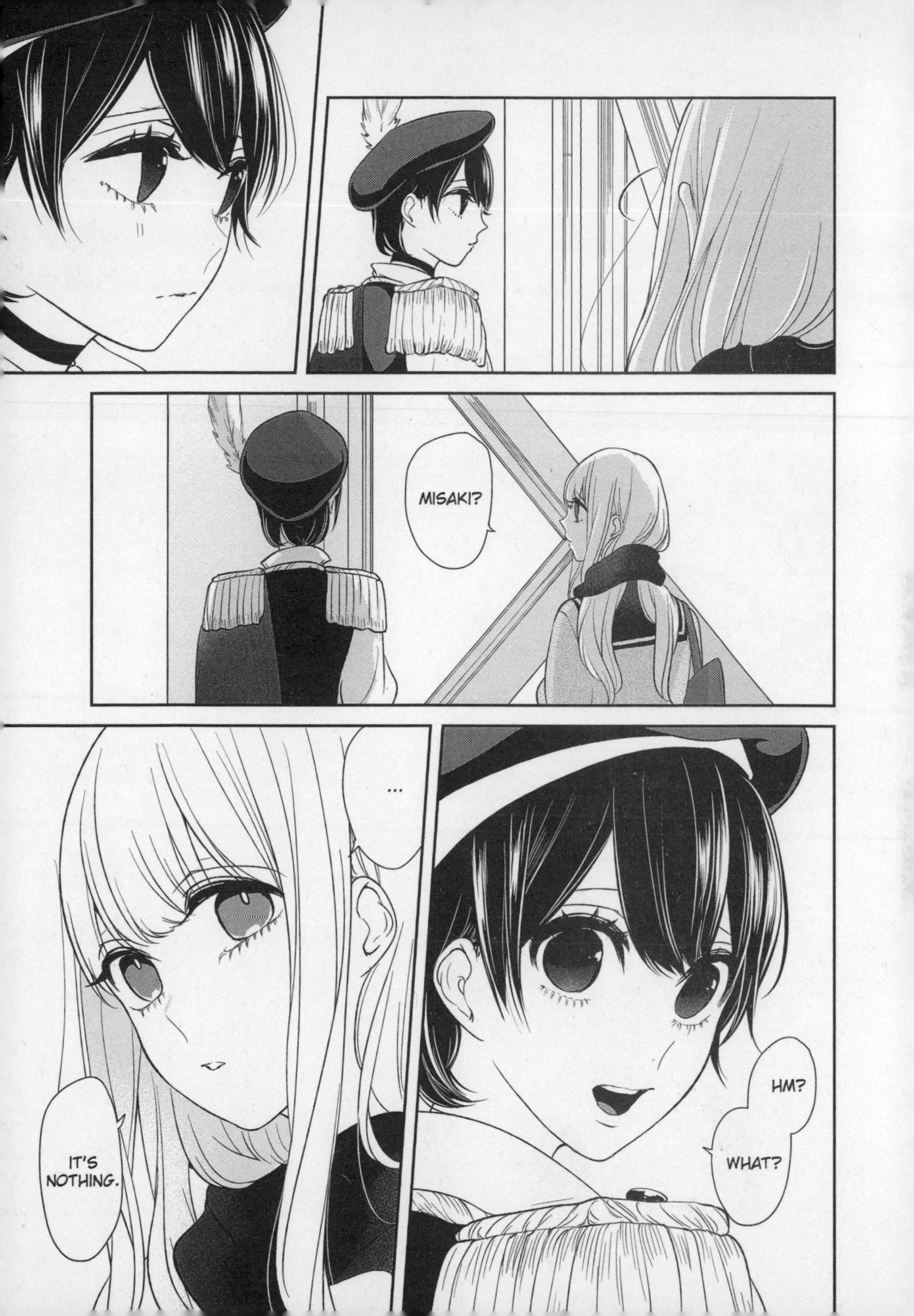
MISAKI?
HM?
WHAT?
...
IT'S NOTHING.

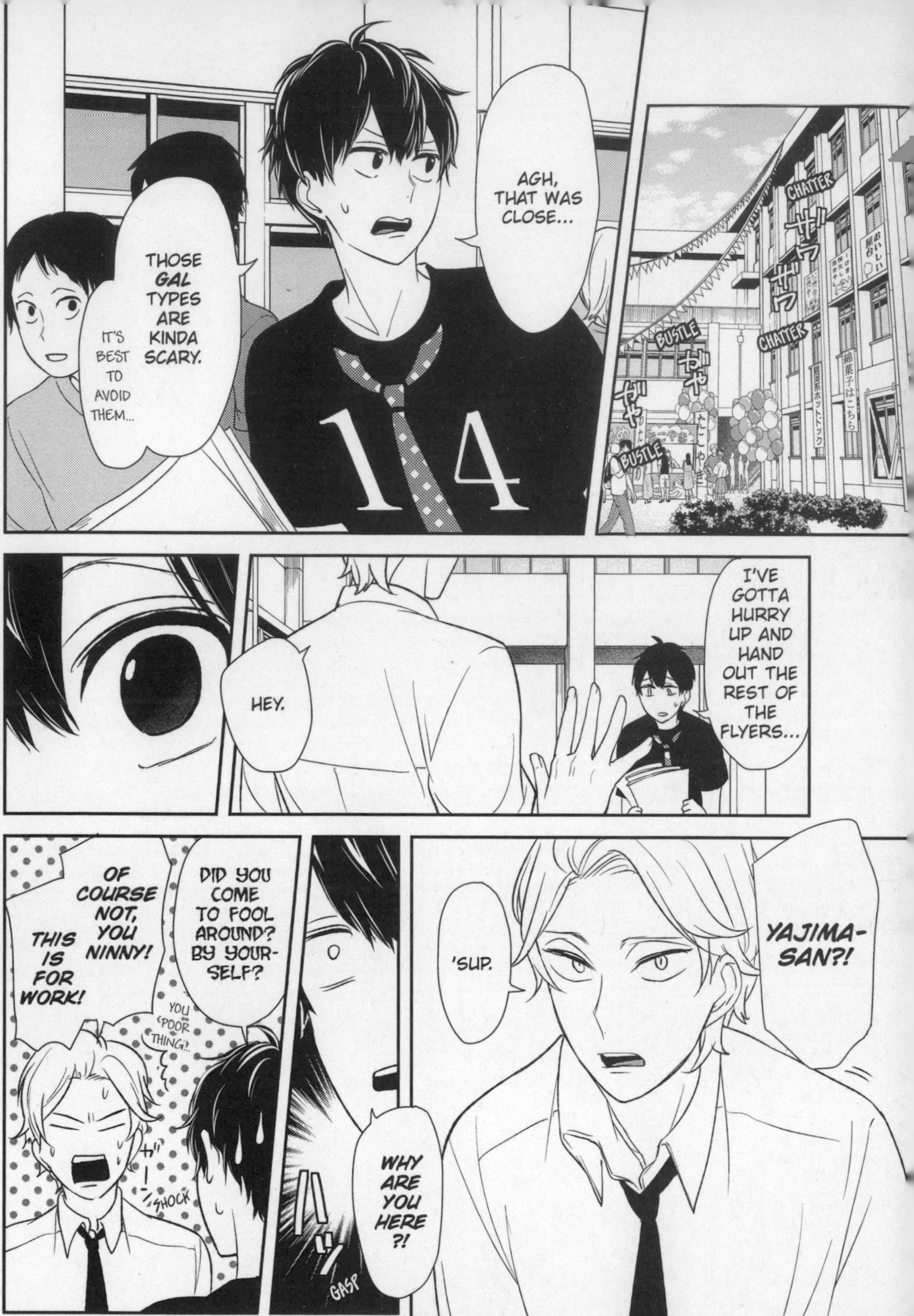
CHATTER
ザワ
ザワ
CHATTER
BUSTLE
ガヤ
ガヤ
BUSTLE
たこやき
AGH, THAT WAS CLOSE...
THOSE GAL TYPES ARE KINDA SCARY.
IT'S BEST TO AVOID THEM...
I'VE GOTTA HURRY UP AND HAND OUT THE REST OF THE FLYERS...
HEY.
YAJIMA-SAN?!
'SUP.
WHY ARE YOU HERE?!
GASP
DID YOU COME TO FOOL AROUND? BY YOURSELF?
YOU POOR THING...
OF COURSE NOT, YOU NINNY! THIS IS FOR WORK!
SHOCK

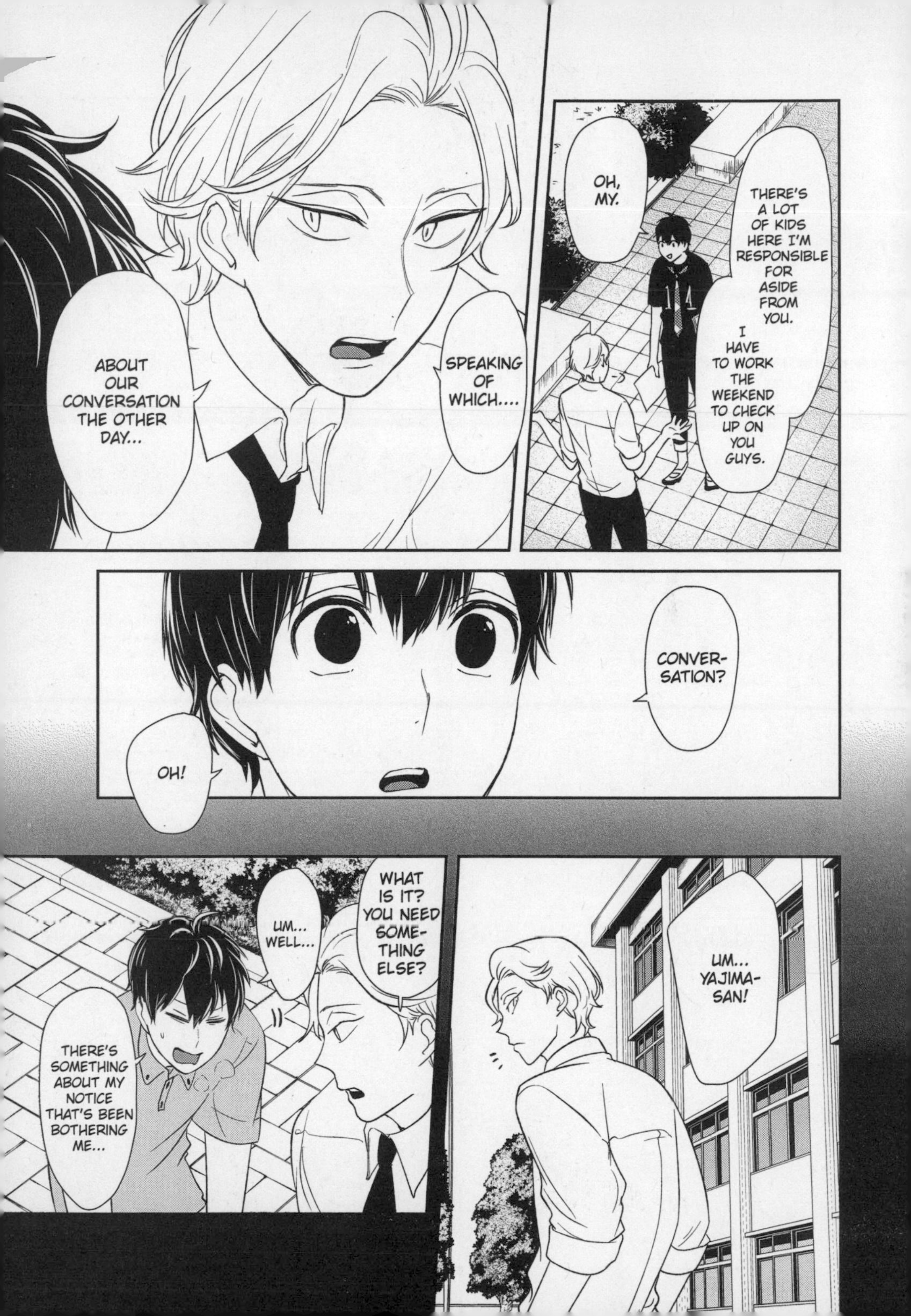
THERE'S A LOT OF KIDS HERE I'M RESPONSIBLE FOR ASIDE FROM YOU.
I HAVE TO WORK THE WEEKEND TO CHECK UP ON YOU GUYS.
OH, MY.
SPEAKING OF WHICH....
ABOUT OUR CONVERSATION THE OTHER DAY...
CONVER-SATION?
OH!
UM... YAJIMA-SAN!
WHAT IS IT? YOU NEED SOME-THING ELSE?
UM... WELL...
THERE'S SOMETHING ABOUT MY NOTICE THAT'S BEEN BOTHERING ME...

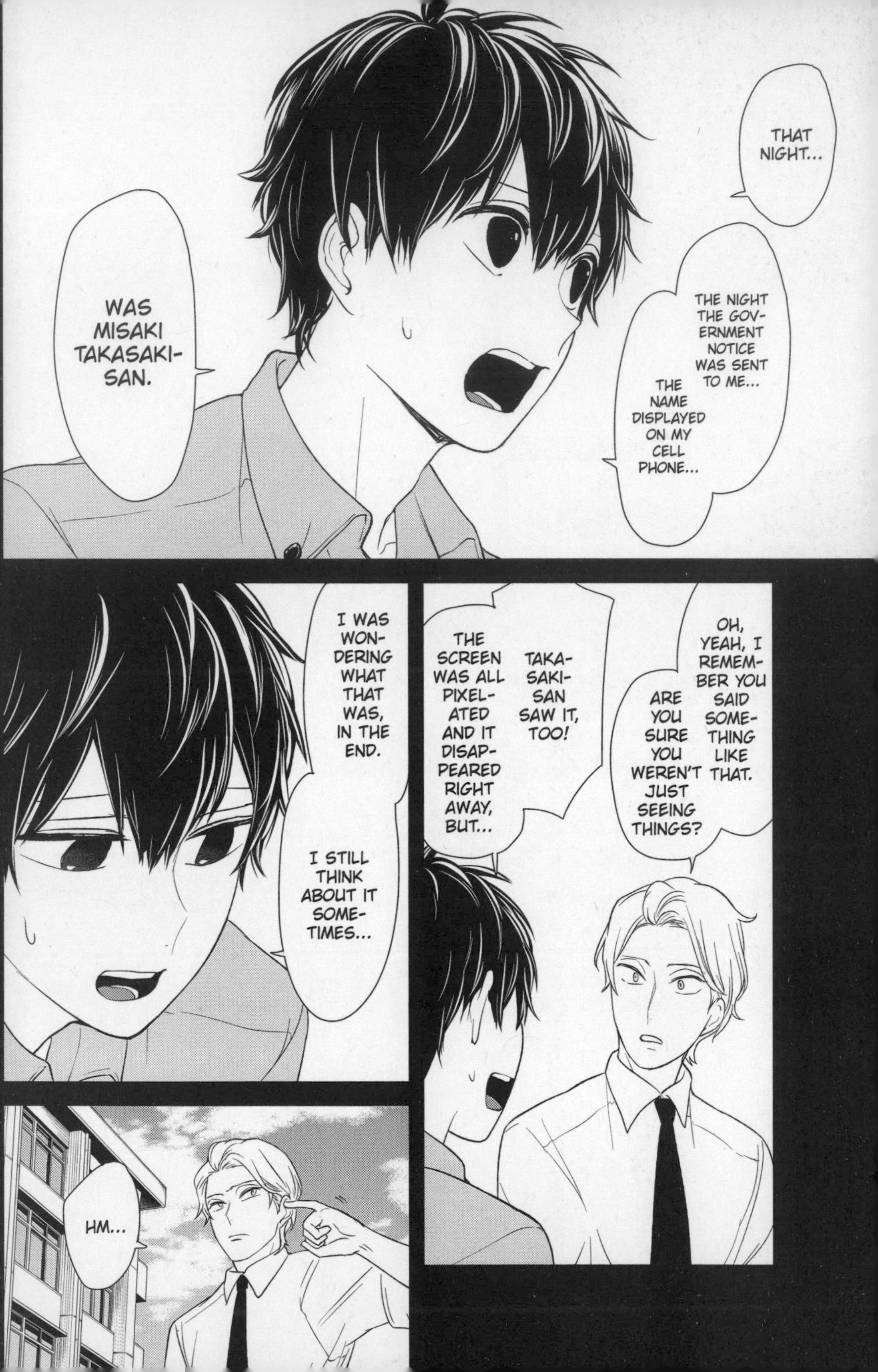
THAT NIGHT...
THE NIGHT THE GOVERNMENT NOTICE WAS SENT TO ME...
THE NAME DISPLAYED ON MY CELL PHONE...
WAS MISAKI TAKASAKI-SAN.
OH, YEAH, I REMEMBER YOU SAID SOMETHING LIKE THAT.
ARE YOU SURE YOU WEREN'T JUST SEEING THINGS?
TAKASAKI-SAN SAW IT, TOO!
THE SCREEN WAS ALL PIXELATED AND IT DISAPPEARED RIGHT AWAY, BUT...
I WAS WONDERING WHAT THAT WAS, IN THE END.
I STILL THINK ABOUT IT SOMETIMES...
HM...

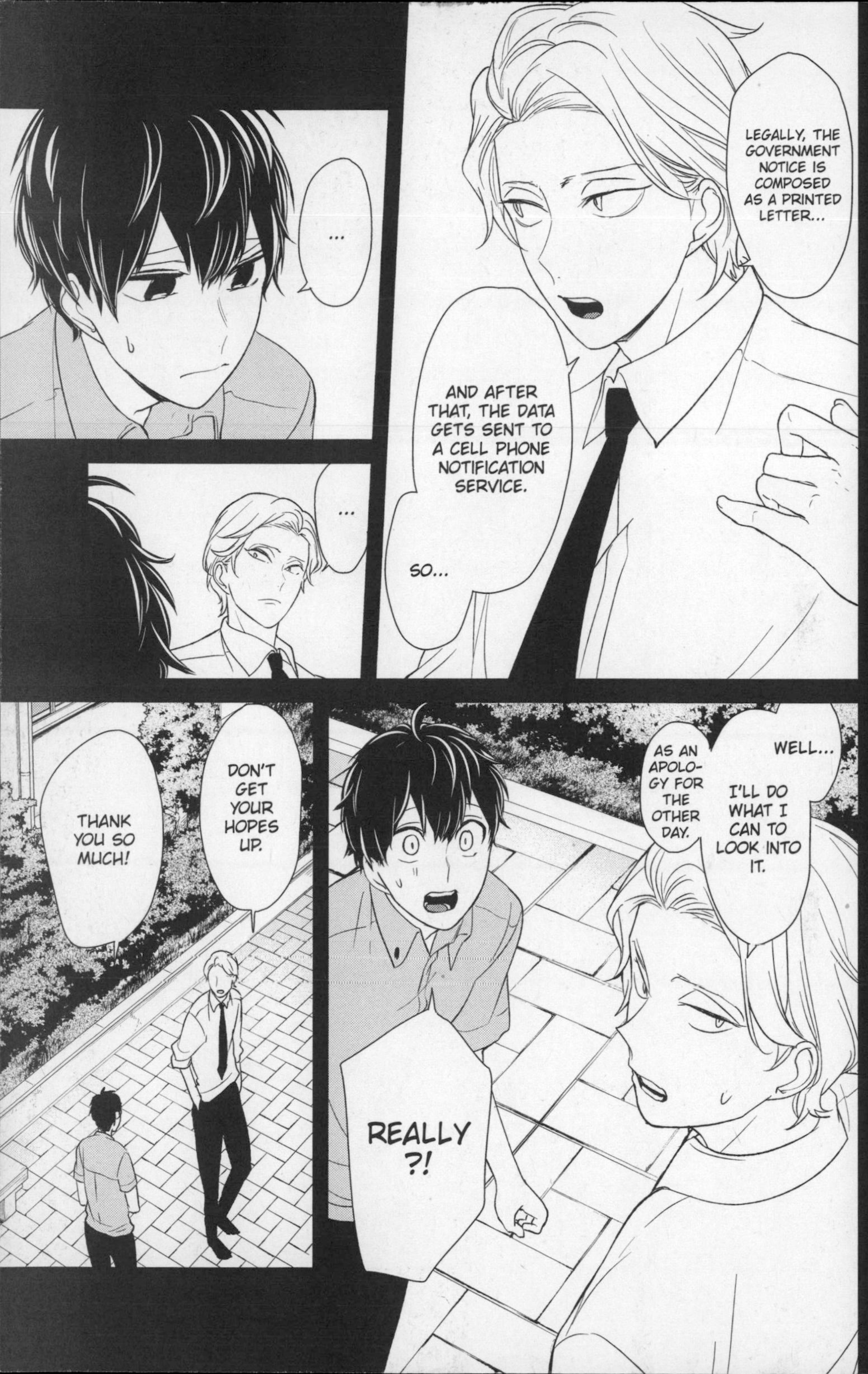
LEGALLY, THE GOVERNMENT NOTICE IS COMPOSED AS A PRINTED LETTER...
AND AFTER THAT, THE DATA GETS SENT TO A CELL PHONE NOTIFICATION SERVICE.
SO...
...
...
WELL...
I'LL DO WHAT I CAN TO LOOK INTO IT.
AS AN APOLOGY FOR THE OTHER DAY.
REALLY ?!
DON'T GET YOUR HOPES UP.
THANK YOU SO MUCH!

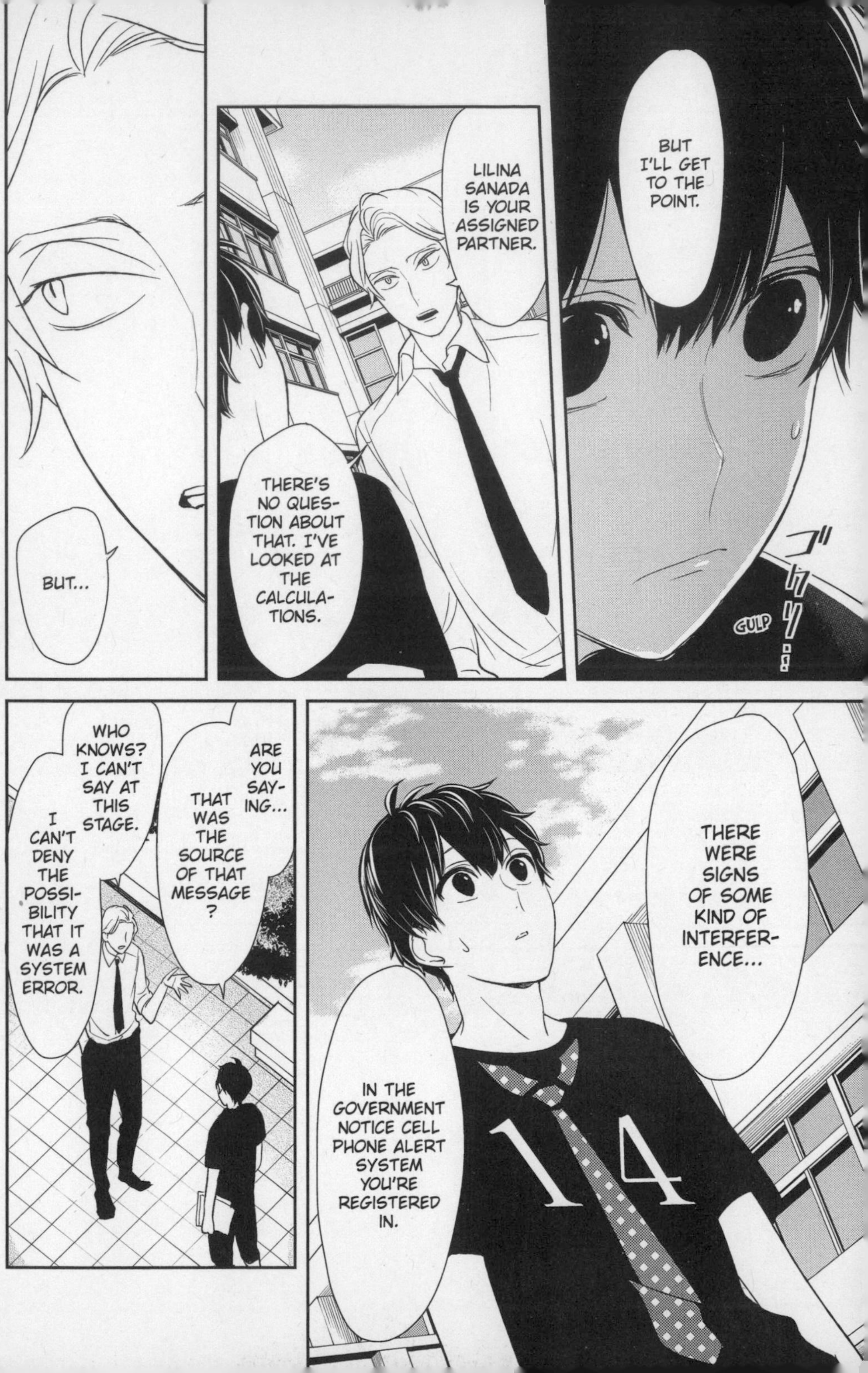
BUT I'LL GET TO THE POINT.
GULP
LILINA SANADA IS YOUR ASSIGNED PARTNER.
THERE'S NO QUESTION ABOUT THAT. I'VE LOOKED AT THE CALCULATIONS.
BUT...
THERE WERE SIGNS OF SOME KIND OF INTERFERENCE...
IN THE GOVERNMENT NOTICE CELL PHONE ALERT SYSTEM YOU'RE REGISTERED IN.
ARE YOU SAYING... THAT WAS THE SOURCE OF THAT MESSAGE?
WHO KNOWS? I CAN'T SAY AT THIS STAGE.
I CAN'T DENY THE POSSIBILITY THAT IT WAS A SYSTEM ERROR.

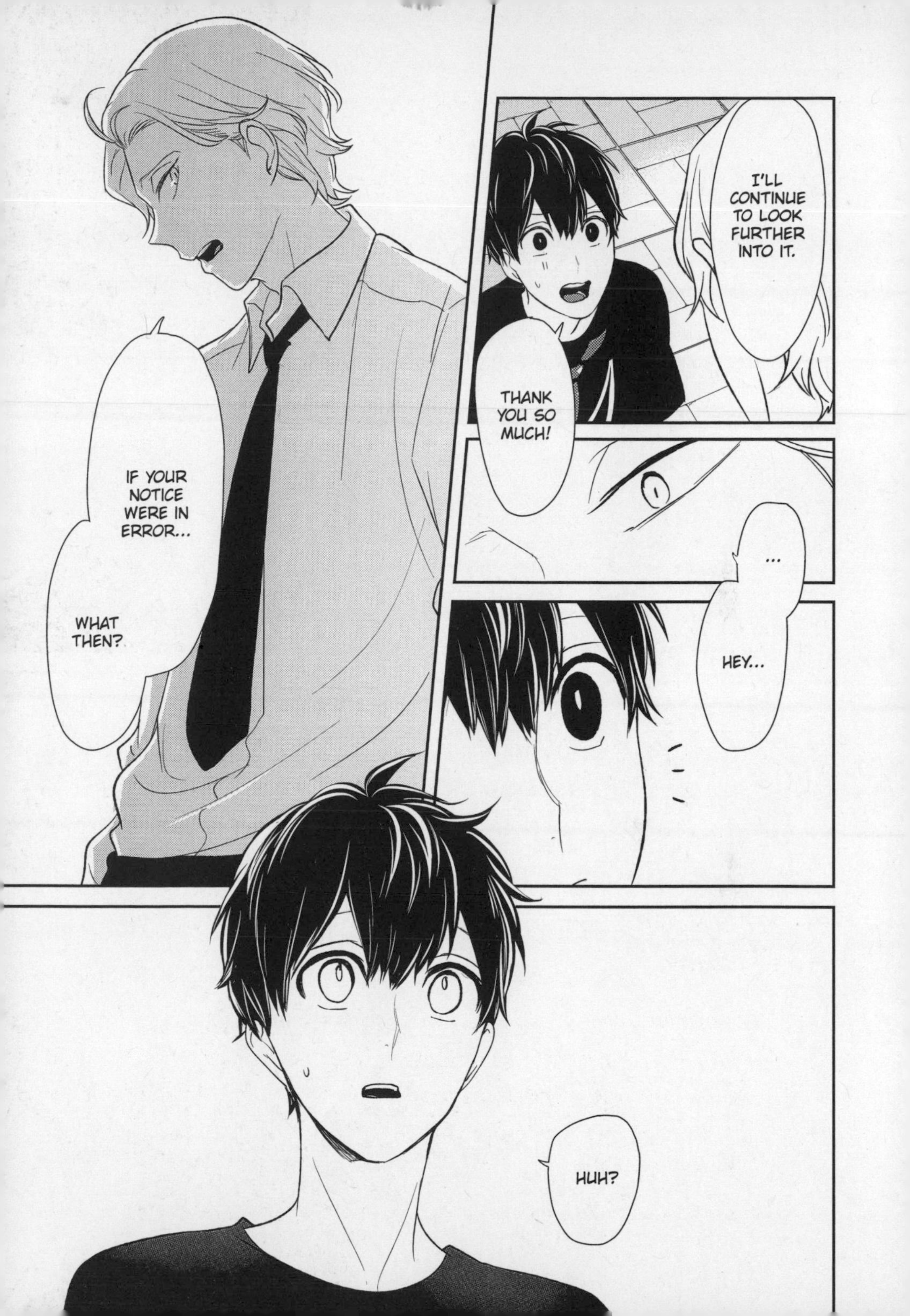
I'LL CONTINUE TO LOOK FURTHER INTO IT.
THANK YOU SO MUCH!
...
HEY...
IF YOUR NOTICE WERE IN ERROR...
WHAT THEN?
HUH?

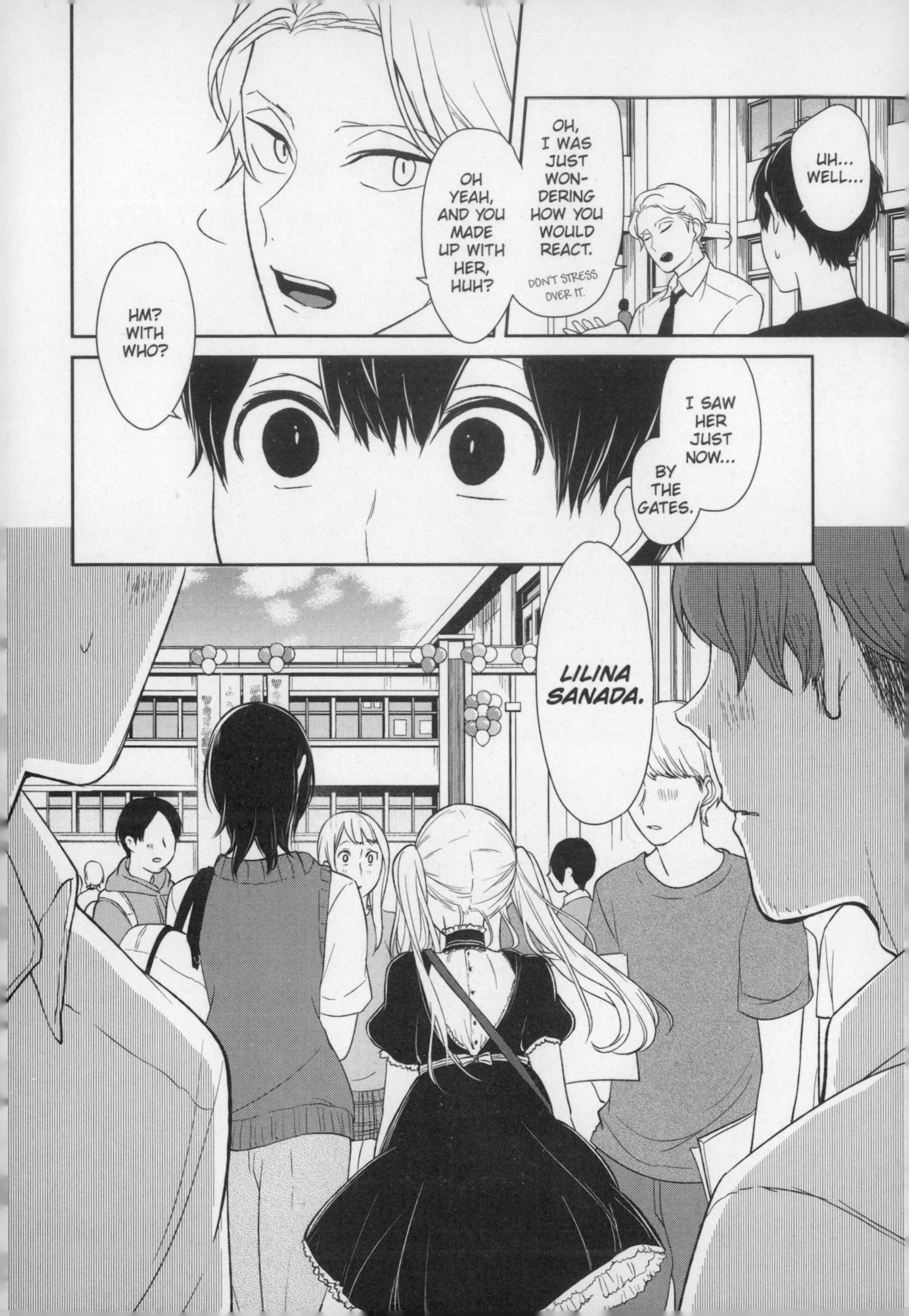
UH... WELL...
OH, I WAS JUST WONDERING HOW YOU WOULD REACT.
DON'T STRESS OVER IT.
OH YEAH, AND YOU MADE UP WITH HER, HUH?
HM? WITH WHO?
I SAW HER JUST NOW...
BY THE GATES.
LILINA SANADA.

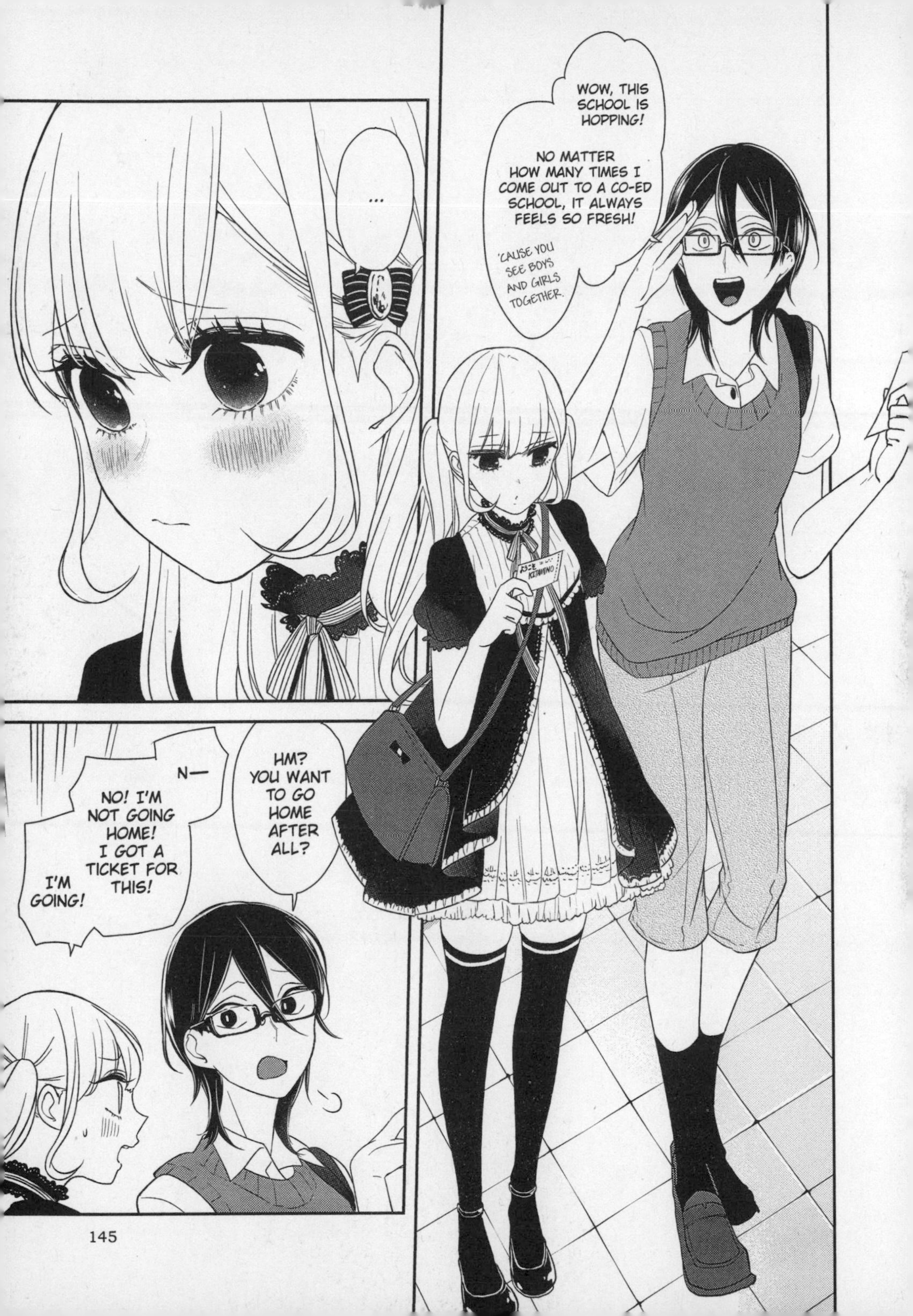
WOW, THIS SCHOOL IS HOPPING!
NO MATTER HOW MANY TIMES I COME OUT TO A CO-ED SCHOOL, IT ALWAYS FEELS SO FRESH!
'CAUSE YOU SEE BOYS AND GIRLS TOGETHER.
...
HM? YOU WANT TO GO HOME AFTER ALL?
N—
NO! I'M NOT GOING HOME! I GOT A TICKET FOR THIS!
I'M GOING!

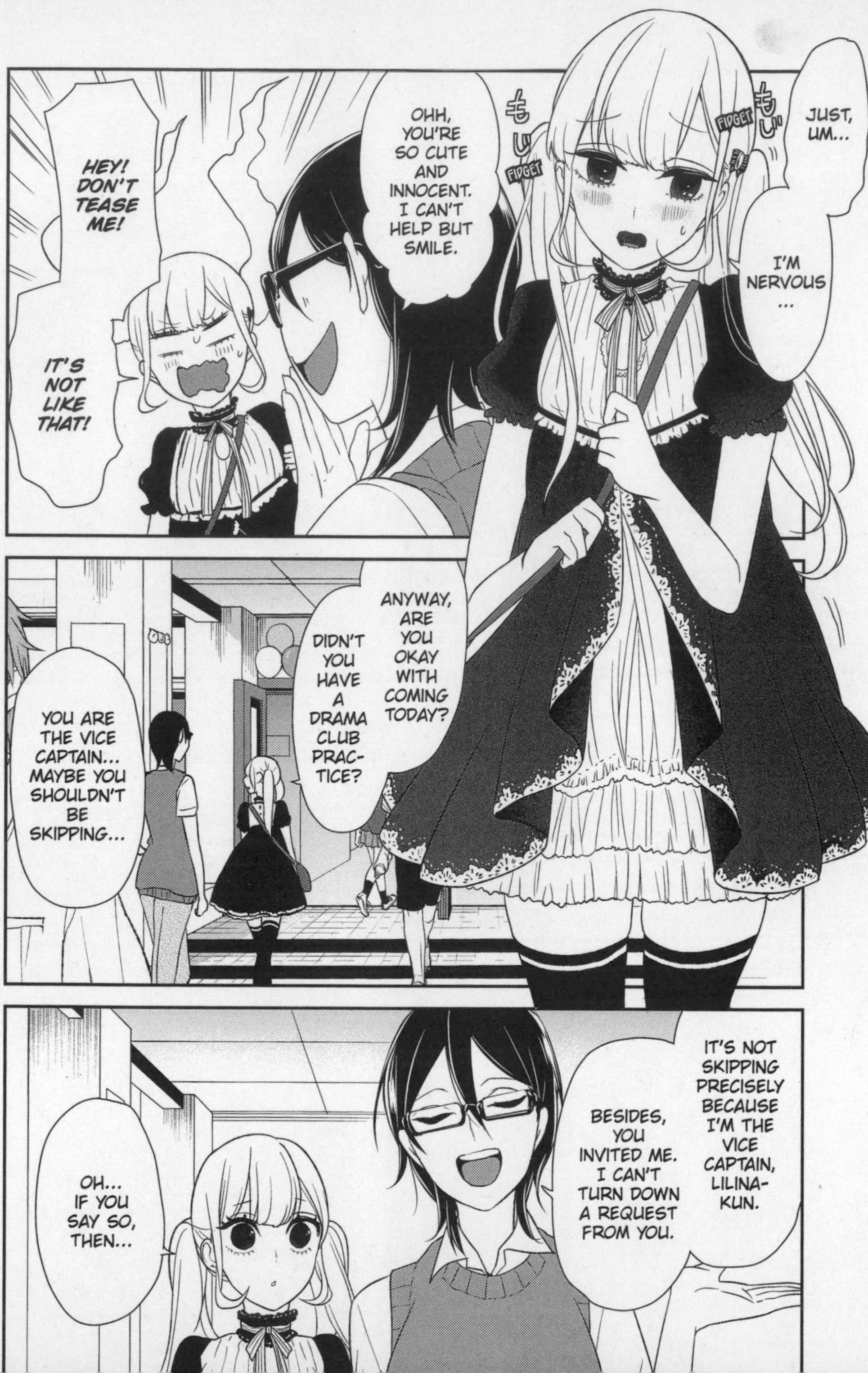
JUST, UM...
もじ
FIDGET
もじ
FIDGET
I'M NERVOUS...
OHH, YOU'RE SO CUTE AND INNOCENT. I CAN'T HELP BUT SMILE.
HEY! DON'T TEASE ME!
IT'S NOT LIKE THAT!
ANYWAY, ARE YOU OKAY WITH COMING TODAY?
DIDN'T YOU HAVE A DRAMA CLUB PRAC-TICE?
YOU ARE THE VICE CAPTAIN... MAYBE YOU SHOULDN'T BE SKIPPING...
IT'S NOT SKIPPING PRECISELY BECAUSE I'M THE VICE CAPTAIN, LILINA-KUN.
BESIDES, YOU INVITED ME. I CAN'T TURN DOWN A REQUEST FROM YOU.
OH... IF YOU SAY SO, THEN...

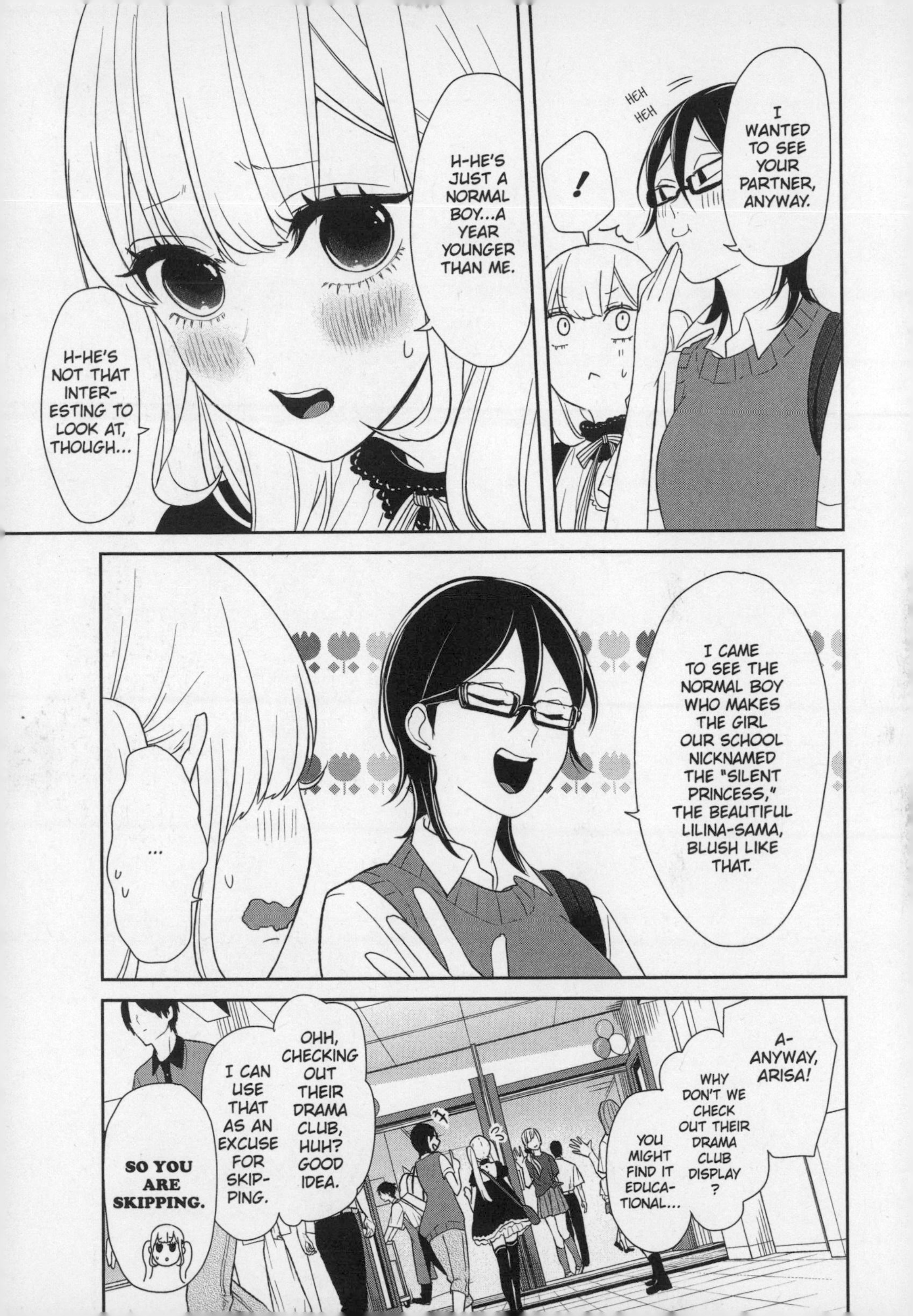
I WANTED TO SEE YOUR PARTNER, ANYWAY.
HEH HEH
!
H-HE'S JUST A NORMAL BOY...A YEAR YOUNGER THAN ME.
H-HE'S NOT THAT INTER-ESTING TO LOOK AT, THOUGH...
I CAME TO SEE THE NORMAL BOY WHO MAKES THE GIRL OUR SCHOOL NICKNAMED THE "SILENT PRINCESS," THE BEAUTIFUL LILINA-SAMA, BLUSH LIKE THAT.
...
A-ANYWAY, ARISA!
WHY DON'T WE CHECK OUT THEIR DRAMA CLUB DISPLAY?
YOU MIGHT FIND IT EDUCA-TIONAL...
OHH, CHECKING OUT THEIR DRAMA CLUB, HUH? GOOD IDEA.
I CAN USE THAT AS AN EXCUSE FOR SKIP-PING.
SO YOU ARE SKIPPING.

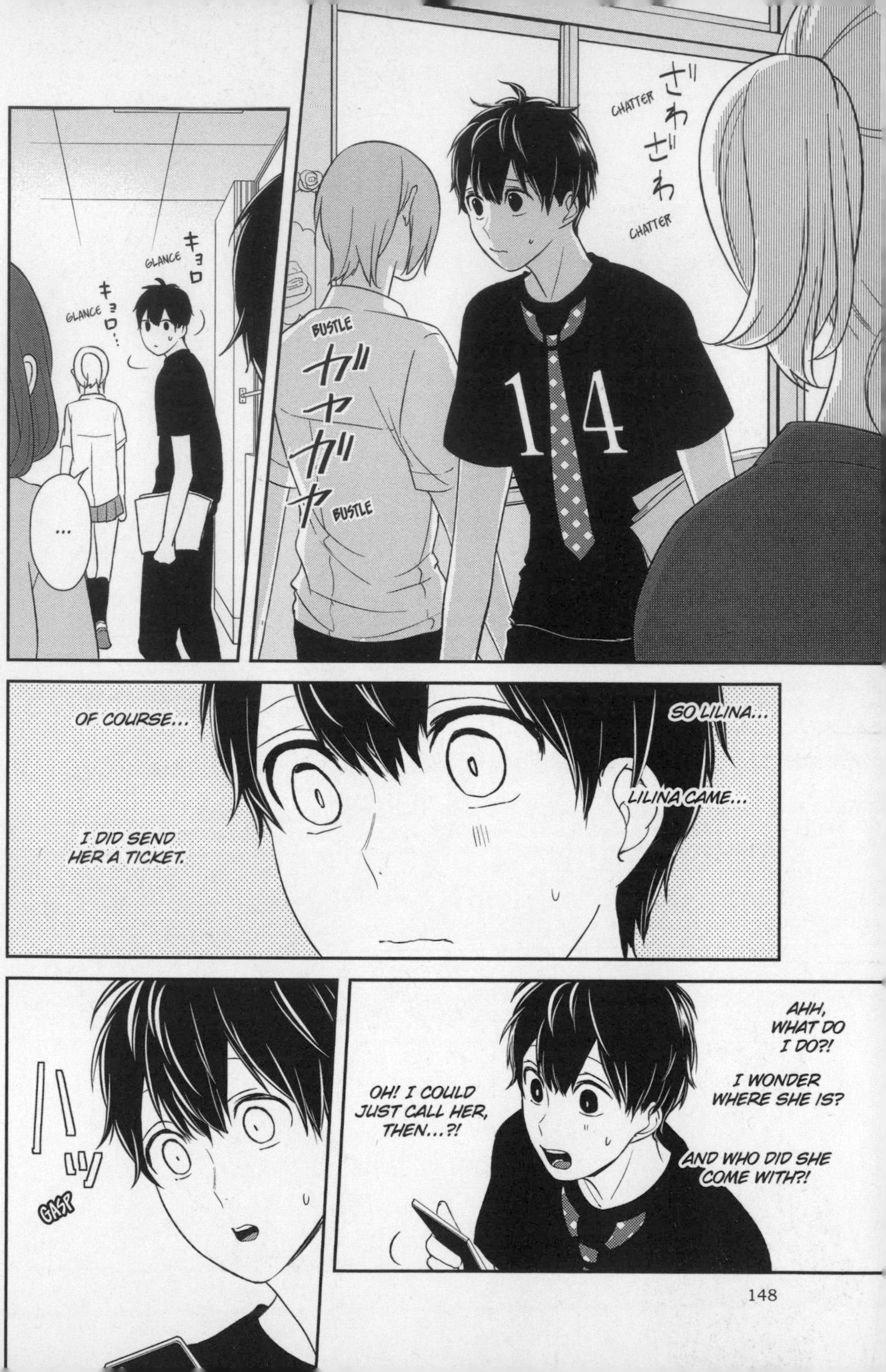

ざわざわ
CHATTER
CHATTER
ガヤガヤ
BUSTLE
BUSTLE
キョロキョロ…
GLANCE
GLANCE
…
SO LILINA…
LILINA CAME…
OF COURSE…
I DID SEND HER A TICKET.
AHH, WHAT DO I DO?!
I WONDER WHERE SHE IS?
AND WHO DID SHE COME WITH?!
OH! I COULD JUST CALL HER, THEN…?!
ハッ
GASP

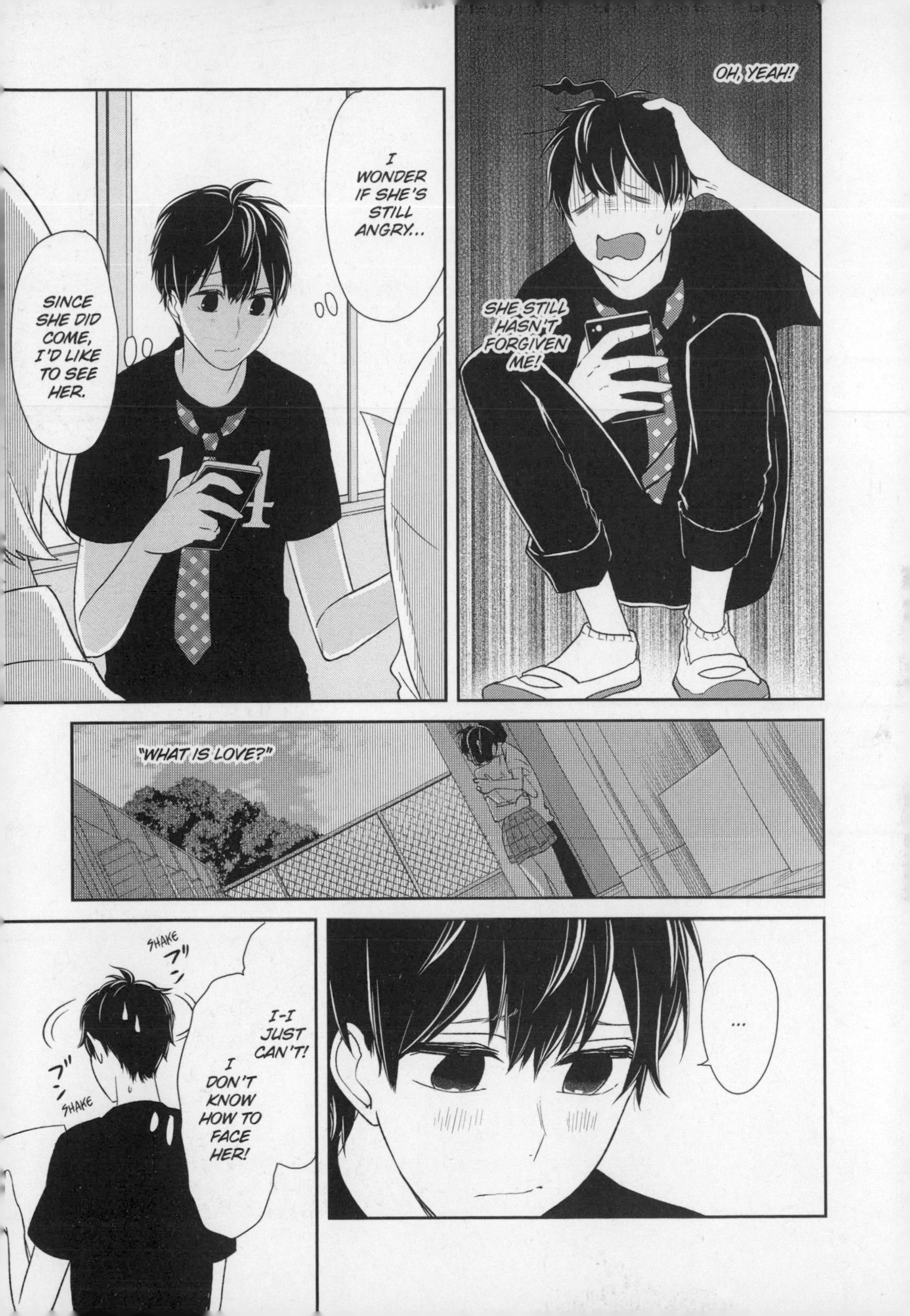
OH, YEAH!
SHE STILL HASN'T FORGIVEN ME!
I WONDER IF SHE'S STILL ANGRY...
SINCE SHE DID COME, I'D LIKE TO SEE HER.
"WHAT IS LOVE?"
...
SHAKE
I-I JUST CAN'T!
I DON'T KNOW HOW TO FACE HER!
SHAKE

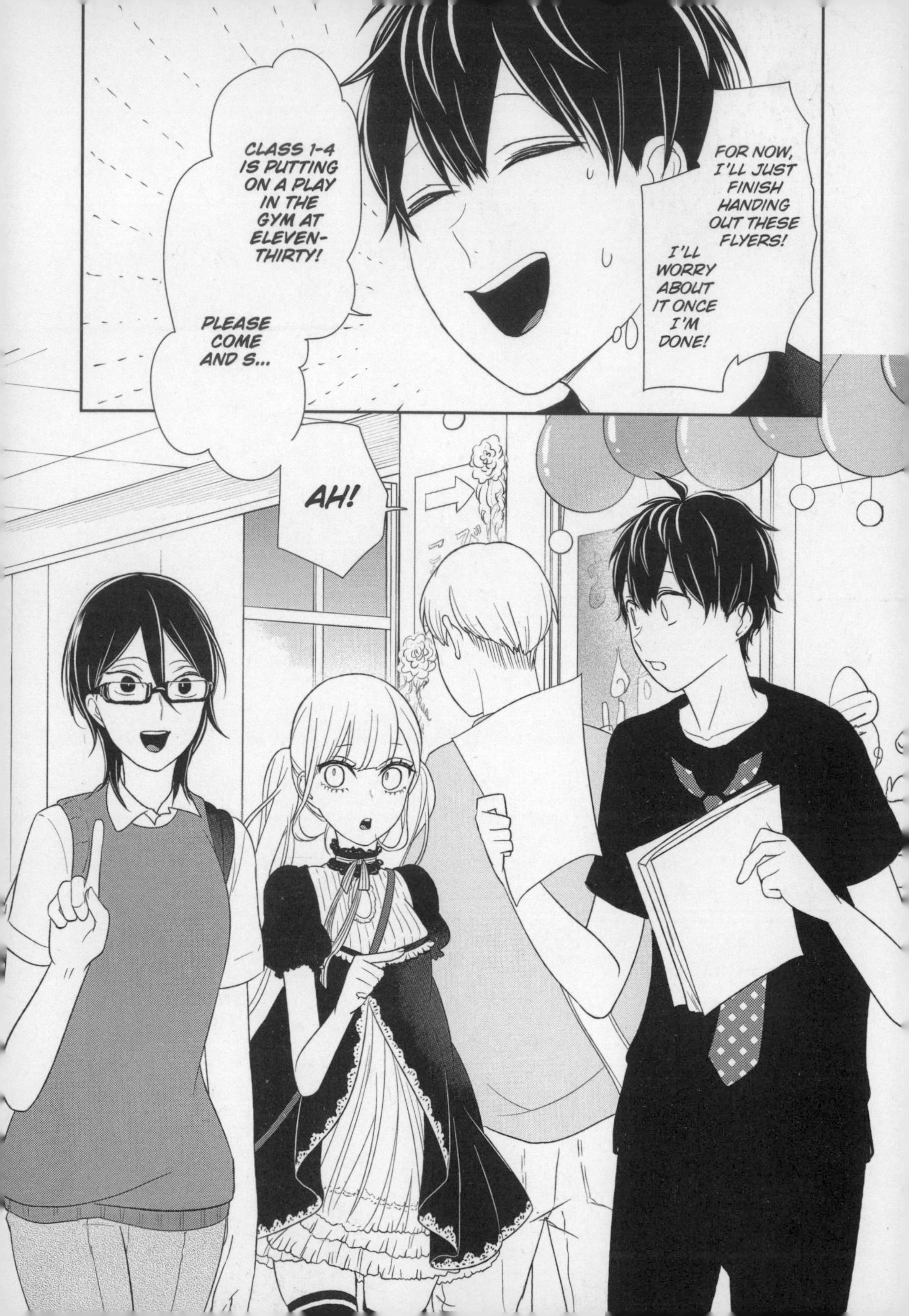
FOR NOW, I'LL JUST FINISH HANDING OUT THESE FLYERS!
I'LL WORRY ABOUT IT ONCE I'M DONE!
CLASS 1-4 IS PUTTING ON A PLAY IN THE GYM AT ELEVEN-THIRTY!
PLEASE COME AND S...
AH!

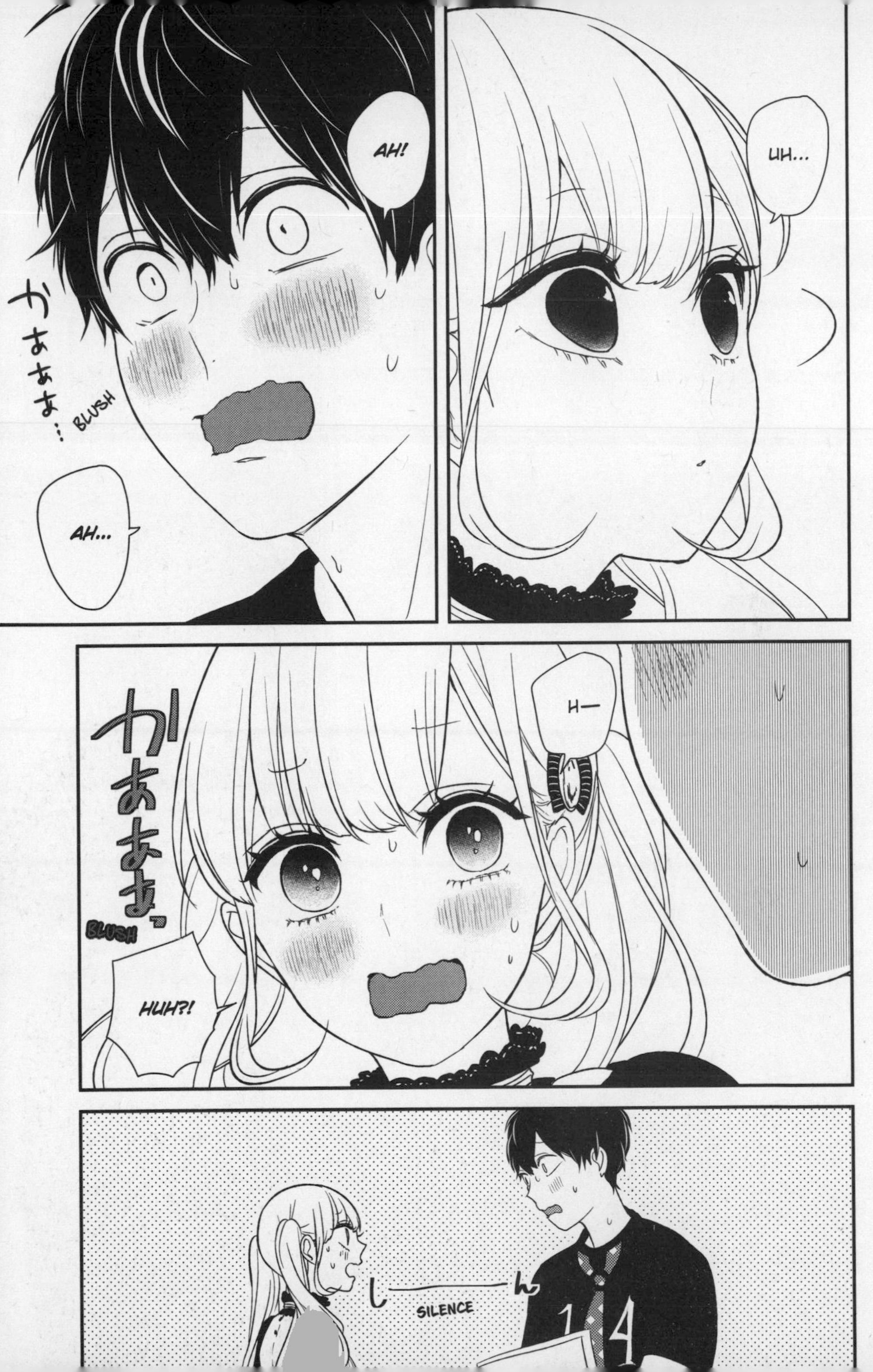
UH...
AH!
かぁぁぁ…
BLUSH
AH...
H—
わぁぁぁ
BLUSH
HUH?!
しーーん
SILENCE

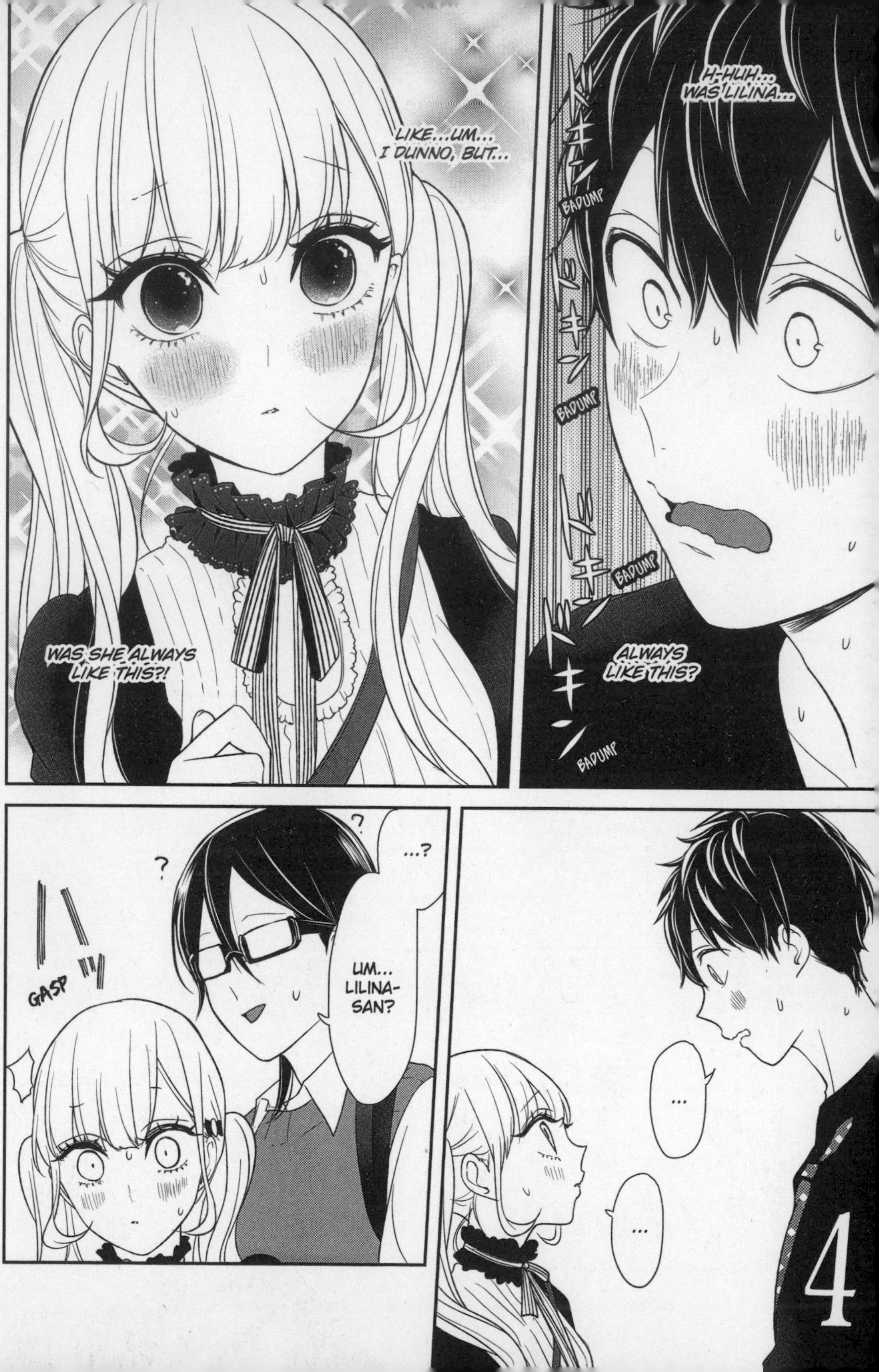
H-HUH... WAS LILINA...
BADUMP
BADUMP
BADUMP
ALWAYS LIKE THIS?
BADUMP
LIKE...UM... I DUNNO, BUT...
WAS SHE ALWAYS LIKE THIS?!
...
...
4
...?
?
?
UM... LILINA-SAN?
GASP

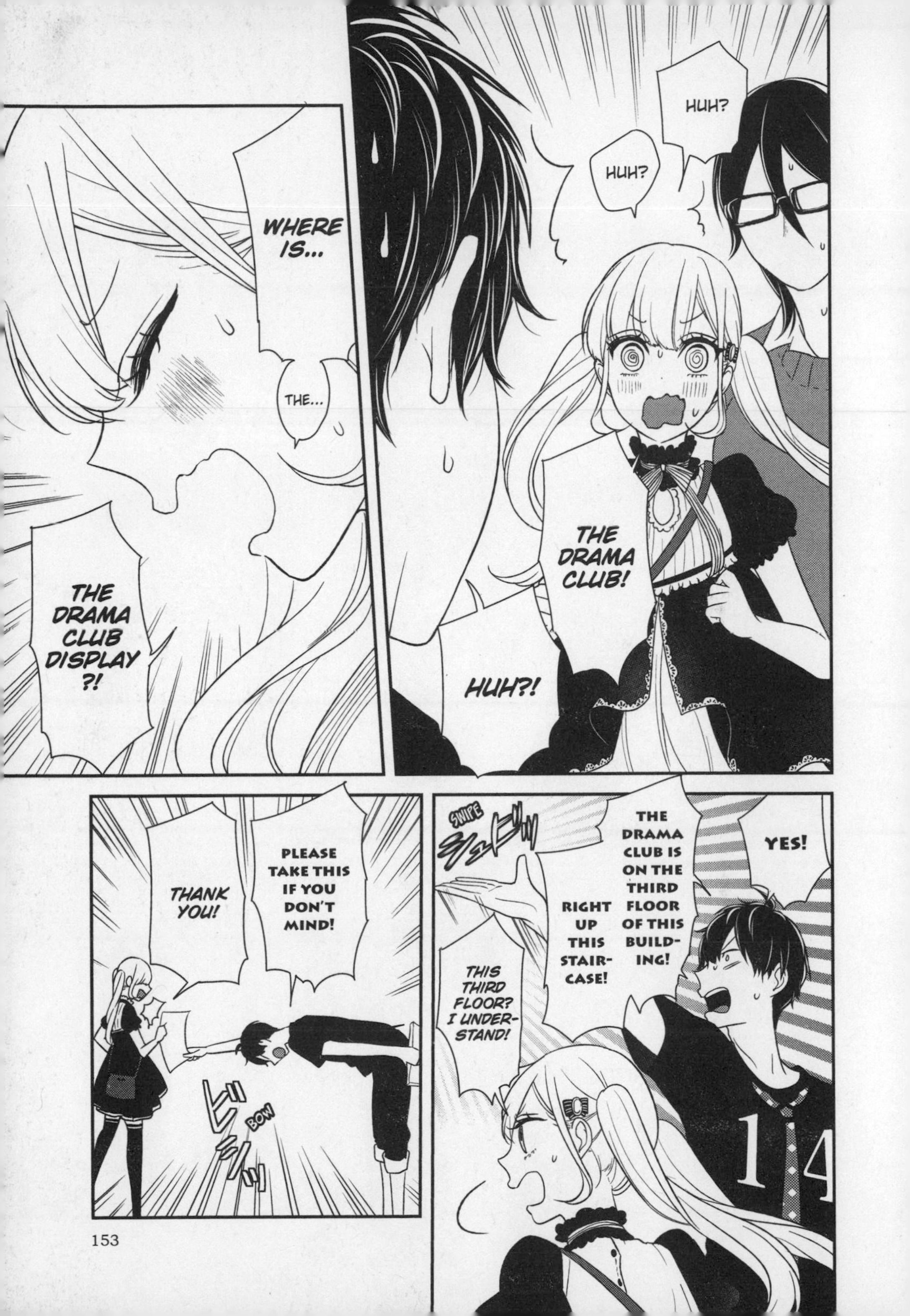
HUH?
HUH?
THE DRAMA CLUB!
HUH?!
WHERE IS...
THE...
THE DRAMA CLUB DISPLAY ?!
SWIPE
YES!
THE DRAMA CLUB IS ON THE THIRD FLOOR OF THIS BUILDING!
RIGHT UP THIS STAIRCASE!
THIS THIRD FLOOR? I UNDERSTAND!
PLEASE TAKE THIS IF YOU DON'T MIND!
THANK YOU!
BOW

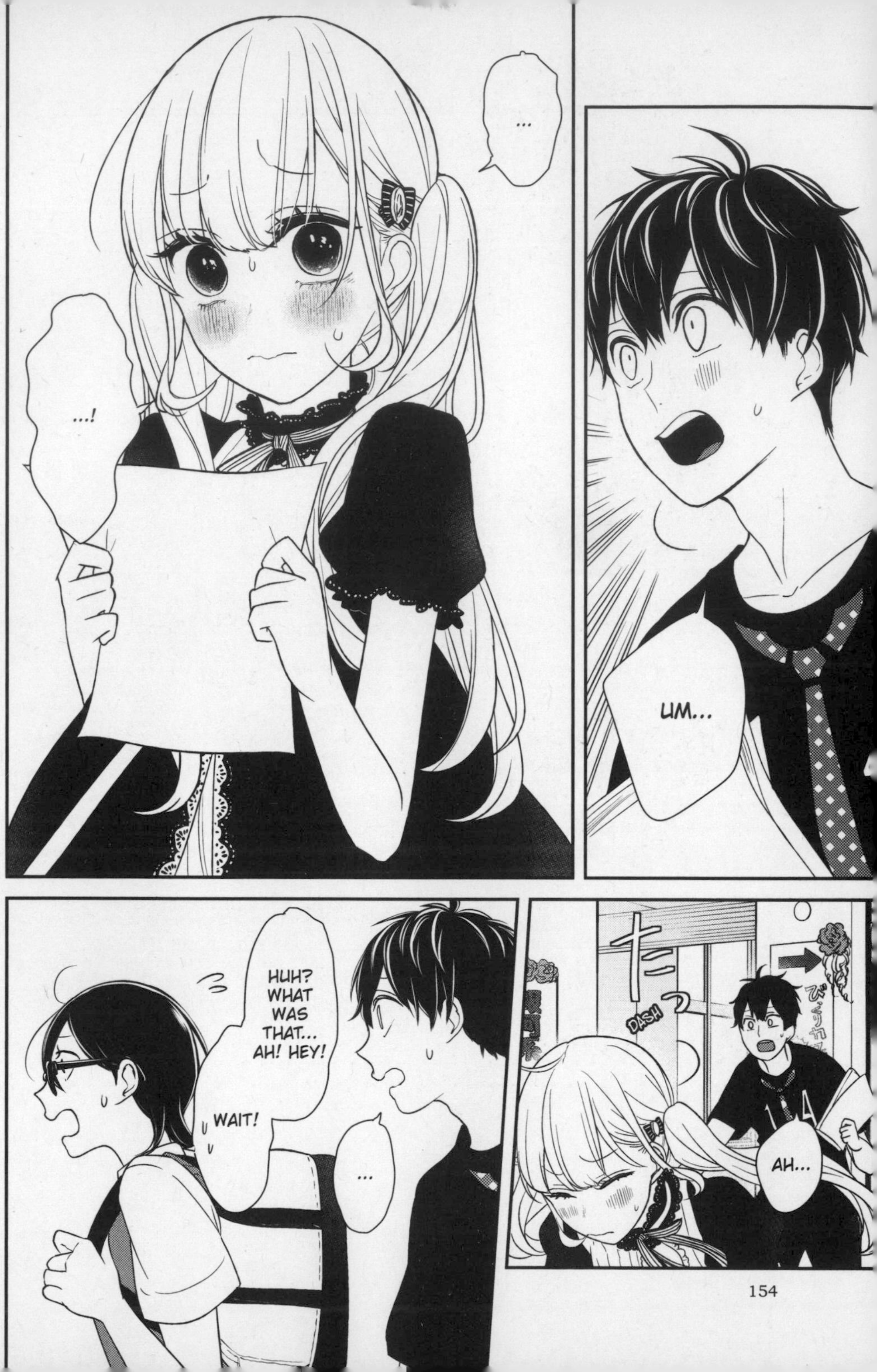
UM...
...
...!
DASH
AH...
HUH? WHAT WAS THAT... AH! HEY!
WAIT!
...

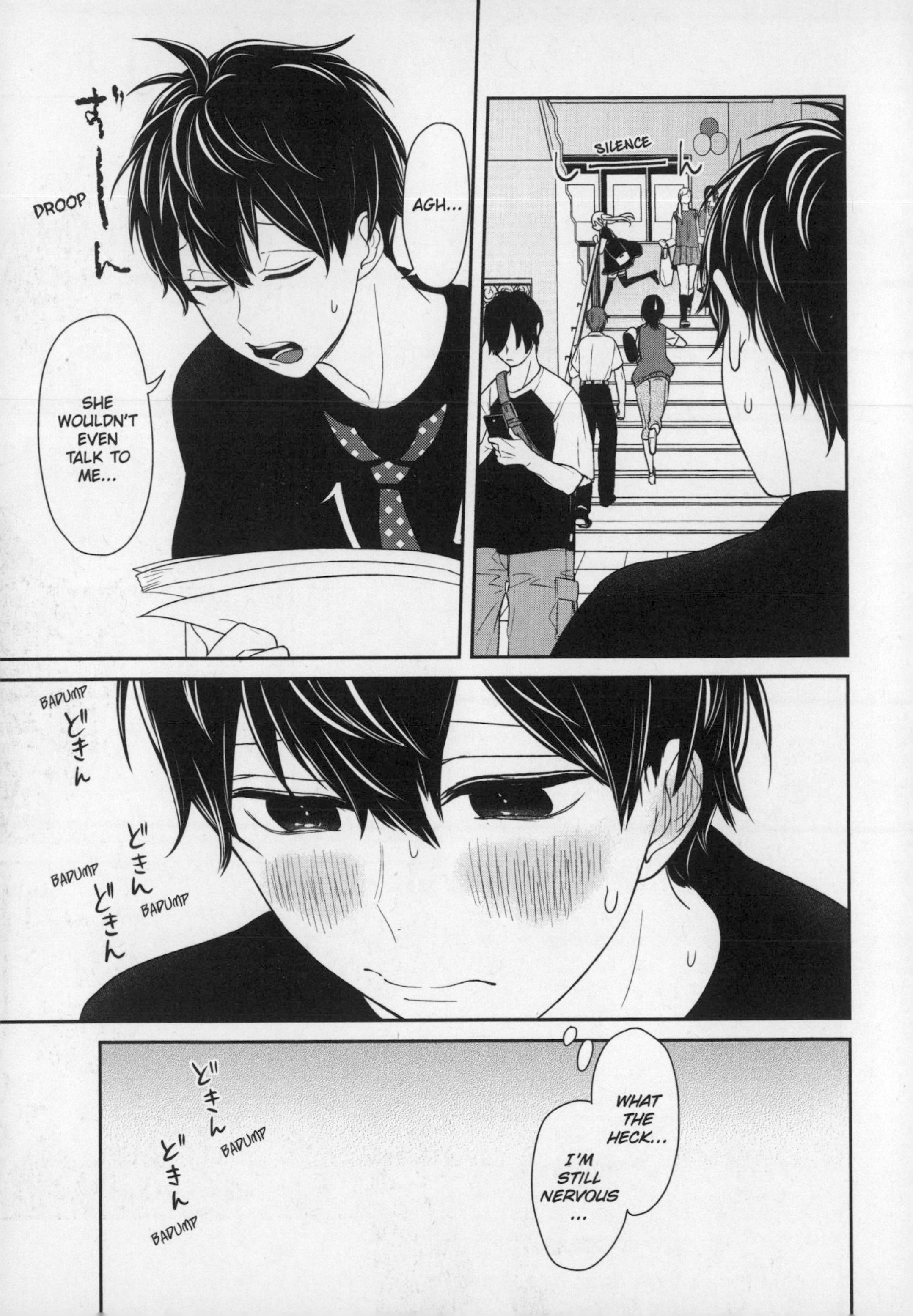
SILENCE
しーん
AGH...
DROOP
ずーん
SHE WOULDN'T EVEN TALK TO ME...
BADUMP
どきん
BADUMP
どきん
BADUMP
どきん
どきん
BADUMP
どきん
BADUMP
WHAT THE HECK... I'M STILL NERVOUS...

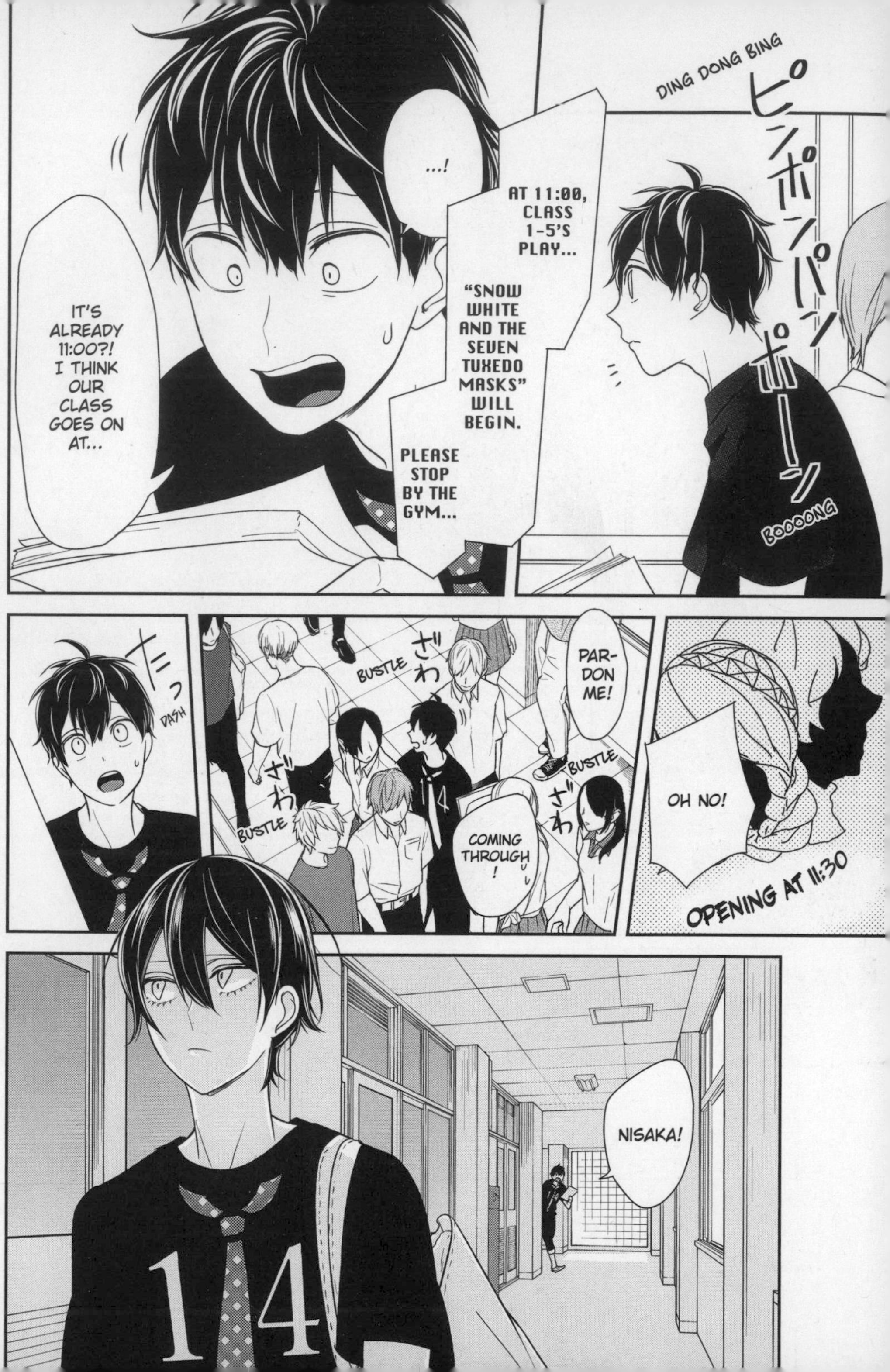
DING DONG BING
ピンポンパンポーン
BOOOONG
AT 11:00, CLASS 1-5'S PLAY...
"SNOW WHITE AND THE SEVEN TUXEDO MASKS" WILL BEGIN.
PLEASE STOP BY THE GYM...
...!
IT'S ALREADY 11:00?! I THINK OUR CLASS GOES ON AT...
OH NO!
OPENING AT 11:30
PAR-DON ME!
ざわ
BUSTLE
ざわ
BUSTLE
ざわ
BUSTLE
COMING THROUGH!
たっ
DASH
NISAKA!

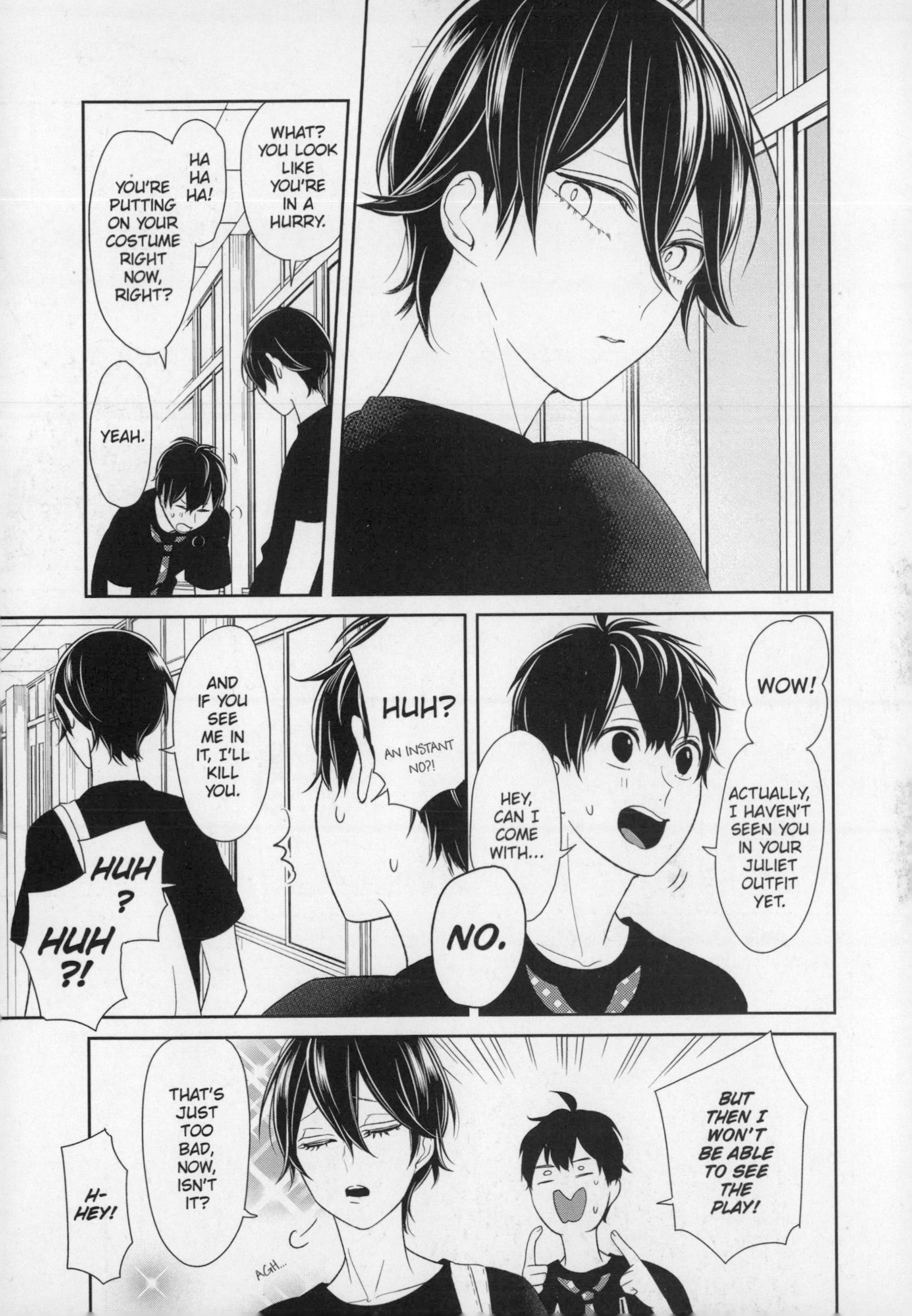
WHAT? YOU LOOK LIKE YOU'RE IN A HURRY.
HA HA HA!
YOU'RE PUTTING ON YOUR COSTUME RIGHT NOW, RIGHT?
YEAH.
WOW!
ACTUALLY, I HAVEN'T SEEN YOU IN YOUR JULIET OUTFIT YET.
HEY, CAN I COME WITH...
NO.
HUH?
AN INSTANT NO?!
AND IF YOU SEE ME IN IT, I'LL KILL YOU.
HUH? HUH?!
BUT THEN I WON'T BE ABLE TO SEE THE PLAY!
AGH...
THAT'S JUST TOO BAD, NOW, ISN'T IT?
H-HEY!

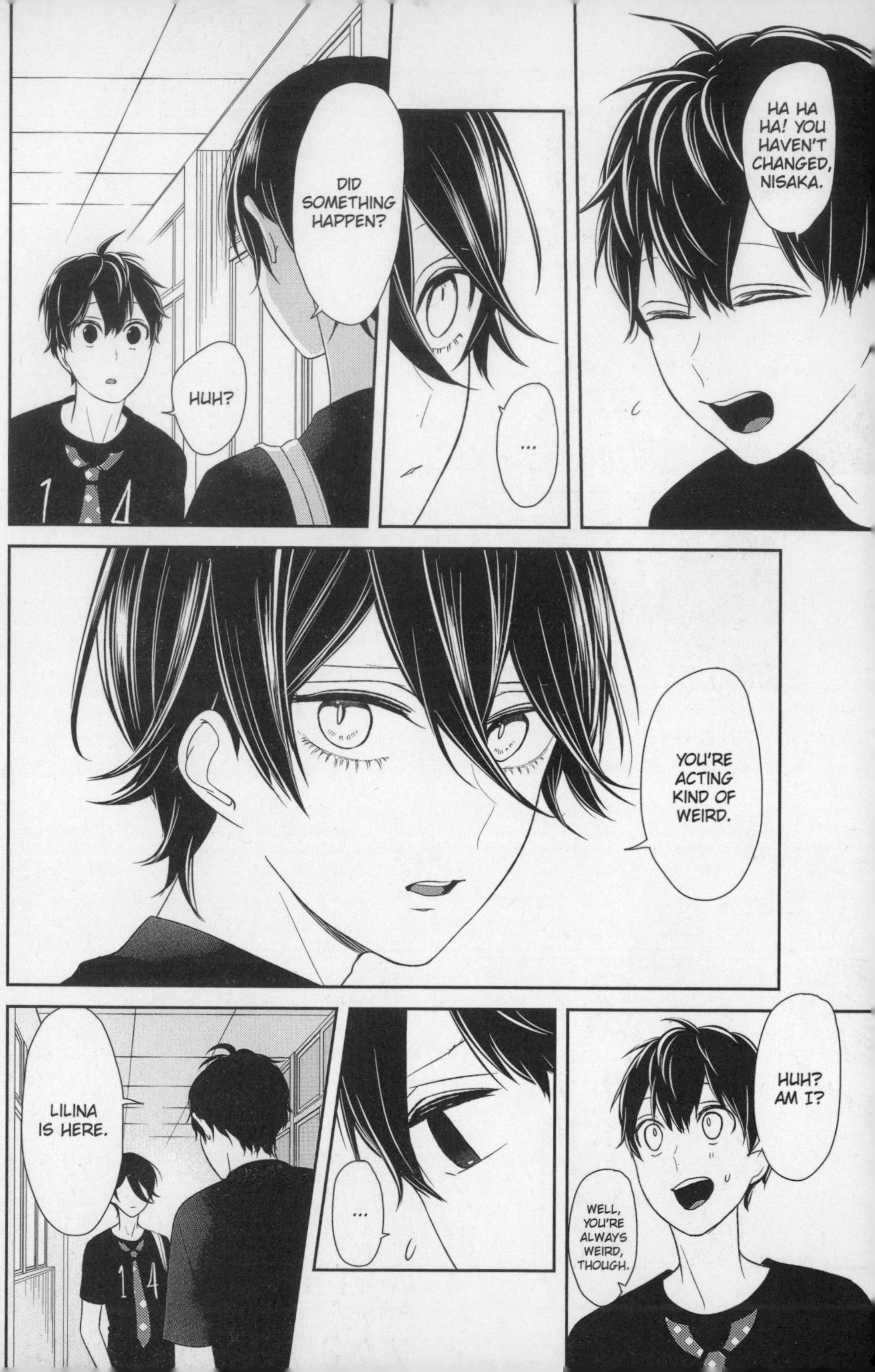
HA HA HA! YOU HAVEN'T CHANGED, NISAKA.
...
DID SOMETHING HAPPEN?
HUH?
YOU'RE ACTING KIND OF WEIRD.
HUH? AM I?
WELL, YOU'RE ALWAYS WEIRD, THOUGH.
...
LILINA IS HERE.

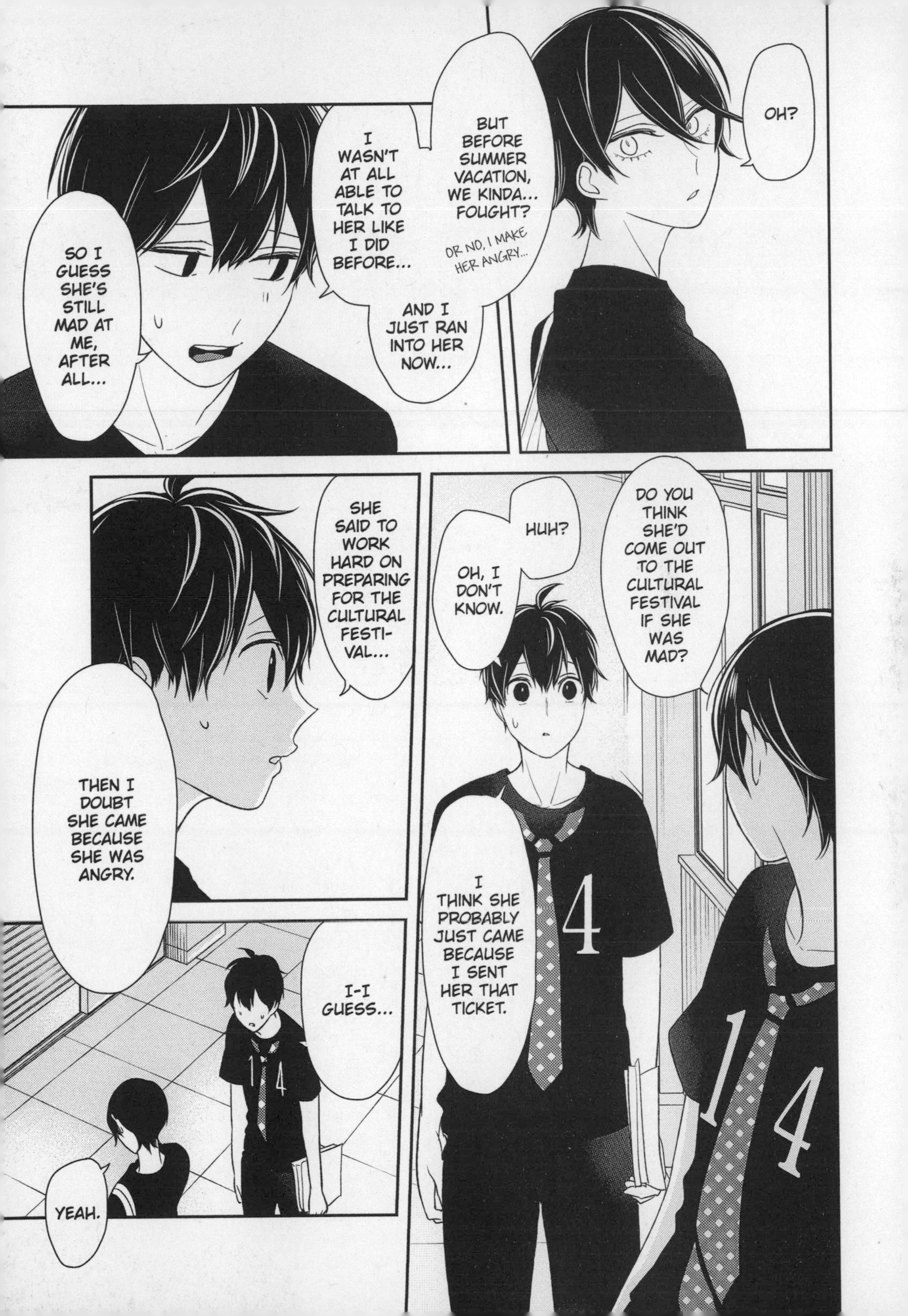
OH?
BUT BEFORE SUMMER VACATION, WE KINDA... FOUGHT?
OR NO, I MAKE HER ANGRY...
I WASN'T AT ALL ABLE TO TALK TO HER LIKE I DID BEFORE...
AND I JUST RAN INTO HER NOW...
SO I GUESS SHE'S STILL MAD AT ME, AFTER ALL...
DO YOU THINK SHE'D COME OUT TO THE CULTURAL FESTIVAL IF SHE WAS MAD?
HUH?
OH, I DON'T KNOW.
I THINK SHE PROBABLY JUST CAME BECAUSE I SENT HER THAT TICKET.
SHE SAID TO WORK HARD ON PREPARING FOR THE CULTURAL FESTI-VAL...
THEN I DOUBT SHE CAME BECAUSE SHE WAS ANGRY.
I-I GUESS...
YEAH.

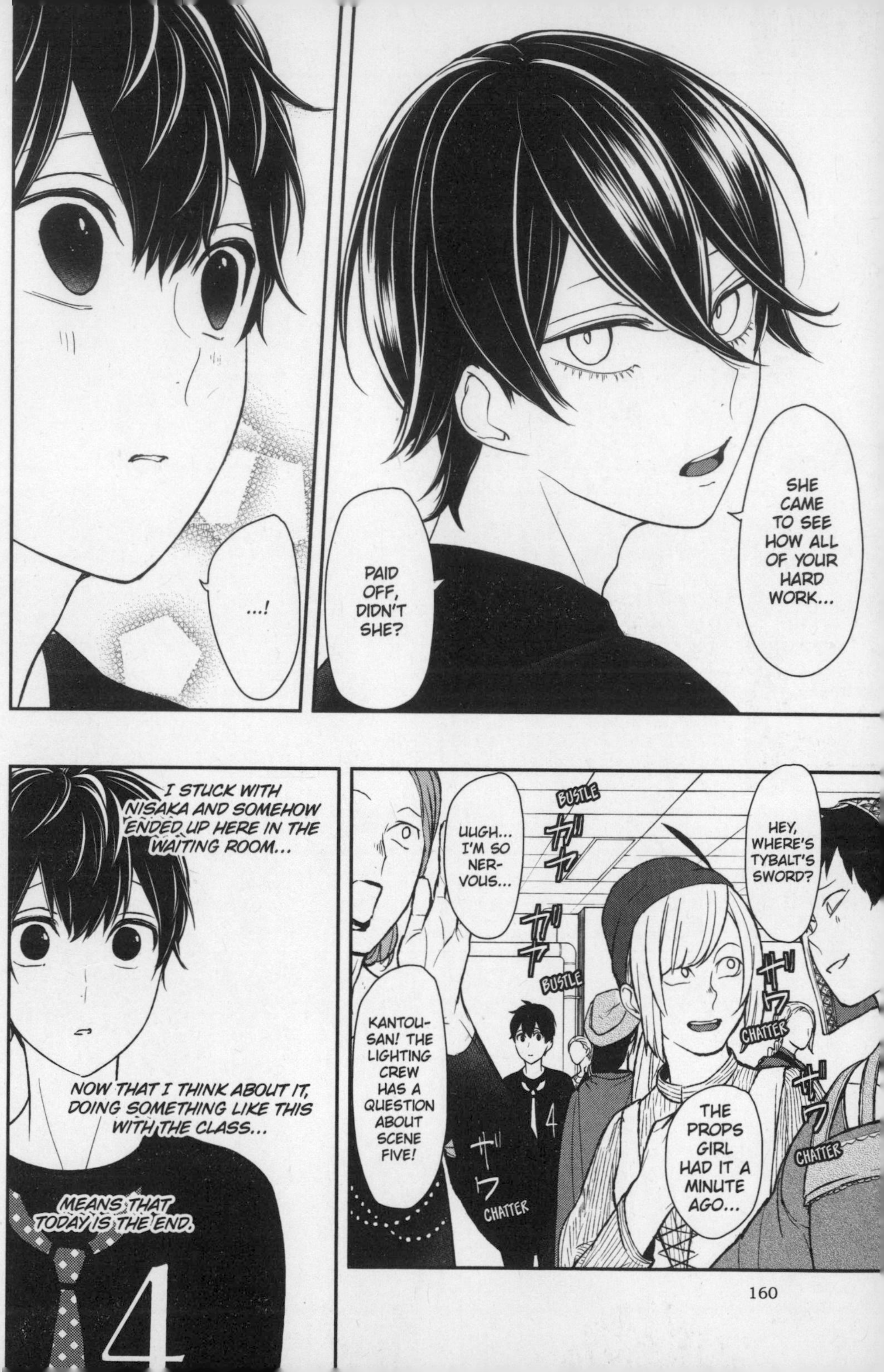
SHE CAME TO SEE HOW ALL OF YOUR HARD WORK...
PAID OFF, DIDN'T SHE?
...!
HEY, WHERE'S TYBALT'S SWORD?
BUSTLE
UUGH... I'M SO NER-VOUS...
BUSTLE
THE PROPS GIRL HAD IT A MINUTE AGO...
CHATTER
CHATTER
KANTOU-SAN! THE LIGHTING CREW HAS A QUESTION ABOUT SCENE FIVE!
CHATTER
I STUCK WITH NISAKA AND SOMEHOW ENDED UP HERE IN THE WAITING ROOM...
NOW THAT I THINK ABOUT IT, DOING SOMETHING LIKE THIS WITH THE CLASS...
MEANS THAT TODAY IS THE END.

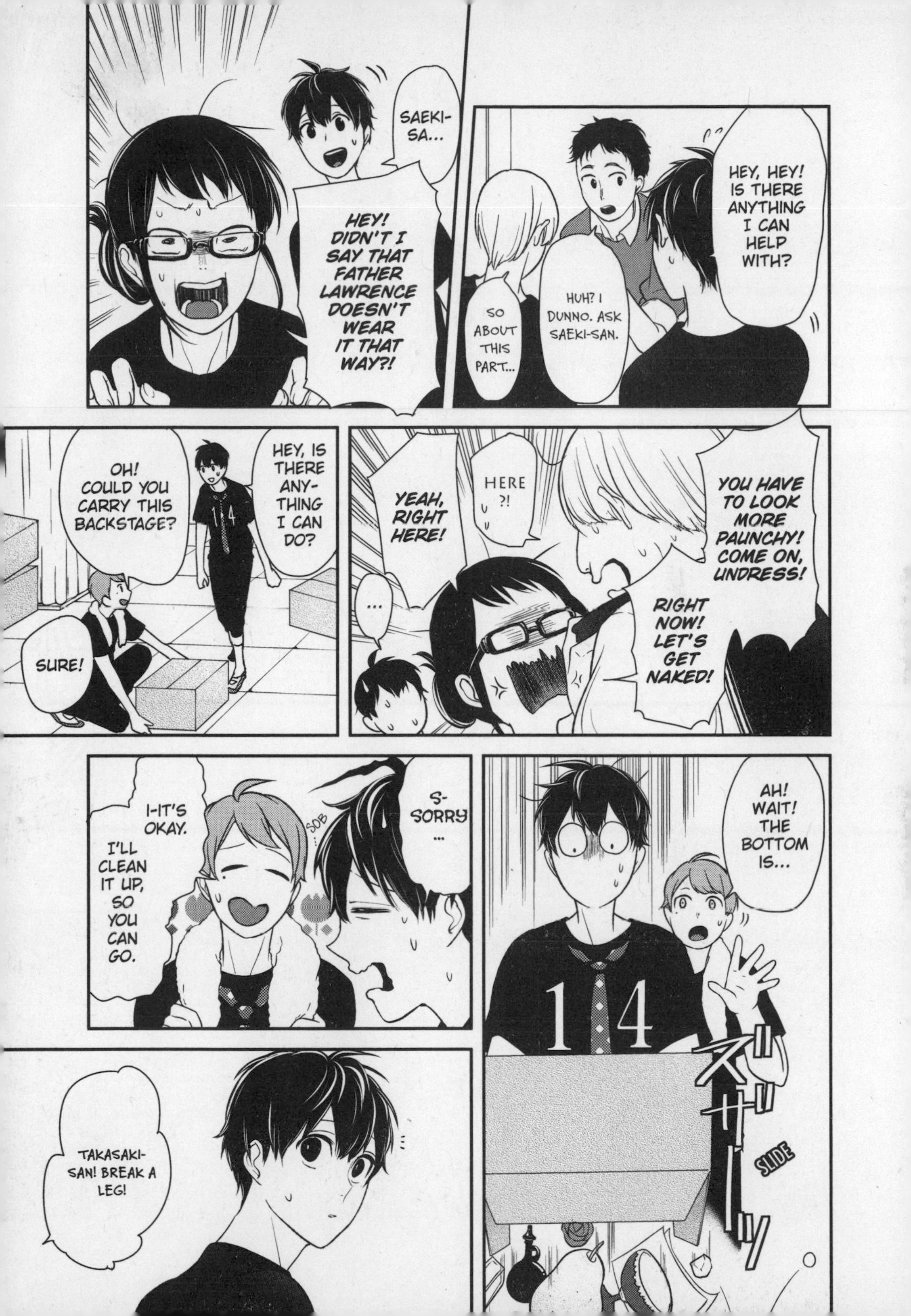
HEY, HEY! IS THERE ANYTHING I CAN HELP WITH?
HUH? I DUNNO. ASK SAEKI-SAN.
SO ABOUT THIS PART...
SAEKI-SA...
HEY! DIDN'T I SAY THAT FATHER LAWRENCE DOESN'T WEAR IT THAT WAY?!
YOU HAVE TO LOOK MORE PAUNCHY! COME ON, UNDRESS!
HERE ?!
YEAH, RIGHT HERE!
RIGHT NOW! LET'S GET NAKED!
...
HEY, IS THERE ANY-THING I CAN DO?
OH! COULD YOU CARRY THIS BACKSTAGE?
SURE!
AH! WAIT! THE BOTTOM IS...
SLIDE
S-SORRY...
SOB
I-IT'S OKAY. I'LL CLEAN IT UP, SO YOU CAN GO.
TAKASAKI-SAN! BREAK A LEG!

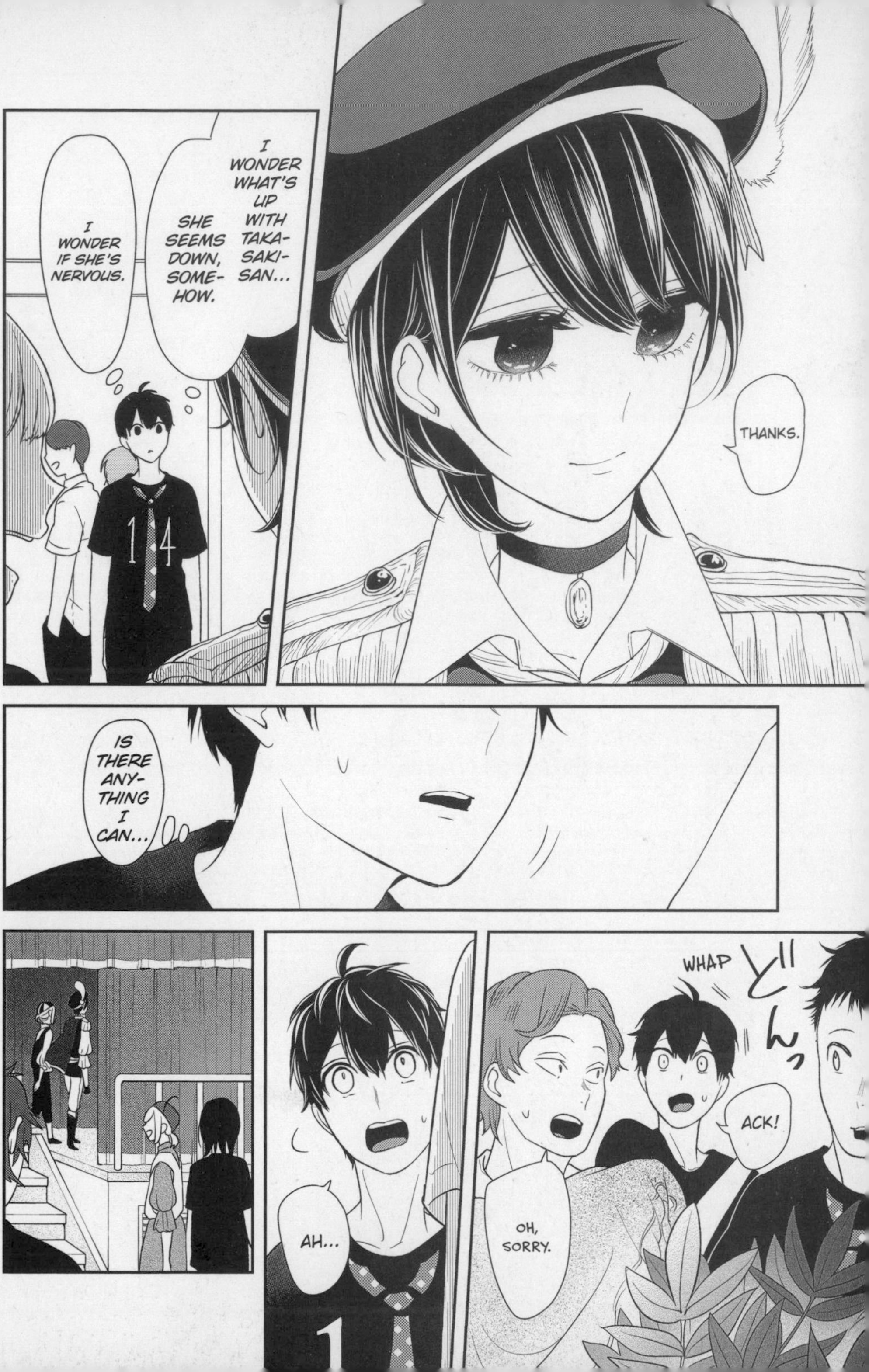
THANKS.
I WONDER WHAT'S UP WITH TAKASAKI-SAN...
SHE SEEMS DOWN, SOMEHOW.
I WONDER IF SHE'S NERVOUS.
IS THERE ANYTHING I CAN...
WHAP
どんっ
ACK!
OH, SORRY.
AH...

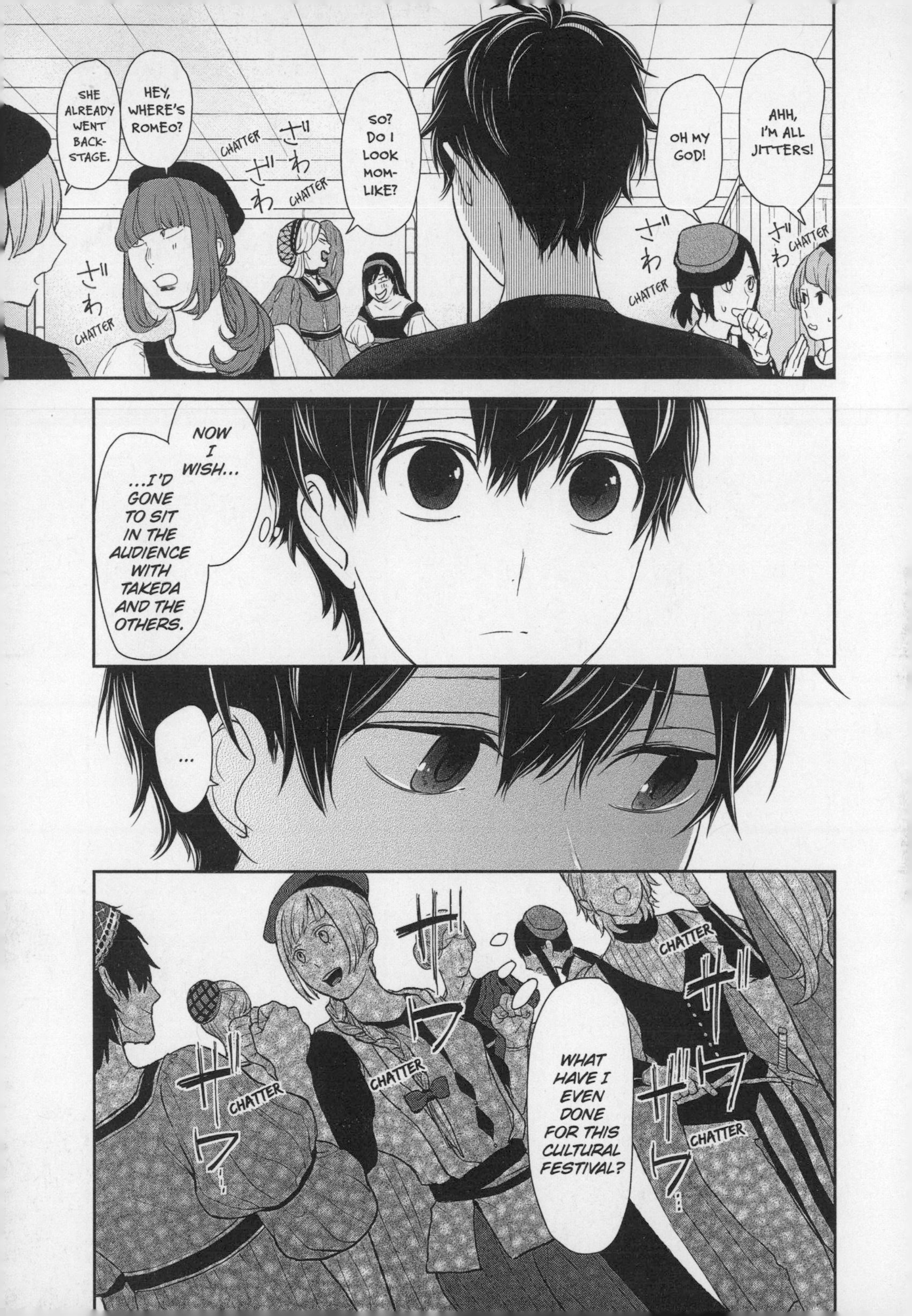
AHH, I'M ALL JITTERS!
ざわ CHATTER
OH MY GOD!
ざわ CHATTER
SO? DO I LOOK MOM-LIKE?
ざわ CHATTER
ざわ CHATTER
HEY, WHERE'S ROMEO?
SHE ALREADY WENT BACK-STAGE.
ざわ CHATTER
NOW I WISH...
...I'D GONE TO SIT IN THE AUDIENCE WITH TAKEDA AND THE OTHERS.
...
ザワ CHATTER
ザワ CHATTER
WHAT HAVE I EVEN DONE FOR THIS CULTURAL FESTIVAL?
ザワ CHATTER
ザワ… CHATTER

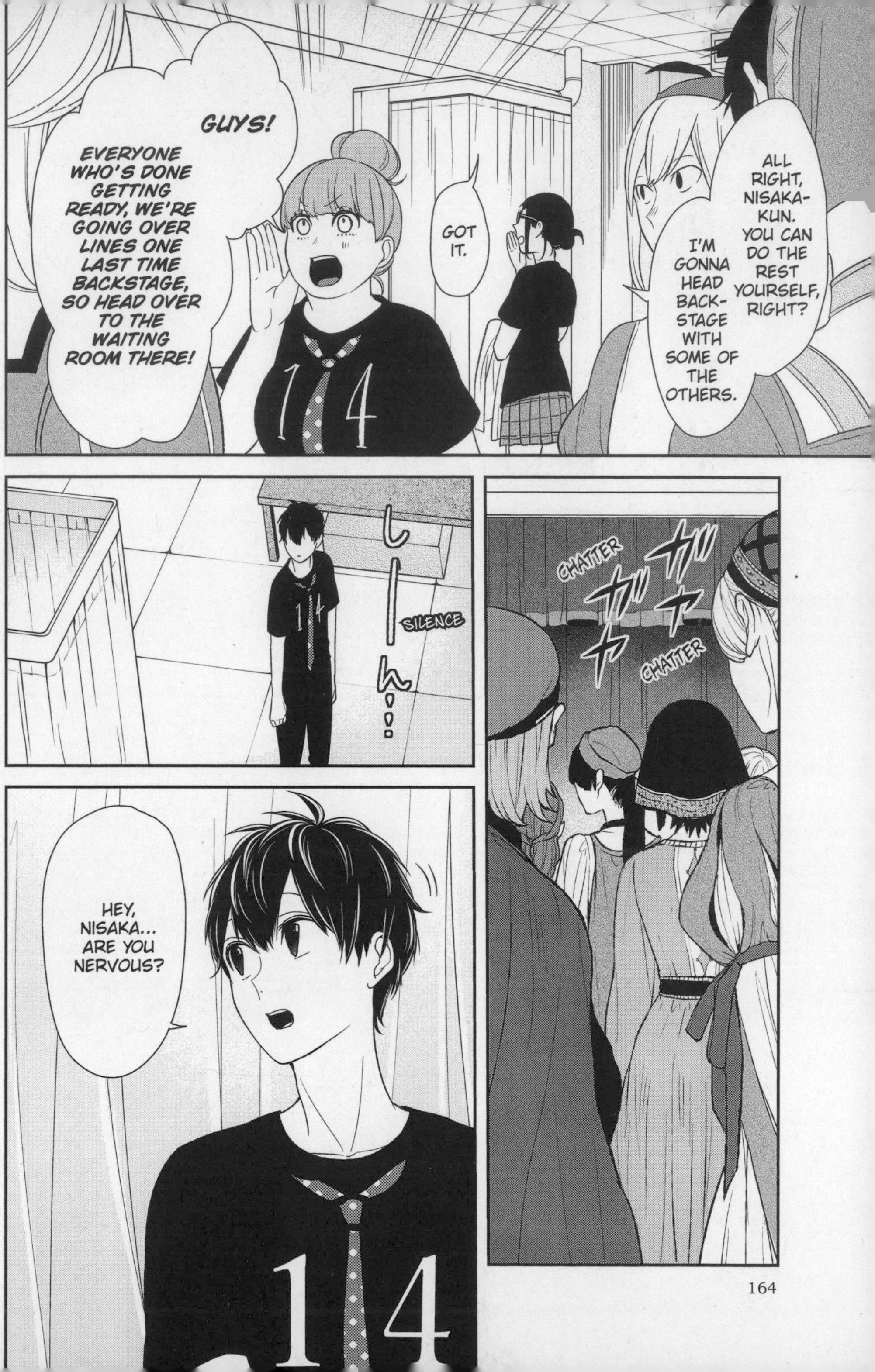
ALL RIGHT, NISAKA-KUN. YOU CAN DO THE REST YOURSELF, RIGHT?
I'M GONNA HEAD BACKSTAGE WITH SOME OF THE OTHERS.
GOT IT.
GUYS!
EVERYONE WHO'S DONE GETTING READY, WE'RE GOING OVER LINES ONE LAST TIME BACKSTAGE, SO HEAD OVER TO THE WAITING ROOM THERE!
ガヤ
CHATTER
ガヤ
CHATTER
しーん!!
SILENCE
HEY, NISAKA... ARE YOU NERVOUS?

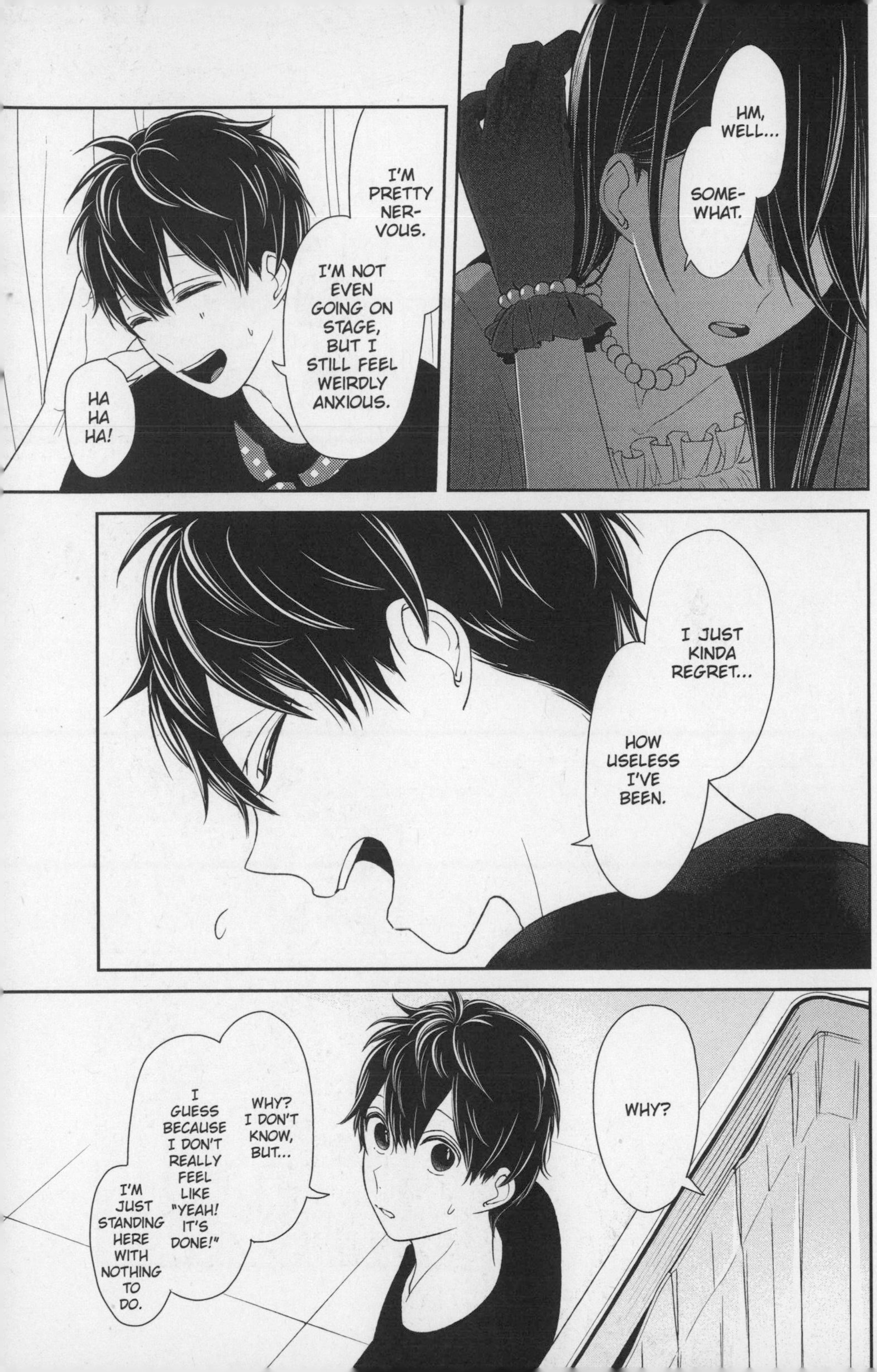
HM, WELL...
SOME-WHAT.
I'M PRETTY NER-VOUS.
I'M NOT EVEN GOING ON STAGE, BUT I STILL FEEL WEIRDLY ANXIOUS.
HA HA HA!
I JUST KINDA REGRET...
HOW USELESS I'VE BEEN.
WHY?
WHY? I DON'T KNOW, BUT...
I GUESS BECAUSE I DON'T REALLY FEEL LIKE "YEAH! IT'S DONE!"
I'M JUST STANDING HERE WITH NOTHING TO DO.

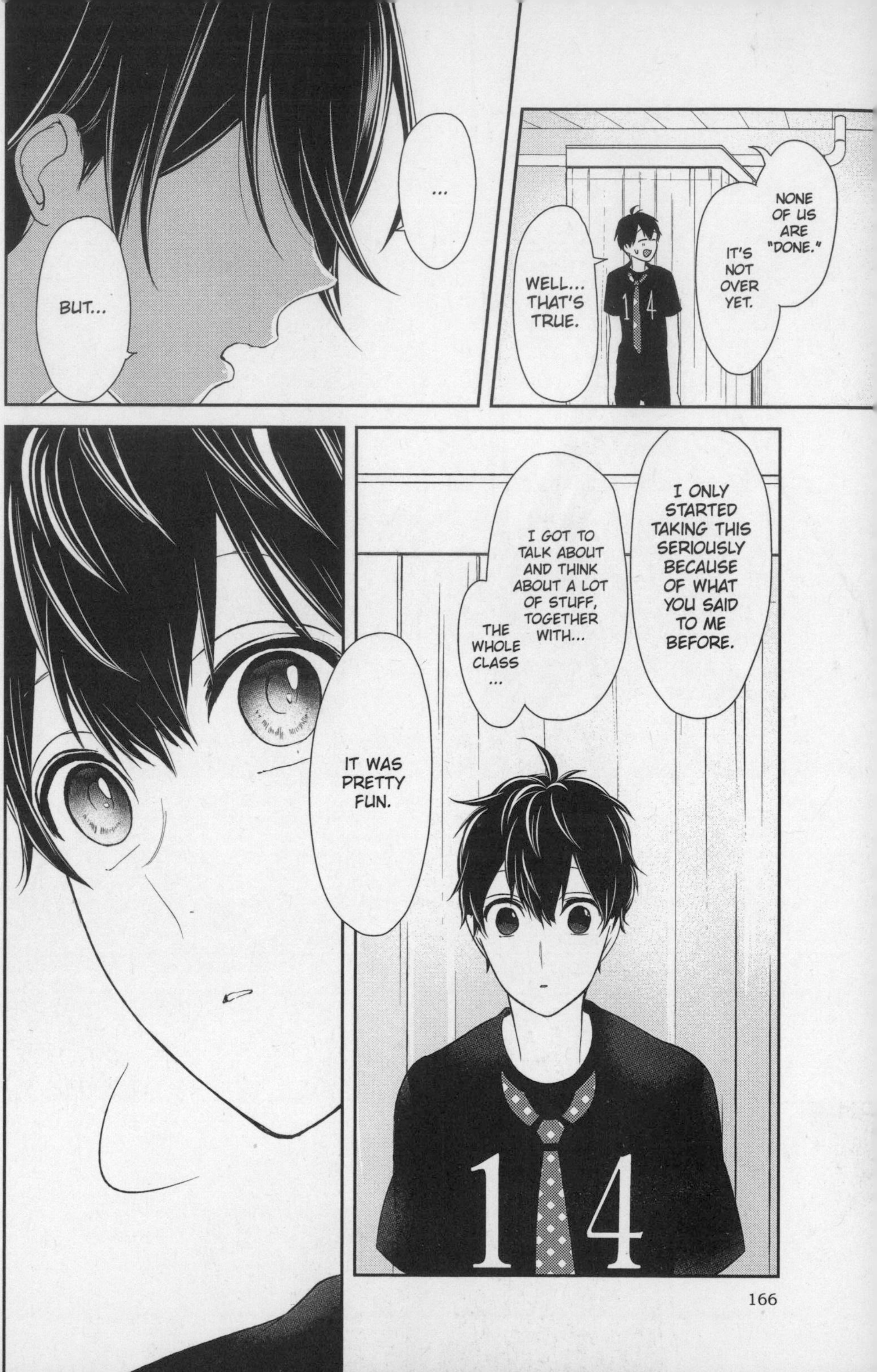
NONE OF US ARE "DONE."
IT'S NOT OVER YET.
WELL... THAT'S TRUE.
...
BUT...
I ONLY STARTED TAKING THIS SERIOUSLY BECAUSE OF WHAT YOU SAID TO ME BEFORE.
I GOT TO TALK ABOUT AND THINK ABOUT A LOT OF STUFF, TOGETHER WITH...
THE WHOLE CLASS ...
IT WAS PRETTY FUN.

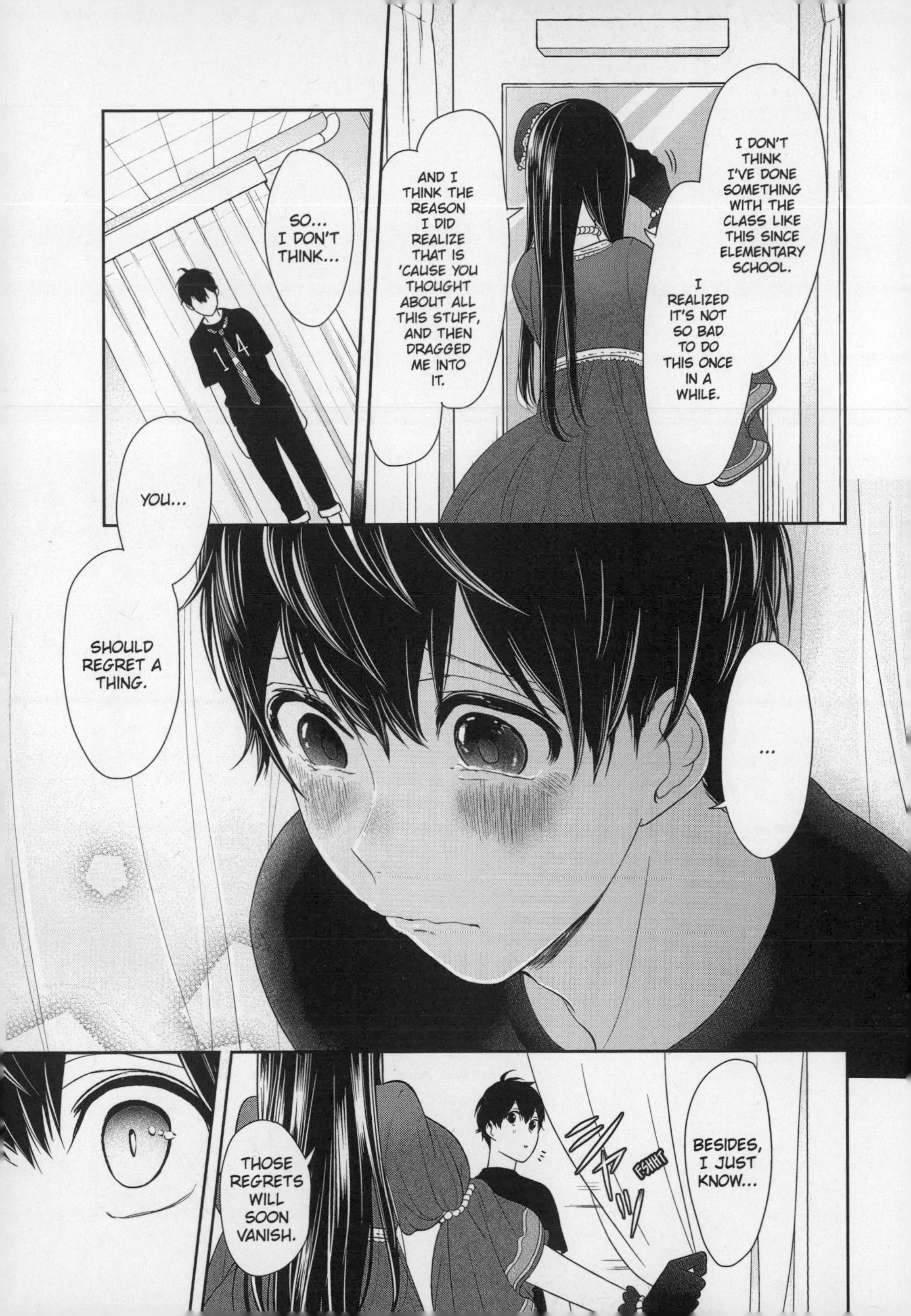
I DON'T THINK I'VE DONE SOMETHING WITH THE CLASS LIKE THIS SINCE ELEMENTARY SCHOOL.
I REALIZED IT'S NOT SO BAD TO DO THIS ONCE IN A WHILE.
AND I THINK THE REASON I DID REALIZE THAT IS 'CAUSE YOU THOUGHT ABOUT ALL THIS STUFF, AND THEN DRAGGED ME INTO IT.
SO... I DON'T THINK...
YOU...
SHOULD REGRET A THING.
...
BESIDES, I JUST KNOW...
FSHHT
THOSE REGRETS WILL SOON VANISH.

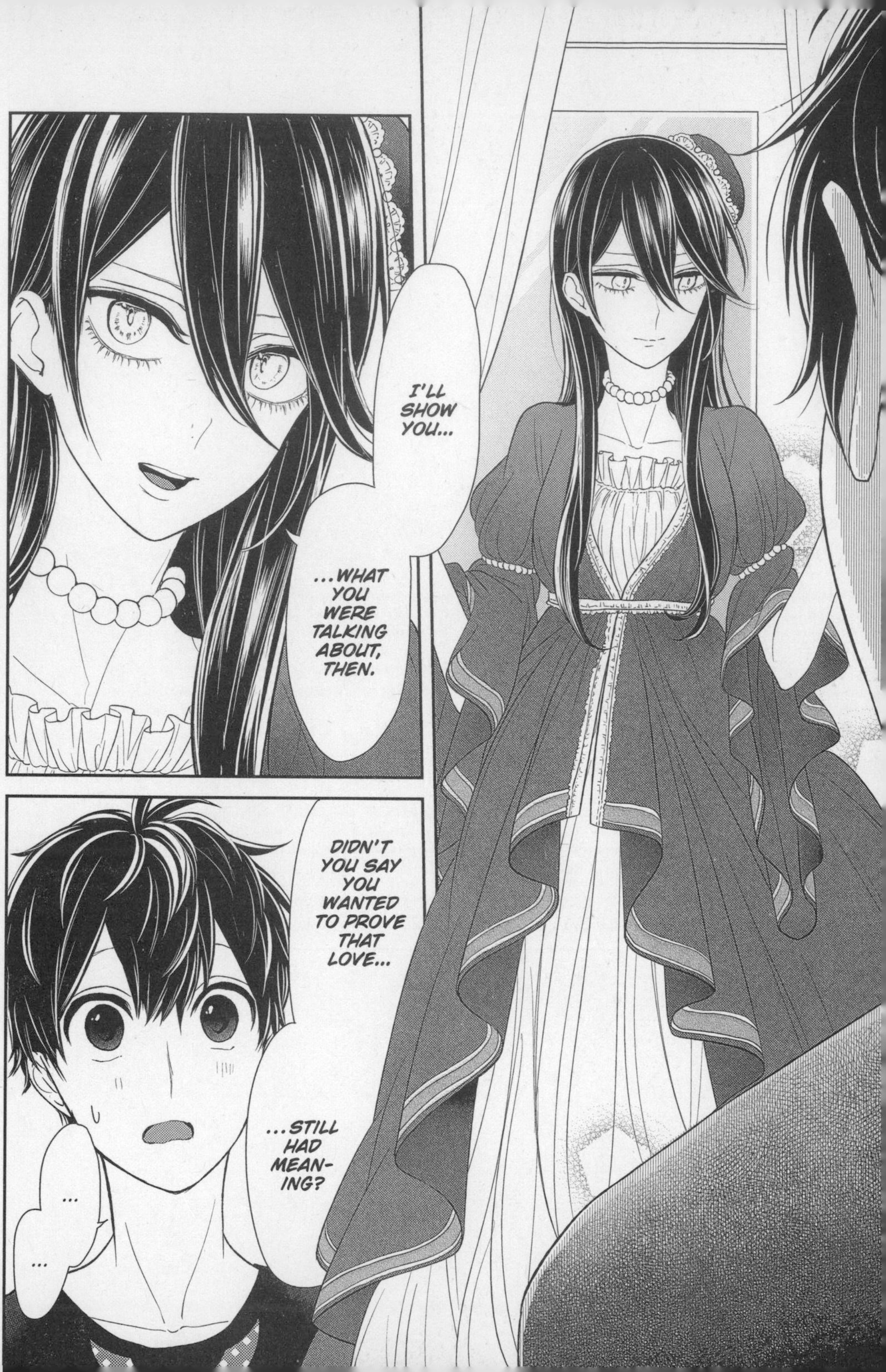

I'LL SHOW YOU...
...WHAT YOU WERE TALKING ABOUT, THEN.
DIDN'T YOU SAY YOU WANTED TO PROVE THAT LOVE...
...STILL HAD MEANING?
...
...

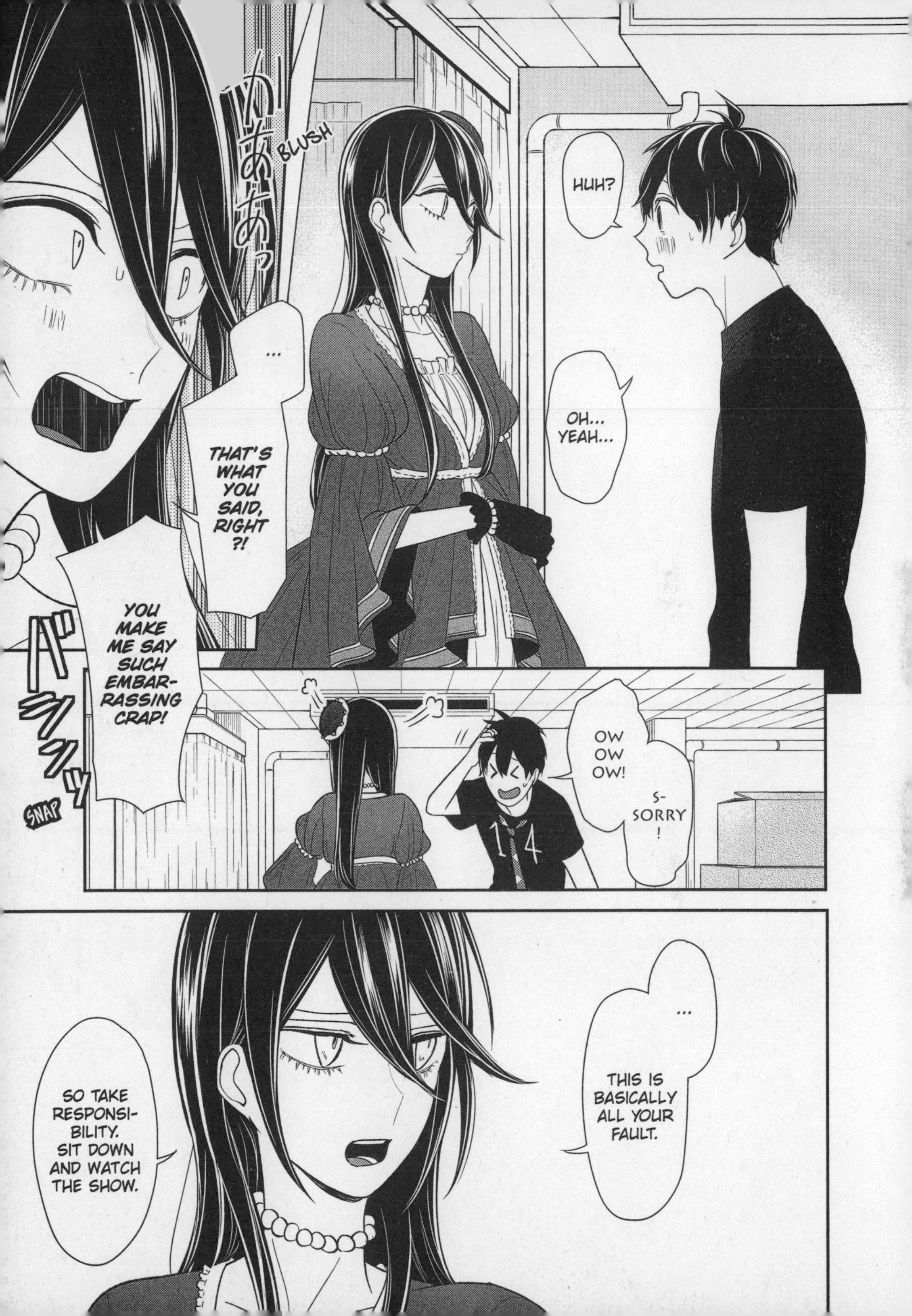
HUH?
OH... YEAH...
...
BLUSH
THAT'S WHAT YOU SAID, RIGHT?!
YOU MAKE ME SAY SUCH EMBARRASSING CRAP!
SNAP
OW OW OW!
S-SORRY!
...
THIS IS BASICALLY ALL YOUR FAULT.
SO TAKE RESPONSIBILITY. SIT DOWN AND WATCH THE SHOW.

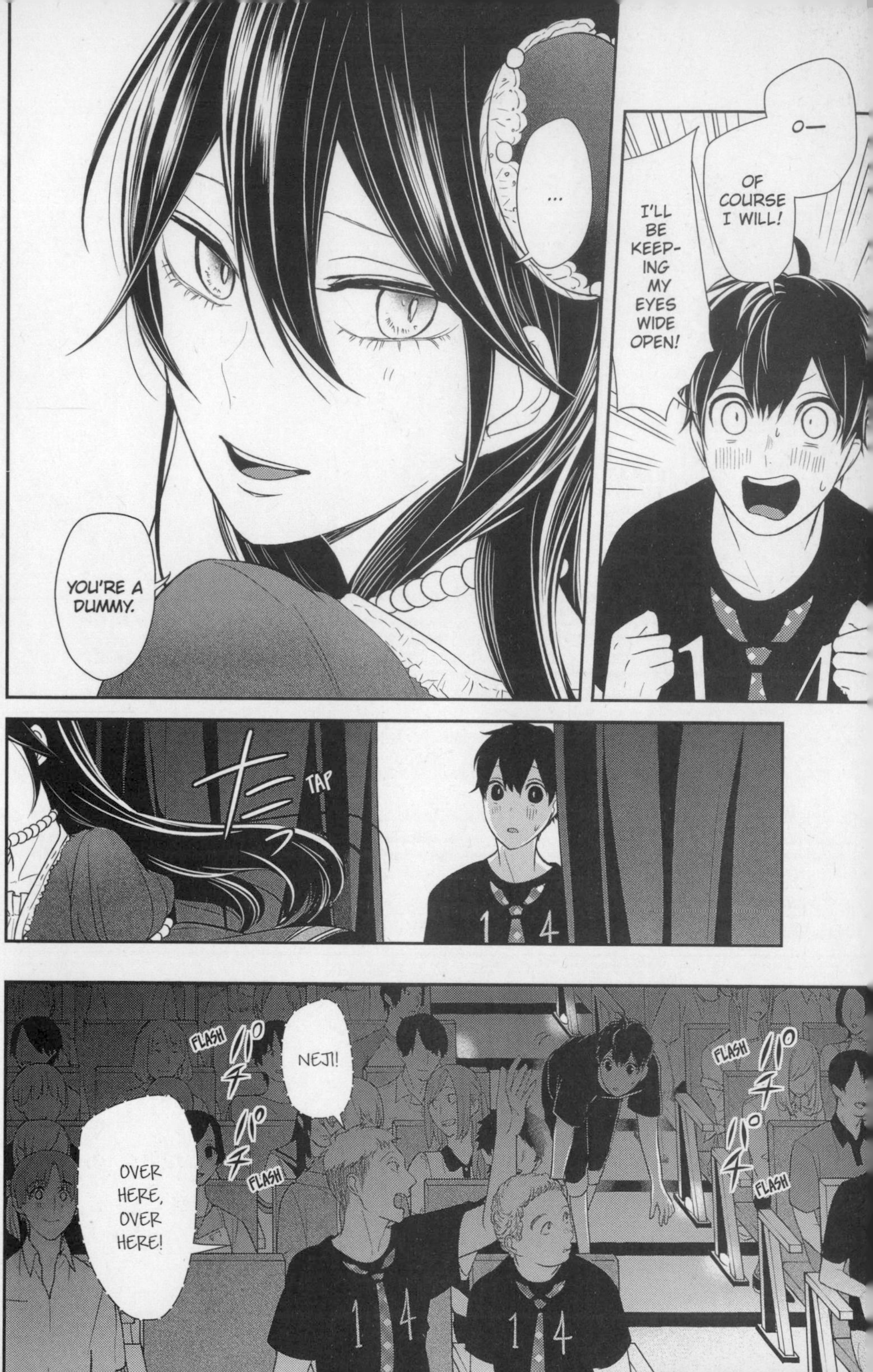
O—
OF COURSE I WILL!
I'LL BE KEEPING MY EYES WIDE OPEN!
...
YOU'RE A DUMMY.
TAP
FLASH
FLASH
NEJI!
OVER HERE, OVER HERE!
FLASH
FLASH

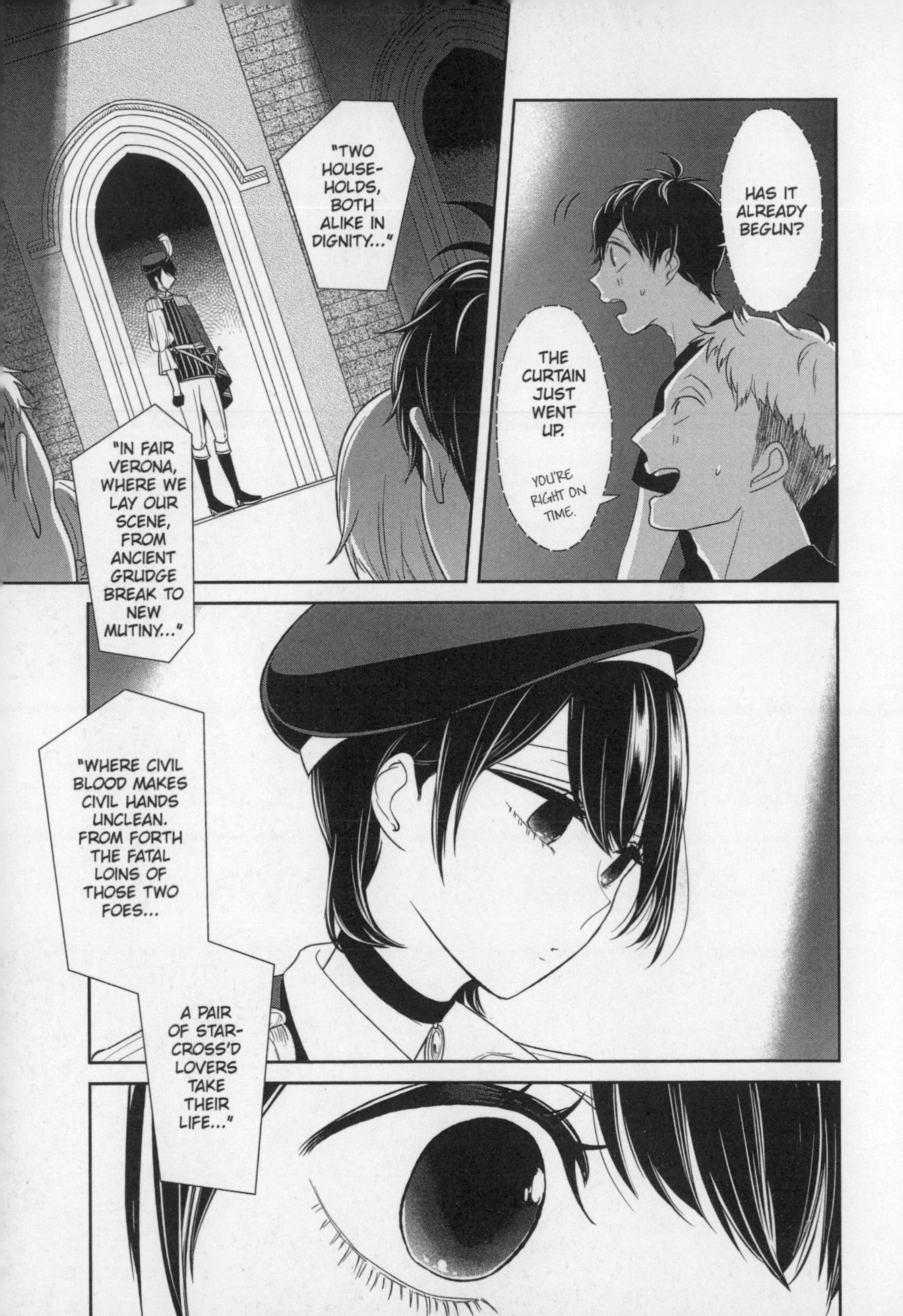
HAS IT ALREADY BEGUN?
THE CURTAIN JUST WENT UP.
YOU'RE RIGHT ON TIME.
"TWO HOUSE-HOLDS, BOTH ALIKE IN DIGNITY..."
"IN FAIR VERONA, WHERE WE LAY OUR SCENE, FROM ANCIENT GRUDGE BREAK TO NEW MUTINY..."
"WHERE CIVIL BLOOD MAKES CIVIL HANDS UNCLEAN. FROM FORTH THE FATAL LOINS OF THOSE TWO FOES...
A PAIR OF STAR-CROSS'D LOVERS TAKE THEIR LIFE..."

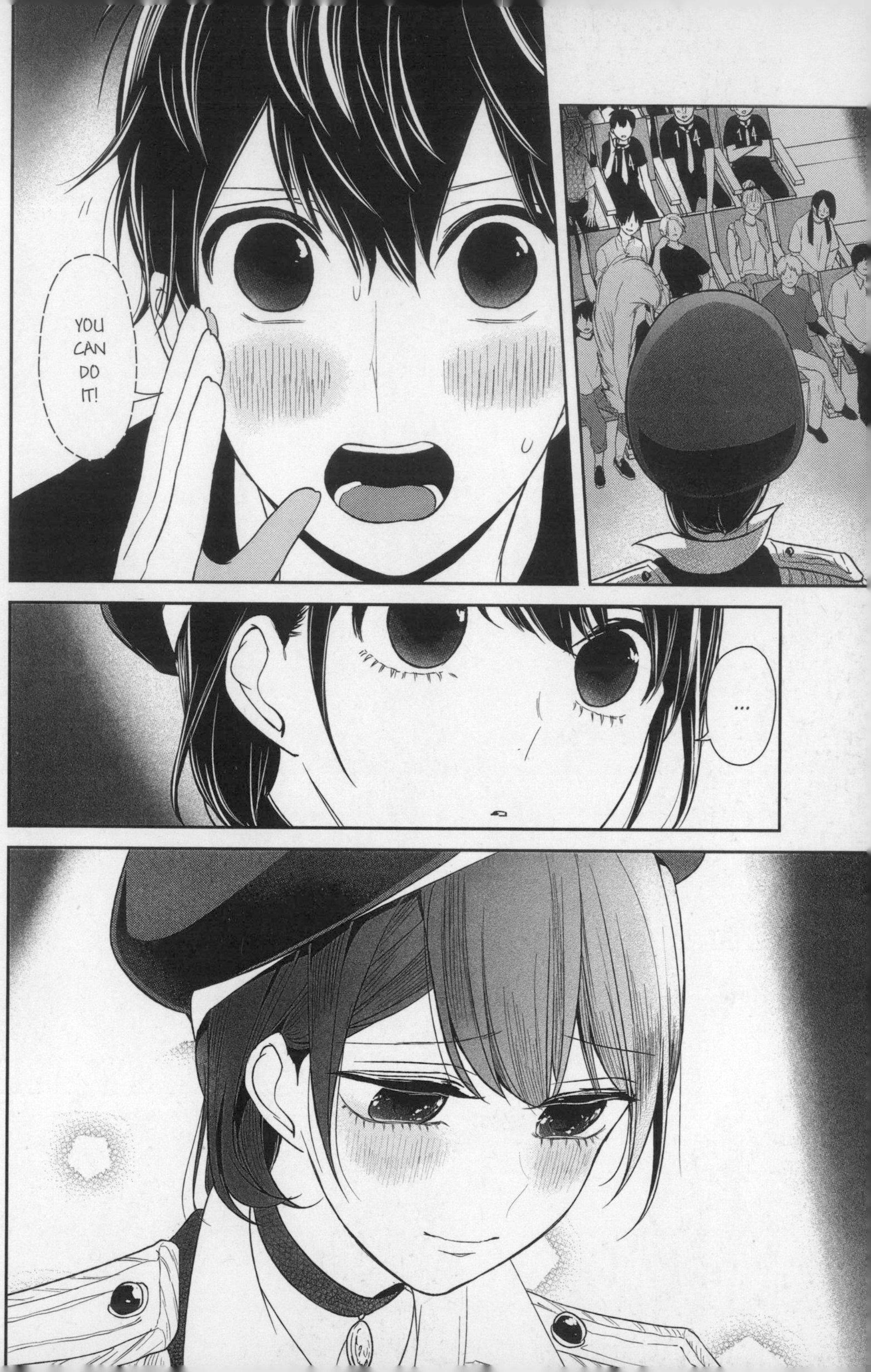
YOU CAN DO IT!
...

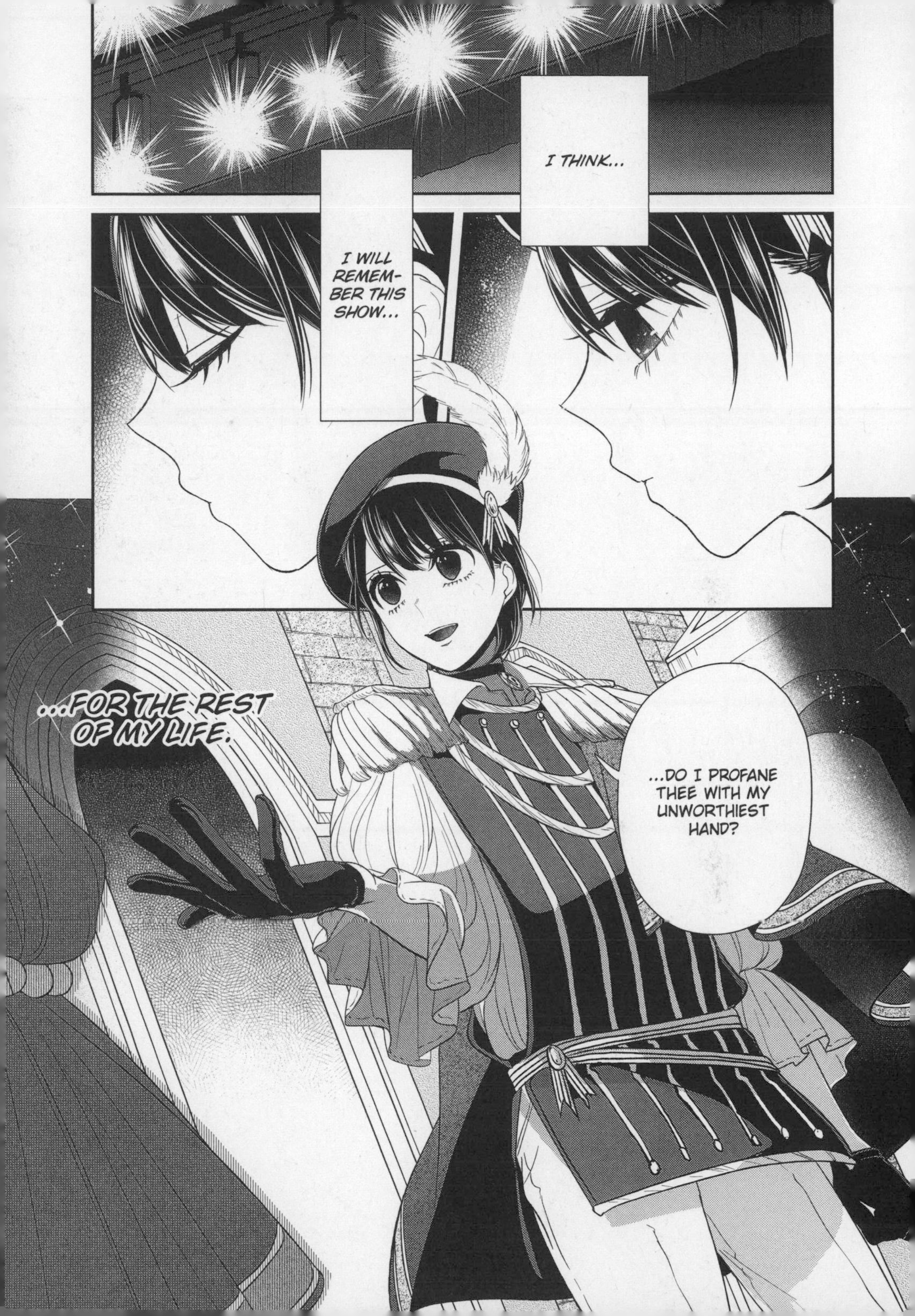
I THINK...
I WILL REMEMBER THIS SHOW...
...DO I PROFANE THEE WITH MY UNWORTHIEST HAND?
...FOR THE REST OF MY LIFE.

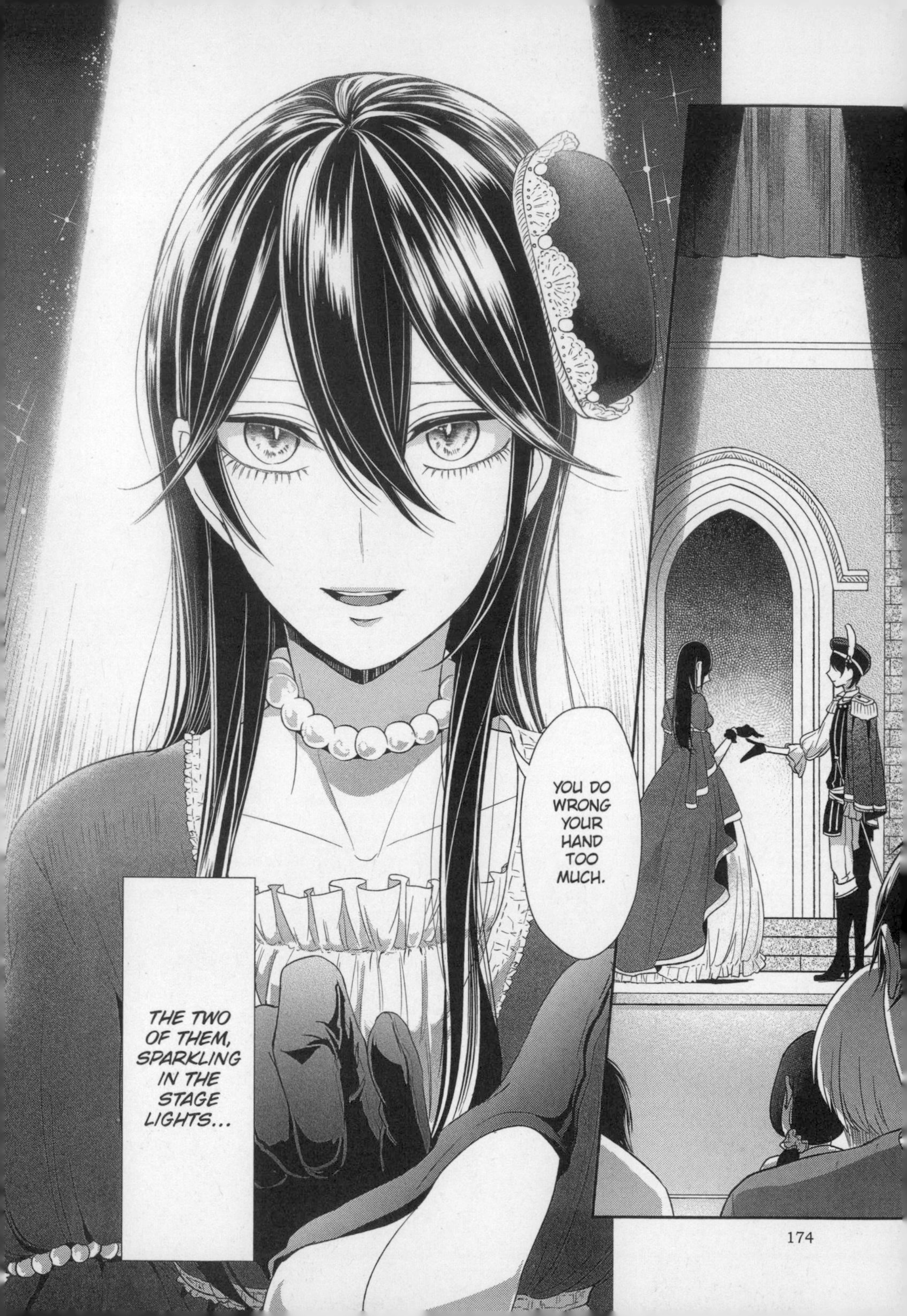
YOU DO WRONG YOUR HAND TOO MUCH.
THE TWO OF THEM, SPARKLING IN THE STAGE LIGHTS...

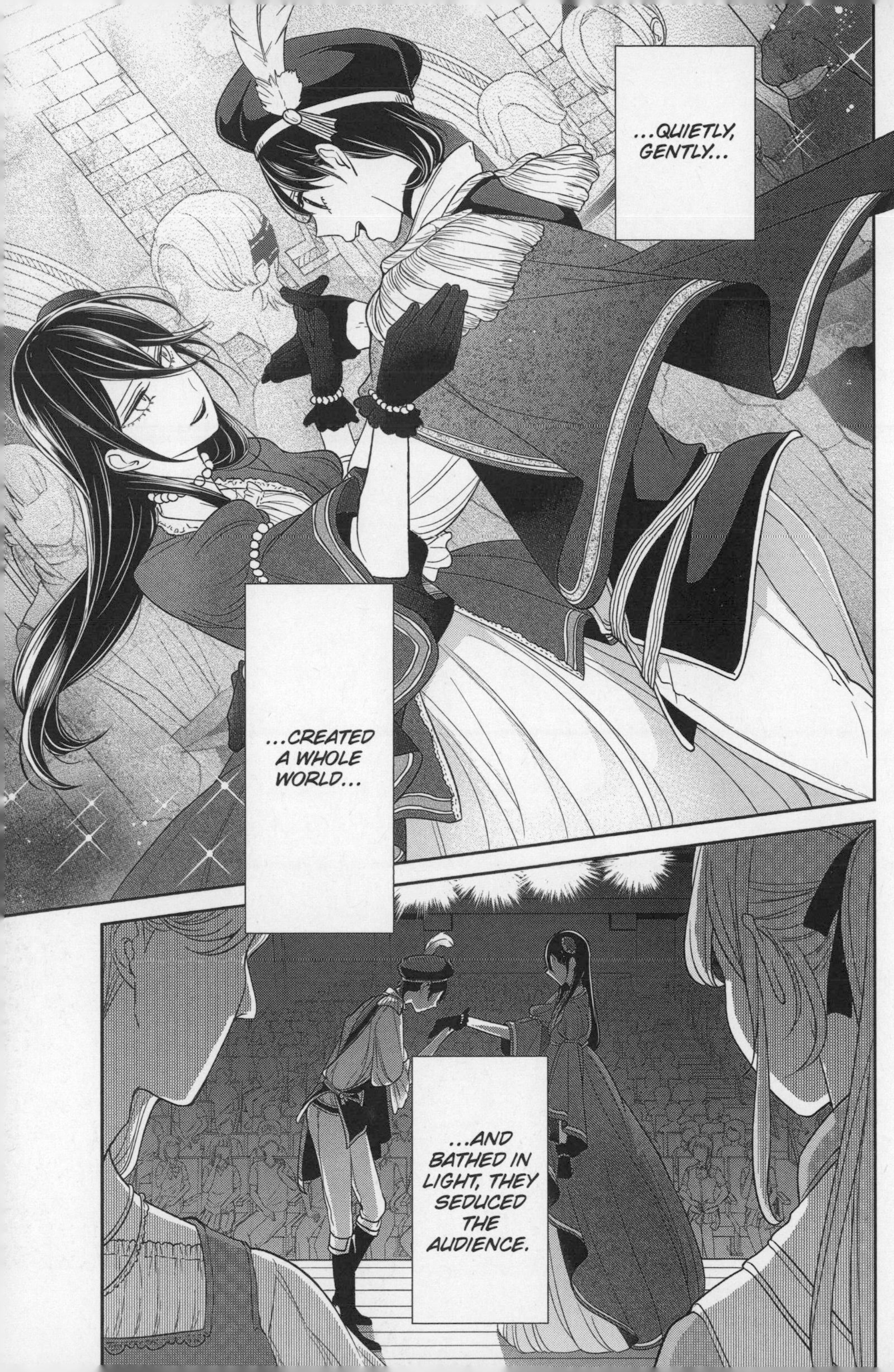
...QUIETLY, GENTLY...
...CREATED A WHOLE WORLD...
...AND BATHED IN LIGHT, THEY SEDUCED THE AUDIENCE.

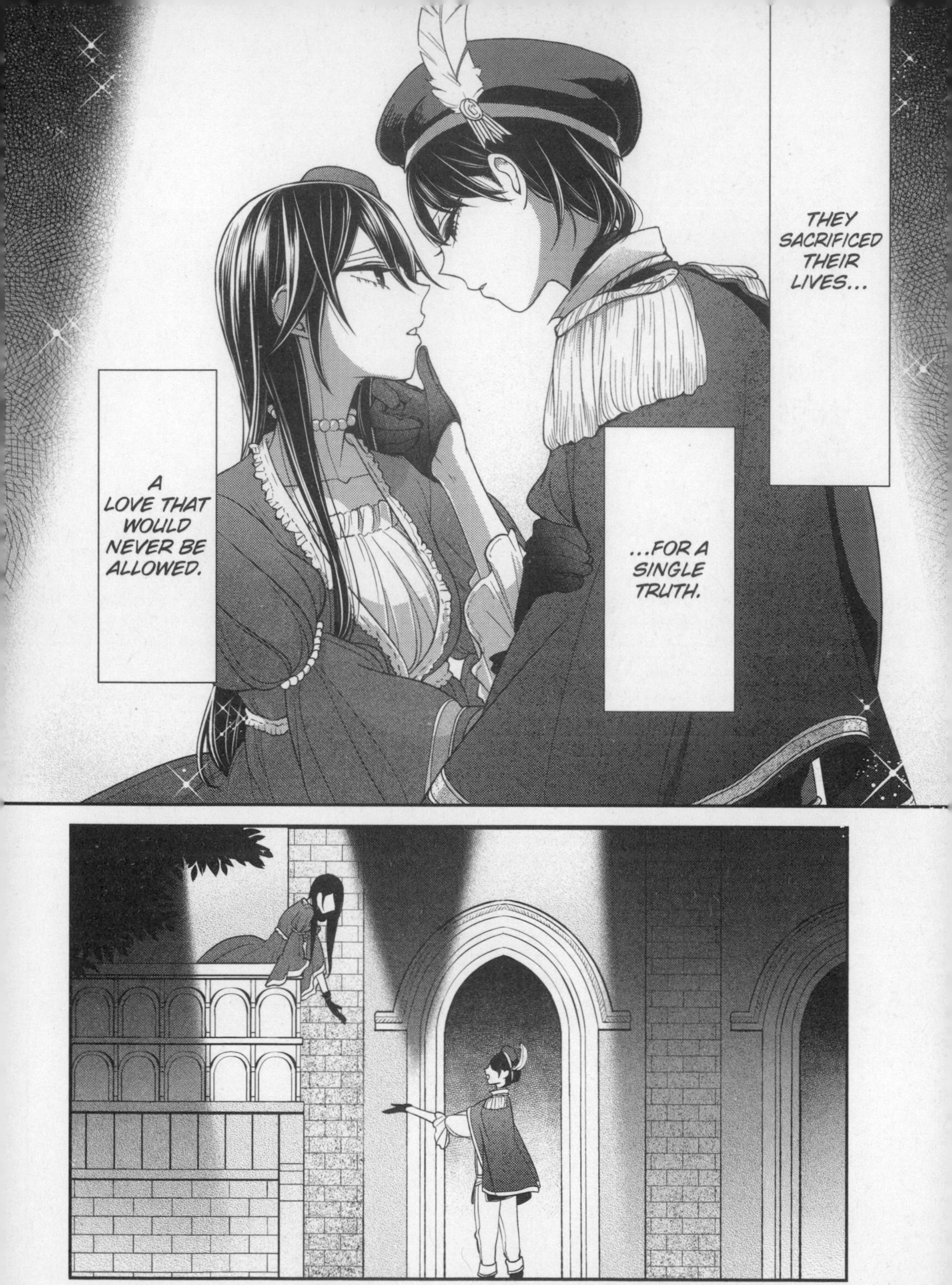
THEY SACRIFICED THEIR LIVES...
...FOR A SINGLE TRUTH.
A LOVE THAT WOULD NEVER BE ALLOWED.

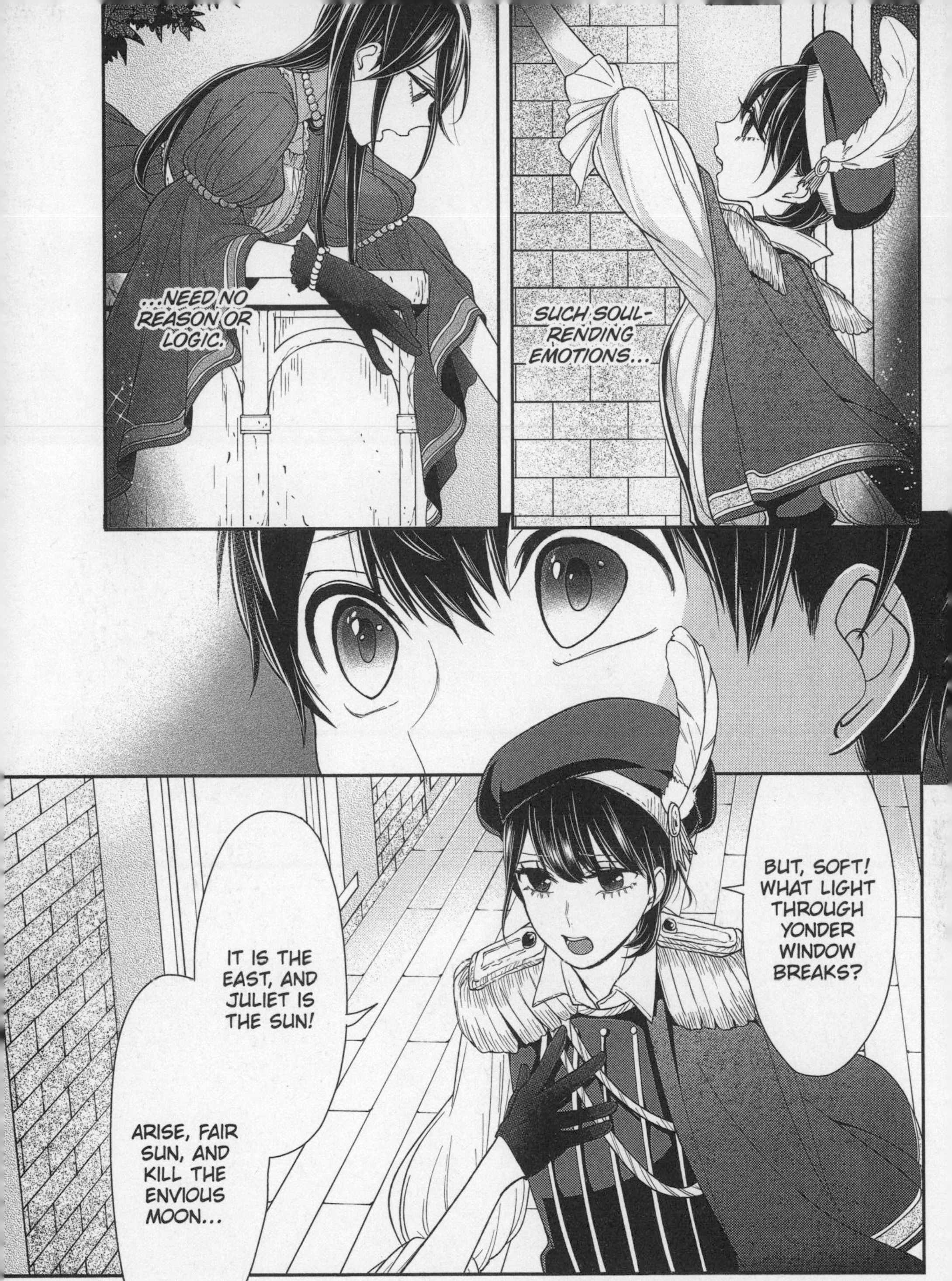
SUCH SOUL-RENDING EMOTIONS...
...NEED NO REASON OR LOGIC.
BUT, SOFT! WHAT LIGHT THROUGH YONDER WINDOW BREAKS?
IT IS THE EAST, AND JULIET IS THE SUN!
ARISE, FAIR SUN, AND KILL THE ENVIOUS MOON...

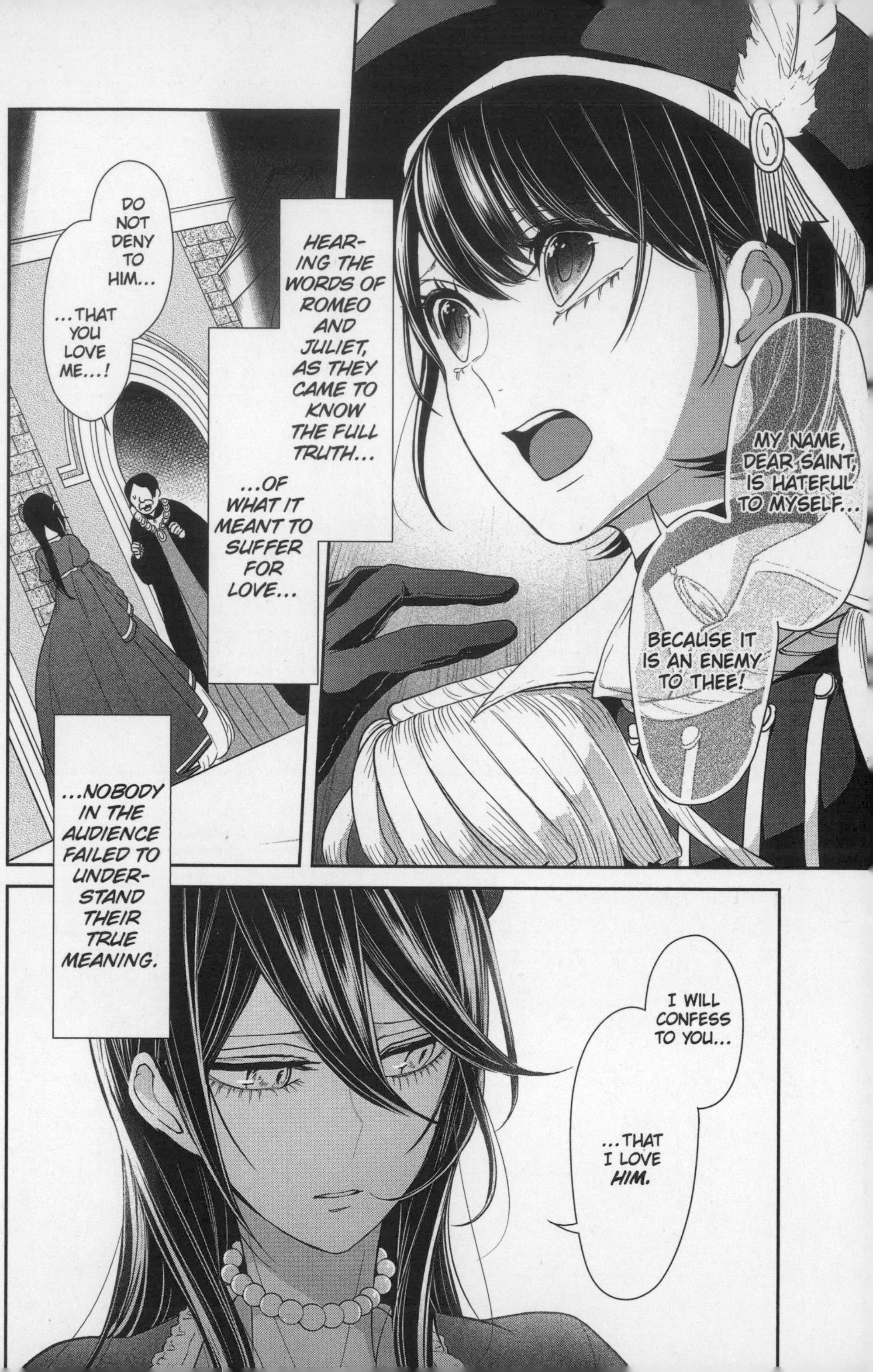
MY NAME, DEAR SAINT, IS HATEFUL TO MYSELF...
BECAUSE IT IS AN ENEMY TO THEE!
HEARING THE WORDS OF ROMEO AND JULIET, AS THEY CAME TO KNOW THE FULL TRUTH...
...OF WHAT IT MEANT TO SUFFER FOR LOVE...
DO NOT DENY TO HIM...
...THAT YOU LOVE ME...!
...NOBODY IN THE AUDIENCE FAILED TO UNDERSTAND THEIR TRUE MEANING.
I WILL CONFESS TO YOU...
...THAT I LOVE *HIM*.

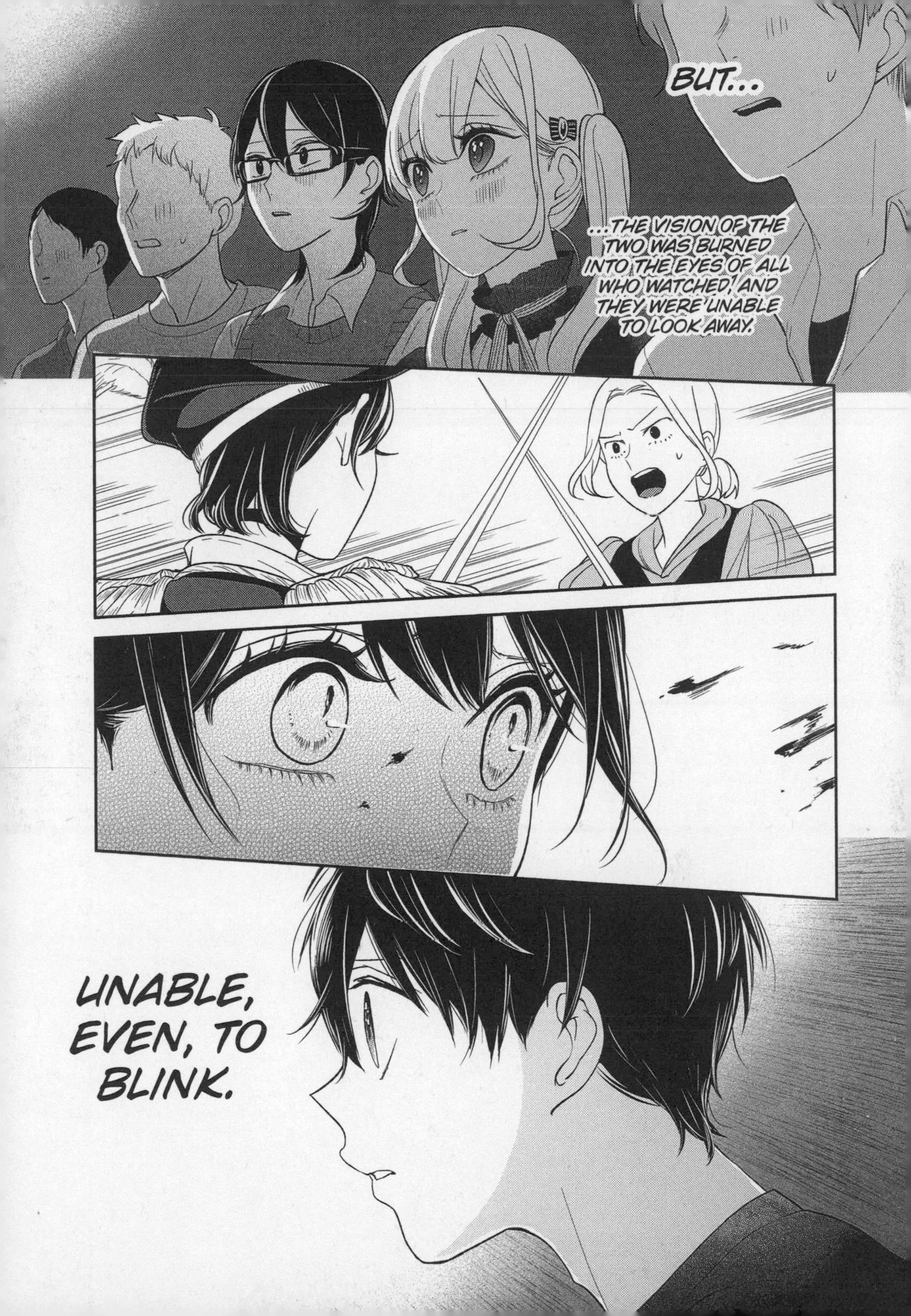
BUT...
...THE VISION OF THE TWO WAS BURNED INTO THE EYES OF ALL WHO WATCHED, AND THEY WERE UNABLE TO LOOK AWAY.
UNABLE, EVEN, TO BLINK.

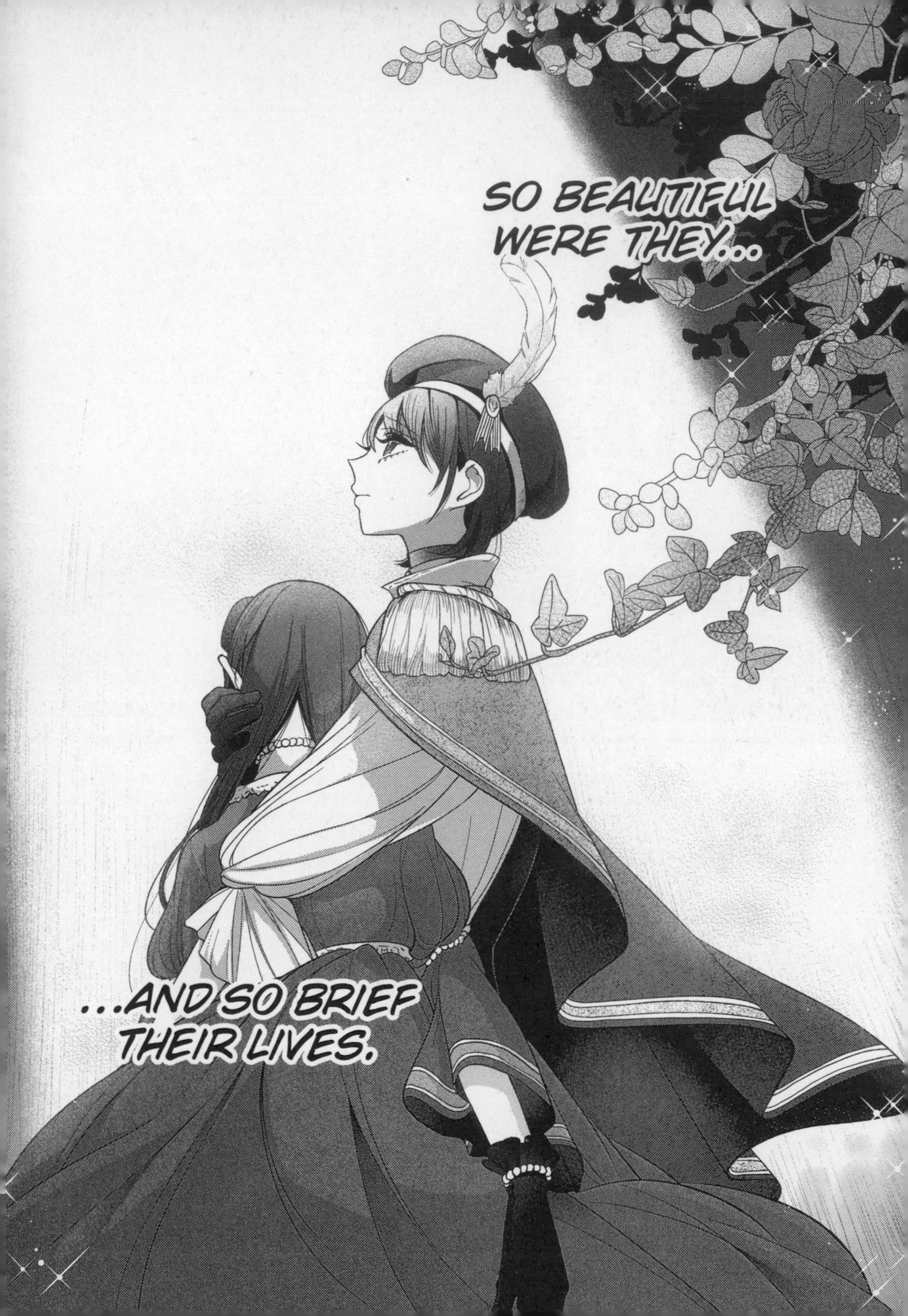
SO BEAUTIFUL WERE THEY...
...AND SO BRIEF THEIR LIVES.

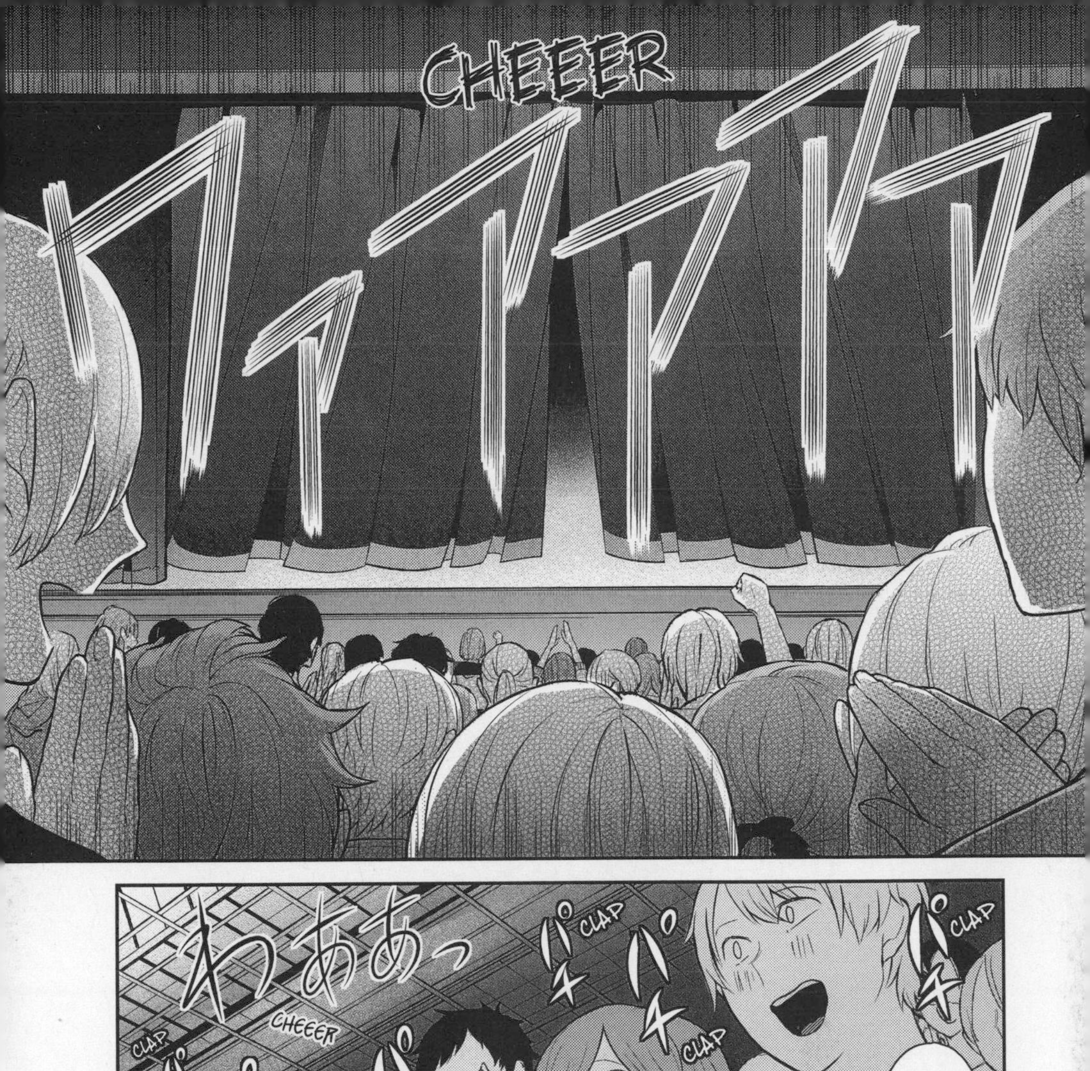
CHEEER

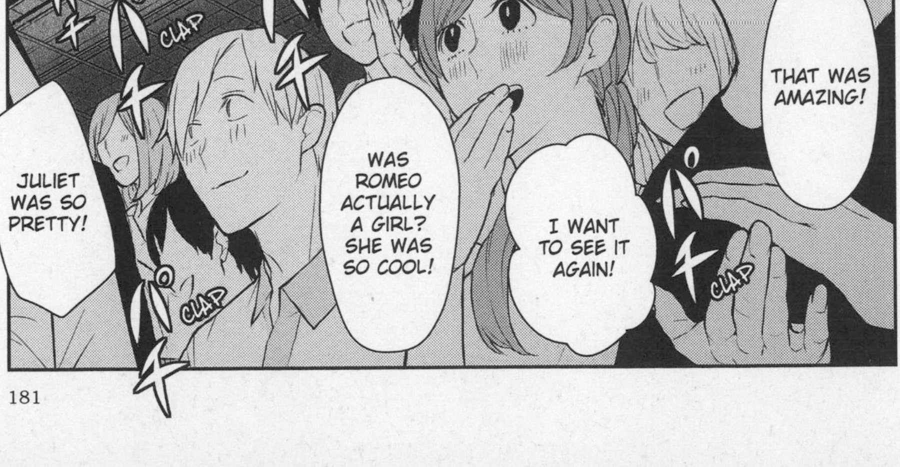
わああっ
CHEEER
CLAP
CLAP
CLAP
CLAP
CLAP
CLAP
CLAP
THAT WAS AMAZING!
I WANT TO SEE IT AGAIN!
WAS ROMEO ACTUALLY A GIRL? SHE WAS SO COOL!
JULIET WAS SO PRETTY!

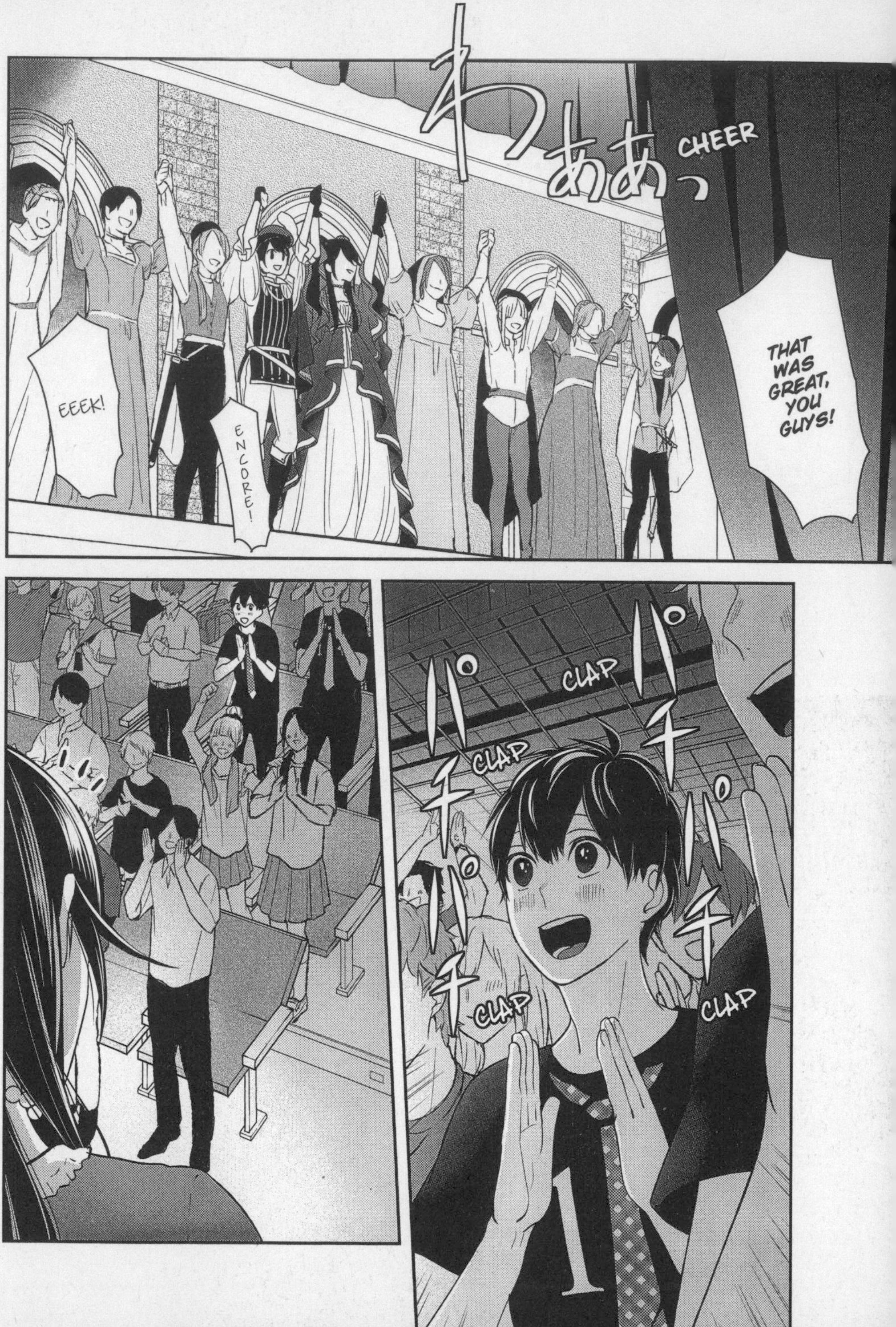
わああっ
CHEER
THAT WAS GREAT, YOU GUYS!
ENCORE!
EEEK!
パチパチ
CLAP
パチパチ
CLAP
CLAP
CLAP

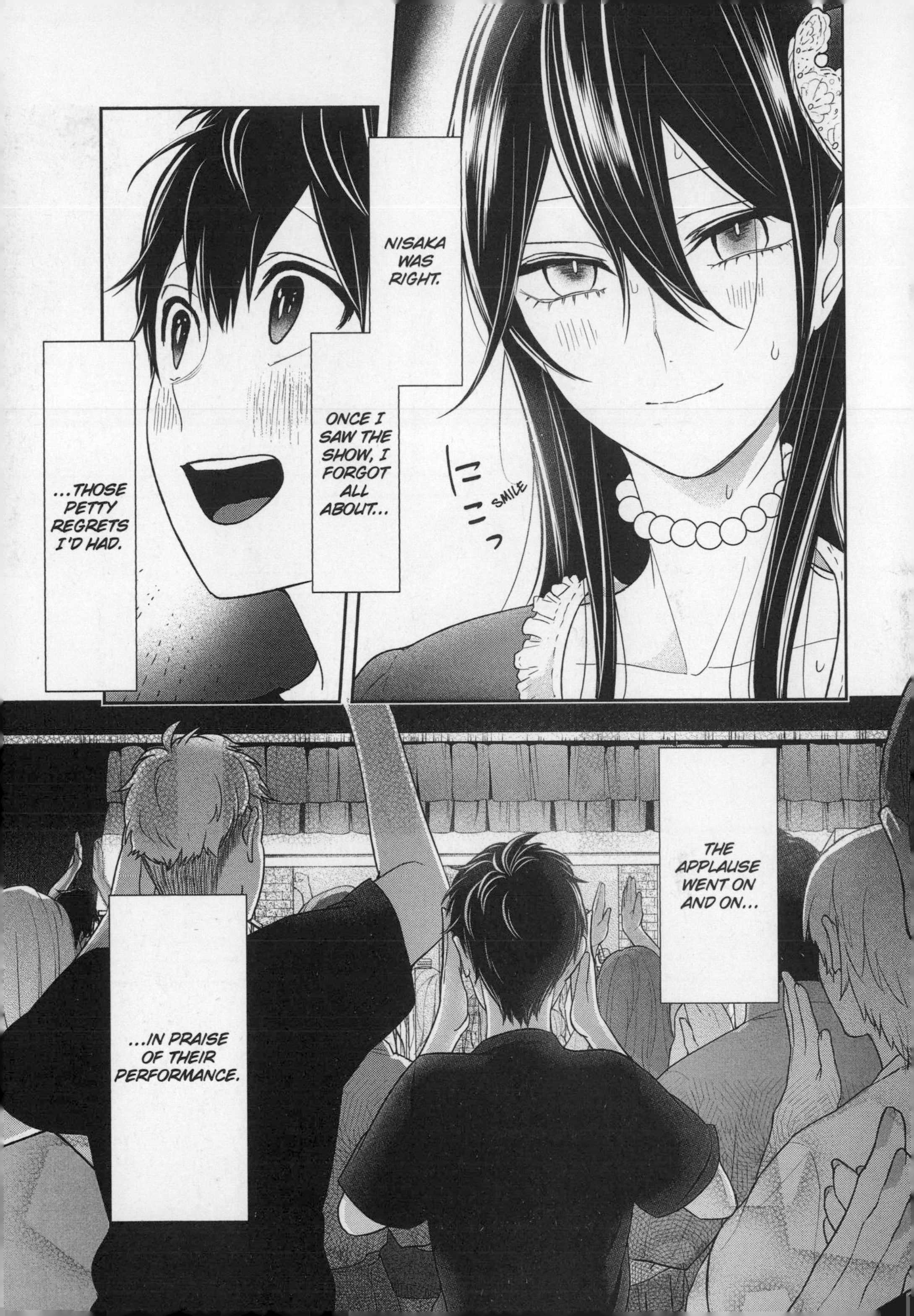
NISAKA WAS RIGHT.
ONCE I SAW THE SHOW, I FORGOT ALL ABOUT...
SMILE
...THOSE PETTY REGRETS I'D HAD.
THE APPLAUSE WENT ON AND ON...
...IN PRAISE OF THEIR PERFORMANCE.

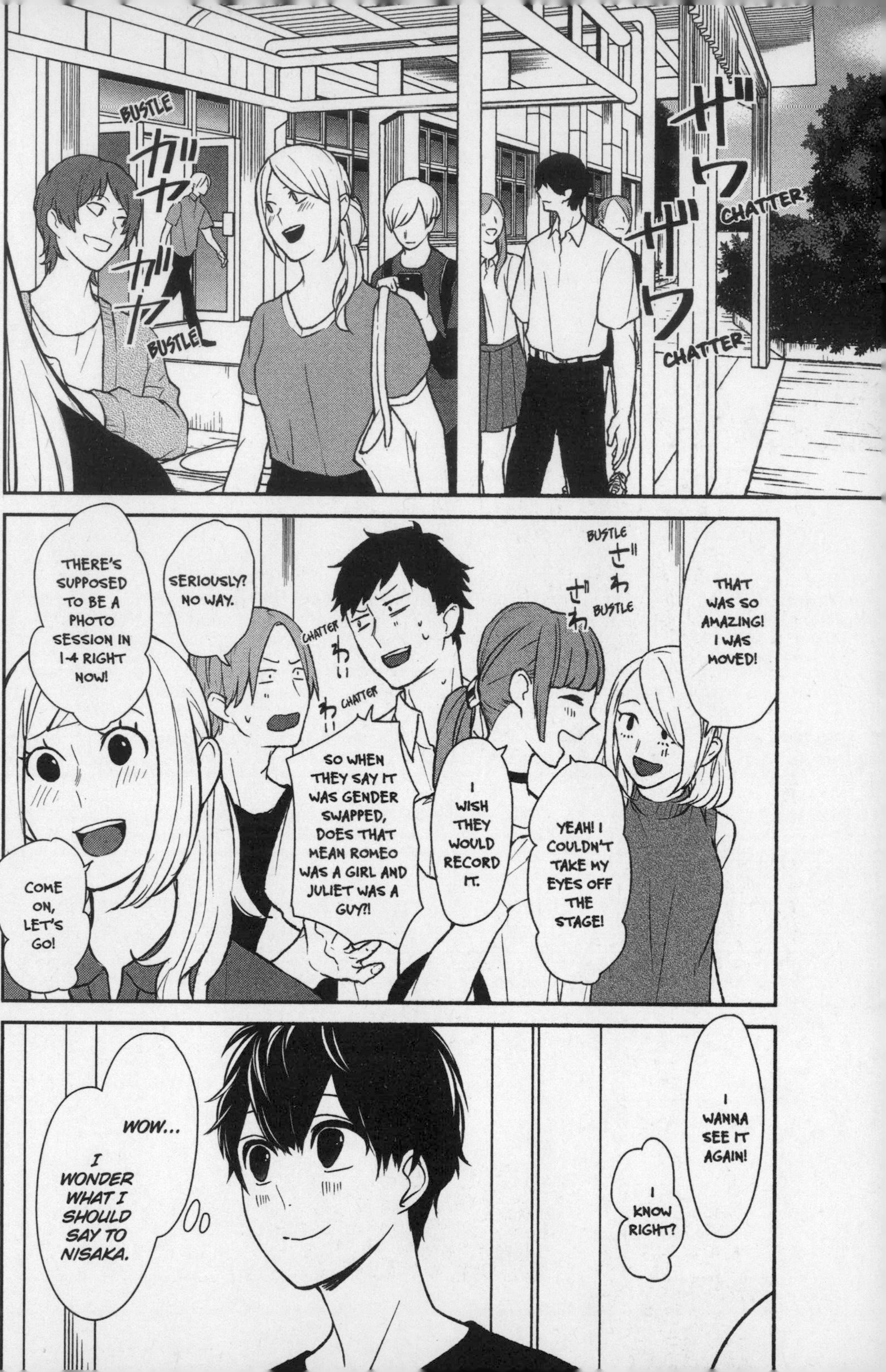
ザワ
ザワ
CHATTER
CHATTER
BUSTLE
ガヤ
ガヤ
BUSTLE
THAT WAS SO AMAZING! I WAS MOVED!
BUSTLE
ざわ
ざわ
BUSTLE
YEAH! I COULDN'T TAKE MY EYES OFF THE STAGE!
I WISH THEY WOULD RECORD IT.
SERIOUSLY? NO WAY.
CHATTER
わい
わい
CHATTER
SO WHEN THEY SAY IT WAS GENDER SWAPPED, DOES THAT MEAN ROMEO WAS A GIRL AND JULIET WAS A GUY?!
THERE'S SUPPOSED TO BE A PHOTO SESSION IN 1-4 RIGHT NOW!
COME ON, LET'S GO!
I WANNA SEE IT AGAIN!
I KNOW RIGHT?
WOW...
I WONDER WHAT I SHOULD SAY TO NISAKA.

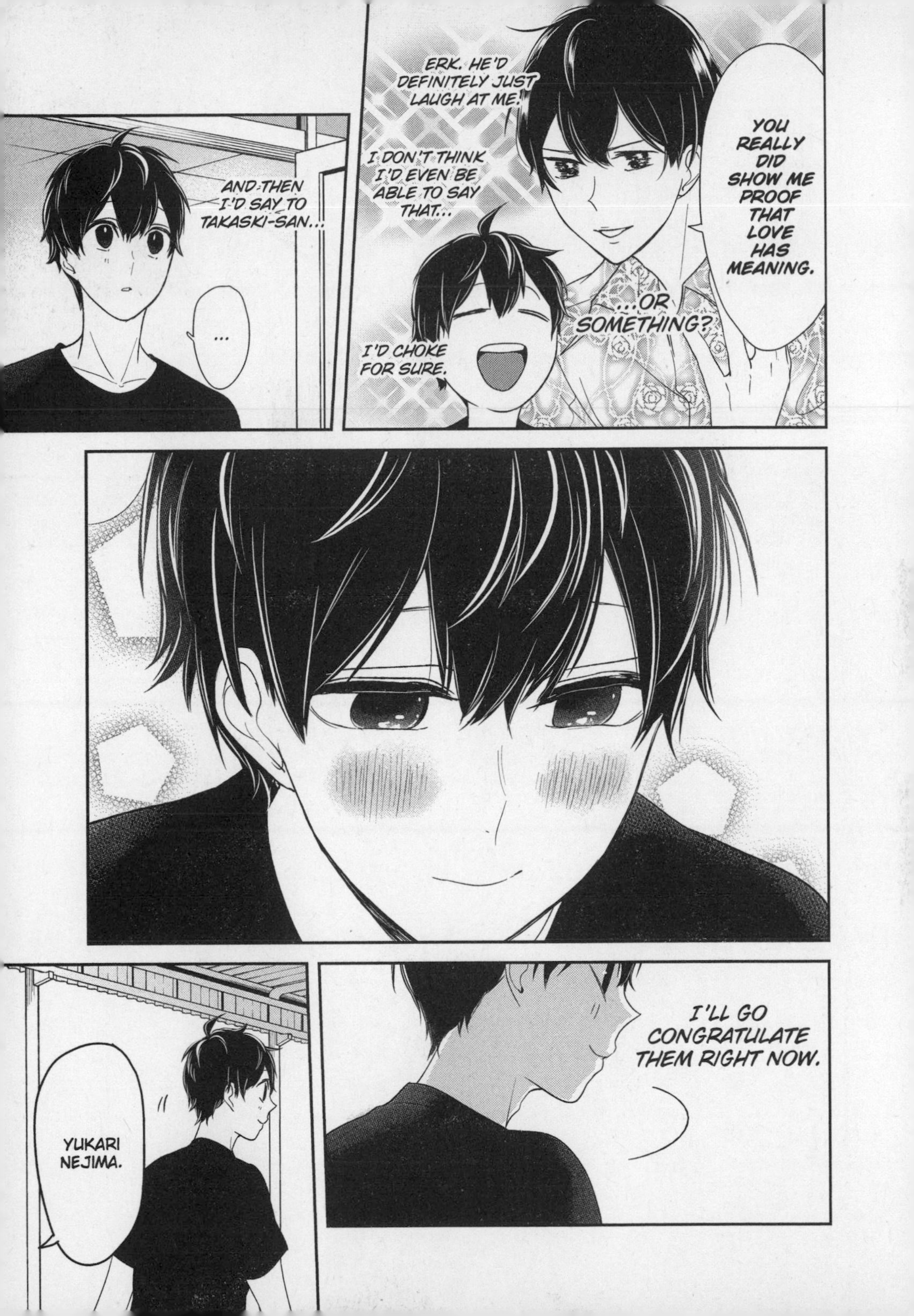
YOU REALLY DID SHOW ME PROOF THAT LOVE HAS MEANING.
...OR SOMETHING?
ERK. HE'D DEFINITELY JUST LAUGH AT ME.
I DON'T THINK I'D EVEN BE ABLE TO SAY THAT...
I'D CHOKE FOR SURE.
AND THEN I'D SAY TO TAKASKI-SAN...
...
I'LL GO CONGRATULATE THEM RIGHT NOW.
YUKARI NEJIMA.

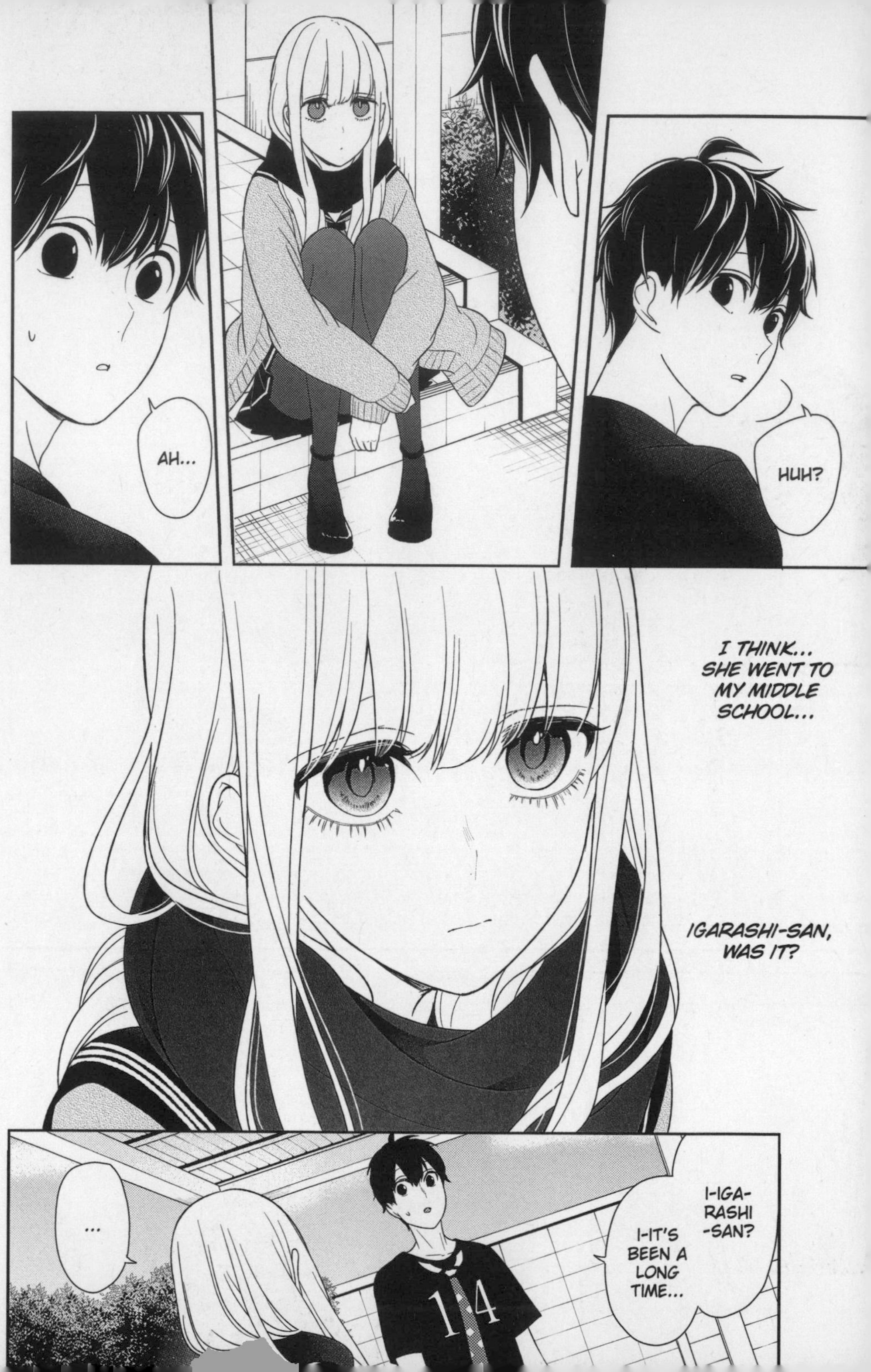
HUH?
AH...
I THINK... SHE WENT TO MY MIDDLE SCHOOL...
IGARASHI-SAN, WAS IT?
I-IGA-RASHI-SAN?
I-IT'S BEEN A LONG TIME...
...

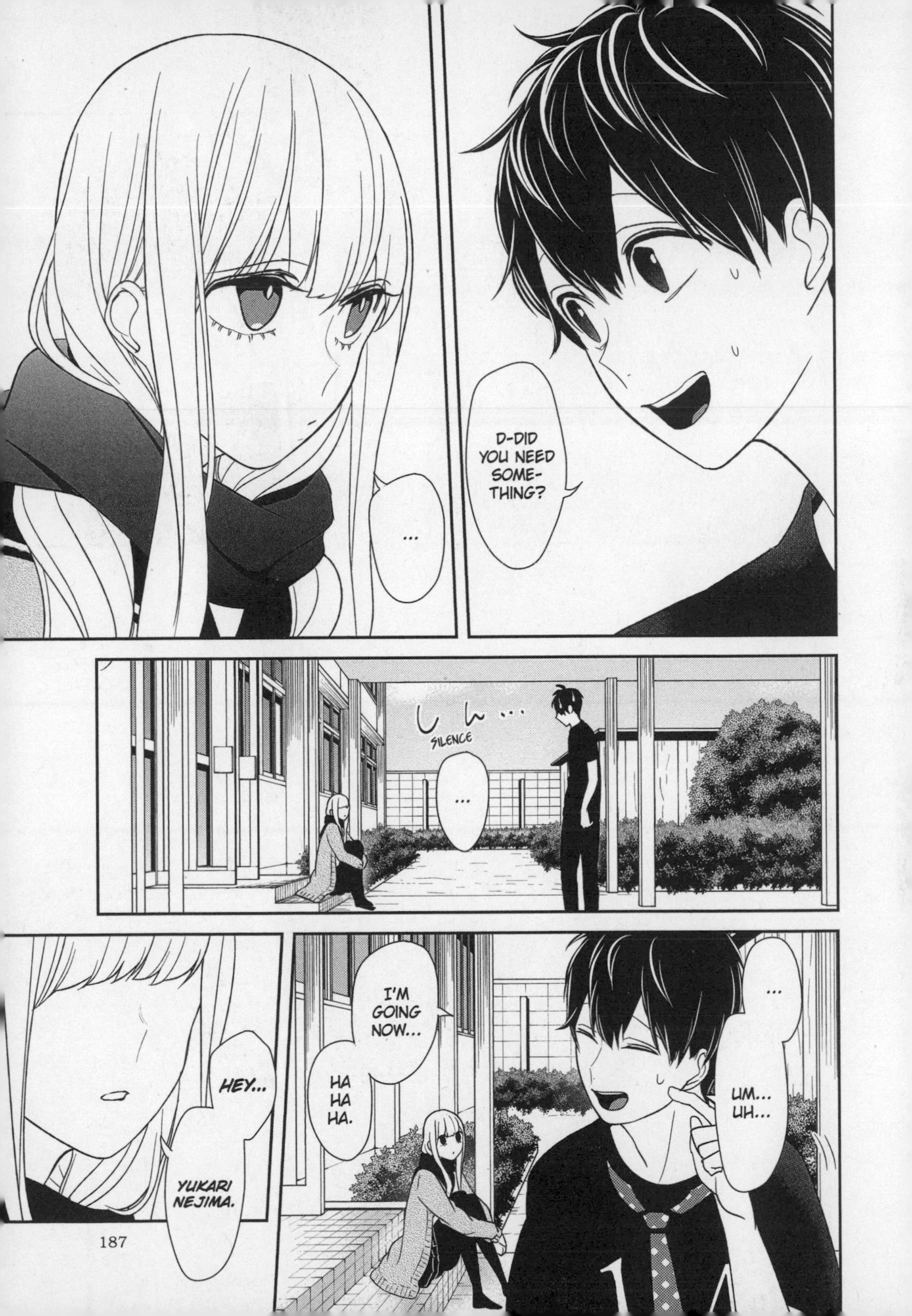
D-DID YOU NEED SOME-THING?
...
しん…
SILENCE
...
...
UM... UH...
HA HA HA.
I'M GOING NOW...
HEY...
YUKARI NEJIMA.

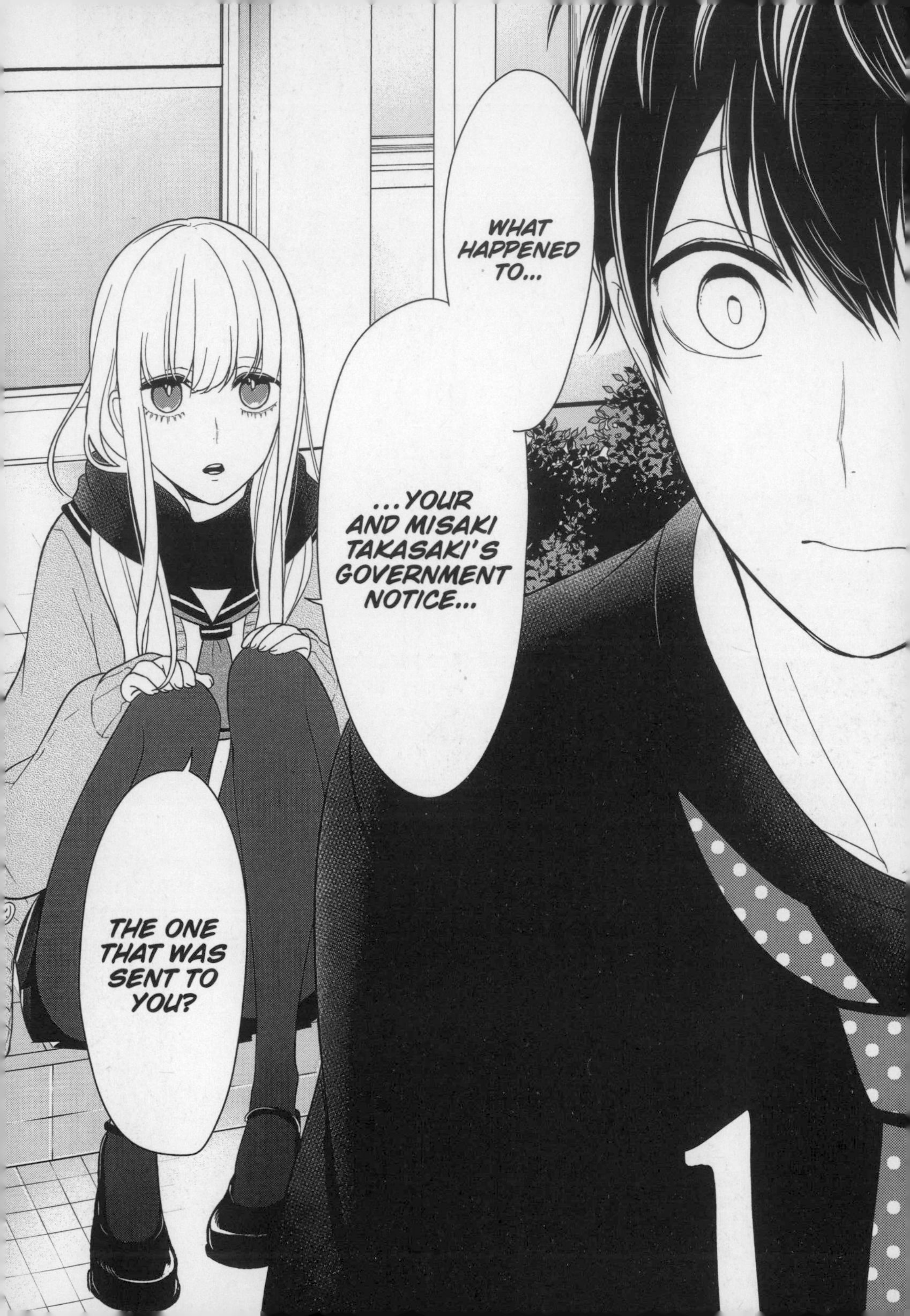
WHAT HAPPENED TO...
...YOUR AND MISAKI TAKASAKI'S GOVERNMENT NOTICE...
THE ONE THAT WAS SENT TO YOU?

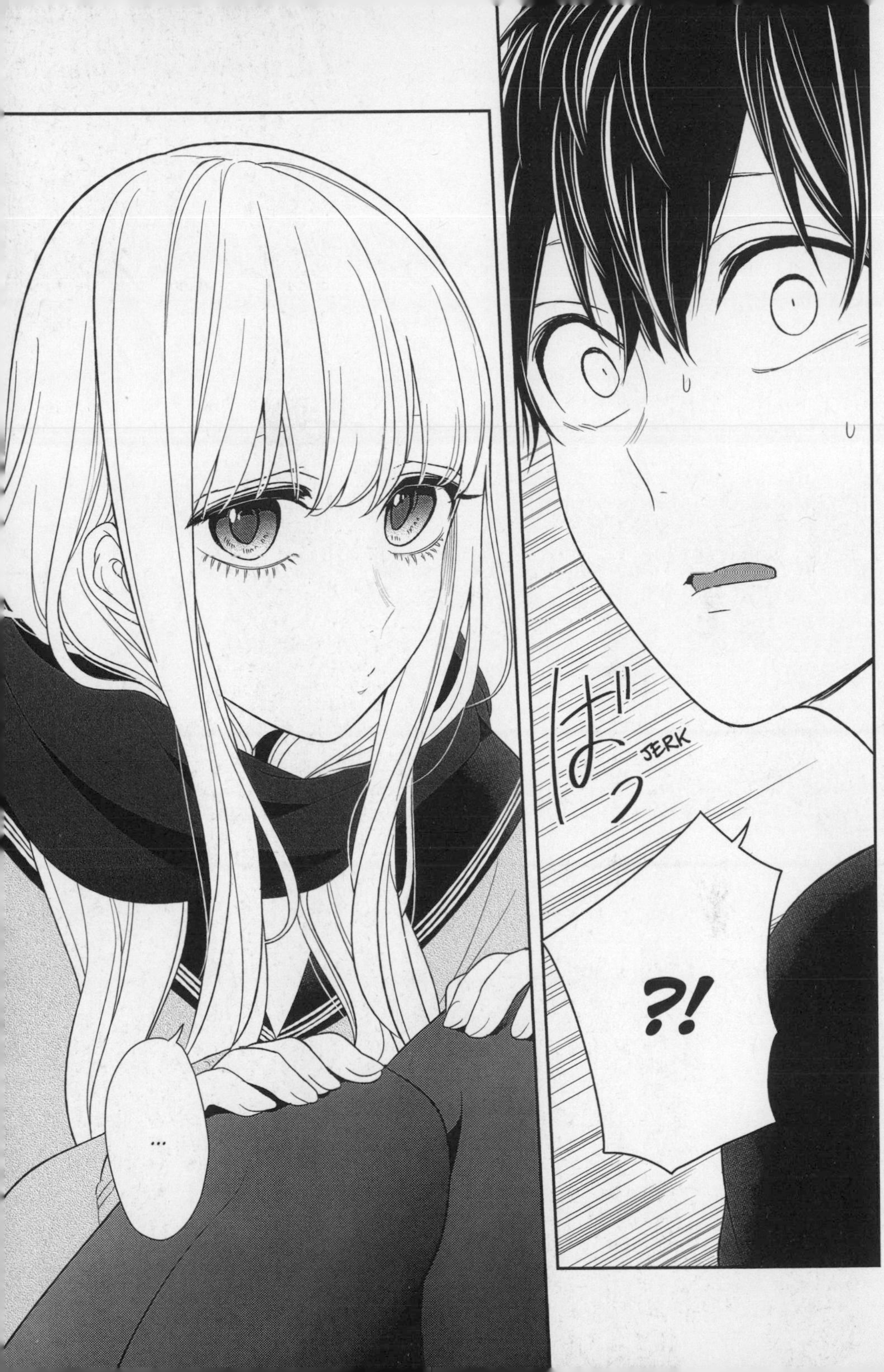
ぱっ
JERK
?!
...

NEXT VOLUME...

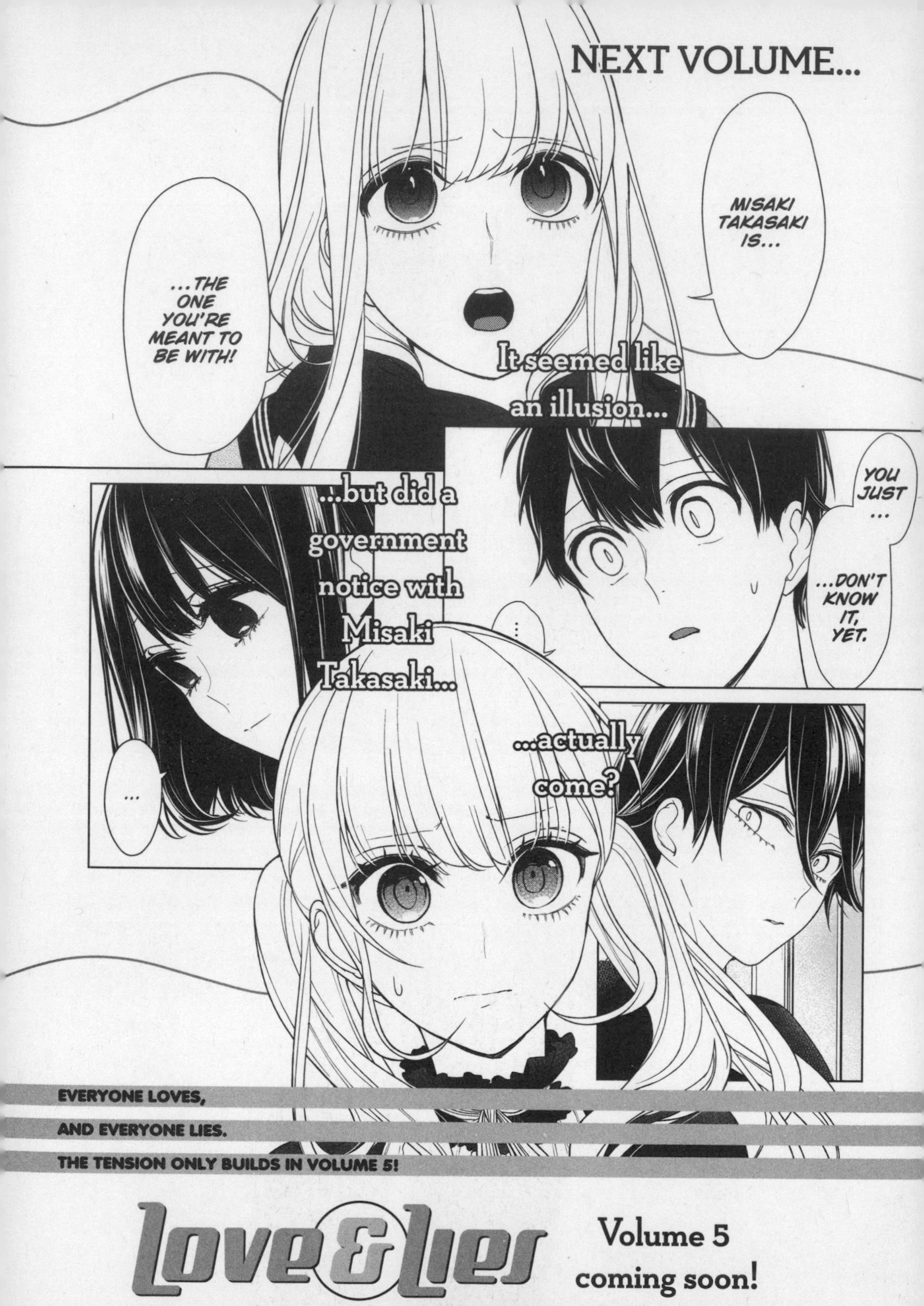
MISAKI TAKASAKI IS...
...THE ONE YOU'RE MEANT TO BE WITH!
It seemed like an illusion...
YOU JUST ...
...DON'T KNOW IT, YET.
...
...but did a government notice with Misaki Takasaki...
...
...actually come?

EVERYONE LOVES,

AND EVERYONE LIES.

THE TENSION ONLY BUILDS IN VOLUME 5!

Love&Lies

Volume 5
coming soon!

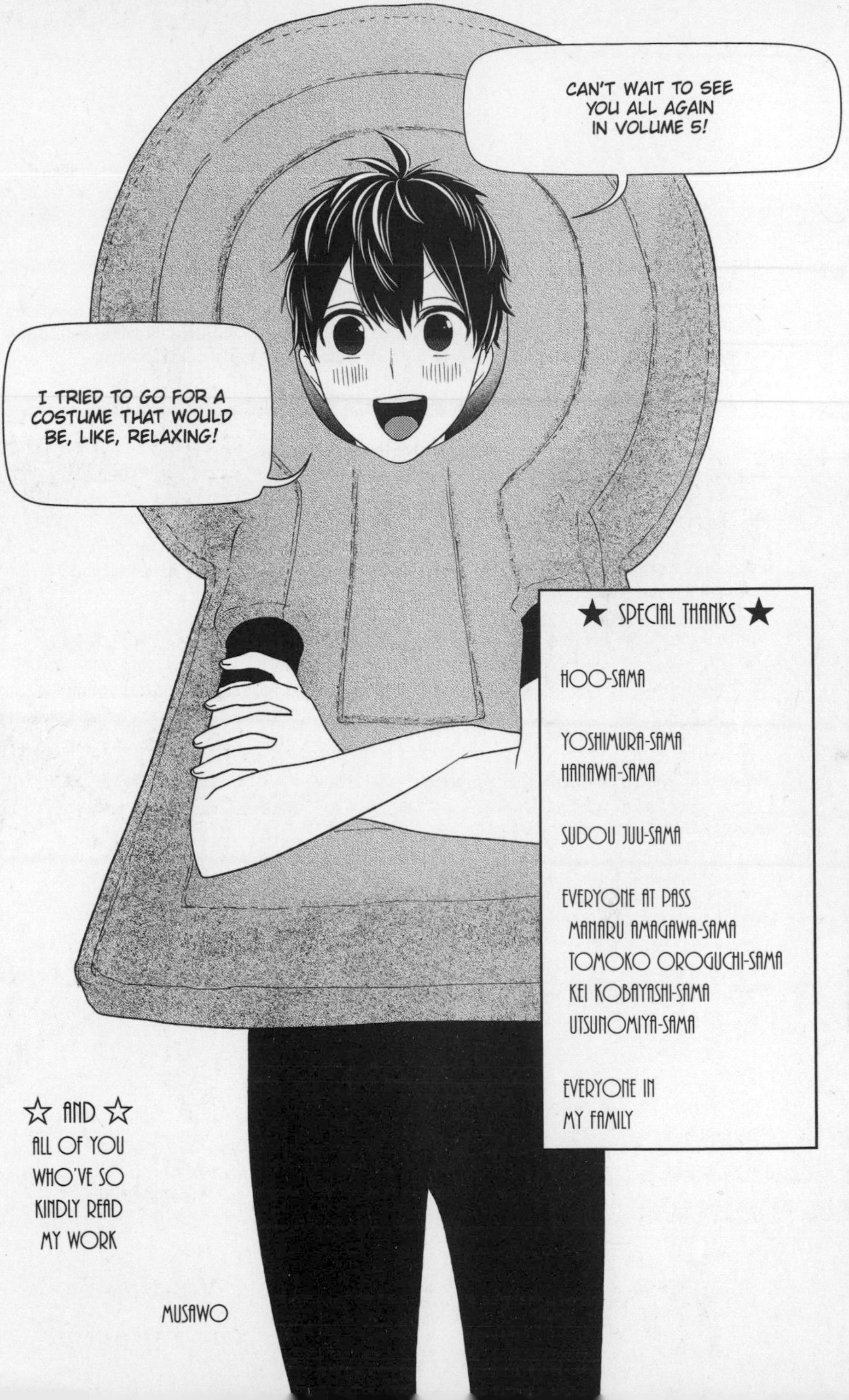
CAN'T WAIT TO SEE YOU ALL AGAIN IN VOLUME 5!
I TRIED TO GO FOR A COSTUME THAT WOULD BE, LIKE, RELAXING!

★ SPECIAL THANKS ★

HOO-SAMA

YOSHIMURA-SAMA
HANAWA-SAMA

SUDOU JUU-SAMA

EVERYONE AT PASS
MANARU AMAGAWA-SAMA
TOMOKO OROGUCHI-SAMA
KEI KOBAYASHI-SAMA
UTSUNOMIYA-SAMA

EVERYONE IN MY FAMILY

☆ AND ☆
ALL OF YOU WHO'VE SO KINDLY READ MY WORK

MUSAWO

A Kodansha Comics Trade Paperback Original.

Love and Lies Volume 4 copyright © 2016 Musawo
English translation copyright © 2018 Musawo

All rights reserved.

Published in the United States by Kodansha Comics, an imprint of Kodansha USA Publishing, LLC, New York.

Publication rights for this English edition arranged through Kodansha Ltd., Tokyo.

First published in Japan in 2016 by Kodansha Ltd., Tokyo, as *Koi to Uso* Volume 4.

ISBN 978-1-63236-560-6

Printed in the United States of America.

www.kodanshacomics.com

9 8 7 6 5 4 3 2 1

Translator: Jennifer Ward
Lettering: Daniel CY
Editing: Paul Starr
Kodansha Comics edition cover design by Phil Balsman